HUMAN RIGHTS UNC
RELIGIOUS FAMILY L
AND INDIA

About one-third of the world's population currently lives under pluri-
legal systems where governments hold individuals subject to the purview
of ethno-religious rather than national norms in respect of family law.
How does the state enforcement of these religious family laws impact
fundamental rights and liberties? What resistance strategies do people
employ in order to overcome the disabilities and limitations these religious laws impose upon their rights? Using archival research, court
observations and interviews with individuals from three countries,
Yüksel Sezgin shows that governments have often intervened in órder
to impress a particular image of subjectivity upon a society, while people
have constantly challenged the interpretive monopoly of courts and
state-sanctioned religious institutions, renegotiated their rights and
duties under the law and changed the system from within. He also
identifies key lessons and best practices for the integration of universal
human rights principles into religious legal systems..

YÜKSEL SEZGIN is an assistant professor of Political Science at Maxwell
School of Citizenship and Public Affairs, Syracuse University, where his
research and teaching interests include legal pluralism, informal justice
systems, comparative religious law and human and women's rights in the
context of the Middle East, South Asia and Sub-Saharan Africa.

CAMBRIDGE STUDIES IN LAW AND SOCIETY

Cambridge Studies in Law and Society aims to publish the best scholarly work on legal discourse and practice in its social and institutional contexts, combining theoretical insights and empirical research.

The fields that it covers are: studies of law in action; the sociology of law; the anthropology of law; cultural studies of law, including the role of legal discourses in social formations; law and economics; law and politics; and studies of governance. The books consider all forms of legal discourse across societies, rather than being limited to lawyers' discourses alone.

The series editors come from a range of disciplines: academic law; socio-legal studies; sociology; and anthropology. All have been actively involved in teaching and writing about law in context.

Series editors

Chris Arup
Monash University, Victoria
Martin Chanock
La Trobe University, Melbourne
Sally Engle Merry
New York University
Susan Silbey
Massachusetts Institute of Technology

A list of books in the series can be found at the back of this book.

HUMAN RIGHTS UNDER STATE-ENFORCED RELIGIOUS FAMILY LAWS IN ISRAEL, EGYPT AND INDIA

Yüksel Sezgin

CAMBRIDGE
UNIVERSITY PRESS

University Printing House, Cambridge CB2 8BS, United Kingdom

Cambridge University Press is part of the University of Cambridge.

It furthers the University's mission by disseminating knowledge in the pursuit of education, learning and research at the highest international levels of excellence.

www.cambridge.org
Information on this title: www.cambridge.org/9781107636491

© Yüksel Sezgin 2013

First published 2013
First paperback edition 2015

A catalogue record for this publication is available from the British Library

Library of Congress Cataloguing in Publication data
Sezgin, Yüksel.
Human rights under state-enforced religious family laws in Israel, Egypt and India / Yüksel Sezgin.
pages   cm. – (Cambridge studies in law and society)
ISBN 978-1-107-04140-0
1. Human rights – Israel.   2. Human rights – Egypt.   3. Human rights – India.   4. Domestic relations – India.   5. Domestic relations – Israel.   6. Domestic relations – Egypt.   7. Religion and law – India.   8. Religion and law – Israel.   9. Religion and law – Egypt.   I. Title.
K3240.S49   2013
342.08′5–dc23

2013002792

ISBN 978-1-107-04140-0 Hardback
ISBN 978-1-107-63649-1 Paperback

*Bu kitap, gözlerimi dünyaya açtığım ilk andan itibaren beni sürekli bir bilim ve
düşün adamı olma yolunda teşvik eden ve bu amaç uğruna hiçbir fedakarlıktan
kaçınmayan, anne ve babam*

Sevinç ve İbrahim Sezgin,

*uzun yıllar önce zeytin ağaçları ve mavi dalgalar ülkesinde aşık olduğum,
gülüşüyle dünyamı aydınlatan biricik hayat arkadaşım, her daim ilham
kaynağım*

Gökçe Doğanay Sezgin

ve

*hayatının ilk iki senesinde, belki de bana en fazla ihtiyaç duyduğu anda,
kendisinden çaldığım günler ve haftalar ile bu kitabı yazdığım canım oğlum*

Derin Ege Sezgin'e

sevgi ve minnetle atfolunmuştur.

§

This book is dedicated with love and gratitude to

my parents Sevinç and Ibrahim Sezgin,

*who, starting the day I opened my eyes to this world, have sacrificed everything to
nurture and encourage me to be a man of thought and intellect,*

*my one and only partner in life whom I fell in love with in the land of olive trees
and blue tides long ago, my eternal source of inspiration with a beautiful
smile that brightens my world*

Gökçe Doğanay Sezgin

and my son, Derin Ege Sezgin

*to whom I still owe the days and weeks I stole from him to write this book
during his first two years in life when he probably needed me the most.*

CONTENTS

TABLES AND FIGURES

ACKNOWLEDGMENTS

This book was made possible with the assistance, generous support and encouragement of many colleagues, friends, family members and institutions. The list of people that I need to thank – if that is possible at all – is so long that I cannot possibly fit their names in a few pages. I am grateful and indebted to all of these selfless and generous people whose names will be eternally carved in gold in my heart.

Among these people a fascinating group of advisors whom I worked with at the University of Washington was more intimately involved with this project. Perhaps the person who deserves most credit for his role in this endeavor is Joel S. Migdal. Joel has been a terrific teacher, supervisor, mentor, a true friend and an "intellectual father" who has been there for me whenever I needed help. Joel spent countless hours reading, editing and criticizing earlier drafts of this project. Thus, for all of this, I will always be grateful and indebted to him. Additionally, Michael McCann, who opened my eyes to the world of "law and society," has been very influential in shaping the theoretical thinking and socio-legalistic approach that I adopted in this study. Michael has been a great source of intellectual inspiration and encouragement at every stage of this project. Another person to whom I owe thanks for his role in the project is Ellis Goldberg. Ellis has always inspired me with his creative thinking and extensive knowledge, and greatly influenced my training at the University of Washington. Last but not least I am also thankful to Gad Barzilai, who served on my committee, read earlier drafts of this book and always provided me with constructive feedback and recommendations.

Evolution of the dissertation, which received both the American Political Science Association's Aaron Wildavsky and the Middle East Studies Association's Malcolm H. Kerr best dissertation awards, into this book took place in several stages, especially during 2010–2012 when I spent time first as a visiting assistant professor at the Women's Studies in Religion Program (WSRP) at Harvard Divinity School, and later as a

Luce Fellow at Princeton University's Institute for International and Regional Studies (PIIRS). I completed the first draft at Harvard and the final draft at Princeton. In this respect I am particularly thankful to William A. Graham and Ann Braude of Harvard Divinity School, and Mark R. Beissinger of Princeton Institute for International and Regional Studies for the intellectual, financial and administrative support they made available to me during the writing stages of this book. I am also grateful to my colleagues Ann Braude, Pamela Voekel, Hauwa Ibrahim, Bethany Moreton and Zhange Ni, and the graduate students who were enrolled in my seminar at the Harvard Divinity School, who generously read and insightfully commented on various parts of the book and greatly contributed to its intellectual evolution. I was able to take on the fellowships at Harvard and Princeton thanks to the generous support and understanding of Jane Bowers and Harold J. Sullivan, then provost and chair respectively, at my former institution, John Jay College, City University of New York. I am truly grateful to Jane and Harold for giving me these opportunities to grow both professionally and intellectually.

The field research and writing stages of this work have also been financially sponsored by the following institutions and programs, in no particular order: the National Science Foundation (#0318497), the Henry Luce Foundation, Harvard Divinity School WSRP Fellowship, the Institute for Humane Studies, the University of Washington Graduate School Dissertation Grant, the University of Washington Chester Fritz Grant, the American Institute of Indian Studies, the Horowitz Foundation for Social Policy, the American University in Cairo Research Grant, the Acton Institute for the Study of Religion and Liberty, the City University of New York Research Foundation, the Association for Israel Studies and the Law and Society Association.

I would also like to acknowledge the support and assistance of the following people who generously helped me at both research and writing stages of the project. Some aided me with arranging my interviews, some helped me obtain access to courts or archives, and some generously read various versions of the manuscript and lent me their wisdom. These people include, in no particular order: Menachem Hofnung, Moussa Abou Ramadan, Ido Shahar, Issa Jabber, Enid Hill, the late Ibrahim Abaza, Reem Leila, Nivedita Menon, Ludo and Rosanne Rocher, Werner Menski, Gordon Woodman, Anne Griffiths, Keebet and Franz von Benda-Beckmann, Arzoo Osanloo, Abdullahi An-Naim, Gopika Solanki, Marc Galanter, Hanna Lerner, Nathan Brown, Tamir Moustafa and Martin Chanock. Ahmet Kuru and Turan Kayaoğlu are two friends and colleagues whom I knew that I could always count upon for their generosity, encouragement, positive energy and wisdom. Another person who has played a pivotal role in shaping my thinking, especially during the revision process, is Mirjam Künkler. Mirjam was not only a source of inspiration and role model for me but also a generous friend and colleague who meticulously commented on various aspects of the book. Two people who came to play an indirect but important role in shaping the final version of the manuscript are Laura Turquet of UN Women and Vijay Nagaraj of the International Council on Human Rights Policy, who challenged and encouraged me to think about policy-relevant implications and lessons of my case studies.

I also thank the editors at Cambridge University Press – Finola O'Sullivan, John Haslam and Richard Woodham – and Sally Engle Merry, the series editor, for believing in this project and seeing it through. Five anonymous reviewers also provided critical comments and feedback, and their suggestions greatly improved the manuscript. The bibliography contains a list of people with whom I exchanged conversations (both electronic and personal) on various aspects of the Israeli, Egyptian and Indian personal status systems as well as a long list of interviewees – those who consented to be identified in the study – who gave me their time and generously shared with me their experiences, stories and opinions without which this project would never have come to fruition. I cannot thank them enough with mere words. This book is for them. This book is a humble attempt to tell their stories, and rectify widespread inequalities I observed during the undertaking of this project. Hence I am donating all royalties from the book (hardback, paperback and electronic versions) to the UN Women's Fund for Gender Equality. The Fund for Gender Equality is a grantmaking fund exclusively dedicated to the advancement of women's economic and political empowerment across the globe. Further information about the Fund can be obtained at www.unwomen.org.

Some portions of the book previously appeared in the following essays, and I am grateful to the publishers for granting me permission to use them here: "The Promise and Pitfalls of Women Challenging Muslim Family Laws in India and Israel" in *Sexuality in Muslim Contexts: Restrictions and Resistance*, Anissa Helie and Homa Hoodfar (eds.) (London: Zed Books, 2012), 98–123; "Triangulating Reform in Family Law: State, Religion and Women's Rights in Comparative Perspective" in *Self-Determination and Women's Rights in Muslim Societies*, Chitra Raghavan and James

. Levine (eds.) (Waltham, MA: Brandeis University Press, 2012), 243–272; "The Role of Alternative Legalities in Bringing About Socio-Legal Change in Religious Systems," *Journal of Comparative Law*, 5(2) (2010), 245–259; "The Israeli Millet System: Examining Legal Pluralism Through Lenses of Nation-Building and Human Rights," *Israel Law Review*, 43(3) (2010), 631–654; "How to Integrate International Human Rights Principles into Religious and Customary Legal Systems?," *Journal of Legal Pluralism*, 60 (2010), 5–40; "Theorizing Formal Pluralism: Quantification of Legal Pluralism for Spatio-Temporal Analysis," *Journal of Legal Pluralism*, 50 (2004), 101–118; "A Political Account for Legal Confrontation Between State and Society: The Case of Israeli Legal Pluralism," *Studies in Law, Politics, and Society*, 32 (2004), 199–235; "Women's Rights in the Triangle of State, Law, and Religion: A Comparison of Egypt and India," *Emory International Law Review*, 25 (2011), 1007–1028.

Last but not least, I would like to thank family members and friends who have always supported and encouraged me in this long and painful process by blessing me with their sincere and unconditional love. I am thankful to Aslıhan Bıyıkoğlu who helped me with the tables and figures included in the book. Pride of place in the acknowledgment must go to my beautiful wife and son who put up with my long absences while I was working on this project. It is to them and my parents that I dedicate this book.

ABBREVIATIONS

Israel

CEIL	Citizenship and Entry into Israel Law, 2003
DRCL	Druze Religious Courts Law, 1962
FCL	Family Courts Law, 1995
FLAML	Family Law Amendment (Maintenance) Law, 1959
ILL	Israel Land Law, 1969
ISL	Israel Succession Law, 1965
LAO	Law and Administration Ordinance, 1948
LFCA	Law of Family Courts (Amendment No. 5), 2001
LMDM	Law of Matters of Dissolution of Marriage (Jurisdiction in Special Cases), 1969
LPSDCI	Law of Personal Status of the Druze Community of Israel, 1961
LPSDCL	Law of Personal Status of the Druze Community of Lebanon, 1948
MAL	Marriage Age Law, 1950
MDRO	Marriage and Divorce (Registration) Ordinance, 1919
MK	Member of Knesset (Israeli Parliament)
OLFR	Ottoman Law of Family Rights, 1917
OLPSC	Ottoman Law of Procedure for Shariʿa Courts, 1917
OLS	Ottoman Law of Succession, 1913
NwA	Nissa wa Afaq (Women and Horizons)
PLABL	Penal Law Amendment (Bigamy) Law, 1959
POC	Palestine Order in Council, 1922
QL	Qadis Law, 1961
QLA	Qadis Law (Amendment No. 10), 2002
RCEDDL	Rabbinical Courts (Enforcement of Divorce Decrees) Law, 1995
RCJL	Rabbinical Courts Jurisdiction (Marriage and Divorce) Law, 1953
SCVAL	Shariʿa Courts (Validation of Appointments) Law, 1953
SO	Succession Ordinance, 1923

WERL   Women's Equal Rights Law, 1951
WGEPSI   Working Group for Equality in Personal Status Issues

Egypt
CCCP   Code of Civil and Commercial Procedure, 1968
ORSC   Ordinance on Regulation of Shariʿa Courts, 1931
PSOCOC Personal Status Ordinance of the Coptic Orthodox
           Community, 1938

India
AIMPLB   All India Muslim Personal Law Board
AIMPLB-J   All India Muslim Personal Law Board-*Jadeed*
AIMWPLB   All India Muslim Women Personal Law Board
AISPLB   All India Shiʿa Personal Law Board
AMA   The Anand Marriage Act, 1909
BMMA   Bharatiya Muslim Mahila Andolan
CMRA   The Child Marriage Restraint Act, 1929
Cr. PC   The Criminal Procedure Code, 1973
DMMA   The Dissolution of Muslim Marriages Act, 1939
DPA   The Dowry Prohibition Act, 1961
HAMA   The Hindu Adoptions and Maintenance Act, 1956
HCB   Hindu Code Bill
HMA   The Hindu Marriage Act, 1955
HMDRA   The Hindu Marriage Disabilities Removal Act, 1946
HMWRSRMA The Hindu Married Women's Right to Separate
           Residence and Maintenance Act, 1946
HSA   The Hindu Succession Act, 1956
HWRA   The Hindu Widows' Remarriage Act, 1856
HWRPA   The Hindu Women's Rights to Property Act, 1937
ICMA   The Indian Christian Marriage Act, 1872
IDA   The Indian Divorce Act, 1869
IPC   The Indian Penal Code, 1860
ISA   Indian Succession Act, 1925
MLAA   Marriage Laws (Amendment) Act, 1976
MPLSAA   The Muslim Personal Law (Shariat) Application Act,
           1937
MWPRDA   The Muslim Women (Protection of Rights on
           Divorce) Act, 1986
MWRN   Muslim Women's Rights Network
PCMA   The Prohibition of the Child Marriage Act, 2006

PISA	The Parsee Intestate Succession Act, 1865
PLA-IV	The Punjab Laws Act IV, 1872
PMDA	The Parsee Marriage and Divorce Act, 1936
UCC	Uniform Civil Code

Others

ASK	Ain o Shalish Kendra
BRAC	Bangladesh Rural Advancement Committee
CEDAW	The Convention on the Elimination of All Forms of Discrimination Against Women, 1979
ECtHR	The European Court of Human Rights
ICCPR	The International Covenant on Civil and Political Rights, 1966
ICESCR	The International Covenant on Economic, Social and Cultural Rights, 1966
ICHRP	The International Council on Human Rights Policy
UDHR	Universal Declaration of Human Rights, 1948
UN Women	United Nations Entity for Gender Equality and the Empowerment of Women
USAID	The United States Agency for International Development

INTRODUCTION

Manikyamma and Sudarsana, two Hindus, married according to Hindu rites in 1977 and had two children, one of whom died in infancy. In September 1983, the husband, Sudarsana, while still legally married to Manikyamma, married another Hindu woman, Lakshmi, in a religious ceremony. Fearing that Manikyamma, who did not consent to her husband's second marriage, could take legal action – the law prohibits bigamy for Hindus while allowing it for Muslims – Sudarsana and Lakshmi converted to Islam and remarried in February 1984, this time following Muslim rites.

When Manikyamma lodged a complaint under Section 494 of the Indian Penal Code, the trial court convicted the husband and the second wife for the crime of bigamy. In appeal, the Sessions Court, however, acquitted the husband and the second wife and recognized their Muslim marriage on grounds that Manikyamma, the first wife, had failed to produce proof of her 1977 marriage to Sudarsana, even though he never denied that Manikyamma was his wife and that he was the father of her child. Later, the High Court of Appeals also affirmed the acquittals and dismissed Manikyamma's petition, but on completely different grounds. This time the court recognized the validity of the first marriage between Manikyamma and Sudarsana but denied the validity of the Hindu and Muslim marriages between the husband and the second wife. The court held that the couple's conversion to Islam was not "valid" because the couple reportedly did not attend the mosque on Fridays, and the wife continued wearing Hindu symbols such as *mangalasuthram* (a necklace considered as a symbol of marriage among

Hindus), *metlu* (toe rings) and *tilakam* (mark on the forehead), thereby their marriage under the Muslim law was invalid. The court also ruled that the couple's Hindu marriage from September 1983 was not valid, either. Thus, the crime of bigamy never occurred. Even though the court recognized the factual existence of the September 1983 marriage between the husband and the second wife, which took place at a Hindu temple in front of witnesses, the judge eventually dismissed the bigamy charges because the complainant (the first wife) failed to provide evidence proving that necessary formalities such as *homam* (offering made to the fire-god Agni) and *saptapadi* (the taking of seven steps by the bridegroom and the bride jointly before the sacred fire) were actually performed by the husband and his second wife during the ceremony in the temple in order for the court to deem this as a "validly solemnized" marriage under the Hindu law, and thereby convict the accused of bigamy.[1]

The 23-year-old Russian immigrant to Israel, Sergeant Nikolai Rappaport, was a combat soldier in southern Lebanon when he was killed in a Hezbollah ambush in 1998. His family expected their son to be honored as a "martyr" and buried in a military ceremony like other fallen soldiers. But Nikolai's funeral was a bit different. There was no open grave for his comrades to lower the flag-draped casket into, but a military vehicle waiting outside to take his body to the airport for a journey to Russia where he was eventually buried (Schmemann 1998). Sergeant Rappaport could not be interred in a Jewish cemetery in Israel because, according to the state-enforced Jewish law, Nikolai was not considered a Jew as he had not been born to a Jewish mother.

Hala Sidqi, a famous Orthodox Copt actress in Egypt, was married to an Orthodox Copt man. For nearly a decade in the 1990s, she tried to divorce her husband but repeatedly failed to get a divorce under the Coptic Orthodox family laws that the court was applying in her case. Thereafter, her lawyer suggested she try to obtain it under Islamic law by filing for *khul'* or no-fault divorce recently made available to Muslim women. The Egyptian law required application of *shari'a* to Christian couples when each spouse belonged to a different sect and rite. Both Hala Sidqi and her husband were Orthodox Copts. In order to obtain a *khul'* divorce under *shari'a*, Sidqi had to become a member of another

---

[1] B. *Chandra Manikyamma* v. B. *Sudarsana Rao*, Andhra Pradesh High Court (1988), accessed in May, 2012, from http://indiankanoon.org/doc/686235/.

denomination. So, she migrated to the Syrian Orthodox Church, while her husband remained a Copt. By doing so, she was able to not only get a divorce under the Islamic law, but also obtain permission to remarry in the church, as, unlike the Coptic Orthodox Church, her new church allowed remarriage for people who had been divorced for reasons other than adultery (El-Alami 2001–2002).

These are not unusual or peculiar stories, but everyday-life stories of hundreds of millions of people who live under "personal status" or "personal law" systems around the globe. In fact, about one-third of the world population currently lives under such legal systems. In this respect, the three countries under examination – Israel, Egypt and India – belong to a group of (mostly postcolonial or post-imperial) countries which do not have a unified or territorial system of family law, but, instead, a particular system of personal status in which individuals are held subject to jurisdiction of state-enforced religious family laws rather than national norms in regard to such matters as marriage, divorce, maintenance and inheritance. To exemplify, under a personal status system, a Jew will be subject to (state-enforced) *halakhah*, a Muslim to (state-enforced) *shari'a*, a Christian to (state-enforced) canon law, and so forth.

Like most other nations, the three countries under examination had inherited existing pluri-legal (legally plural) personal status systems from their imperial or colonial predecessors. Although personal status systems did not always originate under colonial or imperial rule, most did; and this is particularly true for the three countries analyzed in the study. For instance, the origins of the Israeli and Egyptian personal status systems can be traced back to the Ottoman Empire, while the foundations of the Indian personal law system were laid down by Turkish/Mughal dynasties which controlled the subcontinent from the thirteenth century until the arrival of the British in the eighteenth century. In the past, imperial and colonial rulers employed the pluri-legal personal status systems to compartmentalize their subjects into ethno-religious and confessional groupings, and to distribute goods and services accordingly while denying certain populations the benefits of full membership in the political community. Thus, we can understand why multi-ethnic empires or colonial rulers, which often had a "divide and rule" approach towards their subject populations, may have employed pluri-legal personal status systems in the past. But it is not easy to understand why contemporary nation-states like Israel, Egypt or India, which are all constitutionally committed to treat their citizens equally before the law,[2] would ignore their constitutional obligations and hold people to different standards and laws by distinguishing on the basis of gender, ethnicity and religion.

Moreover, even though all three countries apply different communal laws to persons with different ethno-religious backgrounds, and hold men and women to different legal standards, the way each country does this varies considerably. In other words, there are systemic (both institutional and procedural) differences across personal status systems. For instance, in Israel, personal status laws are applied directly by state-appointed-and-salaried communal judges in religious courts (e.g., rabbinical courts, *shari'a* courts, Druze courts, etc.) whereas in Egypt and India they are implemented by secular judges in civil courts. Furthermore, while Muslim men in India are allowed to contract polygynous marriages, their coreligionists in Israel are prohibited from exercising the same "right." While a Christian man in Egypt can divorce his Christian wife under Muslim personal status law (through *talaq*) by simply switching to another Christian denomination (because the Egyptian law requires application of Islamic law to Christian couples when spouses belong to different sects and rites), a non-Muslim man in India who is married to a non-Muslim woman cannot enjoy the "benefits" of Muslim personal law (i.e., the ability to contract a bigamous marriage or repudiate a wife by means of *talaq*) even if he willingly and sincerely embraces the Islamic faith.

Therefore, there is an intriguing puzzle here: why do these three countries, as well as many other postcolonial/post-imperial nations, continue to apply different sets of norms to people from different ethno-religious backgrounds, and hold men and women to different

---

[2] The equal protection clauses in each country's constitutional documents are:

The Declaration of the Establishment of the State of Israel (1948): "The State of Israel ... will ensure complete equality of social and political rights to all its inhabitants irrespective of religion, race or sex ..."

The Constitution of the Arab Republic of Egypt (1971), Article 40: "All citizens are equal before the law. They have equal public rights and duties without discrimination due to sex, ethnic origin, language, religion or creed." Article 33 of the new Egyptian Constitution, adopted in December 2012, which replaced Article 40 above, no longer explicitly lists the grounds on which discrimination is prohibited: "All citizens are equal before the law. They have equal public rights and duties without discrimination." Although Article 33 falls short of explicitly stating on what grounds discrimination is prohibited, Clause 5 of the Preamble still prohibits discrimination on ground of sex, and Article 6 on grounds of sex, origin or religion.

The Constitution of India (1950), Article 14: "The State shall not deny to any person equality before the law or the equal protection of the laws within the territory of India." And Article 15: "(1) The State shall not discriminate against any citizen on grounds only of religion, race, caste, sex, place of birth or any of them."

legal standards despite their constitutional commitments to treat everyone equally before the law? Furthermore, when countries distinguish among their citizens on the basis of sex, religion or ethnicity, why do they do it so differently from one another? Why, for example, are religious laws applied by state-appropriated communal courts in Israel but by civil courts in Egypt and India? How can we explain such cross-national variation? Second, how does the state enforcement of religious personal status laws under these pluri-legal systems impact the fundamental rights and liberties of individuals who are subject to their jurisdiction? Finally, what strategies do people use to respond to any restrictions or disabilities of their rights and liberties, if and when they are imposed by state-enforced personal status laws? These are the three main questions the present study aims to answer.

REFORMING PLURI-LEGAL PERSONAL STATUS SYSTEMS IN THE PROCESS OF STATE- AND NATION-BUILDING

Postcolonial/post-imperial nations which inherited pluri-legal personal status systems upon independence faced more or less the same challenges: what were they going to do with these fragmented legal systems, which were not necessarily conducive to building a modern bureaucratic machinery or a civic sense of national identity? Were they going to preserve them, or eradicate and replace them with completely new bodies of law and legal institutions? A close analysis of the experiences of postcolonial nations which inherited such pluri-legal systems shows that some countries opted for institutional unification (unifying the courts of different religious groups under an overarching system of national courts), some for normative unification (abolishing different bodies of religious and customary or communal laws and enacting in their place uniform territorial laws that applied to everyone equally), some did both and some did neither (see Fig. 1.1).

For instance, both Israel and Egypt upon independence inherited similar "fragmented confessional" personal status systems whose origins can be traced back to the Ottoman *millet* system.[3] Under these fragmented confessional systems, in both countries religious courts of state-recognized ethno-religious communities were granted autonomy to apply state-enforced religious laws in regard to community members' matters of personal status such as marriage, divorce, maintenance and inheritance.

---

[3] For information on the Ottoman *millet* system, see Boogert (2012).

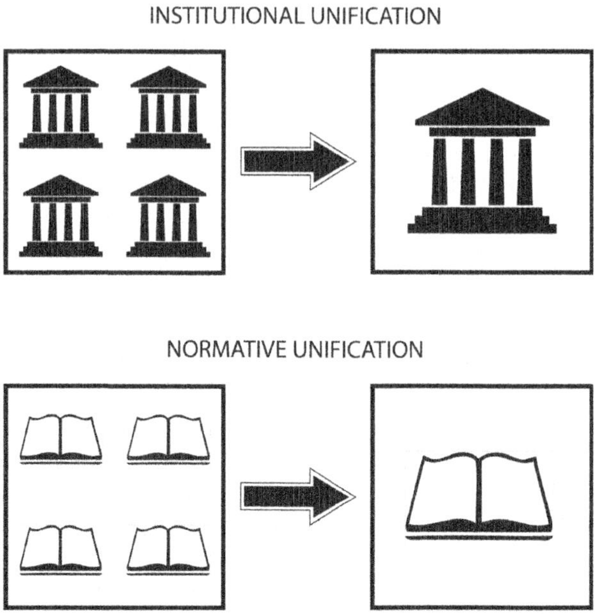

INSTITUTIONAL UNIFICATION

NORMATIVE UNIFICATION

Fig. 1.1 Institutional vs. normative unification

That is to say, as far as family law is concerned, *shari'a* courts applied Islamic law to Muslims, rabbinical courts applied *halakhah* to Jews, and various ecclesiastical courts applied canon laws to Christians. The courts were formally integrated into each country's legal system, and their decisions were directly executed by respective governments. To this day, Israel has more or less preserved this fragmented confessional structure, and refrained from introducing changes that would normatively or institutionally unify its personal status system. As a result, there presently remain fourteen state-recognized religious communities in Israel whose religious family laws and courts (where applicable) are formally recognized and integrated into the country's legal system, and the decisions of these religious courts are directly executed by the government.

Even though Egypt inherited a fragmented confessional system similar to Israel's, its personal status system no longer resembles this ideal type but rather the "unified confessional" model under which different bodies of religious laws are directly applied by civil judges in secular state courts. This is because the Egyptian government during the reign of Nasser abolished all religious courts in 1955 and unified them under an overarching network of national courts; it also placed the application of religious laws in the hands of state-trained secular judges. In fact, this is

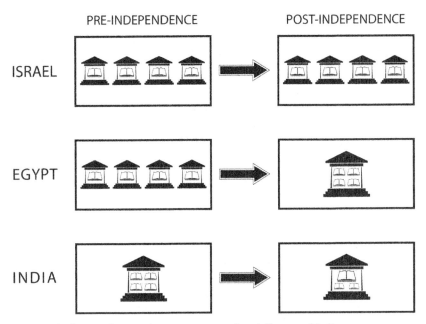

Fig. 1.2 Evolution of personal status systems in Israel, Egypt and India

the very same type of personal status system that Indian leaders found in place when India gained its independence from the British in 1947 (see Fig. 1.2). However, the Indian government under Nehru put forth a drastic agenda for reform, and contemplated complete normative unification in the field of personal status by abolishing all state-enforced religious laws and enacting a Uniform Civil Code (UCC) in their place which would apply to all Indians equally, irrespective of religion. Nevertheless, for various reasons that I elaborate in Chapter 6, the Indian government only half succeeded in its goal of normative unification. As a result, the Indian personal law system today rather resembles the "unified semi-confessional" type under which secular judges at civil courts continue to apply to religious minorities their own communal laws (i.e., *shariat* to Muslims, Christian law to Christians, and Parsi law to Zoroastrian Parsis), and the Hindu law – which was considerably unified across different communities and codified into four separate Acts in 1955–56 – to the rest of the population, which consists mainly of Hindus, Sikhs, Jains and Buddhists, plus anyone else who is not a Muslim, Christian, Parsi or Jew by religion.

The institutional, substantive and procedural differences that we observe across the personal status systems of these three countries give rise to a number of important questions about different states' responses to the challenges of regulating or reforming pluri-legal personal status systems in the state- and nation-building process. For instance, why do Israel and Egypt have two different types of personal status today, even though after independence they inherited very similar fragmented confessional systems closely resembling the Ottoman *millet* system? How can we explain different motives and strategies that each government adopted in regulating and creating its own personal status system? Why did Israel opt for a fragmented confessional system? Why did Egypt not settle for a similar system but aimed for a unified confessional system by means of normative unification? Why did India set for itself the goal of complete normative unification? By the time India gained its independence, it already had the very same form of personal status system (i.e., unified confessional) that Egyptian leaders had aspired to and attained only after their drastic intervention in 1955. Then why was the Nehruvian government not content with the unified confessional system that it had inherited from the British Raj, but instead desired a complete unification? What was it that set Nehru's India apart from Nasser's Egypt? And more importantly, what impact did these different choices of reform have on state–society relations and the rights and freedoms of individuals in each country? In addition to the three main questions posed above, these constitute a second set of enquiries that the present study aims to engage and answer.

HUMAN RIGHTS UNDER STATE-ENFORCED PERSONAL STATUS LAWS

Personal status laws do not exist in isolation. They not only interact with one another, but also are closely intertwined with the general or territorial laws of the state such as criminal law, domestic violence law, housing law, social security law, welfare law, immigration law, labor law and even the constitutional law (Brown 1997). From this point of view, it can be argued that a government may pursue multiple policy objectives as it attempts to intervene in its personal status system. With this understanding, however, the present study primarily focuses on the ideological and political objectives that post-independence Israeli, Egyptian and Indian governments sought to achieve by means of institutional, normative and substantive interventions into their respective personal status systems in the process of state- and nation-building, and the implications of these interventions and state-enforced religious family laws on fundamental rights and liberties of their citizens.

For instance, Israeli leaders maintained a variant of the Ottoman *millet* system in order to homogenize and preserve the Israeli-Jewish identity while segregating and bolstering communal divisions among the country's non-Jewish inhabitants. Nasser abolished religious courts to centralize and systematize his country's legal system, and reportedly to break down the independent political power of religious authorities who had opposed his revolutionary agenda (Crecelius 1966, p. 35). Likewise, the post-independence Indian government sought normative unification of personal laws to build a secular state and eradicate communal sentiments, and thereby inculcate among Indians a sense of common national identity. These varying motivations (differing regimes' choices and ideological orientations) to intervene in personal status systems, different modes of reform, as well as varying configurations of state–community relations, have led to the emergence of a distinct form of personal status in each country (i.e., "fragmented confessional" system in Israel; "unified confessional" system in Egypt, and "unified semi-confessional" system in India). But what about the effects of these divergent personal status systems on the rights and liberties of people who are subject to their purview? Can any particular system be said to be more favorable to or protective of individual rights and liberties in contrast to others? I shall deal with these questions at great length later in the book; however, at this point it should suffice to note that insofar as their impact on human rights is concerned, as corroborated by empirical findings, I have not observed much significant difference between various forms of personal status systems (e.g., fragmented confessional vs. unified semi-confessional, etc.). In other words, empirically speaking, state-enforced religious family laws – no matter which ideal type they resemble – tend to affect human rights in a similar vein by imposing various limitations and disabilities upon four groups of rights and liberties in particular: *the freedom of religion* (which encompasses: the right to have religion, the right to change religion, the right not to profess any religion, the right to profess religion without government intervention, and the right to be free from religious coercion); *equality before the law*; *marital and familial rights* (including right to marry, right to divorce, right to inheritance, etc.); and *procedural rights* (these include individuals' right to fair trial, due process and the right to seek effective remedy when their rights are violated) (An-Naim, Gort *et al.* 1995; van der Vyver and Witte 1996; Gearon 2002; Runzo, Martin *et al.* 2003;

Temperman 2010; Witte and Green 2012). This is especially true when people are forcibly subjected to the jurisdiction of state-sanctioned religious laws and authorities without their explicit or implied consent, as in Israel or Egypt.

However, as explained in greater detail in Chapter 3, this contention should not mislead the reader to assume that there is an inevitable or irreconcilable conflict between "religion" per se and fundamental rights and liberties. This book is not about the treatment of human rights under certain religious traditions (e.g., Islam, Judaism, Christianity or Hinduism), or "classical" religious laws and precepts derived from ancient scriptural or prophetic sources of these traditions. Instead, the book primarily concerns itself with state-appropriated and enforced religiously inspired family or personal status laws – because in personal status systems the state, which is an innately secular institution (An-Naim 2008), codifies and legislates the so-called religious laws, incorporates institutions of certain ethno-religious communities into its legal system, and takes it upon itself to interpret and enforce these laws through its agencies. In this respect, the findings of my investigation across the Israeli, Egyptian and Indian personal status systems reveal that when the state becomes the interpreter and enforcer of religious family laws this usually results in the erosion of fundamental rights and liberties – particularly affecting the four groups of rights mentioned above. With this in mind, the following chapters identify and analyze common human and women's rights concerns occurring under the Israeli, Egyptian and Indian personal status systems.

Even though state-enforced religious family laws impose similar restrictions and disabilities upon all persons who are subject to their jurisdiction (especially when people do not consent to application of religious laws), their impact tends to be harsher on certain groups. These include women, non-religious people, religious dissidents, individuals who do not belong to a recognized religious community (e.g., Baha'i in Egypt), and last but not least the religious people or the believers. As noted earlier, most personal status-related human rights concerns occur in respect of equality before the law (especially gender inequality in regard to marriage, divorce, maintenance, alimony and inheritance), freedom of religion and marital and familial rights. Since male-dominated political authorities who oversaw etatization processes in the three countries under examination often adopted restrictive and gender-unequal aspects and interpretations of sacred texts, religious narratives and customs, the resultant personal status laws have often negatively impacted women's familial, social and bodily rights (Mir-Hosseini 2009; Sonbol 2009). For instance, under the state-enforced Muslim family laws, Egyptian and Indian Muslim men have a legally recognized right to marry up to four wives and divorce them anytime by uttering *talaq* thrice – without even appearing before a court (Esposito and Delong-Bas 2001, pp. 27–34, 49–61; Subramanian 2008). Under the Israeli state-enforced Jewish law, a child who is born to an *agunah* – a woman who is denied a *get* or divorce writ by her husband – is known as *mamzer* (bastard). *Mamzerim* (plural of *mamzer*) and their descendants are forbidden from marrying other Jews for ten generations (Halperin-Kaddari 2004). In order to identify *mamzerim* and implement this religious restriction, the Interior Ministry in Israel maintains a national registry and keeps the names of all *mamzerim* in a database. Similarly in India, under the traditional *Mitakshara* system, which constitutes the backbone of the Hindu Succession Act (HSA), women were long denied equal rights to inheritance and property. The law, even after the recent gender-equalizing changes, continues to grant Hindu parents a testamentary freedom to disinherit their daughters from their self-acquired property and bequeath everything to their male descendants (Agarwal 2005). Lastly, although the rights of non-religious people and religious dissidents are believed to be at greater risk under state-enforced religious laws, the rights of religiously observant people (even those who adhere to the state-sponsored majority faith) should not be overlooked (Temperman 2010, p. 192). In other words, contrary to common belief, the state application of religious laws does not necessarily do a service to religious people or communities, either. On the contrary, as Osanloo demonstrates in the context of state-enforced *shari'a* regulations in Iran, when the state takes it upon itself to interpret and apply religious laws, besides affecting rights of non-religious people this also interferes with the faithful's right to profess their own religion and freely interpret its tenets without state intervention (Osanloo 2009).

The story presented in this book is not just one of how people's rights and freedoms are affected by state-sanctioned religious laws and institutions, but is also of how people respond to limitations and disabilities imposed upon their rights, and what tactics and strategies they use to challenge and reform religious laws and advance their rights and freedoms under personal status systems. In this regard, I maintain that pluri-legal personal status systems can be as much enabling as constraining. They provide a nurturing ground for a variety of resistance strategies from forum-shopping to hermeneutic and rule-making communities which in turn enable and empower individuals to challenge the very foundation and legitimacy of state-sanctioned religious laws, renegotiate with secular and religious authorities rules pertaining to marriage, divorce, maintenance, etc., and make and remake personal status systems to overcome limitations and disabilities imposed upon their rights and freedoms. In other words, people do not just sit on the sidelines and silently accept the imposed limitations and disabilities, they constantly resist and try to find ways to change the system and promote their rights and liberties from within.

As already said, states intervene in their personal status systems in order to impress a particular vision of subjectivity upon society, regulate social and familial relations and ascertain the rules of membership in the political community. However, as individuals engage in the above-mentioned strategies of resistance to escape disabilities imposed upon their rights, they constantly find themselves not only contesting the legitimacy of state-imposed religious norms and institutions, and hegemonic narratives of gender and subjectivity, but also opposing and undermining the state's overall personal status policy and the specific designs and objectives that it aims to achieve through its interventions into the field of personal status. In other words, people who continuously interact, renegotiate with, and make rights demands from personal status institutions decisively interfere with the fate of government's designs to manipulate and turn the personal status field into an instrument of state power. In this connection, I suggest that beyond its most obvious normative and theoretical value there is also an added methodological value in investigating human rights discourses, talks,[4] and particular strategies people devise in response to limitations and disabilities imposed upon their rights under state-imposed religious laws, as this may allow us to closely examine whether a particular government has achieved the objectives that originally led it to intervene in its personal status system. I call this innovative and pragmatic use of human rights "the field of human rights as a testing ground" approach, and harness it throughout the book to illusrate whether the Israeli, Egyptian and Indian governments have succeeded or failed in attaining the ideological and political objectives that initially led them to undertake or

---

[4] "Rights talk" is an essential concept for understanding how individuals and groups in various socio-political and cultural settings articulate their grievances and mobilize existing institutions and channels to make rights claims (Osanloo 2009, p. 6).

refrain from certain interventions in their personal status systems. Lastly, there is also a didactic and practical value in investigating the emerging human rights discourses and methods that human rights actors employ under the Israeli, Egyptian and Indian personal status systems, as they may offer valuable policy-relevant lessons to human rights defenders who struggle to uphold individual rights and liberties under similar religio-legal and customary systems elsewhere. I revisit the pedagogical value of the three case studies and sum up their policy-relevant lessons in the concluding chapter.

METHODOLOGY AND RESEARCH DESIGN

In this book I employ a comparative qualitative methodology through in-depth analyses of three countries, namely Israel, Egypt and India. The reason why these three countries were chosen is threefold: First, they offer an opportunity to closely observe various phases of judicial and legal consolidation and differing reform strategies adopted by postcolonial/post-imperial nations in the process of state-building. For example, Israel maintained a highly fragmented personal status system and refrained from both institutional and normative unification. Egypt inherited the same form of personal status system as Israel but undertook institutional unification which included an overarching network of national courts. India, whose courts were already unified by the British, sought normative unification by abolishing religious laws and enacting a UCC in their place. Second, the case selection also yields a considerable degree of variation on the dependent (form of personal status system) and independent variables that the present study employs (Geddes 1990; King, Keohane *et al.* 1994, pp. 128–132). Moreover, the selection of these countries also allows me to observe the three largest religio-legal systems in the world (Muslim, Hindu and Jewish) and study their impact on human and women's rights from a comparative perspective. Third, Israel, Egypt and India are similar countries in many regards – they share a similar colonial/imperial history: At one point, they were all ruled by grand Islamic empires (the Ottomans in Israel and Egypt, and the Mughals in India) and later by the British Empire. Also, they are all multi-ethnic and multi-religious societies with a long-established tradition of formal plurality, particularly in the field of personal status.

In addition to cross-national comparisons among these three countries, I also employ cross-communal, cross-temporal within-case analyses in each country in order to increase the number of observations and infer more generalizable results on state policies towards pluri-legal personal status systems (Ragin 1987, pp. 69–84; King, Keohane *et al.* 1994, pp. 51–53; George and Bennett 2005, pp. 151–180). I simultaneously harness Mill's methods of agreement and difference for my spatio-temporal cross-case and within-case analyses throughout the book (Lieberson 1991, 1994). The limitations of both methods are well-known (i.e., they tend to result in spurious correlations and omit some variables, etc.). Thus, in order to overcome these limitations, I employ the method of process-tracing as well (Goldstone 2003, pp. 47–52; Mahoney 2003, pp. 363–365; Munck 2004, pp. 107–112; George and Bennett 2005, pp. 205–232). The advantage of process-tracing is that it allows me to analyze diachronically the changes in the composition of independent variables over time (e.g., choice of regime type or relative balance of power between the state and ethno-religious groups) and account for corresponding variations on the dependent variable.

This book primarily relies on data that I gathered during my fieldwork in Israel, Egypt, India and the United Kingdom between 2003 and 2005, and later in 2010. In each country I visited major libraries, various government offices and private and non-governmental agencies in search of historical and archival data. I collected a number of documents, including various government publications, parliamentary debates, judgments of both secular and religious courts, as well as newspapers, pamphlets, newsletters and reports published by various organizations in these four countries. In addition, when possible, I observed court proceedings at various civil and religious courts, from informal *shari'a* courts in India to ecclesiastical courts in Israel. More importantly, I also interviewed 185 individuals, including religious leaders, civil and religious court judges, lawyers, litigants, politicians, clergy-members and human and women's rights activists from 20 different ethno-religious communities in Israel, Egypt and India.

Another major source of information is secondary sources, such as books, journals and dissertations written at major research universities as well as conference papers and several unpublished manuscripts which were kindly made available to me by their authors. Perhaps I should also add to this list my email correspondences with a number of Israeli, Egyptian, Indian, British, American and European scholars who have tirelessly and patiently responded to my questions and shared their expertise with me on many different issues that arose during both the research and writing stages of this book.

AN EXPLANATORY NOTE REGARDING THE USE OF TERMINOLOGY

This book analyzes personal status systems of Israel, Egypt and India. At the outset it should be noted that in this study I adopt a narrower definition of "personal status" which includes only the matters of marriage, divorce, spousal maintenance and, to some extent, succession or inheritance. Historically, "personal status" has been a much broader concept that included all matters of family law and succession as well as religious endowments. Although personal status systems still continue to exist in many parts of the world today, their content varies widely from one country to another. Hence, by narrowing the scope of the concept, I aim to increase its portability or comparability across the cases analyzed in the book (Sartori 1970, 1984). At this point, it should also be noted that the system which is known as "personal status" or "*al-ahwal al-shakhsiyya*" in the Middle East is referred to as personal law in India and other South Asian countries colonized by the British in the past. Hence, throughout the text I use both terms interchangeably. Another important note regarding local usage differences is that the Arabic term "*shari'a*" (often used to refer to Islamic law in Israel and Egypt), is transliterated as "*shariat*" in India. Similarly, due to transliteration differences, the term *qadi* (*shari'a* judge in Israel or in Egypt before 1955) is known as *qazi* in India.

While investigating personal status systems of the three countries, I limit the scope of my analysis exclusively to the norms and institutions of the two most populous communities in each country, namely, the majority and the largest minority community. However, this does not mean that other communities are completely ignored or excluded from the analysis. Instead, it only means that smaller communities are not necessarily studied in detail, while the existence of their norms and institutions are still accounted for as part of a broader analysis of formal plurality in each country.

Regarding the term "fundamental rights and liberties" used throughout the book, I do not offer a definition of my own, but simply refer to the rights and freedoms enshrined in the national constitutional documents and basic laws[5] (of Israel, Egypt and India) and the Universal Declaration of Human Rights of 1948 (UDHR) as "fundamental" or

---

[5] Israel – the Declaration of the Establishment of the State of Israel (1948), and Basic Law: Human Dignity and Liberty (1992); Egypt – the Constitution of the Arab Republic of Egypt (1971); India – the Constitution of India (1950).

"basic" human rights. As noted earlier, some of the rights and liberties which are negatively affected by state-enforced personal status laws include equality before the law (Articles 1, 2 and 7 of the UDHR), marital and familial rights (Articles 12 and 16 of the UDHR), procedural rights (Articles 8 and 10 of the UDHR) and the freedom of thought, conscience and religion (Articles 18 and 19 of the UDHR), which include the right to change religion and the right to be free from religious coercion and persecution.

Regarding the geographical definitions of the countries employed in the book, it should be noted that the word "Israel" is exclusively used in the meaning of Israel's pre-June 5, 1967 borders over which its sovereignty is internationally recognized; while the word "India" is used to include all Indian states but the State of Jammu and Kashmir, which has been granted a special status under the 1950 Indian Constitution (Article 370) and excluded from the purview of Indian personal laws in force. Similarly, Indian personal laws (Hindu, Muslim, etc.) do not apply in Goa and the enclaves of Daman and Diu on the Arabian Sea coast where civil family codes – largely based on the Portuguese Civil Code – uniformly apply to all citizens irrespective of religion. In consonance with Schedules 5 and 6 of the 1950 Constitution, scheduled tribes or indigenous populations are also excluded from the purview of Indian personal laws.

Lastly, regarding the historical periodization (i.e., pre-/postcolonial/imperial or pre-/post-independence) that I employ in the book, the following are the dates on which Israel and India won their independence respectively: May 14, 1948 and August 15, 1947. The cutoff date that I use for Egypt is June 18, 1953 on which date the country was proclaimed a republic. In the next three years the Suez Canal was nationalized and British troops were forced to leave the country, which brought British occupation to an abrupt end and granted Egypt full independence. I also refer to Israel, Egypt and India as postcolonial or post-imperial states throughout the book. Without engaging in a lengthy discussion about whether the Ottoman state was a colonial state on a par with the British colonial state in India, or whether the British Mandate in Palestine or Protectorate in Egypt was a form of colonial rule, or whether Israel can be considered a postcolonial state – as such questions are beyond the scope of this book – I simply define the postcolonial or post-imperial state as a state that upon independence inherited a bureaucratic apparatus as well as a legal system and culture that had been imposed upon the native institutions and populations by an occupying foreign government (Young 1994; Benton 2002).

ORGANIZATION OF THE BOOK

This introductory chapter has summarized the main research questions and theoretical arguments and briefly discussed case selection, research design and methodology. The next two chapters present the theoretical foundations of my argument about the political origins of contemporary personal status systems and their impact on human and women's rights. Chapter 2, questioning the universality of the so-called Western European trajectory of state-building and judicial consolidation, offers an alternative view on state-building in the postcolonial world. The chapter then identifies three ideal, typical personal status systems (i.e., fragmented confessional, unified confessional and unified semi-confessional) and explains what factors (i.e., ideological orientation, regime choice and relative balance of power between the state and ethno-religious groups) contribute to the formation of each type.

Chapter 3 examines the impact of state-sanctioned religious family laws and institutions on human and women's rights under personal status systems. The chapter also discusses various resistance strategies and tactics (i.e., forum-shopping, hermeneutic and rule-making communities) that people frequently employ under personal status systems in order to overcome the limitations and disabilities imposed upon their rights and liberties by state-enforced religious laws. The chapter also shows that through use of these resistance strategies people often challenge the foundations and legitimacy of personal status systems, and in some instances successfully reform the system from within by renegotiating with secular and religious authorities rules pertaining to marriage, divorce, maintenance and inheritance. That is to say, through their everyday interactions with state-sanctioned religious laws and institutions, individuals constantly make and remake personal status systems, and challenge and subvert specific designs and objectives that governments hope to achieve by intervening in their personal status systems. By the same token, the chapter concludes by outlining "the field of human rights as a testing ground" approach that I harness throughout the book to probe whether the Israeli, Egyptian and Indian governments succeeded in attaining the objectives that had originally led them to intervene in their respective personal status systems.

Chapters 4, 5 and 6 are the empirical chapters, which test the theoretical propositions presented in Chapters 2 and 3 by focusing on the cases of Israel, Egypt and India respectively. Each empirical chapter begins with a detailed description of the prevailing personal status system in the specified country, explaining relevant laws, jurisprudence and the court systems in detail. These descriptive sections aim to familiarize the reader with the legal and institutional intricacies of personal status systems, and provide a historical analysis of how these pluri-legal structures were established or solidified under colonial rule and how they were reformed and manipulated by the nationalist leaders after independence. The second sections of the empirical chapters are devoted to an explanation of why and how each country has ended up with a particular type of personal status system – fragmented confessional in Israel, unified confessional in Egypt and unified semi-confessional in India – by closely looking at contributing factors such as regime choice, ideological orientation and the balance of power between the state and ethno-religious communities. The third section of each empirical chapter addresses the questions of how these particular forms of personal status affect the rights and freedoms of individuals in each society, how individuals interact with religious norms and institutions, what tactics and strategies they employ to defend and advance their rights and liberties, and how they renegotiate and remake the personal status systems through their interactions with state-sanctioned religious laws and institutions. Empirical chapters conclude with a brief assessment of each government's performance in attaining the goals that originally led it to intervene in its personal status system.

If even democracies (i.e., Israel and India) cannot sufficiently shield their citizens against restrictive practices of state-enforced religious norms and authorities, then what are the chances of upholding fundamental rights and liberties under religious legal systems elsewhere? Are there any best practices or lessons to be learned from the experiences of these three countries? The concluding chapter engages these vital questions and summarizes policy-relevant lessons learned from the three case studies. Since it is written with policy-makers and human rights defenders in mind, the chapter also makes a number of policy recommendations. Recommendations are primarily based on my fieldwork in Israel, Egypt and India and on recent field research in Sierra Leone, as well as the experience and knowledge that I gained in my capacity as an adviser on two United Nations and ICHRP projects that dealt with questions of human rights under pluri-legal religious and customary systems.

2

PERSONAL STATUS, NATION-BUILDING AND THE POSTCOLONIAL STATE

Why do personal status systems exist? How did Israel, Egypt, India and other postcolonial/post-imperial nations respond to pluri-legal systems that they inherited upon independence? What factors influenced their choice of reform or their decision whether or not to carry out institutional or normative interventions? As noted in the previous chapter, differing regime choices and varying configurations of state–community relations gave rise to a distinct personal status system in each country. But what socio-political factors and considerations specifically contributed to the emergence of each type of personal status system? Put in concrete terms, given both Israel and Egypt inherited almost the same *millet* system from the Ottomans, why is there so much difference between their personal status systems today? For instance, personal status laws are applied by state-sanctioned religious courts in Israel, but by civil courts in Egypt because the Free Officers abolished religious courts and unified them under an overarching network of national courts in 1955. Then why did Egypt undertake unification of religious courts while Israel deliberately refrained from doing so? In spite of their strong desire to unify the court system, however, the Egyptian leaders never tried to defragment scattered communal laws and unify them under a uniform civil code, as their Indian counterparts attempted to do in the 1950s. Why did the revolutionary Nasserist government in Egypt merely confine itself to institutional unification, and not aspire to undertake normative unification as the Indian government did? Or what differentiated the Nehruvian regime's policy towards pluri-legal personal status laws from the policies of Egyptian and Israeli governments? For instance, why did India set for itself the goal of Uniform Civil Code (UCC) (embodied in Article 44 of the 1950 Constitution) while the other two governments remained completely silent on the issue of normative unification?

The present chapter aims to answer these very important questions. In this vein, the chapter opens with a brief discussion of state-building and legal unification in the postcolonial world. It then moves on to discuss specific socio-political and ideological objectives that various postcolonial governments have aimed to attain through their interventions in the field of personal status. Right at this point, the chapter introduces the three typical forms of personal status (i.e., fragmented confessional; unified confessional; and unified semi-confessional), and concludes by detailing what confluence of factors (historical, social, political, etc.) has contributed to the emergence of each model, and how they differed from one another, with specific references to various postcolonial nations including the three case studies.

AN ALTERNATIVE TRAJECTORY OF STATE-BUILDING AND LEGAL UNIFICATION

Students of Western European political history often define the modern state as a centralized and autonomous organization "which controls the population occupying a definite territory" (Tilly 1975a, p. 70). The state establishes its control over society by utilizing the law as a coercive and constitutive force (Kelsen 1945, p. 190; Allott 1980, pp. 45–46; Young 1994, p. 20). According to this centralist point of view that has come to dominate the literature, a government without an exclusive mandate to legislate and adjudicate is not considered a "full-fledged state," as it is assumed to lack the ability to effectively control the normative universe and the subject population on its territory (Nettl 1968; Jackson 1990; Spruyt 1994). In other words, the ability to establish a monopolistic control over the legal affairs of a subject population (i.e., the state being sole law-giver and enforcer on its territory) has come to be viewed as an inseparable aspect of stateness (Smith 1987, p. 135). Those who subscribe to this centralist view report that, from the thirteenth century onwards, Western European states began to gradually subdue rival normative orderings and establish their monopoly on rule-making in their societies (Kelsen 1945; Weber 1954; Galanter 1966; Poggi 1978; Shapiro 1981; Bentzon and Brøndsted 1983; Berman 1983; Durkheim 1984; Migdal 1988; Poggi 1990; Soto 2000). In fact, as some argue, by the end of the seventeenth century England and France had already achieved considerable levels of legal unification through formation of an extensive network of national courts, staffed with professionally trained, state-salaried and appointed judges who applied uniform laws throughout the national territory (Pollock and Maitland 1898, pp. 136–173; Holdsworth 1944, pp. 32–34; Smith 1979, pp. 237–241; Shapiro 1981, pp. 65–125; Kaeuper 1988; Caenegem 1992, p. 100).

Later, in the eighteenth and nineteenth centuries, Germany, Austria, Switzerland, Belgium, Italy, Spain, Portugal and others were reported to have followed course and undertaken a similar process of state-building and judicial consolidation (Arthurs 1985, p. 8).[1] Galanter, for instance, argues that the development, expansion and consolidation of the national legal systems in Europe often involved common directions of change. Codified and uniform "laws [were] applied over wider spatial, ethnic and class areas; personal law [was] replaced by territorial law" (Galanter 1966, p. 154). The legal systems were standardized in the sense that the application of rules became reproducible and predictable. "Disorderly" plural jurisdictions were to a great extent replaced by a single set of national courts with layers of appeal and review to ensure that the actions of individual courts would conform to national standards. Moreover, the system was also put in the hands of full-time professionals who were appointed and salaried by the state. This oft-repeated and mythified narrative of judicial consolidation and rationalization – based on a retrospective fallacy[2] that this was a carefully planned and fully self-conscious process – has been closely associated

---

[1] For further information on judicial consolidation in Europe, see: Pollock and Maitland (1898, pp. 136–173); Brissaud (1912); Huebner (1918); Holdsworth (1944, pp. 32–34, 638); Cassin (1956, pp. 46–48); Smith (1979, pp. 237–252); Shapiro (1981); Watson (1981, p. 112; 1984, pp. 99–130); Katz (1986a, b); Kaeuper (1988, pp. 134–183); Caenegem (1992, pp. 100–102); Kelly (1992); Baumgartner (1995); Wieacker (1995, pp. 72–84); Zweigert and Kötz (1998); Glendon et al. (1999); Crubaugh (2001); and Baker (2002).

[2] The "retrospective fallacy" which creates the illusion that the centralization of legal institutions and political authority was complete and a direct result of a carefully planned and fully self-conscious process of state-building in Europe has been repeatedly refuted in the last several decades (Tilly 1975a, 1975b). Many scholars have argued that, although the Western European states achieved considerable degrees of judicial consolidation in the past, in effect their legal systems have never been "fully" centralized because the process of legal unification is a continuous process and it can never practically be completed. In other words, there is no such thing as complete unification in the normative universe. Thus, every society, including the so-called industrialized Western nations, demonstrates characteristics of legal plurality, albeit at different levels and forms (Pospisil 1967, 1978; Santos 1980; Galanter 1981; Greenhouse 1982; Fitzpatrick 1983, 1984; Arthurs 1985; Merry 1988; Resnik 1989; Dane 1991; Greenhouse and Strijbosch 1993; Halperin-Kaddari 1993; Harring 1994; Tsuk 2001; Morse 2004; Richland and Deer 2004; Woodman 2004; Yılmaz 2005).

with the emergence of the modern Western European state (Kelsen 1945; Weber 1954; Strayer 1970; Anderson 1974; North 1981; Giddens 1985; North 1990; Cutler 2003).

Because the Western state was long portrayed as "the" model for state-building, many scholars have deterministically viewed the so-called European path to judicial centralization and bureaucratization as the only possible direction for the development of the state (Nettl 1968; Jackson 1990; Spruyt 1994). However, in recent years the universality of the European trajectory of state-making through varying forms of contestation and centralization of political power has been increasingly questioned by scholars (Barkey 1994; Kohli 1994; Daloz and Chabal 1999; Herbst 2000; Lopez-Alves 2000; Boone 2003a, 2003b). In fact, some of these studies have successfully shown that the Western model did not exhaust all possible forms of state consolidation, and the experiences of the Western European states applied only partially to other parts of the world.

Along similar lines, this study makes its own contribution to this new generation of scholarship not only by challenging the universality of the European path to centralization,[3] but also by identifying and explaining an alternative mode of state-making and judicial consolidation for the postcolonial world. In this regard, I assert that the process of state-building and legal centralization is diverse, and that non-Western states have improvised their own means and forms of state development in accordance with the special needs of their social structures and political realities. Thus, as I illustrate in the rest of the book, most postcolonial states have not followed the so-called Western European trajectory of "wholesale" judicial consolidation but rather opted for "selective" unification. In other words, as they worked towards greater degrees of centralization and systematization throughout their legal systems,[4]

---

[3] State-building, especially the process of judicial consolidation, is neither unidirectional nor without variation even within the Western world. For instance, in the last three decades the myth of the Western state with an undivided domestic sovereignty presiding over a fully uniform and centralized legal system has been increasingly challenged in the literature. For some representative examples of this scholarship, see Galanter (1981); Arthurs (1985); Merry (1988); Resnik (1989); Dane (1991); Tsuk (2001); Morse (2004); Richland and Deer (2004); Woodman (2004); Yılmaz (2005).

[4] Like their Western counterparts, most postcolonial states undertook large-scale legal reforms in order to secure the public order, monopolize the means of violence in their societies and establish modern economic institutions to cope with the demands of the global market. In this regard, they also codified and unified various sources of unwritten and customary norms, set up hierarchically structured networks of national courts and established modern law schools to staff these courts with a new cadre of legal professionals. Yet, as noted above, postcolonial nations did not pursue a

postcolonial governments simultaneously allowed for differing levels and forms of decentralization and fragmentation by maintaining plural institutions and practices in various issue areas such as personal status or family law (Guillet 1998; Scharf and Nina 2001; Crook 2004).[5] This state of decentralized and fragmented rulemaking and application is widely known as "legal pluralism" (Griffiths 1986; Merry 1988).

In its broadest sense, the term "legal pluralism" refers to the simultaneous existence of distinct normative systems within the same socio-legal space (Hooker 1975, p. 6; Moore 1978, pp. 54–81; Tamanaha 1993, p. 192; Chiba 1998, p. 228; Twining 2001, pp. 52–88). Legal pluralism is a worldwide phenomenon. It takes various forms and occurs at different levels in every society. However, in terms of how state law and non-state normative orderings interact, many instances of legal pluralism can be summarily divided into two broad categories: *informal plurality* and *formal plurality* (Sezgin 2004b) or, in Woodman's terminology, *deep legal pluralism* and *state law pluralism* (Woodman 1999).[6]

Informal plurality refers to a situation where state and non-state normative orderings – each with a different source of content and legitimacy – coexist within the same socio-legal space. Formal plurality, on the other hand, emerges when the sovereign recognizes and incorporates into its central administration of justice different sets of norms and institutions for different groups in the population (Woodman 1999). In many regards, formal plurality can be construed as the embodiment of the state's response to the existing multiple normative orderings that claim to regulate the same socio-legal space simultaneously with state law. The responses of the state to non-state normative orderings usually take two forms: (1) normative

---

process of "wholesale" unification but rather a process of selective unification through which they recognized the jurisdiction of non-state normative orderings along with their rule-making and implementing agencies (Anderson 1958; Carson 1958; Cotran 1965; Verhelst 1968; Seidman 1978; Bennett and Vermeulen 1979; Prinsloo 1990; Schacht and Layish 1991; Mirow 2004; Perkins 2004).

[5] In this respect, most postcolonial nations, including the three under examination in the present study, exhibit what Menski calls "Type III" legal systems, combining elements of both general and personal laws. In Menski's classification, in the world as a whole there are three types of legal systems: Type I, Type II and Type III. As noted, Type III systems combine general laws with group-specific personal laws. Type I systems are the so-called uniform systems which claim to apply one law for all, but in reality they always make exceptions and accommodate various ethno-religious and cultural claims. For instance, to accommodate the Sikh turban, "English law has permitted Sikhs to ride a motorcycle without a crash helmet, and to work on building sites without hard hats" (Menski 2009, p. 38). Type II, on the other hand, is often observed in countries like the United States, Canada, Australia and New Zealand which maintain fairly centralized legal systems but grant a special status to indigenous populations (Menski 2012, p. 220).

[6] Griffiths (1986) employs similar taxonomy and respectively calls these two categories "weak" and "strong" legal pluralism.

recognition; and (2) institutional recognition. In the case of normative recognition, the central authority requires its institutions to
give effect to the norms of non-state law (e.g., the recognition of
Coptic Christian personal status laws at the Egyptian courts), whereas
in the case of institutional recognition it incorporates the institutions
of non-state orderings into its administration of law and courts (e.g.,
the incorporation of *shari'a* courts into the Israeli legal system)
(Woodman 1999). Instances of legal pluralism that are observed in
the field of personal status usually appear in the shape of formal
plurality or state law pluralism. Thus, with this in mind, in the rest
of the book the term "legal pluralism" is exclusively used to refer to
instances of formal plurality or state law pluralism.

HISTORICAL AND POLITICAL ORIGINS OF PERSONAL
STATUS SYSTEMS

The constant renegotiation of the rules of the game in the normative
universe between the state and society often leads to an accommodation
that takes the shape of formal plurality, through which central governments recognize and incorporate various sources of non-state law and
institutions into their legal systems for regulation of a wide array of
policy issues from land tenure, property rights and natural resources
management to succession and family law (Wiber 1993; Guillet
1998; Scharf and Nina 2001; Meinzen-Dick and Pradhan 2002;
Benda-Beckmann *et al.* 2006). The issue area that is most commonly
observed to be formally plural across the postcolonial world is the field
of personal status. In fact, the field of personal status epitomizes a
quintessential instance of formal plurality, as it is historically one of
the earliest issue areas in which various sources of non-state norms and
institutions were recognized and incorporated by the central authorities
(Hooker 1975; Griffiths 1986, p. 6; Menski 2000, p. 131).

In brief, a personal status system, for the purposes of the present study,
can be defined as a system in which members of various ethno-religious
communities that are specifically recognized as such by central authorities
are subject to jurisdiction of state-sanctioned communal norms and institutions in regard to personal or familial matters such as marriage, divorce,
spousal maintenance, inheritance and so forth. Such systems often exhibit
not a unified or a territorial body of family law that is uniformly applied to
all citizens irrespective of ethno-religious considerations, but instead a
pluri-legal system in which a Muslim is subject to state-enforced *shari'a*,

a Jew to state-enforced *halakhah*, a Christian to state-enforced canon law, a Hindu to state-enforced Hindu law, and so on.

Not all, but most personal status systems historically descend from personal law systems that had been widely employed by multi-ethnic empires in the past (i.e., the Roman, Ottoman, British, French and Dutch Empires). In particular, the system was popularized by the Ottomans as the "*millet*" system (Benjamin 1982; Karpat 1982; Goffman 1994). In many regards, contemporary personal status systems, widely observed in the Middle East, North Africa and Asia, may be said to resemble this historical model. The tangential resemblance, however, has misled many to construe the survival and persistence of formal plurality in the field of personal status as an anachronistic legacy of colonialism (Hooker 1975; Bennett and Peart 1983; Fitzpatrick 1983; Griffiths 1986; Roberts and Mann 1991; Young 1994; Bogdan 2000; Larson 2001; Benton 2002). For example, such scholars as Hooker (1975, pp. 454–479), Griffiths (1986, pp. 7–8) and Vanderlinden (1989, p. 153) argue that plural personal status systems have survived because, after independence, most postcolonial states, despite their strong desires to unify their legal system under an overarching network of law and courts, failed to overcome the resistance of ethno-religious groups and thereby were forced to continue to recognize the communal jurisdictions which were originally granted autonomy by their colonial or imperial predecessors.

The "colonial legacy" explanations can be harnessed as a powerful catalytic variable to understand the range of options and strategies which were available to postcolonial leaders in encountering challenges of formal plurality. But they cannot alone suffice to explain the reason why variant forms of personal status still continue to exist, as they suffer two major shortcomings. First, they neglect the agency of the postcolonial state and the interests of its leaders in preserving, controlling and manipulating colonial institutions of personal status by consistently treating postcolonial states as disempowered or incapacitated entities. Second, they also present a homeostatic vision of formal plurality as if institutions of personal status were permanently "frozen" in the time of colonialism, and afterwards not open to alteration by the postcolonial agency.

The colonial period was critical because it was within that period that the foundations of current personal status systems were laid out. But this does not mean that postcolonial states were permanently "locked in" to a self-reinforcing path that predestined their options and forced them to accept pre-existing institutions of personal status (Kuper and

Kuper 1965, pp. 15–17; Opoku 1970; Charrad 2001, p. 7; Pierson 2004, p. 52; Thelen 2004, p. 8). On the contrary, as evidence suggests, rulers of many postcolonial nations pursued policies in the realm of personal status that considerably differed from those of their colonial predecessors. In this regard, experiences of many postcolonial nations suggest that modern – as well as pre-modern – personal status systems have come into existence not as a result of historical contingency, but as a direct outcome of a dynamic interplay between the ruling elites' choice of regime type and ideological orientation on the one hand, and the relative balance of power between central authorities and ethnoreligious groups on the other. Personal status systems are ever-changing dynamic constructions. They constantly evolve, emulating changes that occur in the composition of these forces that initially contributed to their very formation. Moreover, as explained in Chapter 3, individuals who regularly interact with personal status institutions also play a pivotal role in their constant remaking. In the final analysis, as the following chapters demonstrate, personal status systems of postcolonial/post-imperial nations have constantly evolved and taken new forms in response to changes in political preferences of the ruling elites, the capacity of the ethno-religious groups to resist government meddling, and the challenges posed by individuals who used these pluri-legal constructs.

REGULATING PLURAL PERSONAL STATUS SYSTEMS IN THE NATION-BUILDING PROCESS

The regulation of family law or personal status matters has always been of great interest to political authorities throughout the world (Westermarck 1922; Weber 1954; Dewar and Parker 1992; Mirow 2004). Family law has long been considered by political elites as a useful instrument to ascertain the rules of inclusion and exclusion within the political community by dictating to their subjects who could marry whom or who could inherit from whom through juridification of reproductive relations in society (Grubbs 1995, pp. 261–316; Stevens 1999; Basson 2004; Bell 2004, pp. 253–288). Particularly with the advancement of capitalist production relations and the monopolization of bureaucratic administration from the nineteenth century onwards, the family has further become the subject of stricter state regulation and control (Goody 1983; Chartier 1989; Glendon 1989; Perrot 1990). The governance of family as an "institution" was increasingly brought under state control and surveillance for the efficient utilization of a cheap labor force, the accumulation of capital (Leacock 1977; Hegel 1991, pp. 199–219), the transformation of production relations (Tucker 1978; Weber 1978, pp. 356–384), the reduction of social transaction costs by creating self-controlled individuals (Donzelot 1997; Rose 1999), the profanization of public life (Caldwell 1991; Garvey 1993; Bradley 1996) and the emancipation of women and children from patriarchal oppression (Freeman 1984).

In short, as Diamant (2000, p. 3) so eloquently puts it, "modern state rulers have both envisioned a new family order and devoted considerable resources to remolding family structure and relations according to this vision," which, by and large, has reflected their choice of regime type and ideological orientations (Zimmerman 1940; Nimkoff 1965; Gittins 1985). Among these rulers, none has tried harder than those who rose to power by revolutionary means and subsequently undertook a wholesale transformation of societal structures in order to create a new political, legal and moral order. For example, from France to Russia, China and Iran, the very first move of the revolutionary cadres in their quest for creation of a new order was to promulgate new family codes, radically altering the rules of marriage, divorce and succession in their respective societies (Hazard 1939; Timasheff 1965; McAleavy 1968; d'Encausse 1974; Bennigsen and Lemercier-Quelquejay 1979; Traer 1980; Semidyorkin 1988; Hunt 1992; Mir-Hosseini 1993; Diamant 2000).

Similarly, postcolonial/post-imperial leaders, particularly the ones who led their nations to freedom by revolutionary means, have also attempted similar socio-economic and moral transformations in their societies by reforming plural personal status systems that they inherited upon independence (Sezgin 2012c). In terms of objectives that they have sought to achieve, postcolonial nations' interventions into pluri-legal personal status systems can be divided into three groups: (1) interventions that aimed to redefine the provisions of membership in the political community; (2) interventions that aimed to redefine the role of religious norms and institutions in public life; and (3) interventions that were initiated with purely mechanical or non-ideological considerations, such as systematization of law and justice administration or reclamation of full sovereignty by terminating non-state jurisdictions on the national territory.

Redefining provisions of membership in the political community: inclusionary vs. exclusionary regimes

Plural personal status systems were historically employed by imperial regimes to identify and categorize their subject populations according to their racial and ethno-religious differences. As Mamdani (1996) convincingly demonstrates, the preservation and prolongation of such pluri-legal structures by postcolonial rulers have usually brought about further ossification of the colonial categories of race, gender and ethnicity, and by and large subverted their attempts to redefine the terms of membership in the political community (Ahluwalia 2001; Canning and Rose 2002). In this respect, it was often assumed that the survival of the postcolonial nations depended upon their ability to generate a new sense of national identity and belonging among their populations; and for that to happen, racial, sectarian, ethnic and gendered categories of subjectivity and citizenry built under colonial rule had to be completely removed by terminating the socio-political and legal institutions that generated and sustained these categories in the first place (Anderson 1991; Brubaker 1996, pp. 85–89).

In fact, this conviction was particularly common among the leaders of what I call inclusionary regimes,[7] which were – at least rhetorically – committed to the idea of building an egalitarian, homogenous and civic citizenry.[8] The leaders of inclusionary regimes, who firmly believed in the instrumental value of legal uniformity to generate a common sense of nationhood among their citizens, have often deemed the colonial institutions of personal status inconsistent with their political goals and preferences, and thus have taken steps to abolish these pluri-legal systems and replace them with a territorially unified system of law and courts. For instance, as I explain in greater detail in Chapter 6, the post-1947 rulers of India considered the colonial personal law system, which emboldened divisive communal sentiments, inhibitive to their nation-building project, and wanted to replace it with a Uniform Civil Code (UCC) that would help inculcate a sense of national unity among their citizens. Similarly, in the 1960s, both Kenya and Ivory Coast tried – albeit unsuccessfully – to unify their legal systems in order

---

[7] Inclusionary regimes have been strongly committed to the idea that "group-specific identities within a political community are irrelevant when it comes to each individual member's status and rights vis-à-vis the state" (Butenschøn 2000, p. 26), and thus need to be ruled out as valid criteria for membership of the political community.

[8] The type of citizenry that I describe here does not necessarily denote a liberal or democratic form of citizenship, even though its instances often resemble the characteristics of what many call the "liberal" or "universalist" model (Turner 1990; Smith 1997; Shafir and Peled 2002, pp. 4–11).

to generate a common sense of national identity among their ethno-linguistically and religiously divided populations (Anderson 1969; Derrett 1969; Bennett and Vermeulen 1979; Allott 1980, pp. 176–187; Brown 1994, p. 95; Toungara 1994, p. 45; Cotran 1996, p. 196; Mamdani 1996, pp. 128–137).

Unlike inclusionary regimes, which sought to eliminate communal differences by promoting a common national identity, exclusionary regimes were not concerned with cultivating a common sense of belonging among citizens from different ethno-religious backgrounds (Joseph 2005, p. 162). They rather aimed to preserve and reinforce existing ethnic, sectarian and linguistic divisions among their subjects as they often conceived of their citizenry not as a composite unit but as separate communities. Moreover, in such regimes, the relationship between the citizen and the state was often deemed to be indirect in the sense that individuals were considered to be first and foremost members of their cultural groups; and their status as members of these cultural groups in turn determined the nature of their relationship to the state and their status in the larger political community (Butenschøn 2000, p. 23).

Mamdani has shown that dual legal systems had long been appropriated by exclusionary colonial and postcolonial regimes throughout Africa in order to create stratified categories of subjectivity by excluding certain groups from the spoils of power and denying them the terms of equal membership in the political community (Mamdani 1996, pp. 109–137). In a similar vein, plural personal status systems have also been harnessed by exclusionary regimes to maintain existing group boundaries – sometimes by imposing strict rules of endogamy – in order to sustain demographic and socio-political primacy of dominant ethno-religious groups while denying equal rights and representation to minority communities. Thus, exclusionary regimes have conserved, and whenever possible reinforced, colonial institutions of personal status in order to promote their particular vision of subjectivity and build a web of corresponding hierarchies among the citizens (Brubaker 1996, pp. 85–89; Marx 1996; Chesterman and Galligan 1997; Yiftachel 1997, 1999; Butenschøn 2000; Smooha and Jarve 2005).

For instance, the founding leaders of Israel preserved a variant of the old *millet* system that they had inherited from the Ottoman Empire (through the British Mandate) and appropriated it in the process of state- and nation-building as a powerful instrument of horizontal homogenization within the Jewish community, and of vertical segmentation between Jewish and non-Jewish communities (more on this in Chapter 4). Similarly, the Lebanese state also preserved a variant of the Ottoman *millet* system that it had inherited upon independence. The Lebanese constitutional system is based upon a peculiar power-sharing arrangement that divides major political offices and administrative responsibilities among the six largest ethno-religious groups in the country: Maronite, Greek Orthodox, Greek Catholic, Sunni, Shi'a and Druze. As Saadeh (2002, p. 450) puts it, the mere fact that governmental positions had to be divided proportionally among various communities made keeping the *millet* system imperative in order to know precisely who was a Muslim, Christian or a Druze, and maintain primordial communal identities as they were carved into the National Charter in 1943. In fact, this is what personal status systems are good for, and what the *millet* system did for Lebanon and Israel: to compartmentalize people into ethno-religious and tribal groupings and keep them apart (El-Gemayel 1985; Joseph 1999, 2000; Maktabi 2000; Reinkowski and Saadeh 2006, p. 99).

Redefining the role of religion in public life: secular vs. theocratically inclined regimes

Another ideological goal that some postcolonial states have strived to attain by meddling in existing personal status systems is to redefine the role of state-sanctioned religious norms and institutions in public life. In personal status systems the central authority incorporates religious laws and institutions of certain ethno-religious communities into its legal system and takes it upon itself to apply and enforce these laws through its agencies. This is what I call the process of "etatization," or state appropriation of religious norms and institutions. I explain in greater detail the normative and political implications of etatization on the legitimacy of religious norms and institutions as well as the state's claim to apply preordained "divine" laws and commandments in Chapter 3; however, at this point it shall suffice to note that this aspect of personal status systems has captured the attention of leaders around the world who have wanted to either increase or decrease – depending upon their ideological preferences – the role of religion in the public sphere (Loimeier 1996; Ezzat 2000b). As individual experiences of many countries as diverse as Turkey (Lewis 1968; Berkes 1998), India (Smith 1963), Ethiopia (David 1962; Allott 1980, p. 185; Idris 1994; Menski 2000, pp. 480–484), Tanzania (Ghai 1975; Rosen 1978; Rwezaura and Wanitzek 1988; Jeppie, Moosa *et al.* 2010, pp. 273–303), Mozambique (Sachs and Welch 1990, pp. 17–20), the People's Democratic Republic of Yemen (Molyneux 1991), Tunisia (Borrmans 1977, pp. 325–328; Charrad 2001, pp. 202–222; Webb 2007, pp. 297–302) and Yugoslavia (Cohen 1985) illustrate, regimes with secular[9] inclinations have viewed state-enforced religious personal status laws unfavorably and have tried to replace them with non-denominational territorial laws and institutions to secularize socio-legal institutions and practices. In India, for instance, secular considerations, in addition to inclusionary motivations, played a pivotal role in forging the founding elite's attitudes towards state-enforced communal and religious laws and led them to insert Article 44, which directs the union government to enact a secular civil code, into the 1950 Constitution. Likewise, in 1972 the Senegalese government abolished its personal status system and promulgated the *Code de la Famille* with the sole purpose of strengthening secular/laicistic characteristics of the regime and creating a homogenous family law system across the country (Sow, Rennick *et al.* 1989, p. 34; Loimeier 1996, p. 187; Sow 2003, p. 72).

In contrast, regimes which have lacked secular credentials or displayed theocratic propensities have usually been inclined to preserve and even reinforce the existing pluri-legal personal status systems in order to heighten the stature and influence of state-enforced religious precepts and institutions within their legal systems. Regimes with theocratic inclinations are, by default, exclusionary regimes, because they not only identify themselves with a particular belief system and propagate its supremacy, but also relegate individuals who do not profess the "official" faith to a second-class status (e.g., the Ottoman *millet* system) and exclude them from the religio-political community. Thus there has been an added incentive for theocratically oriented regimes to maintain plural personal systems, for they helped them not only keep track of who belonged to what religious community, but also police ethno-religious boundaries in order to prevent interfaith unions which could potentially undermine the dominance and purity of the preponderant religious groups. This latter concern was particularly

---

[9] For the purposes of the present study an ideal-typical secular state is defined as "a state which guarantees individual and corporate freedom of religion, deals with the individual as a citizen irrespective of his religion, is not constitutionally connected to a particular religion ..." (Smith 1963, p. 4). In other words, a secular state should, first, guarantee its citizens' freedom *from* organized religion in the sense that individuals should not be forcibly subjected to the jurisdiction of religious norms and institutions without their explicit consent. Second, a secular state must view the individual as a right-bearing citizen, not as a member of a particular religious group. Stated differently, the link between the state and citizen must be unequivocal and based on considerations other than those of religion. For an elaborate discussion of secularism, see Kuru (2009).

visible in the Israeli leaders' decision to preserve and appropriate the Ottoman *millet* system as one of the main pillars of their nation-building project. In fact, as shown in Chapter 4, the Israeli leaders have employed the *millet* system in its modified form to ensure the survival of Israel as a "Jewish State" and guarantee the endurance of ethno-genealogical, demographic and political primacy of the Jews within it. Similar dynamics have also been at work in Iran and Pakistan – self-proclaimed Islamic states – which, to this day, continue using *millet*-like systems in order to separate non-Muslims from Muslims and ensure the continued predominance of the latter group in the political community (Coulson 1957; Binder 1963; Higgins 1984; Sanasarian 2000, p. 75; Dalacoura 2002, p. 88; Tsadik 2003; Yılmaz 2005, pp. 125–142; Gabriel 2007; Abghari 2008, p. 131; Butt 2008; Ahmed 2010, p. 194).

Interventions motivated by mechanical considerations: technocratic-authoritarian regimes

Beyond such ideological motivations as redefining the provisions of membership in the political community and reevaluating the place of religion in public life, some postcolonial nations have been motivated by rather mechanical or non-ideological concerns while reforming their pluri-legal personal status systems. These were mostly technocratic-authoritarian regimes with developmentalist outlooks.[10] Technocratic-authoritarian regimes were principally characterized by a relative lack of ideological interest in personal status issues. Instead, they were largely propelled by such considerations as consolidating the power of central government, systematizing the administration of law and justice (i.e., lowering its transaction costs, increasing its effectiveness, etc.) and neutralizing religious authorities, preventing them from becoming alternative power foci in the society by divesting them of their personal status-related privileges and powers – an important source of legitimacy among their adherents (Sezgin 2004a, 2009).

Many postcolonial leaders from Egypt's Nasser to Indonesia's Sukarno and the post-1966 military rulers of Nigeria similarly viewed their plural legal systems as an undesirable legacy of colonialism and extra-territoriality which, they thought, had to be completely wiped out for attainment of full sovereignty (Kayaoglu 2010). For instance, the post-independence Indonesian government – particularly during the

---

[10] The concept of "technocratic-authoritarian regime" used in this study is partly inspired by Juan J. Linz's and Guillermo O'Donnell's analyses (O'Donnell 1973, 1979; Linz 2000, pp. 159–208).

period 1947–1960 – systematically replaced *adat* courts with a unified national court system in order to dismantle remnants of Dutch colonialism and expand the power and reach of the new state throughout the archipelago (Lev 2000, pp. 33–70). In fact, for the Sukarno regime, "a unified court system was a prelude to a united sovereign state" (Lukito 2003, p. 20). Likewise, the military regime in Nigeria after 1966 abolished the customary courts and reorganized them under the Ministry of Justice. The Nigerian regime was primarily concerned with the inefficiency, inconsistency and prohibitive cost of customary jurisdictions and resolved to put an end to this "juridical anarchy" by means of institutional unification (Obilade 1969; Nwogogu 1976). The reasons for the abolition of customary courts in Nigeria were detailed in a government-issued white paper in 1971. The Nigerian white paper closely resembled the memorandum issued sixteen years earlier by the Free Officers in Egypt explaining the considerations that led them to abolish *milliyah* (communal) courts and unify them under an overarching network of national courts (Safran 1958). Both documents were written in a strongly "Weberian" tone and emphasized typical concerns of technocratic-authoritarian regimes that motivated them to intervene in their plural personal status systems, i.e. to consolidate the power of emerging parastatal organizations, systematize the administration of justice and put an end to the multiplicity of customary and communal jurisdictions for the attainment of full sovereignty.

The balance of power and social opposition to state intervention

As discussed, differing motives and regime choices have influenced the ways and means through which governments chose to intervene in their personal status systems. Broadly speaking, in terms of the objectives many governments have sought to achieve, we could talk about three prototypical modes of intervention across personal status systems: (1) Normative Intervention; (2) Institutional Intervention; and (3) Substantive Intervention.

Normative interventions were usually undertaken by governments seeking to either extinguish or augment the normative plurality of their personal status systems. To suppress normative plurality, governments have often taken steps to minimize the presence and reach of religious and customary laws in their personal status systems; more ambitious governments have tried to abolish religious laws entirely in order to achieve complete normative unification (that is, the dream or myth of having "one law for all"). In contrast, when they have wanted to embolden or increase normative plurality, they have extended formal recognition to religious and customary laws which were not previously recognized, and incorporated them into their legal systems. For instance, Turkey normatively unified its personal status system in 1926 when the Kemalist regime abolished separate religious laws for Muslims, Christians and Jews, and replaced them with a secular civil code that uniformly applied to all citizens irrespective of religion. Israel, on the other hand, further deepened the normative plurality of its personal status system by recognizing and incorporating religious laws that had not been recognized before 1948, i.e., the recognition of Druze personal status laws in 1957.

Institutional interventions, on the other hand, were implemented by governments that sought to eliminate or boost institutional plurality of their personal status systems. When the goal was to suppress institutional plurality or achieve complete institutional unification, governments have usually tried to terminate separate communal tribunals and install in their place a system of uniform and hierarchically structured national courts with layers of appeal and review that would exercise jurisdiction over all citizens irrespective of their ethno-religious backgrounds. When they have sought to increase institutional plurality, they have instead granted formal recognition to communal courts, which were previously denied such a status, and incorporated them into their legal systems. As I explain in detail later, the Nasserist regime's abolition of the religious courts of fifteen religious communities and transfer of their jurisdiction to national courts in 1955 was a quintessential example of interventions that intended to suppress plurality and achieve institutional unification. By contrast, Israel's recognition and incorporation of Druze courts in 1962 was a typical example of interventions that led to further institutional deunification or fragmentation in personal status systems.

Substantive interventions were implemented by nearly all governments to affect change in material laws of personal status – without due concern for abrogating or augmenting institutional or normative plurality of their legal systems (e.g., enactment of laws to ban bigamy or raise the minimum age for marriage, etc.).[11]

---

[11] Theoretically speaking, substantive interventions can also be used to decrease normative plurality of personal status systems by standardizing certain legal practices across different communities. For example, a law declaring a nationwide ban on polygamous marriages would affect the religious law of each community and effectively decrease the level of the normative plurality in the system by imposing nationwide common standards binding upon all citizens, irrespective of communal affiliation.

TABLE 2.1 Modes of intervention and regime typologies

	Exclusionary and/or theocratically oriented	Technocratic-authoritarian	Inclusionary and/or secular
Normative Intervention	Tend to preserve or reinforce normative plurality by granting recognition to religious laws which were not previously acknowledged	Do not intervene to abolish or reinforce normative plurality	Seek to abolish normative plurality by abolishing religious laws and unifying them under a civil code
Institutional Intervention	Tend to preserve or reinforce institutional plurality by granting recognition to religious courts which were not previously incorporated	Seek to abolish institutional plurality by eliminating religious courts and unifying them under national courts	Seek to abolish institutional plurality by eliminating religious courts and unifying them under national courts
Substantive Intervention	Change material laws of personal status	Change material laws of personal status	Change material laws of personal status

Since each mode of intervention was intended for a particular purpose, governments with differing ideological orientations normally opted for the type of intervention that would best serve their political objectives (see Table 2.1). In fact, individual experiences of many governments have shown that while institutional interventions have often been undertaken by regimes with mere efficiency or sovereignty considerations in mind (i.e., technocratic-authoritarian regimes), normative interventions, which require a strong ideological commitment on the part of governments, have frequently been the choice of ideologically motivated inclusionary or exclusionary regimes (Seidman 1978, pp. 211–212; Bennett and Peart 1983, p. 147).[12] However,

---

[12] This distinction is made here solely for analytical purposes. Especially in systems where communal courts apply their own laws, normative intervention cannot be made in isolation. It has to be made in tandem with institutional intervention. This is because communal courts essentially exist to apply their own laws. Thus there would not be a need for separate communal courts if communal laws had already been abolished and unified under a civil code. Therefore normative unification in a system where there are separate courts for different communities logically entails undertaking institutional unification as well.

all countries – regardless of their regime type – have made substantive interventions in response to internal and external forces demanding changes in the laws of personal status.

Interventions in personal status systems or family laws never take place in the absence of social opposition. Throughout history, governments attempting to alter the way their citizens wed, divorce and inherit have always encountered substantial opposition from religious authorities and conservative forces in society (Goody 1983; Freeman 1984; Glendon 1989; Bradley 1996; Bonfield 2001, 2002; Htun 2003; Maxwell 2003; Cretney 2005). Similarly, interventions by postcolonial governments into their personal status systems have also drawn fierce resistance from ethno-religious communities whose norms and institutions were being threatened by government actions. In essence, personal status laws function as identity markers or virtual border stones that demarcate communal boundaries among various ethno-religious communities. Hence, the preservation of these structures has often been deemed vital for the protection of the communal identity and the conservation of the community's socio-economic resources. Therefore any government that wished to intervene in its personal status system in any form (i.e., normative, institutional or substantive) had to have the upper hand vis-à-vis communal forces and overcome their resistance in order to successfully carry out its designs. Put this way, the fate of a government's interventions into its personal status system was originally decided by the relative balance of power[13] between the state and societal forces – or on the one hand by the government's ability to impose its political will upon communal forces, and on the other the capacity of communal forces to resist government meddling in order to preserve their juridico-political autonomy.

---

[13] The relative balance of power can be measured by the extent to which the political leaders depend upon resources controlled by the religious groups whose norms and institutions are targeted by the government's interventions (Sezgin 2004a). Stated differently, the capacity of religious groups to oppose and alter the government's intervention program is positively correlated with the amount of resources in their control upon which the ruling elite depends. These resources could be economic, political, or even simply numerical power in a system where it matters (e.g., electoral support in a democratic system). Similarly, the political and economic resources that a government allocates and appropriates solely for the purpose of formulating and executing its intervention policy constitute the backbone of that government's strength in its encounter with the communal forces. Moreover, a government's capacity to dictate its preferences and surmount the opposition also greatly depends upon such factors as the existence of a relatively coherent leadership that throws its undivided support behind interventions, the effectiveness of state institutions coordinating the intervention process, and the willingness of bureaucratic agencies to support the government's views and comply with its objectives (Bunce 1999; Charrad 2001; Peled 2001).

Although communal forces have always resisted government intervention in personal status systems, the intensity and severity of opposition they fomented seem to have been correlated with the type of intervention in question. A close scrutiny of the experiences of postcolonial nations as diverse as India, Tunisia and Ethiopia suggests that in comparison to institutional and substantive interventions, normative interventions that sought to abrogate religious laws often instigated a greater amount of resistance from communal forces. The colossal size and rigidity of the social opposition mounted against normative interventions necessitated not only mobilization of larger amounts of government resources but also an unshakable moral and ideological commitment on the part of the ruling elite. Perhaps this is why normative unification in personal status systems has been rather rare, and very difficult to undertake for nations with limited capabilities.

Categorization of personal status systems

As heretofore shown, postcolonial governments often approached inherited personal status systems instrumentally, and attempted to intervene in these pluri-legal structures in order to impress a particular ideological vision upon the society, while ethno-religious communities fiercely resisted government meddling in order to preserve their juridical autonomy and communal identity. Governments succeeded in their objectives only to the extent that they were able to co-opt, neutralize or suppress the opposition of religious groups and authorities. Of course, governments varied widely in their ability to overcome social opposition. Moreover, differing regime structures also meant differing motives and means of intervention. Thus, on the one hand, diverging regime choices, ideological orientations and governments' varying levels of ability to intervene successfully in pluri-legal systems, and on the other the ethno-religious groups' varying capacities to resist government interventions, gave rise to multiple forms of personal status across the postcolonial/post-imperial world. Even though the exact form and composition of personal status systems always vary from one country to another and over time, in this study I introduce three ideal types which are shown in Fig. 2.1 below: (1) fragmented confessional; (2) unified confessional; and (3) unified semi-confessional.

In fragmented confessional systems, each state-recognized ethno-religious community has its own network of state-enforced courts, which are staffed with (often state-appointed) communal judges who apply the state-appropriated communal norms (customary and

FRAGMENTED
CONFESSIONAL

UNIFIED
CONFESSIONAL

UNIFIED
SEMI-CONFESSIONAL

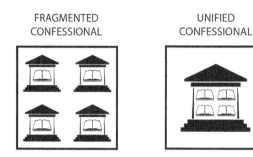 

Fig. 2.1 Types of personal status systems

religious laws which are incorporated into the state's legal system) (e.g., *qadis* applying Islamic law at *shari'a* courts or *dayanim* applying Jewish law at rabbinical courts, etc.). This type of personal status system has generally emerged in countries with strong exclusionary or theocratic inclinations. As mentioned earlier, postcolonial nations with such proclivities have viewed plural personal status systems as useful tools for turning their vision of building an ethno-religiously stratified and segmented citizenry into reality, and augmenting the role of religious norms and institutions in public life. Thus, they have usually preserved – and even reinforced – institutional and normative plurality of personal status systems that they had inherited from colonial rule. In other words, they attempted neither to unify communal courts under an overarching network of civil courts nor abolish state-enforced religious laws and replace them with a civil code that would apply to all citizens equally. As a result, fragmented confessional personal status systems that we observe across the postcolonial world today usually exhibit high levels of institutional and normative plurality.

As explained below, social and institutional opposition has played an important role as a centrifugal force in the formation of the other two types of personal status systems. However, since exclusionary or theocratically inclined regimes were usually not concerned with unification of religious courts or laws, social opposition thus did not come to play a significant role in shaping fragmented confessional systems. However, it should be noted that in some rare instances, fragmented confessional systems may come about as a result of a balance of power tilting strongly in favor of religious groups and institutions rather than the desires of the government in question to maintain such a pluri-legal system. For example, in cases of total state failure, some elements in the society may set up a pluri-legal system based on religious and customary laws, and impose it upon the powerless state and people against their will.

Personal status systems of Lebanon and Israel, where state-recognized religious communities have separate courts and apply their own communal laws, closely resemble the fragmented confessional model. In this book, I focus on the latter case and explain, in Chapter 4, how and why the Israeli state has maintained a variant of the *millet* system and actively refrained from institutional and normative unification. Briefly, I argue that Israeli leaders preserved and reinforced the old *millet* system, realizing the ideological and instrumental value of the existing institutions of personal status as a means of horizontal homogenization among Jews and vertical segmentation between Jews and non-Jews.

In unified confessional systems, different bodies of state-appropriated religious laws are directly applied by civil judges at secular state courts (e.g., the same secularly trained judge at a civil court applying *shari'a* in the case of a Muslim litigant and *halakhah* in the case of a Jewish litigant). The main difference between fragmented and unified confessional systems is that, in the latter, communal courts are abolished and replaced with an overarching network of civil courts, while in the former each community has a separate state-sanctioned court. Unified confessional systems have usually come about in technocratic-authoritarian regimes, which have been primarily motivated by such mechanical considerations as achieving bureaucratic efficiency, centralizing the power of state institutions by terminating non-state jurisdictions, fighting against remnants of colonialism and weakening the power and status of religious authorities. In order to succeed in these objectives, technocratic-authoritarian regimes essentially relied on institutional measures – while shying away from normative interventions preferred by ideologically motivated regimes (secular or inclusionary) – to facilitate drastic socio-legal, political and legal transformations in their societies. Regimes attempting institutional unification mostly encountered resistance from smaller but decisively powerful groups (i.e., religious court judges, clergy, etc.) whose professional and economic interests were directly threatened by unification schemes. Governments have achieved their objectives to the extent they were able to co-opt and neutralize the opposition of these groups.

Close approximations of unified confessional systems can be found in, for example, Morocco and Egypt (Liebesny 1975, pp. 113–114; Buskens 2010, p. 103). Both countries abolished religious courts and established unified court systems without undertaking accompanying reform that would unify the diverse religious laws under a secular civil code. Both regimes were moved by a desire to centralize and systematize their legal systems. Particularly in Egypt, as I demonstrate in Chapter 5, the sovereignty and systematization concerns were so central to the reform process that the explanatory memorandum accompanying Law No. 462 of 1955, which abolished religious courts and transferred their jurisdiction to national courts, read like a "Weberian" manifesto.

Unified semi-confessional systems are the most centralized personal status systems, as one may consider them just a few steps short of complete unification. As in unified confessional systems, courts in semi-confessional systems are fully unified. The law, however, is only partially unified. Some segments of the population are subject to a single unified code while the others continue to be governed by their own separate laws (e.g., the same secularly trained judge at a civil court applying *shari'a* in the case of a Muslim litigant, and non-denominational civil law in the case of Jewish and Christian litigants). Unified semi-confessional systems have often appeared in countries with strong inclusionary and/or secular inclinations that were principally committed to the idea of building a civic citizenry by eradicating ethno-religious differences among their citizens and diminishing the role of religion in public life. With these goals in mind, many inclusionary and/or secular regimes have attempted both institutional – unless their courts were already unified – and normative unification in order to attain "full" legal unification. Although most of them were fairly successful at institutional unification – as it was relatively easy to co-opt and suppress the opposition of religious authorities who were directly impacted by this type of reform – their efforts at normative unification were more often than not only partially successful. Most postcolonial/post-imperial governments did not possess the immense amount of power and resources required to neutralize the opposition of religious communities who unmistakably viewed the government's actions as an assault on their faith, way of life and values they held "sacred." In the end, even though most inclusionary/secular regimes wished to completely unify their personal status systems by eliminating all communal laws and courts, many of them have instead settled for unified semi-confessional systems due to their inability to fully neutralize communal elements which opposed and forestalled their attempts at further normative unification (see Table 2.2).

The Indian and Senegalese personal status systems closely resemble this ideal type. Senegal, a secular (*laïque*) democratic republic, moved aggressively to create a unified family law system after independence. It first abolished separate religious and customary courts, and then undertook codification of a new secular family code that would apply

TABLE 2.2 Factors contributing to emergence of personal status systems

	Fragmented confessional	Unified confessional	Unified semi-confessional
Regime structure (ideological orientation)	Theocratically inclined and/or exclusionary	Technocratic-authoritarian	Secular and/or inclusionary
Balance of power between the state and religious groups	The state has no interest in unifying the field of personal status. So there is no opposition from religious groups. Or: The balance of power favors religious groups which impose a pluri-legal personal status system despite the state's opposition (regardless of regime type).	The state has no ideological interest in personal status; but motivated by mechanical considerations. Seeks only institutional unification. Institutional unification fully successful. Limited resistance from religious groups and authorities which the state is able to neutralize.	Seeks both normative and institutional unification. Institutional unification fully successful. Normative unification partially successful due to resistance of some religious groups and authorities which the state fails to overcome.

to all Senegalese irrespective of religion. However, in the face of strong resistance from *marabouts* (*sufi* teachers and living saints) the government was forced to make an exception for the Muslim community and create a separate section on Islamic succession law in the new *Code de la Famille* (1972), an Act otherwise uniformly applied to all Senegalese regardless of religion (Villalón 1995, pp. 227–229). India, too, is a secular inclusionary regime. Unlike Senegal, however, its court system was already unified at the time of its independence, thanks to British colonial rule. To complete the process of legal unification that was initiated by the British a century before, the post-independence rulers of India needed to undertake normative unification by abolishing dispersed personal laws. In fact, this is what the founding elite – who believed in the instrumental value of uniform secular laws for eliminating communal sentiments and generating a common national identity – had planned for even before independence. This desire of the early Indian leaders was embodied in Article 44 of the 1950 Constitution, which directed the union government to enact a UCC that would be applicable to all Indians regardless of caste or religion. However, as I demonstrate in Chapter 6, in the face of muscular opposition from religious minorities (especially the Muslim community), the Indian leaders completely gave up on their dream of a UCC, and carried out instead a limited version of the normative unification originally envisaged by the framers of the constitution. They unified the law for Hindus, Sikhs, Buddhists and Jains through 1955–1956 Hindu Code Bill reforms, while willy-nilly agreeing to continuance of separate personal laws for Muslims, Christians and Parsis.

It seems only appropriate to conclude the current section with a cautionary remark regarding the use of ideal types employed in the study. Regime typologies (e.g., inclusionary, exclusionary, etc.), as well as the three distinct forms of personal status introduced above, are all ideal types. Ideal types cannot be found in their purest form in the real world. That is to say, it is extremely rare for states to fit entirely within a single category and have no common characteristics with other states belonging in different categories. Instead, at different times countries tend more toward one set of characteristics than another. What is important in the categorization of real-life examples is the extent to which a state exhibits the characteristics that predominate in one category as opposed to another.

This chapter has laid out the theoretical foundation of my argument that differing regime choices and varying configurations of state–community relations gave rise to a different form of personal status in each country. But what about their impact on fundamental rights and liberties? Are there any differences between variant types of personal status system in terms of their effects on human and women's rights? How do people interact with state-sanctioned religious laws and authorities, and respond to limitations and disabilities imposed upon their rights and liberties? What normative and political implications do their actions carry for the long-term survival of the system, and the fate of government's interventions into the field of personal status? The next chapter answers these questions.

3

THE IMPACT OF STATE-ENFORCED PERSONAL STATUS LAWS ON HUMAN RIGHTS

In the previous chapter, I argued that in the process of nation- and state-building, leaders of postcolonial nations adopted an instrumental approach towards institutions of personal status, and modified these pluri-legal structures in accordance with their ideological orientations. However, it would be plainly wrong to analyze matters of personal status merely from an angle of social engineering or judicial consolidation, as they are intimately related to the fundamental rights and freedoms of individuals who live under such systems. In other words, questions of who can marry whom or whether one can obtain a divorce are not just questions of identity or "border stones" demarcating communal boundaries. For a Christian woman who needs to change her denomination to be able to divorce her husband in Egypt, for a Russian Jew forbidden to marry within Israel because he is not considered a "proper" Jew by rabbinical authorities, for a Hindu woman who is disinherited (by her father) in favor of her male siblings or nephews, or for an Indian Muslim woman who is entitled to inherit only half the share of her brother, these questions are of utmost significance, as they carry substantive financial, legal and emotional implications.

In personal status systems, the central authority incorporates religious laws and institutions of certain ethno-religious communities into its legal system and takes it upon itself to apply and enforce these laws through its agencies. In *Islam and the Secular State*, An-Naim argues that *shari'a* principles cannot be enforced by the state, and if such an enforcement is attempted the outcome will not necessarily be the religious law of Islam binding upon the faithful, but the political will of the state (An-Naim 2008, p. 1). Following An-Naim, I likewise hold that the state appropriation of religious family laws strips them of their divine authority and legitimacy, and turns them into ordinary enactments of the temporal political authority. In other words, I do not view state-enforced religious personal status laws as "divine" laws in their own right, but as socio-political constructions – not any different than secular enactments of the state, which essentially embody its coercive power and political will rather than those of a "heavenly" authority. Thus, if and when personal status laws – applied either directly by state courts, or by religious authorities operating under the auspices of the state – encroach upon individuals' constitutional rights and freedoms, it is the state that we should hold responsible for violations of human rights, not the religious tradition that these laws are supposedly drawn from. After all, it is the state authorities who appropriate and apply rather restrictive and less liberal interpretations of religious norms – assuming there are competing more egalitarian and enlightened interpretations – which infringe upon the very rights and freedoms that the state is obligated to protect under both domestic and international law.

Based on empirical evidence gathered through my field research in Israel, Egypt and India, I claim that state-enforced personal status laws often have a negative impact on fundamental rights and freedoms, especially when people are not presented with alternative civil or non-denominational institutions of marriage, divorce, maintenance or inheritance, and are forcibly subjected to the jurisdiction of religious norms and authorities. In this regard, as both my empirical findings and the prevailing consensus in the literature evince, state-enforced religious laws tend to have detrimental impact particularly on those four groups of rights and freedoms mentioned earlier in the introductory chapter: the freedom of religion; equality before the law; marital and familial rights; and procedural rights (An-Naim, Gort et al. 1995; van der Vyver and Witte 1996; Gearon 2002; Runzo, Martin et al. 2003; Temperman 2010; Witte and Green 2012). In this connection, it is worth noting that the aforementioned quadripartite classification and sequential ordering should not be construed as a presumption of normative hierarchy among different rights or categories of rights, as they are primarily intended for analytical purposes. Otherwise, it is the contention of the present study that human rights are indivisible, interdependent and interrelated, which means that each and every right is equally important and necessary for overall enjoyment of human rights.

People do not silently accept the restrictions and disabilities imposed upon their rights by state-sanctioned religious norms and institutions. In order to remove these limitations and disabilities, they resort to various resistance strategies, from forum-shopping to formation of hermeneutic and rule-making communities. As individuals engage in these resistance strategies, they constantly challenge the legitimacy of state-run religious norms and institutions, renegotiate their rights and duties under the law and try to reform the system from within. For instance, as shown later in the book, hermeneutic communities usually offer deviant interpretations of state-enforced personal status laws by rendering enlightened and emancipatory readings of original scriptural and prophetic sources in order to promote and protect rights and liberties that are either denied or not sufficiently protected under the existing state-sanctioned interpretations of personal status laws. In other words, as people work towards overcoming disabilities and limitations imposed upon their rights, they try to not only renegotiate with the authorities the terms on which existing personal status systems are founded, but also remake these very structures in the process.

As noted earlier, governments intervene in their personal status systems in order to impress a particular ideological vision and reorganize social relations in accordance with their political preferences. However, people who continuously interact with, renegotiate with and make rights demands from personal status institutions decisively interfere with the intent of government's designs to manipulate and turn the personal status field into an instrument of state power. By the same token, I suggest that beyond its most obvious normative and theoretical value there is also an added methodological value to studying human rights discourses, violations, and the particular strategies people devise to respond to these violations under personal status systems. In this respect, I argue that what is later in the chapter called "the field of human rights as a testing ground" approach enables us to probe the extent to which each government has succeeded or failed in attaining the objectives that had originally led it to intervene in its personal status system, by specifically studying personal status-related human rights violations, sites where these violations occur, people's responses and state–society contestations that these responses give rise to.

This chapter is comprised of four sections. First, I discuss whether personal status laws are "divine" religious laws or secular enactments of the state. Second, I turn my attention to impact of personal status laws on fundamental rights and liberties by giving specific examples from the three case studies under examination. Third, I describe how people respond to limitations and disabilities placed upon their rights by state-sanctioned religious laws and institutions, and the resistance strategies they resort to in order to advance their rights to marriage, divorce, maintenance, etc. Fourth, I introduce "the field of human rights as a testing ground" framework that I harness throughout the book to evaluate the performances of Israeli, Egyptian and Indian states in attaining the objectives they originally set out to achieve through their interventions into their personal status systems.

ARE PERSONAL STATUS LAWS "DIVINE" RELIGIOUS LAWS?

The modern state is inherently and historically a mundane political institution. The laws and policies of the state represent the political will and power of the secular authority – this is true even when the rulers of the state make claims to the contrary and pretend to exercise their authority in the name of a "god" or legitimize their rule in reference to certain religious norms and precepts (i.e., the so-called theocratic or religious states in the Middle East). In this respect, one of the main assumptions of the present study is that whenever the state appropriates religious norms and takes it upon itself to apply them through its own institutions – which may be civil state courts as in Egypt or India, or state-appropriated and controlled communal courts as in Israel – religious laws are stripped of their divine authority and legitimacy, and become ordinary laws of the state, just like any of its other enactments that symbolize the coercive power and will of its temporal rulers rather than a heavenly or spiritual authority. Put this way, as An-Naim eloquently points out, the etatization or state-enforcement of religious norms "will distort the meaning, abuse the methodology, weaken the moral authority of these norms, and ultimately . . . [cut] them off from their religious foundations and sources of communal development." (An-Naim 2011, p. 787).[1]

---

[1] It is often argued that the etatization of religious (and customary) laws leads to ossification and fossilization of rather flexible and constantly evolving legal edicts and practices (Kosambi 2007, p. 243). For instance, colonial and postcolonial authorities usually froze religious and customary norms in time and space by adopting arbitrary formulations of those norms as interpreted by state judges and legislators, and denied them "the possibility of evolving and adapting as part of [an] integrated . . . social system" (An-Naim 2011, p. 787). For example Sonbol (2009, p. 193) points out that before the modernization and codification of Islamic law in the late nineteenth and early twentieth centuries Egyptian *qadis* enjoyed vast discretionary powers as they "could refer to a wide

In this respect, etatization or state appropriation of religious norms is a violent and invasive process through which the secular authority selectively adopts and codifies certain interpretations and aspects of religious norms, traditions and narratives, and labels them as "divine law" or "God's word," while leaving out certain other aspects and interpretations of the tradition as unworthy of adoption, for they may not suit the immediate interests and needs of the ruling elite. In other words, etatization of religious laws and institutions is a fundamentally distortive and corruptive process that eventually brings about desacralization of religious norms and institutions. The resultant laws are no longer "divine" as they are forcefully separated from their original foundation and communities, which serve as their main source of moral authority and vitality (Berman 2000), and are rather reduced to enactments of the secular authority upon which they now depend for not only their continued existence but also legitimacy and ascribed "holiness." For instance, classical Islamic law bestows upon a Muslim wife the right to no-fault divorce known as *khulʿ* through which the wife could ask a *qadi* for divorce provided that she forfeits her financial claims and returns the dower she received at the time of marriage (*nikah*). Even though *khulʿ* – believed to be originally made available to women by Prophet Mohammad – is a well-established principle of Islamic law, the Egyptian government, despite its official claims to adhere to Islamic law and the tradition of the Prophet (*sunna*) in the field of family law, openly neglected the existence and application of this very principle, and did not consider it as part of its "divine law" until the legislature finally codified it into Law No. 1 in 2000 (more on this in Chapter 5) (An-Naim 2008, p. 29). From this point of view, what seems to be the source of "holiness" or "divinity" attributed to the practice of *khulʿ* becomes, under the Egyptian law of 2000, not its prophetic source but the legislative activity and political will of the state. Thus, despite the claims of the Egyptian state to the contrary, the Khulʿ Law of 2000 – like all other personal status laws applied by the state – was not in itself an inviolable sacrosanct law but a religiously inspired secular enactment, detached from its original source and foundation and completely dependent upon the political authority for its legitimacy.

number of divergent sources in making judgments, based on precedent, judicial discretion and general interest." However, codification, Sonbol argues, destroyed the flexibility enjoyed by *qadis* and led to gradual rigidification of their rulings while considerably limiting their options in terms of which *madhhab* or precedents they could use. For a similar discussion of the impact of codification of Islamic laws in Iran, see Osanloo (2009).

As the following pages attest, not only the three countries that are the subjects of the current study, but all countries that apply religion-based personal status laws, undertake similar processes of etatization through which they distort, desacralize and appropriate religious norms and mold them into profane enactments that no longer represent the original source and divine foundation but the coercive power and political will of the state. Despite the governments' and state-sponsored religious institutions' contrary claims and pretenses to apply religious laws – as mandated by the divine will of "God" – the current study treats personal status laws as religiously inspired enactments of the political authority, devoid of any divine source or legitimacy. However, since personal status laws in all three countries under examination are both officially and popularly referred to as "religious laws," I also frequently refer to them as such throughout the text for the sake of brevity and consistency. Nonetheless, the reader should be constantly reminded of the afore-mentioned premise that these laws are not sacrosanct immutable laws in their own right, but state-enforced, religiously inspired man-made laws which are open to reinterpretation and amendment.

In this regard, personal status systems are neither natural nor divinely ordained institutions but socio-political constructions (Sonbol 2009). In fact, as Chapter 2 has argued, these pluri-legal structures were often targeted and manipulated by colonial and postcolonial governments as instruments of state- and nation-building. Whether in the colonial or postcolonial era, however, construction and regulation of personal status systems has always been a political project steered by hegemonic masculine forces which have selectively adopted and codified more restrictive interpretations of religious texts and narratives that entrenched existing socio-economic gender disparities and transposed them into the legal arena (Mir-Hosseini 2009; Sonbol 2009). That is to say, whether it was a secular, inclusionary or bureaucratic-authoritarian regime, or whether it was a Muslim, Jewish or Hindu government, the architects of personal status systems were predominantly male. Female and subaltern voices and inputs were rarely sought and almost never taken into consideration, as men – both in the center and at the periphery – continuously negotiated and renegotiated among themselves the rules pertaining to marriage, divorce, maintenance and inheritance (Wadud 1995, p. 48). It was men who interpreted the holy scripture and ascertained "God's" commands regarding what was required of a woman to release her from the bond of marriage, when she could be declared a disobedient wife and denied her maintenance, how many days she would have to wait following her divorce before making herself available to another man, and so forth (Sezgin 2012a). In brief, personal status laws are not just secular socio-political constructions, but also andro- (and often ethno-) centric legalities built through selective interpretations of sacred texts, traditions and narratives that came to heavily influence the rights and freedoms of women and subaltern groups while denying them terms of equal membership in the political community. The next two sections will look at the impact of state-enforced personal status laws on the rights and freedoms of individuals in detail.

HOW DO PERSONAL STATUS SYSTEMS AFFECT FUNDAMENTAL RIGHTS AND LIBERTIES?

The empirical evidence presented in the following chapters, which I gathered through my field research in the three countries under examination, shows that regardless of which ideal type they resemble personal status systems are often detrimental to the rights and freedoms of people who are subject to their jurisdiction. In other words, as far as the impact of state-enforced religiously inspired personal status laws on human rights is concerned, I have not found much significant difference between variant types of personal status systems (e.g., fragmented confessional vs. unified semi-confessional), nor for that matter between exclusionary/theocratically oriented and inclusionary/secular regimes. In fact, as Table 3.1 denotes, I did not find personal status laws in secular India to be necessarily less restrictive of human rights than personal status laws in Egypt – a Muslim majority country where *shari'a* is the principal source of legislation – or in Israel, a Jewish state. Having said this, however, it should be noted that unlike Israel or Egypt, the secular Indian state has long provided its citizens with an optional civil code, which not only allows civil marriage and divorce (including interfaith unions), but also supposedly mitigates negative impacts of state-enforced personal status laws by making their application technically consensual. Stated differently, as a secular democratic regime, India, at least theoretically, seeks its citizens' implicit consent before subjecting them to the jurisdiction of religious norms and institutions, and furnishes them with a freedom of exit that would enable individuals to leave the communal track and transfer their disputes to civil law and institutions at their own will (Kymlicka 1995, 1996; Kukathas 1998; Kymlicka and Norman 2000). However, whether the availability of such secular remedies really does provide Indian citizens with a type of exit strategy that Benhabib

49

TABLE 3.1 Human rights under Israeli, Egyptian and Indian personal status systems

	Israel	Egypt	India
Type of personal status system	Fragmented confessional.	Unified confessional.	Unified semi-confessional.
Is application of religious laws consensual or non-consensual?	Non-consensual.	Non-consensual.	Theoretically consensual. There is a secular option which citizens can take advantage of (the SMA of 1954). However most people are either unaware of the law or hesitant to use it. Also, some registrars and court officials are reported to discourage people from marrying under the SMA of 1954.
Impact of state-enforced personal status laws on human rights	Often detrimental.	Often detrimental.	Often detrimental.
Whose rights are most at stake?	People whose Jewishness is contested (e.g., Russian immigrants). Jewish women. Muslim women.	Secular dissidents. Muslim women. Christian women. People who belong to non-recognized communities (e.g., Baha'i).	Muslim women. Hindu women.
Select human rights issues	Who is a Jew? Jewish marriage and divorce. Agunah and mamzer. Muslim maintenance.	Muslim marriage and divorce (talaq). Polygyny. Coptic Orthodox divorce and remarriage. Hisba and apostasy.	Muslim marriage and divorce (triple talaq). Muslim maintenance. Hindu succession.

(2002, pp. 131–132) and Barzilai (2003, pp. 251–253) prescribe, and make them any better off than their Egyptian or Israeli counterparts who do not have access to such remedies, is a pending question. Chapter 6 will answer it by analyzing the effectiveness of such secular remedies as the SMA of 1954 and the Cr. PC of 1973 (Section 125) in helping Indians escape disabilities imposed upon their rights and freedoms by state-enforced religious laws.

As noted above, the main contention of the present study is that state-enforced religious laws in the field of family law negatively impact fundamental rights and liberties. The intellectual risk of writing about human rights in the context of various religiously inspired legal systems is well known: the author's assertions – like the one above – can always be taken out of their context without considering their limitations and stated constraints, and misinterpreted by different audiences, however well intended they may be. Thus, in order to prevent such a risk of misinterpretation, I would like to add the following cautionary note to further delineate the essence and limits of my contention: First, my primary interest in the present study is state-enforced religiously inspired personal status laws. In this respect, I would like to remind the reader of my earlier assertion that I treat personal status laws as essentially secular enactments – devoid of any divine source or legitimacy – that solely represent the power and will of the state, not that of a heavenly authority. Thus, my assertions about Israeli, Egyptian or Indian personal status laws in the rest of the book should be viewed from this vantage point, and not taken as my views or assumptions about a particular religious tradition (i.e., Islam, Judaism or Hinduism) or a sacred legal system – in the most classical sense of the term (i.e., *shari'a*, *halakhah*, Hindu law, etc.). In other words, the present study does not purport to make any assertions about whether Islam or Judaism, or whether classical *shari'a* or Hindu law, is compatible with modern human rights ideas and standards. On the contrary, I purposely shy away from such inquiries and assertions for I think not only that they are misplaced and counter-productive, but also that I am neither comfortable nor competent to pass such judgments on great millennia-old, immensely diverse traditions or legal systems.

This brings me to my second point: that the present study does not treat religious legal systems or traditions (e.g., *shari'a*, *halakhah*, etc.) as monolithic or static, but rather as diverse, flexible and dynamic. For instance there are significant theological, sectarian, jurisprudential, customary, political and ideological differences among and within Muslim societies that inevitably lead to different interpretations and understandings of Islamic law. As will be seen in the following chapters, divergent divorce practices across Muslim societies are particularly demonstrative of vast diversity in understanding and application of the Islamic family or personal status laws, which supposedly derive from the same scriptural and prophetic sources. In this respect, it is more correct to speak of "Muslim laws" in the plural, rather than "the" *shari'a*, as there is not a monolithic understanding of *shari'a* across the one-and-a-half-billion Muslims in the world. The same is also true for other religious legal systems and traditions examined in the book (i.e., Judaism, Hinduism, etc.). As explained in greater detail below, there are numerous hermeneutic and rule-making communities across the personal status systems under scrutiny which constantly challenge the legitimacy and scriptural authority of state-enforced religious family laws, and render emancipatory, feminist and enlightened interpretations of these laws. That is to say, personal status laws are multivocal. There is no single version of *shari'a* or *halakhah*, but rather multiple versions of each competing to become "the" *shari'a* or *halakhah* that authorities come to rely upon in deciding questions of personal status.

Third, since this book is primarily concerned with "state-enforced" religious family laws its findings may not be directly applicable to religious laws applied by autonomous religious communities. There are both theoretical and normative reasons for this. The state is the primary bearer of duty in relation to human rights under domestic and international law. Therefore, when the laws (secular or religious) that the state applies violate such principles as equality before the law or gender equality, it is only normal and expected for us to hold the state accountable because of its constitutional promises and international obligations to uphold those principles in the first place. However, if and when the laws applied by autonomous religious communities encroach upon individual rights and liberties, we may not be able to hold the communities liable for those violations. Because unlike the state, religious communities are not, aside from horizontal obligations, under direct legal obligation to uphold and implement domestic or international human rights law (Gardbaum 2003; Hessbruegge 2005; Knox 2008; Robbers 2010, p. 166). Moreover, from a normative point of view, the community in question may have a different conceptualization and understanding of such principles as "equal treatment", etc. than those embodied in secular domestic and international human rights documents; and thereby it may not consider itself bound by those rules. Therefore, as the US Supreme

Court has recently ruled,[2] the unilateral imposition of those secular norms and values upon autonomous religious groups and organizations that reject those principles on moral grounds may impose an undue burden on them, and impede their right to freely practice their religion and organize their internal affairs. Having said this, however, it should also be noted that the present study does not assume that community-enforced religious laws are bound to be always violative of domestic and international human rights norms. On the contrary, as shown in the following chapters, a considerable number of religious groups – especially the ones which I call "hermeneutic" communities – that I came across during my field research in Israel, Egypt and India either claimed to apply or advocated for application of human and women's rights-compliant interpretations of religious family laws.

Fourth, neither does the present study assume that state-enforced religious laws are categorically violative of human rights. It is true that as a result of my field research I conclude that state-enforced religious laws are often detrimental to the rights and liberties of individuals who are subject to their jurisdiction. But my inferences are only applicable and limited to the three case studies (whatever their merits or short-comings may be) that I present. As I explain in the following chapters, because in these three countries pre- and post-independence authorities that oversaw etatization processes often adopted restrictive and gender-unequal aspects and interpretations of sacred texts, religious narratives and customs, the resultant laws have usually come to negatively impact rights of certain individuals including women, children and religious dissidents. However, I do not suggest that this is always, and has to be, the case in every society where the state takes it upon itself to directly apply religious laws.[3] The state authorities that oversee the process of etatization may adopt and apply more liberal and enlightened interpre-tations of religious norms and customs which comply with nationally and internationally accepted human rights standards. Of course, as sug-gested by many, for this to happen the government must allow space for

---

[2] *Hosanna-Tabor Evangelical Lutheran Church and School* v. *Equal Employment Opportunity Commission*, 565 US (2012) – (Docket No. 10–553).

[3] On a related point, in response to the question of whether the rise of constitutions requiring states to respect *shari'a* norms threatens human rights, Lombardi and Brown, based on their analysis of the Egyptian Supreme Constitutional Court's Article 2 jurisprudence, assert that "constitutional Islamization does not, by itself . . . lead to a serious diminution of women's rights or other human rights" (Lombardi and Brown 2006, p. 434).

and tolerate (and protect, when necessary) cultural dissenters who freely generate alternative interpretations of state-enforced religious laws and cultural norms, make democratic institutions and mechanisms available to dissenters to openly promote their deviant interpretations, and consider these competing notions of justice, equity and equality for adoption and implementation (Shachar 2001; Sunder 2001, 2003; Phillips 2007).

Moreover, the present study also recognizes that state-enforced religious laws may be more protective of certain individual rights and liberties than alternative laws and normative systems. This is reported to be the case particularly in pluri-legal societies in Africa where individuals have simultaneous access to multiple legal systems, and forum-shop between religious, customary and tribal laws (Ezeilo 2000). For instance, even though I did not personally observe this in any of the three countries under scrutiny, I was repeatedly told by women during a recent research trip to Sierra Leone that Muslim women usually prefer Islamic family laws over customary laws because the latter do not confer upon them a right to spousal maintenance or entitle them to a share of a deceased husband's estate, while the former both recognize their right to maintenance and give them a fixed share in the deceased husband's estate.

Lastly, the current study does not assume that secular uniform laws are normatively superior to or better protective of human and women's rights than religious personal status laws (state enforced or otherwise). On the contrary, like Osanloo (2009), I am of the opinion that simplistic dichotomies such as "secular law is good, religious law is bad" must be avoided at all cost in order to locate and better understand the multi-vocal and intersubjective nature of rights talks under personal status systems. Human and women's rights violations can occur under both secular and religious family law systems (Peters and Wolper 1995). Stated differently, secular legal systems are not, by definition, more protective of human rights. In fact, there are many countries where constant human and women's rights violations take place under secular and uniform legal systems. Therefore, with these reservations in mind, next I will discuss in detail some human and women's rights problems that commonly occur in the personal status systems under scrutiny.

WHAT AND WHOSE RIGHTS ARE AT STAKE?

Pluri-legal personal status systems were one of the issues at the heart of the European Court of Human Rights (ECtHR) Grand Chamber decision in *Refah Partisi (The Welfare Party) and Others* v. *Turkey*.[4] "The case involved the forcible dissolution of the Welfare Party in Turkey on several grounds, including the charge that the Welfare Party's advocacy of a plurality of legal systems violated Turkey's Constitution" (ICHRP 2009, p. 137). The particular pluri-legal personal status system advocated by the Welfare Party closely resembled the model currently found in Israel, and to some degree, those in Egypt and India. In response to the Welfare Party's claim that religion-based private law systems were in complete accordance with the terms of the European Convention on Human Rights, the Grand Chamber unequivocally declared that the proposed system, which would entail categorization of all individual citizens on the basis of religion with "rights and freedoms not as an individual but according to his allegiance to a religious movement" (*Refah Partisi*, 2003, para.119), could not be considered to be compatible with the Convention system. The court cited two reasons for its decision. First, it concluded that the proposed personal status system would undermine "the state's role as the guarantor of individual rights and freedoms" since "it would oblige individuals to obey, not rules laid down by the state ... but static rules of law imposed by the religion concerned," and that as a result it could not "ensure that everyone within its jurisdiction enjoys in full, and without being able to waive them, the rights and freedoms guaranteed by the Convention" (*ibid.*). Second, the Grand Chamber reasoned that

> such a system would undeniably infringe the principle of non-discrimination between individuals as regards their enjoyment of public freedoms, which is one of the fundamental principles of democracy. A difference in treatment between individuals in all fields of public and private law according to their religion or beliefs manifestly cannot be justified under the Convention ... Such a difference in treatment cannot maintain a fair balance between, on the one hand, the claims of certain religious groups who wish to be governed by their own rules and on the other the interest of society as a whole, which must be based on peace and on tolerance between the various religions and beliefs (*ibid.*).

The Chamber also noted that the Welfare Party's "policy ... to apply some of *shari'a*'s private-law rules to a large part of the population in Turkey (namely Muslims)" within a pluri-legal framework was "beyond

---

[4] *Refah Partisi (The Welfare Party) and Others* v. *Turkey* (2003) 37 EHRR 1, retrieved in May 2012 from http://hudoc.echr.coe.int/sites/eng/pages/search.aspx?i=001-60936.

the freedom of individuals to observe the precepts of their religion" as it fell "outside the private sphere to which Turkish law" and the Convention "confine religion" (*Refah Partisi*, 2003, para.127). The court further reiterated that "freedom of religion, including the freedom to manifest one's religion by worship and observance, is primarily a matter of individual conscience," and stressed that "the sphere of individual conscience is quite different from the field of private law, which concerns the organization and functioning of society as a whole" (*Refah Partisi*, 2003, para.128).

Many both within and without Turkey have widely criticized the ECtHR's decision in the *Refah Partisi* case, because it not only upheld the banning of a legitimate political party, which many saw as an undemocratic act in itself, but also reached critical conclusions on the advantages and disadvantages of personal status systems without any concrete evidence (Boyle 2004; Macklem 2006; Mayer 2012). It is true that Refah leaders frequently talked about reinstating the old *millet* system, which Atatürk – the founder of the secular Turkish Republic – abolished in 1926. But this did not go beyond electoral rhetoric, as the party leaders made no commitments in their program or took any legislative action, when in power, to set up a personal status system (Moe 2012, p. 243). In other words, when the justices of the ECtHR spoke about implications of pluri-legal personal status systems on the rights and freedoms protected under the Convention, they only expressed an opinion in abstract, primarily relying upon their own and the Turkish Constitutional Court's presumptions about the intentions of Refah leaders, rather than their acts, without any conclusive evidence.

However faulty (technically or substantively) the ECtHR's views about human rights implications of personal status systems may be, the court's fear that state-enforced religious laws within a pluri-legal framework may undermine some essential democratic rights and freedoms is not completely unwarranted. In fact, the view that legal systems which "are premised on state enforcement of religious laws" are usually surrounded and characterized by "systemic human rights problems" seems to be widely accepted in the literature (Temperman 2010, p. 171). As Temperman notes, fundamental human rights concerns under so-called religious systems are often related to the notions of: (1) freedom from religion; (2) equality before the law; and (3) transparency, legal certainty and lack of checks and balances (Temperman 2010, p. 172). In this respect, the findings of my research are largely in agreement with the prevailing position in the literature that state-enforced religious laws – whether Islamic, Jewish or Hindu – negatively impact and limit rights and freedoms of individuals who are subject to their jurisdiction (Don-Yehiya 1999; Agnes 2001; An-Naim 2008; Estin 2011; Sezgin 2011). This is especially true in legal systems, like those of Israel and Egypt, where people are not presented with alternative civil or non-denominational laws of marriage, divorce, maintenance or inheritance, and are forcibly subjected to jurisdiction of state-enforced religious norms and institutions without their explicit or implied consent. As noted earlier, the availability of an alternative secular code (as in India) could mitigate negative implications of state-enforced religious laws by making their application theoretically consensual. Stated differently, whenever religious laws are applied to individual citizens it may be presumed that they either explicitly or implicitly consent to the application of religious laws, as they could simply opt for alternative secular codes which are available to them, if they do not consent. I address the question of whether the availability of alternative secular codes actually ameliorates the harshness of state-enforced religious laws, and equips individuals with a viable exit option, in Chapter 6. But it suffices to note here that, as my findings demonstrate, with regards to the promotion and enjoyment of fundamental rights and liberties under religious systems, the ability to challenge state-enforced religious laws from within, and offer dissenting interpretations of those laws, seems to matter as much as (if not more than) the right to exit (Shachar 2001; Sunder 2001; Benhabib 2002; Phillips 2007).

Although state-enforced personal status laws negatively affect the rights and freedoms of nearly all individuals who are forcibly subjected to their jurisdiction, their impact on some groups tends to be harsher. These include children, religious dissidents, secular individuals, people without a religion, persons who do not belong to a "recognized" community, and most notably, women. Since personal status systems, as a direct result of male-dominated etatization processes, often institutionalize patriarchal interpretations of religious precepts, customs and narratives by giving them formal recognition and state-sanctioned backing, gender-based discriminations and violations are usually among the most common human rights violations that occur not only across the three case studies that I present in this book but elsewhere where similar systems can be found (Women Living Under Muslim Laws 2006). As the study shows, the so-called Muslim, Jewish, Hindu and Christian personal status laws often discriminate against women and deny them equal rights with men in familial affairs such as marriage, divorce, maintenance, inheritance and custody.[5] For instance, as Chapters 5 and 6 show in detail, under the Muslim laws, as they are interpreted and applied by Egyptian and Indian courts, women's right to divorce is severely truncated vis-à-vis men, who enjoy almost unhindered access to extrajudicial and unilateral divorce widely known as *talaq*. The situation is not any better for the Jewish women in Israel who need to pay off their husbands to obtain a divorce writ (*get*) in order to be formally released from the bond of marriage (more on this in Chapter 4) (Bogoch and Halperin-Kaddari 2006); or for the Hindu women who have been traditionally denied an equal share in the allocation of joint family property.[6]

In personal status systems, not every community's laws and institutions are recognized and given effect by the state. Imagine a scenario where the state only recognizes Muslim, Jewish and Christian laws, and does not allow civil marriage and divorce. Then how would people who profess a religion other than those three wed or divorce? In fact, this is the predicament the members of the Egyptian Baha'i community have long faced. Since the Egyptian government does not recognize the Baha'i faith, its adherents cannot officially marry or divorce in the country. In some cases, Baha'is have reportedly even been denied a national ID card. The government, because it does not recognize the validity of Baha'i marriage certificates, often refuses to register applicants' marital status as widows, widowers or divorcees, or issue them national ID cards unless they register as "unmarried" or convert to a "heavenly" faith. Since "a national ID is essential to obtain access to postsecondary schooling, get a job, vote, travel abroad or within Egypt, and conduct the most basic financial and administrative transactions," not having one has dire effects (Human Rights Watch 2007, p. 1; US Department of State 2010).

In other words, under personal status systems religion is not just a matter of personal conviction but of public law and policy. Judges who apply state-interpreted and enforced religious laws, or registrars who register births, marriages and divorces, are both empowered and required

---

[5] There is a sizable literature discussing gender issues under various religious traditions and legal systems. For instance, for women's rights under Muslim, Jewish and Hindu laws see Esposito and DeLong-Bas (2001), Biale (1995) and Mitter (2006) respectively.

[6] Even though the HSA, as amended in 2005, expanded Hindu women's right to property, Hindu succession laws still suffer from major inequalities and shortcomings, mostly due to the inability and unwillingness of the Indian Parliament to do away with the old *Mitakshara* system which still constitutes the backbone of the HSA. In this respect, there remain several areas where the law needs further improvements. For example, restrictions need to be imposed on parents' testamentary freedoms to prevent them from disinheriting their daughters from their self-acquired property by establishing the principle of reserved shares, like in Islamic law. For further information, see Mishra (2009) and Patel (2007, pp. 52–53).

by law to determine what religious community each person belongs to. This often leads to the problem of defining who is a Jew, who is a Muslim or who is a Hindu, as authorities often need to examine whether people truly belong to the community whose faith they claim to profess, on the basis of officially sanctioned interpretations of religious laws and precepts. These inquiries particularly pose a great difficulty for people who do not profess a religion, secular people, and religious dissidents who do not profess or subscribe to officially sanctioned religious laws or dogmas, and inevitably result in denial of their basic rights, from marriage to burial rights. For instance, as I demonstrate in Chapter 4, in Israel rabbinical authorities usually refuse to marry Jewish residents whose Jewishness according to *halachic* criteria is in question (Edelman 1998; Brackman 1999). Given the fact that there is no civil marriage in Israel, these people are permanently denied their fundamental right to marry and found a family within the country. Moreover, due to their forcible subjection to religious law, their freedom of conscience and religion and right to equality before the law are also severely violated. Further, as the discussion of the infamous *Abu Zayd* case in Chapter 5 shows, the inquisitorial powers conferred upon courts or state-controlled religious authorities to determine questions of religious identity and decide whether a person is a member of the fold or an apostate may also have a life-threatening impact besides their dire effects on individual rights and liberties (Olsson 2008; Agrama 2011).

It can hardly be disputed that whenever the state subjects secular individuals or people who do not profess a religion to religious laws against their will, this undeniably leads to the violation of these individuals' religious rights and freedoms. State enforcement of religious laws, however, also violates the religious people's right to profess their religion without state intervention (Temperman 2010, p. 192). In other words, state application of religious laws does not necessarily do a service to religious people or communities. The rights of religious and secular people are equally threatened by the state's hermeneutic monopoly and control over religious institutions. In this respect, it is possible that some religious people – like some ultra-orthodox Jewish groups in Israel – may find the application and manipulation of religious texts and principles by temporal authority completely abominable, while others – like some Muslim groups in India – principally not opposing the idea of state enforcement of religious laws, may detest the particular way and fashion in which authorities choose to apply and interpret the religious laws. Yet some others may also object to the state enforcement of religious laws on grounds that it not only corrupts the religion and tradition in question, but also interferes with the faithful's right to freely interpret and exercise tenets, duties and rituals of their faith. For instance, as Osanloo demonstrates through her rich ethnography of Qur'anic meetings among middle-class Iranian women in the 1990s, most Muslim women with whom she spoke "believed in the basic principle of public modesty but disagreed with the regulation of it, or at least the manner in which it was regulated [by the state]" (Osanloo 2009, p. 87). Many women who willingly wore the *chador* before the revolution objected to the imposition of it by the Islamic regime after 1979 on grounds that it had violated women's bodily freedoms, and it gave rise to hypocrisy and licentiousness rather than promoting decency or modesty: "The *chador* does not mean anyone who wears it is modest . . . We have more prostitutes now than ever before, and the problem is that [since *chador* is mandatory] no one can tell the difference between a regular woman and a prostitute" (Osanloo 2009, p. 87).

State-enforced religious laws may also impinge upon individuals' right to fair trial and due process, and the right to seek effective remedy when their rights are violated. For example, under Muslim personal status laws in Egypt and India, a man can unilaterally divorce his wife without appearing at a court or providing any legal reason for his action (*talaq*). Since *talaq* is an extrajudicial act, the wife cannot challenge or appeal the husband's pronouncement at a court of law. Similarly, under Law No. 1 of 2000, which allows the Egyptian Muslim women to seek no-fault divorce from the court without the husband's consent (*khulʿ*), neither can husbands appeal *khulʿ* decrees at a court of law. Another procedural concern in personal status systems is the relative lack of legal certainty, transparency and checks and balances. Religious laws, which the states officially claim to apply in the field of personal status, were historically jurists' law (*Juristenrecht*) – a body of law that was formulated by the experts and legal scholars rather than the state (Schiller 1958; Peters 2002). Even though in many countries religious rules pertaining to matters of personal status were codified in the late nineteenth and twentieth centuries, most systems continue to recognize unwritten religious rules, narratives and customs as part of jurisprudence which allows both secular and religious judges – *à la* classical jurists – to find laws and even make new ones by drawing upon classical sources that may previously have been unknown to the parties.[7] As exemplified by the

---

[7] Muslim and Christian laws in Egypt, Muslim law in Israel and Hindu law in India are, to a great extent, codified. However, despite codification, they all continue to recognize and apply

Egyptian Court of Cassation's admittance[8] of the *hisba* petition that led to declaration of Professor Abu Zayd as an apostate and subsequently his forced separation from his wife (more on this in Chapter 5), this inevitably introduces an element of arbitrariness and legal uncertainty into personal status systems (Bernard-Maugiron 1999, pp. 178–182).

Another problem commonly observed in personal status systems is the relative lack of institutional and procedural checks on the power of religious tribunals or civil personal status courts. Religious or communal courts usually tend to emphasize their institutional separateness and claim normative superiority vis-à-vis their secular counterparts. For example, Mautner reports that even though rabbinical courts are part of the state court system, unlike civil courts, they almost never cite secular legislation or precedents of the Israeli Supreme Court in their decisions (Mautner 2011, p. 192). Moreover, the rabbinical courts' claims to institutional separateness from the secular system and normative superiority of their laws seem to be recognized by the Israeli Supreme Court, which has actively refrained from inquiring into the nature and substance of the laws applied by these courts. For instance, Justice H. Cohn remarked in *Schtreit v. the Chief Rabbi of Israel,*[9] that "it is … a long established practice in this court that we do not sit in appeal over religious courts, for they decide everything according to their own religious law, and the civil court has not to inquire into their ways as regards the substance and nature of this law" (Shava 1985, p. 5). Although there are no separate religious courts in India, the Supreme Court of India has also embraced a similar attitude towards the so-called religious personal laws applied by civil family courts, and in a number of cases held that these laws were not susceptible to Part III of the constitution, and thereby could not be "challenged as being in violation of fundamental rights especially those guaranteed under Articles 14, 15 and 21 of the constitution" (Desai 2004, p. 15). Thus, especially in countries – like all three countries examined in this book – where there is not a clearly defined hierarchy of national norms or a repugnancy clause in place that subjects personal status laws to constitutional and international rights standards (a good example of which can be found in

---

unwritten rules and customs as part of personal status law. In other words, judges in all three countries are given some leeway to "find" the applicable personal law by drawing upon historical and classical sources of the tradition in question, especially when there is a legitimate need for it (i.e., legal lacuna). Obviously judges enjoy greater discretionary powers when the personal law in question remains largely uncodified (i.e., Jewish law in Israel or Muslim law in India).

[8] Court of Cassation, Case Nos: 475, 478, 481, 65th Judicial Year, August 5, 1996.
[9] HCJ 301/63 *Schtreit* v. *The Chief Rabbi of Israel* [1964] IsrSC 18(1) 598.

Sections 15 and 39 of the 1996 Constitution of South Africa), the impact of state-enforced religious laws on substantive and procedural human rights tends to be graver (Rautenbach 2010; Bennett 2011).

The most serious structural human rights concern raised by pluri-legal personal status systems is that, as justices of the ECtHR declared in the *Refah Partisi* case, they systematically undermine the state's obligation under both domestic and international law to treat all citizens equally before the law and not to discriminate among them on the basis of gender, religion or ethnicity (ICHRP 2009, pp. 73–78). Personal status systems are essentially characterized by intra- and intergroup inequality as they not only apply different sets of norms to people from different ethno-religious backgrounds, but also hold members of the same group (e.g., men and women) to different legal standards. Thus, since the principle that "all are equal before the law and are entitled without any discrimination to equal protection of the law"[10] has long become the main founding principle of international human rights law, one may suggest that pluri-legal personal status systems are thereby inherently incompatible with international human rights law. Such an assertion, from a purely legalistic point of view – which the present study adopts – is not necessarily untrue. Having said this, however, one could very well argue that since general laws have different impacts on people from different religious, normative and cultural backgrounds, it may not always be fair to blindly treat everyone according to the same standards and principles (Barry 2001, p. 34). In other words, the "equal treatment" may sometimes require, as some suggest, the recognition and accommodation of religious and cultural differences among subjects of the law rather than the pretence of treating everyone the same (Young 1990; Taylor and Gutmann 1994; Tully 1995; Kymlicka and Norman 2000; Parekh 2000; Kukathas 2003).

At this point, the question really comes down to the "true" meaning and function of equality, as well as fairness and justice. This is an age-old, profoundly philosophical question whose comprehensive consideration unfortunately lies beyond the scope of this book. However, my desire to eschew this very question is more of a theoretical and epistemological concern rather than a mere practical consideration. In this respect, I strongly believe that such a question would have been more fitting if the subject matter of the present study was not state-enforced personal status laws, but religious laws of autonomous ethno-religious

---

[10] Article 7 of the Universal Declaration of Human Rights (1948).

communities – independent of state control and regulation. Religious communities are normative communities in the sense that they have their own notions of justice and equality, which may well differ from, or even clash with, the equality principle usually enshrined in national constitutions and international human rights documents. Thus, had the present study dealt with religious laws applied by autonomous communities and institutions, instead of state-enforced personal status laws, it would have been more fitting and even necessary for us to engage competing notions of equality advocated by religious communities in order to locate and better understand prevailing rights discourses within them, and avoid the risk of judging them by standards which they may consider "alien" and not adhere to.

Personal status laws are not divinely ordained rules but socio-political constructions and enactments of the state. In personal status systems, the state-incorporated religious authorities and civil courts apply religiously inspired norms within parameters set by the state. Like autonomous religious communities, states also have their own concepts of justice and equality, usually embodied in their founding documents or constitutions, which may sometimes differ from, or clash with, the so-called universal principle of equality prohibiting discrimination on such grounds as race, religion or gender. For example, the 1961 Constitution of South Africa did not contain an equal protection clause as the apartheid regime outrightly rejected the equality of white and colored populations (Rabe 2001, pp. 281–282). If any of the three countries under scrutiny had similarly rejected the universal principle of equality, it would again have been necessary for us to engage and investigate their competing notions of equality, or lack thereof, in order to understand why they choose to apply different sets of laws to members of different ethno-religious groups, and the impact of these laws on individual rights and freedoms from their own point of view. However, this is not the case with any of the three countries, as none of them has ever put forth an alternative vision of equality or justice that would challenge or compete with the universal principle that prohibits discrimination on the grounds of race, sex or religion. On the contrary, they all have – at least constitutionally – internalized the principle of non-discrimination and committed themselves to treat their citizens equally before the law.[11] Moreover all three

---

[11] For equal protection clauses in each country's constitutional documents, see the Declaration of the Establishment of the State of Israel (1948); the Constitution of the Arab Republic of Egypt (1971), Article 40; and the Indian Constitution (1950), Articles 14 and 15.

countries have also adopted and ratified international documents under which they are obliged to not only guarantee equality of all before the law, but also ensure that all enjoy their basic rights and freedoms – such as freedom of religion, right to marry, right to found family and right to fair trial, among others.[12]

Therefore, with these remarks in mind, I maintain throughout the book that states bear the primary responsibility for human rights violations that occur under personal status systems. As shown in Chapter 2, personal status systems are socio-political constructions. The laws applied by state-integrated religious or civil family courts are not divine laws but enactments of the secular authority that essentially symbolize its coercive power and political will. In this regard, I contend that personal status-related human rights violations occur not as a result of divine intervention, but as a result of political choice. It is the political authority that decides which particular aspects or interpretations of religious texts, traditions or narratives are adopted and transposed into law. If the marriage or divorce laws that the state chooses to empower its courts to apply have certain gender-unequal provisions, the culprit here is not the religion these laws were supposedly drawn from but the political authority which adopts restrictive "patriarchal" interpretations of the tradition over its more enlightened and liberal interpretations. In other words, a state that encroaches upon its citizens' fundamental rights by claiming to apply divine laws not only desacralizes the tradition in question, and strips off the divinity of those laws it allegedly applies, but also violates its own constitutional and international obligations.[13]

HOW DO INDIVIDUALS RESPOND TO ENCROACHMENT UPON THEIR RIGHTS AND LIBERTIES?

It has so far been argued that state-enforced personal status laws violate fundamental rights and liberties, especially when people are forcibly subjected to jurisdiction of state-sanctioned religious laws and institutions

---

[12] All three countries signed and ratified the following UN treaties: ICCPR (1966), ICESCR (1966), and CEDAW (1979).

[13] Apparently governments in all three countries under examination are aware that the personal status laws they apply contradict their international obligations to treat everyone equally before the law. For example, all three countries have placed specific reservations or declarations on Article 16 of the CEDAW, which calls for elimination of discrimination against women in matters relating to marriage and family relations, on grounds that the personal status laws in force do not conform with the provisions of the said Article. For specific reservations and declarations placed on CEDAW by each country, see Appendix.

without their consent. This is because most governments – at least the three analyzed here – are either unable or unwilling to reform their personal status systems, and fail to protect vulnerable populations (i.e., women, children, etc.) against encroachments of so-called religious rules and authorities that operate under their auspices. Nevertheless, this does not mean that people just sit on the sidelines, and silently accept disabilities and limitations imposed upon their fundamental rights by state-sanctioned religious laws and institutions. On the contrary, as case studies presented in the following chapters evidence, the failure of the state has led people – especially the ones who are impacted most (i.e., women) – to take matters into their own hands and try to advance their rights to marriage, divorce, maintenance, inheritance, etc. by resorting to various tactics and strategies of resistance.

One of the tactics frequently used by individuals to navigate through and exploit the loopholes of pluri-legal systems is forum-shopping. Forum-shopping usually occurs when there are multiple normative order-ings with parallel jurisdictions. In such pluri-legal settings, litigants, if they are permitted to forum-shop, may alter their strategies accordingly and move their cases from one jurisdiction to another in pursuit of legal gains by exploiting inherent inconsistencies and loopholes of plural systems. Among the cases analyzed in this book, forum-shopping is most visible in Egypt, where Christians occasionally convert to Islam or migrate between different churches in order to escape disabilities imposed upon their rights by their own communal laws. For example, a person who belongs to a church that does not allow divorce could simply switch to another church which permits divorce and subsequently allows remar-riage. Similarly, the availability of independent *shariat* courts (*Dar-ul Qazas*) operated by various Muslim sects and organizations has reportedly enabled Indian Muslims (especially women) to shop between different *shariat* courts as well as between these informal tribunals and state courts (Solanki 2011, p. 313).

In this respect, it can be suggested that the availability of multiple forums principally empowers litigants by increasing their choices and allowing them to escape disabilities imposed upon them under their communal laws.[14] However, the mere existence of multiple forums in

[14] As Keebet von Benda-Beckmann suggests, apart from disputants, forums involved may also benefit from forum-shopping by using disputes for their own, mainly political, ends. That is to say, "besides forum shopping disputants there are also 'shopping forums' engaged in trying to acquire and manipulate disputes from which they expect to gain political advantage" (Benda-Beckmann 1981, p. 117). One may argue that this is particularly the case with forum-shopping in

itself is not always enough to safeguard individual rights and liberties (Solanki 2011, p. 313). First, even though it is often assumed that people migrating back and forth between different religious communities act out of their own will, this may not always be the case. Sometimes people may be compelled to leave their cultural communities to escape the disabilities imposed upon their rights in them because they have no other choice. For example, as explained in detail in Chapter 5, Orthodox Copts who have obtained a divorce from Egyptian family courts on grounds other than adultery – which is the only ground on which the church allows remarriage – are compelled to migrate to another church that allows remarriage for divorcees, or convert to Islam in order to found a family, because there is no other legal venue (i.e., civil marriage) available to them. In other words, the Egyptian personal status system forces Coptic Orthodox divorcees to make a difficult choice: if they want to exercise their right to marry and found a family they need to sacrifice their right to profess and exercise their own faith, and embrace another one. In this respect, forum-shopping is an outcome not of individual choice, but lack thereof. Besides, forum-shopping can be utilized only by skillful litigants who have access to and knowledge of both jurisdictions, and who are willing to bear associated individual costs (monetary, social, psychological, etc.). Individuals who convert to another religion or become a member of another normative community may be subjected to social sanctioning, and forced to bear certain socio-economic costs. For example, a person who has left her normative community may consequently be expelled and prevented by communal authorities from using communal resources and property that she was previously entitled to as a member. Moreover, forum-shopping also has important systemic implications. The ability of people to wander back and forth between different communities by resorting to opportunistic conversions not only undermines the general sense of trust among the populace in the country's justice system and its legal ideology, but also openly challenges the legitimacy of established communal

Egypt. During my field research in Egypt some Christian informants, especially members of the clergy, told me that the Egyptian legal system had actively encouraged Christians to forum-shop by converting to Islam or changing their denomination because the Muslim authorities, who were reportedly interested in subjugating the Christian culture and identity, allegedly wanted to apply Islamic law to Christians whenever possible. However, it is worth noting that clergy of the Coptic Orthodox Church also blamed other Christian churches for enticing their members with relaxed marriage and divorce rules that allegedly encouraged those Orthodox Copts who could not remarry in the Coptic church to migrate to other churches (for more information, see Chapter 5).

boundaries and contests the monopoly of state-imposed religious laws and institutions.

In personal status systems, where some people are systematically denied their fundamental rights by the state which claims to implement "God's" will and orders, rights talks eventually revolve around the question of whose interpretation of the holy scripture and tradition shall be deemed authoritative (Gaay Fortman, Martens et al. 2010). In fact there is a global trend from Morocco to Malaysia, which I also observed, particularly among women's groups, in Israel, Egypt and India, that individuals who live under personal status systems increasingly respond to violations of their rights by forming hermeneutic or interpretive communities that challenge official interpretations of religious precepts and offer emancipatory, egalitarian (i.e., women-friendly) readings of law in hopes of advancing their rights and reforming the system from within (Balchin 2009; Salime 2011). This is the second tactic by which individuals respond to the violation of their rights under personal status systems. In the process of hermeneutic activity, in order to identify and remove disabilities and human rights violations, these communities engage in an An-Naimian "internal discourse" through enlightened interpretations of cultural values and norms (An-Naim 1992, pp. 26–29; Twining 2009, pp. 58–90). However, hermeneutic groups are not just agents who solely engage in internal scriptural activity, but interlocutors (or "knowledge brokers" in Merry's terminology) who also participate in cross-cultural dialogues on a global level, from which they draw intellectual inspiration, resources and moral authority that guide them in locating and retrospectively constructing cultural references and narratives that promote a particular vision and set of rights (Merry 2006b). In effect, this is the very process that Levitt and Merry (2009) refer to as "vernacularization," through which hermeneutic communities translate global human and women's rights discourses and practices by meticulously grafting them onto local rights discourses, culture, tradition, and religious beliefs and teachings of their own societies (Merry 2006a).

Nowadays any discussion of human rights and religion, particularly in the context of non-Western societies, inexorably rotates around the axis of universalism and cultural relativism (Goodale and Merry 2007). However, it is imperative to transcend this false and counterproductive dichotomy to understand the multifaceted and complex nature of human rights talks under personal status systems (Santos 2002, p. 18; Osanloo 2009, p. 2). This is not to deny prevalent structural and conceptual limitations of international human rights law which, in some respects, make it seem less feasible as a framework that can be effectively deployed in pluri-legal or religion-based systems. For example, it is commonly acknowledged that the prevailing operational concept of religion in international human rights documents and discourses essentially embodies a Western understanding of the concept (Sharma 2006, p. 175). As demonstrated by the ECtHR in the above-mentioned *Refah Partisi* case, international law often treats religion as an inherently personal, uncontestable and static matter that falls outside the sphere of private law (Sunder 2003, p. 1419). Although this is a manifest limitation, it does not in itself present, as Sharma convincingly argues, an insuperable barrier to global acceptance and application of human rights law (Sharma 2006, p. 254). Neither does it make human rights a cultural product of the West, by implication unsuitable or alien to non-Western societies – a moral claim that is often invoked by authoritarian regimes in Asia and Africa as an excuse for their violations, and repression of emerging human rights movements, at home (Chanock 2000, p. 19; Afshari 2001, p. 10). At this point, it is worth noting that even in the West human rights ideas, when they first emerged, stirred profound ideological and cultural debate and opposition (Afshari 2001, p. 10). For example, at the time when they were first articulated, both racial and gender equality were similarly described as alien to Western culture – just as to non-Western ones – and were rejected by many people on cultural grounds. In fact, as Chanock notes, the achievement of both color and gender equality in the West, especially in the USA, has required and continues to require political and cultural transformation of many institutions from workplaces to schools, churches and political parties (Chanock 2000, p. 19). Thus, from this point of view, human rights should be seen not as an abstract cultural construction of any particular civilization, but as a product of intense political struggle and "a response to the universality of the modern state as a globally convergent mode of governance" (Afshari 2001, p. 10) – and an indispensable insurance policy to protect the ruled against the excesses of the executive branch.[15]

[15] Similarly, An-Naim and Hammond (2002, p. 19) suggest that "the present articulation of human rights emerged in Western countries in response to particular models of the centralized powers of the nation-state and certain forms of economic development. Since these models now prevail in all parts of the world ... the same articulation of rights would probably be necessary everywhere for the same reasons those formulations were adopted by Western societies. Generally speaking, all human rights ... are designed to help people to ensure that the centralized powers and economic resources of the state are used in full accord with their human dignity and for the satisfaction of their basic needs."

In every society, knowledge of human rights comes from within the experiences of human rights violations and the experiences of working against these violations. In other words, as Ackerly suggests, human rights are both immanent and universal in the sense that underwear is universal. "Not everywhere in the world do people wear cotton or linen undergarments, but where they wear wool (which itches the skin of most humans), they wear undergarments" (Ackerly 2008, p. 22). Likewise, she argues, "not everywhere and at all times have people made rights claims and called them 'human rights' when doing so," but almost everywhere they have resisted oppression, striven for social justice – as they understood and conceptualized it – and made specific claims through their words and actions that may contribute to our understanding of the universality of human rights as a manifestation of shared human experience in resisting oppression and injustice (*ibid.*). This is not to say that "all human societies have actually articulated and applied human rights norms in the modern sense of the term" (An-Naim and Hammond 2002, p. 19). But the need and desire for protection against government repression has been universal (Chanock 2000, p. 19); and people have expressed their grievances and claims in a familiar "rights language" that globally – or at least across the three countries that I studied – emphasizes individual (and communal) rights, duties and responsibilities of the state, and the need for restraints to be placed upon its powers.

I conducted 185 interviews with people from 20 different ethno-religious communities in 3 different countries. My informants included *qadis*, *dayanim*, *imams*, priests, gurus, secular judges, lawyers, community leaders, litigants from all walks of life and women's and human rights activists, among others. Notwithstanding national, religious, gender, sectarian and cultural differences, most people whom I talked to were fairly familiar with, if not fully conversant in, the emerging language of rights. If they did not speak it with the same fluency, they used a strikingly similar lexicon transcending national and communal boundaries. For instance, both a Russian Jew in Tel-Aviv, Israel, who was not allowed to marry the woman he loved because state-controlled rabbinical authorities did not consider him a "proper" Jew, and a Christian woman in Alexandria, Egypt, who was not allowed to marry her fiancé because her church did not recognize her divorce from a previous marriage, demonstrated a similar affinity and understanding of the language of rights, and constantly talked about the right to marry and found a family not in abstract terms but in human terms as they lived and experienced it.

Put this way, everyday disputants and practitioners have not seen rights – or lack thereof – in abstract terms but as lived, concrete realities. Neither have they seen rights through cultural lenses. For example, among people I interviewed not even a single person rejected outright the so-called global values of human or women's rights because they were "Western" constructs or "imperialist" impositions (Schwab and Pollis 1982; Ignatieff and Gutmann 2001; Mutua 2002). Neither did I come across informants who advocated an Islamic, Jewish, Hindu, Buddhist, Asian, African or, in Donnelly's terminology, "non-western conception of human rights," and asserted its supremacy over "universal" human rights law (Donnelly 2002, pp. 71–88). Nevertheless, this does not mean that the so-called universal human rights principles were uncritically embraced and fully internalized by people in different cultural, religious and political settings. It rather means that the universal/ cultural dichotomy and other binaries frequently used in academic, and some policy, circles to frame human rights debates in non-Western societies were often brushed aside by people who took a "fairly strategic and pragmatic [non-ideological] approach to using human rights values and technologies" and employed them as politico-legal tools to advance their own ends (Levitt and Merry 2009, p. 6). That is to say, people were usually more pragmatic and end-oriented than culturally or ideologically motivated in their usage and application of the rights language. People reacted to what they perceived to be injustice. If they were denied permission to marry the person they fell in love with, then justice simply meant obtaining permission to marry, which they were denied in the first place. To that end, they selectively exploited the language of rights to express their grievances, make a moral claim and undo injustice they thought they had been subjected to; otherwise people did not make claims in abstract for wholesale adoption of inalienable, indivisible human rights in their totality, as this would not necessarily offer them immediate assistance in finding practical solutions to practical problems.

Human rights talks under personal status systems usually take a multi-vocal and intersubjective form (Preis 1996). Some elements, which are certainly in the minority (especially in Egypt and India), wholeheartedly embrace secular, liberal and individualistic core values and principles embedded in international human and women's rights documents (e.g., UDHR, CEDAW), and resort to their language to challenge existing "discriminatory," "patriarchal" laws and practices. However, as already said, the majority of people – activists and non-activists alike – are more selective in their adoption and use of international human rights values and practices. Rather, they seem to pick and choose certain rights and practices from the list strategically, and disarticulate, transmute and fuse these into certain normative frames that would empower them to tackle personal status-related limitations and disabilities (e.g., right to marriage, divorce, maintenance, etc.). In other words, in personal status systems human rights are deconstructed and reconstructed into a culturally and politically hybrid (or *mestizo*, as Santos likes to call it) concept of rights organized as a constellation of intelligible local meanings and empowering normative references (Santos 2002, p. 19). In this way of conceptualization, however, the normative axis of rights shifts slightly away from secular individualism of the West – a distinct marker of international human rights documents – while fairness, equity, dignity and compassion; communal, individual and spousal obligations; and a mutated and contested form of equality emerge as core values of rights schemes in personal status systems. Despite the shift in normative axis, however, the political axis of human rights largely remains unchanged from its original message that obliges the state to act in certain ways or to refrain from certain acts in order to fulfill and protect rights and freedoms of citizens. Since in all three countries under scrutiny personal status laws are applied by civil courts or state-sanctioned communal courts, most people I encountered consistently held the state responsible for what they considered to be violation of their rights by personal status courts. For example, this is what an orthodox Jewish woman who had been denied *get* by her husband told me in reference to her ongoing divorce case:

> This is not Tehran ... this is Jerusalem. This is supposed to be a democratic country, not a theocracy ... I have nothing against the religion. I believe in God ... And God is fair and compassionate ... He has nothing to do with what is happening to me right now ... I blame it on those judges who side with that awful man [referring to her husband]. And I hold no one responsible, but the government which pays their [rabbinical judges'] salaries, and never fails to reward them for their intransigence.[16]

The emerging (*mestizo*) language of rights is communicated to the masses and put into action by hermeneutic communities through various programs that are intended to raise individuals' awareness of their rights, entitlements and protections, and boost their agency to stand up for

---

[16] Personal interview (Jerusalem, January 2005). Informant declined to be identified.

themselves and solve personal status-related disputes by mobilizing innovative tools and strategies made available largely as a result of hermeneutic activity. In doing so, hermeneutic groups build cross-communal alliances by transcending ethno-religious divides (e.g., Muslim–Jewish alliances in Israel, Muslim–Hindu alliances in India), lobby for judicial and legislative change, mobilize courts, educate the public and seek behavioral change by framing gender and human rights issues in terms that resonate with prevailing religious and cultural notions.

As mentioned earlier, in personal status systems, governments usually claim that they apply "sacred" laws that represent the power and will of divine authority. Despite the deceptiveness and falseness of such claims, the majority of people – most are religiously illiterate – tend to take them at face value and unquestionably accept the divine source and origin of state-enforced personal status laws. In this respect, framing becomes vital for promotion and acceptance of human rights among people who view government-enforced personal status laws as "sacred". Since people are more likely to accept human rights norms when they are presented as consistent with their values and belief systems, rather than as moral and political obligations binding upon them "regardless of inconsistency with their religious beliefs" (An-Naim 2012, p.58), the role that hermeneutic communities play in framing personal status-related human rights concerns in familiar religious terms becomes of critical importance.

In this respect, through framing and interpretive activity, hermeneutic communities lay the seeds for long-term acceptance and internalization of human rights norms by encouraging new ways of thinking about religion, personal status laws, cultural norms and gender roles in the society. During my field research I came across a number of hermeneutic communities from Kolech in Israel to the Bharatiya Muslim Mahila Andolan (BMMA) in India, all having achieved varying degrees of success. The ability of each organization to instigate meaningful change seemed to be closely correlated with such factors as the objectives of the group, the political and legal culture of the country, prevailing ideologies of justice, suitability of the tradition in question to exegetical and hermeneutical activity, institutional constraints/opportunities, and the relative existence, or lack, of a broader support structure with access to political allies and financial and legal resources. Hermeneutic communities were also visibly more prevalent and successful in environments where there already existed other civil society organizations that challenged the legitimacy of state-enforced religious laws and advocated adoption of liberal human rights principles and norms by employing non-religious or secular references and frameworks. The experiences and strategies of these groups and their human rights talks and discourses served as an important source of inspiration and point of reference for hermeneutic communities.

Hermeneutic communities usually adopt moderate means and strive for incremental change by working within existing personal status systems. However, some groups whose rights are disenfranchised under the existing system may adopt a more activist or assertive agenda and refuse to engage with state-controlled personal status institutions (they may even call for their complete abolition). Moreover, as governments and state-sponsored religious authorities repeatedly fail to address their concerns, some disillusioned groups, both secular and religious, may steadily evolve into "rule-making" communities by setting up their own personal status institutions that apply their own version of law to members of their self-proclaimed communities. Rule-making communities are best epitomized by such associations as the New Family Organization in Israel, which offers an alternative, non-religious mode of marriage and divorce to secular Jews, and the AIMWPLB, which, after long years of dissatisfaction with the particular versions of Muslim law applied by state courts or *Dar-ul Qazas* run by male-dominated AIMPLB, set up a *mahila adalat* (women's court) in order to promote and apply woman-friendly interpretations of Muslim personal laws. In some regards, however, the emergence of such alternative personal status institutions in a formally plural system can be viewed as the state's failure to regulate the normative and institutional plurality of its personal status field. Transmutation of formal plurality into informal plurality, as one may argue, not only undermines the sovereignty of the state but also deals a blow to the ideological and political goals it seeks to attain through its interventions in the field of personal status.

THE FIELD OF HUMAN RIGHTS AS A TESTING GROUND

Personal status systems are socio-political constructions. Both colonial and postcolonial/post-imperial governments intervened, successfully or unsuccessfully, in their pluri-legal personal status systems in order to impose a particular image of subjectivity upon society, and reorganize social relations in accordance with their political preferences. However, personal status systems are not just instruments of social and political engineering; they also have very important normative implications. They place certain restrictions and disabilities upon individuals, and thereby limit their enjoyment of certain fundamental rights and liberties. As noted, however, people often respond to the limitations and disabilities imposed upon their rights by employing various resistance strategies that include forum-shopping and the formation of hermeneutic and rule-making communities. As individuals engage in these activities, they contest the hegemonic narratives of gender, ethnicity and subjectivity, challenge the interpretive monopoly of state-sanctioned religious institutions, obfuscate communal boundaries, and redefine the role and place of disenfranchised individuals as rights-bearing equal citizens in familial and public space.

In other words, when hermeneutic or rule-making communities produce alternative interpretations of state-enforced religious laws and try to redefine the rights and duties of individuals under the law, or when people migrate back and forth between different ethno-religious communities in search of a favorable forum, they not only challenge the authority of the state and call into question the legitimacy of its regulation of personal status issues, but also deal a serious blow to the ideological and political designs that its rulers may have aimed to achieve through their interventions into the field of personal status. From this point of view, beyond simply informing us how fundamental rights and liberties are affected, the analysis of human rights talks, personal status-related violations and particular strategies people devise in encountering these violations could allow us to probe into the extent to which states succeed in achieving the objectives which originally led them to intervene in their personal status systems. Stated differently, I contend that individuals who interact with personal status systems on a regular basis decisively interfere with governments' attempts to regulate these pluri-legal institutions, and thereby play a pivotal role in their remaking. Thus, gaining insights into people's responses, sites of resistance and the state–society contestations these responses give rise to would equip us with unique lenses through which we could evaluate the performance of each government in attaining the objectives that motivated it to intervene in its personal status system in the first place.

In fact, in the following chapters I employ "the field of human rights as a testing ground" approach that I have just described to illustrate the extent to which Israeli, Egyptian and Indian governments have succeeded or failed in attaining their ideological and political goals. For example, as I explain in greater detail in Chapter 4, one of the main objectives of the Israeli government in maintaining the old *millet* system was the preservation and homogenization of the Israeli-Jewish identity. However, as my analysis of ongoing human rights discourses and struggles shows, particularly within the Jewish sector, the monopoly granted to rabbinical courts over marital affairs has caused profound ideological divisions and further fragmented the Jewish majority by dividing it into two groups of "marriageable" and "unmarriageable" Jews, and has brought about a *Kulturkampf* between the secular and religious elements in the community. Consequently, one may argue that the Israeli government has encountered serious challenges in attaining the goal of homogenization and unification of the Israeli Jewish population that had originally led it to retain a variant of the old *millet* system.

Similarly, the original intent of the Nasserist regime in enacting Law No. 462 of 1955 that abolished all religious courts and unified them under an overarching network of national courts was to systemize its legal system and break down the independent political power of religious groups and authorities. However, through my analysis in Chapter 5 of personal status-related human rights violations and strategies of resistance employed by Egyptian citizens, I demonstrate that the reform of 1955 only partially succeeded in producing its intended goals. This is because the religious activists have still found ways to exploit the current system of personal status in order to discredit and challenge the regime and intimidate secular forces (i.e., the *Abu Zayd* case). At the same time, individuals seeking legal gains continued resorting to forum-shopping as if the 1955 law that denounced this very practice for eroding citizens' trust in the system of justice had never been enacted. Likewise, my analysis in Chapter 6 of human rights issues in the backdrop of the *Shah Bano* case and the ensuing socio-political and legal developments demonstrate that the Indian leaders, who originally tried to intervene in the personal status system (striving for legal uniformity, national unity and secularism), have, to a great extent, failed to turn their uniformist and secularist vision into reality. Moreover, as the growing communal tensions, the reconfessionalization of the personal law system (i.e., a growing number of *shariat* courts, reintroduction of community-specific laws in lieu of secular uniform legislation, etc.) that has been underway since the late 1970s and the limited relevance and impracticality of civil and secular remedies (e.g., the SMA of 1954) in providing Indians with a viable exit option attest (despite simultaneous convergence and harmonization attempts), the Indian government has also somewhat failed in establishing the truly secular, democratic legal system that some of its founders had long envisioned, where everybody would be equal before the law and freely follow the laws of their own choosing without duress of any kind (e.g., customary, religious, tribal, etc.).

Chapter 3 has argued that state-enforced religious personal status laws often negatively impact fundamental rights and liberties, especially when people are forcibly subjected to their jurisdiction. However, as shown, pluri-legal personal status systems can be as much enabling as constraining. They provide a nurturing ground for all sorts of rule-making and hermeneutic communities, which in turn not only challenge the foundation and legitimacy of pluri-legal systems, but also renegotiate them to make room for and support the very rights and liberties they encroach upon. The next chapter tests these theoretical propositions by explaining the historical and political roots of the Israeli personal status system, and analyzing its impact on the rights and freedoms of individuals, as well as the ways the people react to limitations and disabilities placed upon them by state-sanctioned religious laws and authorities.

4

A FRAGMENTED CONFESSIONAL SYSTEM: STATE-ENFORCED RELIGIOUS FAMILY LAWS AND HUMAN RIGHTS IN ISRAEL

Israel formally inherited the personal status components of the Ottoman *millet* system,[1] as modified by the British Mandate, when the Provisional Council of State enacted the Law and Administration Ordinance (LAO) on May 19, 1948. The *millet* system that Israel adopted in its modified form was a fragmented confessional system under which the Ottoman and British authorities had granted juridical autonomy over matters of personal status[2] (e.g., marriage, divorce, succession, maintenance and alimony) to eleven[3] ethno-religious communities in Palestine. Since then, Israel has somewhat preserved this pluri-legal structure, and further extended its limits to include

---

[1] The Ottoman *millet* system, besides the personal status-related privileges that it granted, also recognized the organizational autonomy of Christian and Jewish communities across the empire, which enjoyed extensive freedoms to elect their communal leaders and self-govern their internal affairs (Benjamin 1982; Karpat 1982; Goffman 1994). However, Israel, for various political and ideological reasons, did not adopt the organizational framework of the *millet* system, but only retained its personal status-related aspects – albeit in a modified form.

[2] According to Article 51 of the Palestine Order in Council (POC) of 1922, the term "matters of personal status" means "suits regarding marriage or divorce, alimony, maintenance, guardianship, legitimation and adoption of minors, inhibition from dealing with property of persons who are legally incompetent, successions, wills and legacies and the administration of the property of absent persons" (Wright 1952, p. 118). However, for the purposes of the present study, the concept of personal status is defined more narrowly, and the scope of the term is exclusively confined to the matters of marriage, divorce, succession and spousal maintenance.

[3] According to the Second Schedule to the POC, as amended in 1939, the following communities were officially recognized by the Mandatory regime in addition to the Sunni Muslim community: Eastern (Orthodox), Latin (Catholic), Gregorian Armenian, Armenian (Catholic), Syrian (Catholic), Chaldean (Uniate), Greek Catholic Melkite, Maronite, Syrian Orthodox, Jewish (Wright 1952, p. 127).

three more communities whose jurisdictions were not previously recognized under the Turkish or British rule.[4] In other words, Israel has
never attempted to put an end to the multiplicity of religious courts
and unify them under a network of national courts, as Egypt did in
1955. Nor has it ever attempted to abolish the personal status laws of
various communities and enact a secular and uniform civil code in
their place, as India attempted in the 1950s. Instead, it has preserved
the main framework of the *millet* system through which it has granted
religious courts of fourteen state-recognized communities, staffed with
communal judges who apply state-enforced communal laws, exclusive
jurisdiction over matters of marriage and divorce and concurrent
jurisdiction with civil family courts over matters of maintenance and
succession.

As noted earlier, plural personal status systems – like the one that
Israel inherited upon independence – had historically been harnessed by
imperial powers to segregate and categorize their subject populations
into ethno-religious groupings, exclude the subaltern from the spoils of
power and deny them the terms of equal membership in the political
community. Moreover, such systems also treated people first and foremost as members of their cultural communities, rather than rights-
bearing equal citizens, and this undermined individuals' fundamental
rights and liberties by forcibly subjecting them to the purview of religious
norms and institutions. Against this backdrop, Israel's retention of the
Ottoman *millet* system, which institutionalized gender and religion-
based inequalities, was quite paradoxical given that from the very
moment of its inception the Jewish State pledged itself to guarantee its
citizens' freedom of religion and conscience, and to ensure complete
equality of all its inhabitants irrespective of religion, race or sex. In this
respect, two main questions guide the analysis below: (1) Why has Israel
preserved the old *millet* system and continued differentiating among its
citizens on the basis of ethnicity, religion and gender despite its democratic claims and constitutional obligations to treat everyone equally
before the law? (2) How have the preservation of the *millet* system and
the forcible application of religious laws affected the rights and freedoms
of Israeli citizens, and what tactics and strategies have they devised to

---

[4] Three communities recognized after the establishment of the State of Israel are: the Druze
community (1957), the Evangelical Episcopal Church (1970), and the Baha'i community
(1971) (Shava 1981, pp. 239, 247; Goldstein 1992, p. 145; Edelman 1994, p. 51; Abou
Ramadan 2003, p. 255).

respond to limitations and disabilities imposed upon their rights and freedoms by religious laws and institutions?

In the present chapter, I mainly argue that the adoption and utilization of the *millet* system – albeit in its modified form – was a logical extension of Israel's exclusionary and theocratically inclined founding ideology (Sezgin 2010b). The fragmented confessional system that Israel inherited from the Ottomans through the British Mandate has been appropriated by the Israeli regime as an instrument of nation-building to achieve two complementary objectives in particular: the preservation and homogenization of Israeli-Jewish identity, and the differentiation of non-Jewish identities. Has either of these objectives been achieved? To answer the question, I employ "the field of human rights as a testing ground" approach that I laid out in Chapter 3. In this respect, I next turn my attention to human rights-related concerns that presently occur under the Israeli personal status system, and analyze the responses of various hermeneutic and rule-making communities to evaluate the effectiveness of Israel's interventions into its system of personal status. Through this innovative use of the human rights framework, I first document detrimental impacts of personal status laws on fundamental rights and liberties; second, taking a closer look at ongoing contestations over matrimonial laws between human and women's rights groups on the one hand and state-sanctioned religious authorities on the other, I finally demonstrate that the old *millet* system has, to a significant extent, betrayed the intentions of those who initially endorsed and came to rely upon it as the backbone of their nation-building project.

The chapter is divided into three sections. First, I describe the history and the current state of the Israeli personal status system, specifically drawing on the Jewish, Muslim, Christian and Druze religious courts. Second, to explain what factors have led the Israeli leaders to retain a variant of the Ottoman *millet* system, I examine exclusionary and theocratic proclivities of the Israeli regime and demonstrate how the political elites have harnessed and manipulated the personal status system in the nation-building process. Third, I analyze the impact of state-enforced personal status laws on the rights and freedoms of Israeli citizens, and demonstrate how people have contested the hegemonic narratives and discourses of ethnicity, religion and gender, as well as the scriptural and hermeneutic monopoly of state-sanctioned religious institutions, and how they have remade the state-enforced religious norms and practices through their interactions with and adoption of various strategies of resistance.

I. THE ISRAELI PERSONAL STATUS SYSTEM

Rabbinical courts

All Jewish residents of Israel are subject to mandatory jurisdiction of rabbinical courts in regard to matters of personal status. There are twelve rabbinical courts of first instance, which are spread across the different regions of the country. There is also a Rabbinical Court of Appeals (*Bet Din ha-Gadol*) located in Jerusalem. The LAO of May 19, 1948 formally incorporated all religious courts, including the rabbinical courts as they existed under British rule, into the legal system of the new state. Thereafter, the Israeli government swiftly moved to restructure the organization and jurisdiction of Jewish courts. First, with the enactment of the Rabbinical Courts Jurisdiction (Marriage and Divorce) Law (RCJL) in 1953, they were officially placed under the supervision of the Ministry of Religious Affairs, and remained therein until the ministry was dismantled and the administration of all religious courts was transferred to the Ministry of Justice in 2004 (in 2008, after the (re)establishment of the Ministry of Religious Services, rabbinical courts were placed under its jurisdiction while the Muslim and Druze courts continued to remain as part of the Ministry of Justice). The second major step was taken with the Dayanim Law in 1955, which turned rabbinical court judges (*dayanim*) into state officials "akin to the judges of the civil courts ... with equivalent salaries" (Edelman 1994, p. 53). In addition, the law also set the legal requirements for the appointment, promotion, tenure and other emoluments of *dayanim*. Like civil judges, they are now appointed for life by the President of the State upon the recommendation of a nomination committee.[5] As of 2009, there were 88 active *dayanim* occupying the benches of both rabbinical courts of first instance and the Court of Appeals.[6]

During the Mandate, rabbinical courts were allowed to exercise their jurisdiction only over the Jews "possessing Palestinian citizenship, over 18 years of age, and registered in the Jewish Community Register" (Chigier 1967, p. 159). Jews who were not registered with communal authorities (*Knesset Yisrael*) were simply not subject to the jurisdiction of the rabbinical courts. Yet, with the enactment of the RCJL of 1953, the

---

[5] The nomination committee is composed of the two chief rabbis (*Sephardi* and *Ashkenazi*), two government ministers (one of whom must be the Minister of Justice), two *dayanim* from the Bet Din ha-Gadol, two members of the Knesset and two representatives of the Israel Bar Association.
[6] Israel Central Bureau of Statistics, retrieved in January 2011 from www1.cbs.gov.il/publications/isr_in_n10h.pdf

principle of voluntary association was abolished and the rabbinical courts were granted a nearly universal jurisdiction over all Jewish residents (citizens and non-citizens) of the country (Bentwich 1964, p. 244; Chigier 1967, p. 156; Rubinstein 1967, p. 386).[7]

While the personal jurisdiction of rabbinical courts was extended by the Israeli legislature, their subject matter jurisdiction was reduced as compared to the Mandate period.[8] According to the Palestine Order in Council (POC) of 1922 (Article 53), rabbinical courts had exclusive jurisdiction in matters of marriage and divorce, alimony and confirmation of wills of their registered community members, and concurrent jurisdiction (with civil district courts) in any other matter of personal status, provided that all parties to the action consented to their jurisdiction. Yet, under the current law, the rabbinical courts have exclusive jurisdiction only in regard to matters of marriage and divorce (including *chalitza*).[9] In all other matters, they have concurrent jurisdiction with the specialized family courts. However, the 1953 law states that when a suit for divorce is filed in a rabbinical court, by virtue of the "connection principle" (*iqaron ha-krikhah*), the same court can also claim exclusive

---

[7] Rabbinical courts claim jurisdiction over Jewish foreigners who happen to visit or temporarily reside in Israel. For example, in some cases, Jewish Americans who entered Israel as tourists have become defendants in divorce cases filed against them in local rabbinical courts by their American spouses, even though they may have been civilly divorced in the US (Kempster 1997). Such a case took place in 2004, when a national of Monaco divorced his wife civilly in Monaco without issuing a *get* and moved to Israel. Because his wife had already petitioned the local rabbinical court in Israel, the Monégasque husband was issued an injunction upon his arrival forbidding him to leave the country until he gave his wife a *get*. Although the Supreme Court of Israel ruled in 2004 (HCJ 6751/04 *Sabbag* v. *The Rabbinical Court of Appeals* [2004] IsrSC 59(4) 817) that rabbinical courts cannot exercise jurisdiction over foreign individuals, such cases still continue to cause international embarrassment for the Israeli government. For example, the travel warning issued by the Department of State still cautions Jewish Americans against the excessive jurisdiction claims of the Israeli rabbinical courts – see http://travel.state.gov/travel/cis_pa_tw/cis/cis_1064.html (accessed in February 2011).

[8] As an exception, however, as during the Mandate period, the Arbitration Law of 1968 continued to recognize the rabbinical courts' authority to arbitrate in financial disputes and other civil matters at the consent of both parties (Porat-Martin 1979, p. 43). However, in 2006 in the case of Sima Amir (HCJ 8638/03 *Sima Amir* v. *High Rabbinical Court* [2006] IsrSC 61(1)), the Supreme Court declared that rabbinical courts were not authorized to arbitrate civil disputes even when both sides voluntarily agreed to bring the dispute to their jurisdiction (Barka 2006; Yoaz 2006). In addition to state-run rabbinical courts, there are also private rabbinical courts operated by various Jewish communities across Israel (e.g., Beth-Din-Zedek in Bnei Brak in Tel-Aviv, Eda Haredit rabbinical court in Mea Shearim in Jerusalem) (Porat-Martin 1977, pp. 91–102; 1979, pp. 62–76). Besides arbitration, some of these courts also rule over personal status matters. In fact, the jurisdiction of the Eda Haredit court to rule over its followers' matters of personal status has been recognized by the official rabbinical court system (personal interview with Prof. Aviad Hacohen [Jerusalem, February 2005]); for further information on non-state religious adjudication in Israel, see Hofri-Winogradow (2010).

[9] *Chalitza* is performance of the ceremony by which both a childless widow and her brother-in-law are released from the duty of contracting a levirate marriage.

jurisdiction over such matters as maintenance and custody if they are attached to the original divorce suit by the petitioning party at the time of filing (Porat-Martin 1981–1983; Rosen-Zvi 1989; Shava 1998; Halperin-Kaddari 2004, pp. 233–235).[10] Similarly, in the case of succession (testate and intestate), the rabbinical court's jurisdiction is contingent upon all interested parties' consent in writing; otherwise the primary jurisdiction belongs to the civil courts, which will distribute the property according to provisions of the secular Israel Succession Law (ISL) of 1965.[11,12,13,14]

---

[10] An interesting aspect of this jurisdictional split is that both civil courts and rabbinical courts have to apply the same substantive laws to the matter in hand. This is particularly true for matters of maintenance. There is no secular territorial law of maintenance or alimony in Israel. When such matters are brought to their jurisdiction, the civil courts have to apply the parties' religious laws to the case in hand, under the provisions of the Family Law Amendment (Maintenance) Law (FLAML) of 1959 (Vitta 1947, p. 163; Chigier 1967, p. 165; Shava 1973; Eisenman 1978, p. 90). Although both the rabbinical and civil courts seemingly apply the same substantive Jewish law in matters of concurrent jurisdiction, it is not uncommon for the courts to render opposing interpretations of the same legal principles and rules. The reason behind this is twofold. First, the rabbinical courts and civil courts operate under different laws of procedure and evidence (Shava 1985). Second and more importantly, the legal ideology and value systems that civil court judges rely upon in making their decisions are significantly different from those of *dayanim* (Porat-Martin 1979).

[11] The ISL of 1965 is an optional uniform and territorial piece of legislation that is applicable to members of all religious communities. Even though the 1965 law seemingly aimed to achieve some sort of institutional and normative unification in matters of inheritance, the reality is far from it. On the contrary, the law has further increased the normative plurality of the field in comparison to the British era (see n. 12 below). During the Mandate, by virtue of the Succession Ordinance (SO) of 1923, both religious and civil courts (see n. 13 below) were required to apply the provisions of the Ottoman Law of Succession (OLS) of 1913 to distribution of *miri* land (see n. 14 below) and religious laws of the parties to *mülk* land and other movables. Thus, as far as succession to *miri* land was concerned, there was a considerable degree of normative unity, as all the courts in the country were required to apply the same codified inheritance law. Yet, with the enactment of the ISL in 1965, the relative unity in the field of succession was considerably weakened as religious courts were now allowed to apply their own communal laws to all categories of property without any distinctions (i.e., movable, immovable, *mülk* or *miri*).

[12] The WERL of 1951 extended the application of the OLS to *mülk* property and all movables. The law required both civil and religious courts of recognized communities to apply Ottoman law to all types of property without any distinction. In other words, with the enactment of the WERL, a total normative unification was already achieved in the field of succession throughout the religious and civil courts of Israel. In this regard, the ISL was a step backwards in comparison not only to the British period but also the period from 1951–1965. This is because the ISL led to refragmentation of an already unified legal system by stopping the application of the Ottoman law and granting the communal courts freedom to apply their own particularistic norms and customs in matters of succession.

[13] Both in matters of testate and intestate succession, the 1923 ordinance recognized the primary jurisdiction of the civil courts and concurrent jurisdiction of the Jewish and Christian courts, upon the consent of the interested parties (Reiter 1996, p. 37). Shari'a courts were excluded from the purview of the ordinance, as they had exclusive jurisdiction over matters of succession, with the exception of the distribution of *miri* land, in which case they had to apply the OLS of 1913.

[14] The Ottoman Land Law of 1858 (Article 1) enumerated five distinct categories of land: *mülk, miri, vakıf, metruk* and *mevat. Mülk* lands were held in complete private ownership and exempt

Unlike matters of concurrent jurisdiction, marriage and divorce are left under the exclusive jurisdiction of religious courts. Both the Knesset and the Israeli Supreme Court (sitting as the High Court of Justice) have vigilantly refrained from directly interfering with the religious courts' exclusive jurisdiction in this area.[15] (Mautner 2011, pp. 192–193; Meydani 2011, p. 93.) In particular, the parliament has refused to enact any matrimonial laws that would directly interfere with the substantive laws of religious communities. For instance, the lawmakers usually provided "opt-out" clauses in legislation that dealt with matrimonial issues, such as the Marriage Age Law (MAL) of 1950, the Women's Equal Rights Law (WERL) of 1951,[16] and the Penal Law Amendment (Bigamy) Law (PLABL) of 1959.[17] As a result, the legislative and judicial branches' encroachments upon substantive Jewish matrimonial laws have been kept to a minimum. Therefore, rabbinical courts more or less continue to apply the traditional Jewish law that is

from tithe; *miri* lands were state lands leased to the individuals who held the land by usufruct rather than by title deed; *vakif* lands belonged to religious foundations and were used for pious purposes; *metruk* lands were left for general public use, like highways; and finally, *mevat* lands were unoccupied desert lands, woodlands and grazing spots not held by title deed (Stein 1984, pp. 3–34; Gerber 1987, pp. 67–90).

[15] For example, under Section 7(b)(4) of the Courts Law of 1957 and Article 15(d)(4) of the Basic Law: the Judiciary of 1984, the Supreme Court of Israel, sitting in its capacity as the High Court of Justice, is authorized to hear petitions regarding the competence of religious courts and quash their proceedings and decisions if found *ultra vires* (i.e., HCJ 1842/92 *Naomi Blaugrund v. The Rabbinical Court of Appeals* [1992] IsrSC 46(3) 423; HCJ 5182/93 *Levy v. The Rabbinical Court of Tel Aviv/Jaffa* [1994] IsrSC 48(3) 1; and HCJ 3269/95 *Katz v. The Rabbinical Court of Jerusalem* [1996] IsrSC 50(4) 590). Despite this clear-cut mandate given by the legislature as well as its growing secularist activism and infamous confrontational approach towards the religious authorities, the High Court of Justice has been especially cautious in its dealings with rabbinical courts' exercise of their exclusive jurisdiction in matters of marriage and divorce (Woods 2001; Halperin-Kaddari 2002; Barzilai 2003, pp. 219). The rabbinical courts' rulings, particularly on matters of marriage and divorce, have been effectively exempt from judicial review by civil courts on material grounds, as well. That is to say "even when ... a rabbinical court has [seemingly] erred on a point of Jewish Law" the High Court of Justice still "cannot regard itself as competent to refer the case back to the court of origin, let alone reverse the decision" (Porat-Martin 1979, p. 241).

[16] Section 8 of the WERL of 1951 prescribes divorce against the wife's will a criminal offense that is subject to five years in prison.

[17] For example, although the WERL was to give Israeli women of all faiths equal status with regard to any legal act and proceedings of both secular and religious origin, the matters of marriage and divorce were intentionally excluded from the purview of the law by virtue of Section 5. Similarly, even though the law was theoretically required to be applied by the religious courts of recognized communities, Section 7 deliberately diluted the potential impacts of the law on the jurisdiction of religious courts by making the application of it conditional on the interested parties' consent. According to the legal mechanism devised in Section 7, individuals who are eighteen years of age or over could consent before the competent tribunal to have their case tried according to the laws of their community without the restrictions placed on them by the virtue of the WERL. Likewise, the MAL of 1950 (Porat-Martin 1979, pp. 235–236) and the PLABL of 1959 were also designed to accommodate the specific requirements of *halakhah* (Rubinstein 1967, p. 230) and provided similar opt-out options.

known as *halakhah*. *Halakhah* is uncodified religious law whose main sources traditionally include the Torah, Talmud, *takkanot* (rabbinical enactments), *she'elot u-teshuvot* (questions and answers) and *minhag* (custom) (Elon 1967, 1968a, 1968b, 1969; Chigier 1979; Eliash 1981–1983; Hecht, Jackson *et al.* 1996).[18] Today, the only form of *halakhah* recognized in Israel is the Orthodox (Zucker 1973, pp. 76–86). Non-Orthodox streams (i.e., Conservative, Reform) are left out of the official religious establishment (Abramov 1976, pp. 192–198; Sapir 2001; Shetreet 2002, pp. 169–180; Shifman 2002, pp. 22–26). By implication, when rabbis solemnize marriages or *dayanim* decide on cases of personal status, they primarily rely upon the orthodox interpretation of Jewish law, aside from civil and penal enactments (e.g., age of marriage rules, prohibition of bigamy, etc.) which they are by law required to follow.

Shari'a courts

Shari'a courts, which exercise jurisdiction over the personal status matters of Israeli Muslims (roughly 15 percent of the total population), were also incorporated into the new state's legal system in 1948 (Ghanem 2001, p. 1; Louër 2003, p. 12). There are currently eight regional *shari'a* courts of first instance, as well as a Shari'a Court of Appeals (*Mahkamah al-Isti'naf al-Shar'iyya*) located in West Jerusalem,[19] which was established in 1953.[20] Like rabbinical courts, they have exclusive jurisdiction over marriage and divorce, and concurrent jurisdiction over all other matters of personal status. However, prior to 2001, when the Law of Family Courts (Amendment No. 5) (LFCA) equalized their subject matter jurisdiction to that of rabbinical courts, *shari'a* courts had the broadest jurisdiction

---

[18] Maimonides' compilations of Talmudic Law from the twelfth century, *Mishneh Torah*, and Rabbi Joseph Karo's authoritative commentary on *halakhah* from the sixteenth century, *Shulchan Aruch*, are also among the most popularly consulted sources.

[19] Since the enactment of the Qadis Law (Amendment No. 10) (QLA) in 2002, the Shari'a Court of Appeals has de facto come to be known as the High Shari'a Court of Appeals or the Supreme Shari'a Court of Appeals (Abou Ramadan 2003, p. 276).

[20] In addition to the Israeli *shari'a* court in West Jerusalem, there are three more *shari'a* courts in East Jerusalem, which has been formally considered as part of the national territory by the Israeli government since its occupation and annexation of the city in 1967. Two of these courts are run by the Palestinian National Authority, while the third is still administered by Jordan as a remnant of its rule in East Jerusalem from 1948 to 1967. Rulings of these courts are not currently recognized or executed by the Israeli authorities. However, Palestinians living in East Jerusalem as "permanent residents" (rather than full citizens) of Israel could alternatively resort to the Israeli *shari'a* court of West Jerusalem for their matters of personal status when they want their cases to produce legal consequences that are recognized and enforced by the Israeli government (Welchman 1990; Reiter 1997a; Welchman 2000, 2003, 2004; Shahar 2006, pp. 11–22). Further and up-to-date information on *shari'a* courts – including their recent rulings – can be found at www.justice.gov.il/MOJHeb/BatiDinHashreim/.

among religious courts in the country. This was particularly true before 1948, as the British had defined the jurisdiction of Muslim courts much more generously than they had for the rest of the communal courts by closely following the Ottoman tradition (Ghandour 1990; Abu-Gosh 1991; Natour 2000).[21] However, as I demonstrate below, after 1948 the Israeli government manipulated the organizational structure of Muslim courts and systematically limited their autonomy and jurisdiction (Natour 2009, pp. 8–10).

During the dislocations of 1947–1948, Muslim religious institutions, including *shari'a* courts, were completely destroyed (Kupferschmidt 1987).[22] The system was in need of urgent care and restoration to generate a continued sense of identity, belonging and cohesion among a dislocated and disoriented people. In fact, this was what the Israeli government had started doing as early as August 1948 by establishing two *shari'a* courts, in Nazareth and Acre. Two more courts were to follow, in Jaffa and Tayyiba, in January 1950. The next step was taken in December 1953 with the enactment of the Shari'a Courts (Validation of Appointments) Law (SCVAL), which retroactively validated the formation of the aforementioned courts and the appointment of their *qadis*. The same law also created the Shari'a Court of Appeals in Jerusalem (Eisenman 1978, p. 169). As part of the government's restructuring program, *shari'a* courts, like their Jewish counterparts, were placed under the supervision of the Ministry of Religious Affairs, and remained therein until 2004. Thereafter they were placed under the jurisdiction of the Ministry of Justice.

A more comprehensive law regulating the appointments, promotions and emoluments of *qadis* was enacted in 1961. Under the law, *qadis* were declared salaried state officials who were now required to take the pledge of allegiance to the State of Israel,[23] and appointed by the President of

---

[21] Article 52 of the POC recognized the exclusive jurisdiction of *shari'a* courts over matters of personal status by referring to Article 7 of the Ottoman Law of Procedure for Shari'a Courts (OLPSC) of 1917 (Natour 1997, p. 27). The list of personal status matters mentioned in Article 7 was in fact more comprehensive than Article 51 of the POC (see n. 2 above) which defined what the term "personal status" meant in terms of the jurisdiction of rabbinical and ecclesiastical courts. Moreover, during the Mandate, the Muslim courts were also exempt from the purview of the SO of 1923 (Article 20).

[22] "All but one *shari'a* court judge from Mandate times, Sh. Tahir at-Tabari of Tiberius, had fled" from Palestine during the skirmishes and battles that took place in 1947–1949 (Eisenman 1978, p. 169).

[23] According to Section 7 of the law, prior to his appointment, a *qadi* has to make the following declaration before the President of the State: "I pledge myself to bear allegiance to the State of Israel, to dispense justice fairly, not to pervert the law and to show no favor."

the State upon the recommendation of a nine-member nominations committee.[24] The Qadis Law (QL) of 1961 also stated the minimum requirements to be sought in eligible candidates for appointment as *qadis*. According to Article 2, any Muslim citizen of Israel, who was married and at least 30 years of age, led "a way of life befitting the status of a *qadi*," and had "suitable" training in *shari'a* was qualified to be nominated as an Islamic judge.[25]

Apart from its tampering with their organizational structure, the Israeli government has also consistently reduced the subject matter jurisdiction of Muslim courts through legislative actions. However, these legislative interventions, as Layish (1993, p. 174) notes, have been restrained in two respects: First, as in the case of rabbinical courts, they have never directly encroached upon the substantive Muslim laws of marriage and divorce; instead the legislature has sought to enact procedural provisions or penal sanctions in this area. Second, "even in matters [e.g., succession] in which provisions have been enacted that supersede the religious law, the parties have, with certain reservations, been left an opportunity to litigate under religious law" (Layish 1971,

---

[24] The committee consists of two cabinet ministers (one of which is the Minister of Justice), two current *qadis*, three Members of the Knesset, of whom at least two are Muslims, and two members of the Israel Bar Association, of whom one is also a Muslim.

[25] The QL of 1961 failed to stipulate any objective criteria for appointees other than such vague and discretionary principles as having "suitable" Islamic training or leading a "way of life" befitting the status of a *qadi*. The nominations committee, headed by the Minister of Religious Affairs until 2004 – a position often occupied by members of Orthodox Jewish religious parties (Edelman 1994, p. 78) – made its recommendations mostly on political and security grounds and on the basis of familial connections rather than religious expertise or any other objective criteria (Neuhaus 1991, pp. 35–38; Reiter 1997b; Peled 2001, pp. 68, 121). For example, Dr. Mitkhal Natour, a former professor of *shari'a* at the Islamic College of Baqa al-Gharbiyyah, told me in our meeting that "the question has never been if [a particular] candidate had the knowledge or not ... but which party [he was] from, which minister [was] behind [him] ... or which minister [was] supporting [him]." The appointment of unqualified individuals as *qadis* through political patronage has led to wide criticism of the *shari'a* judicial system and a great erosion of respect for and trust in this traditionally prestigious institution among the Muslim Palestinians in Israel (Reiter 1997b, p. 208). In response to the growing public discontent with the existing system of *qadi* appointments in recent years, the current President of the Shari'a Court of Appeals, Qadi Ahmad Natour, in collaboration with several Muslim members of the Knesset, initiated the passage of the QLA in July 2002. Now, according to the new version of Article 2, candidates must have high religious education in *shari'a* or in Islamic studies, or otherwise be lawyers who are members of the Israel Bar Association and who have practiced law for a period of no less than five years. In addition, nominees are now also required to pass a test given by a three-member Examination Committee, which would include the President of the Shari'a Court of Appeals, a Muslim member of the Knesset, and a person who has been a *qadi* in the past or has been an active lawyer for at least five years (Abou Ramadan 2005, p. 249; Shahar 2006, p. 57). As Qadi Ahmad Natour noted in our meeting in January 2005, in the then most recent *qadi* examination to fill two open positions, forty-five candidates had competed and only five were able to pass the exam.

p. 255). Therefore, the primary source of substantive law applied at *shari'a* courts remains the Ottoman Law of Family Rights (OLFR) of 1917 (Aydın 1985, 2000). For matters not covered by the Ottoman Law, *qadis* often resort to the Egyptian jurist Qadri Pasha's nineteenth-century compilation of Islamic personal status laws (Qadri 1914), and various other commentaries on *Hanafi* jurisprudence. Although *qadis* principally exercise a considerable degree of discretionary freedom in interpreting and applying the *shari'a* law (Edelman 1994, p. 77),[26] they are required to take into consideration the procedural limitations and penal sanctions imposed by such secular legislations as the MAL of 1950, the WERL of 1951 and the PLABL of 1959.[27] Moreover, their decisions are also subject to review by the Shari'a Court of Appeals, and subsequently by the Israeli High Court of Justice (Zahalka 2009, pp. 45–59).[28] However, like in the case of other religious laws, when an issue involving substantive matters of Islamic law comes up for review, the High Court of Justice, not feeling "at ease in its role as a 'high interpreter' for a *shari'a* decision," often exercises judicial restraint, and supports "its position by referring to the Shari'a Court of Appeals [i.e., HCJ 9347/99 *Ali Hamza* v. *Shari'a Court of Appeals and Others* [2001] IsrSC 55(2) 54]" (Abou Ramadan 2005–2006, p. 102).

However, the effectiveness of this approach to induce socio-legal change through indirect interventions into the material laws of the religious communities has been highly equivocal. The questionable performance of penal measures prescribed in the aforementioned legislation (e.g., prohibition of underage marriages, *talaq* or bigamy) can be attributed to their requirement of the Muslim *qadi* to ignore the *shari'a*

[26] Although the *qadis* in Israel theoretically enjoy a considerable degree of discretionary freedom to consult any sources of *shari'a* in their rulings, Dr. Mitkhal Natour, a former professor of *shari'a* at the Islamic College of Baqa al-Gharbiyyah, thinks that, in practice, this freedom does not mean much, because *qadis* are not really able to take advantage of it due to the fact that most of them are not "qualified" or "learned" enough to utilize the original sources of Islamic law. Instead, pointing to his own book (1997), Dr. Natour says *qadis* often make use of readily available secondary sources and compilations of earlier court decisions and laws in force. Personal interview with Dr. Natour (East Jerusalem, January 2005).

[27] These laws provide, respectively, for the dissolution of the marriage of a juvenile girl (under 17), the prohibition against divorcing one's wife unilaterally against her will (*talaq*) and the prohibition against contracting bigamous marriages.

[28] The High Court of Justice occasionally intervenes and overturns the decision of the Shari'a Court of Appeals – most often in cases concerning paternity, maintenance and custody (Abou Ramadan 2008) rather than marital affairs; see, for instance, C.A. 3077/90 *Plonit* v. *Ploni* [1995] IsrSC 49(3) 578; HCJ 9740/05 *Plonit* v. *Shari'a Court of Appeals* [2006] IsrSC 60(1) 1541; and HCJ 1129/06 *Plonit and another* v. *Shari'a Court of Appeals* [2006] IsrSC 60(2) 3313.

and have his coreligionists punished, at the behest of the Jewish State, for exercising their "god-given" rights. Not surprisingly, most *qadis* have circumvented the application of such secular legislation, which they consider "un-Islamic." In particular, the stance of contemporary Islamic judges on the use of Israeli law has been reportedly more recusant than that of earlier generations of *qadis*, who embraced a somewhat compliant approach towards the procedural and criminal provisions imposed by Israeli legislation (Layish 1971, pp. 241, 256; 1975, p. 335; 1993, p. 182; Reiter 1997b).

For example, the incumbent President of the Shari'a Court of Appeals, Qadi Ahmad Natour, openly objects to the implementation of civil laws (including Basic Laws of the State of Israel) in the Islamic courts, not to mention the cooperation with law-enforcement agencies in the prosecution of individuals whose religiously permissible actions violate the provisions of the secular legislation. In an interview that I conducted with him in January 2005, Qadi Natour expressed his objection to the implementation of the Knesset-passed laws at the *shari'a* courts in the following words:

> As *shari'a* judges, I think that one of the most important duties that we have is to apply the *shari'a* law, and try to make it pure *shari'a* . . . not be involved with any particular Israeli law . . . *Shari'a* is part of our identity, character, our belonging, our root . . . If we apply the Israeli law, our identity, character, belonging, and all these will be interrupted . . . Israel calls itself a Jewish and a democratic state. We think that this is very problematic. Most of the positive Israeli laws are derived from the Jewish law . . . And we have nothing to do with the Israeli Jewish Law . . . For instance, in the case of divorce against the wife's will (*talaq*) [which is, according to the WERL of 1951, a criminal offense subject to five years in prison] . . . We believe that the *qadi* has nothing to do with the act of divorce or the crime. Because he does not initiate the divorce . . . When a man comes and tells the judge "I divorced my wife without her consent" . . . According to the *shari'a*, the divorce is there . . . The court did not do it, or participate in any crime. And, according to the law [referring to the OLFR of 1917] the *qadi* has to write down in his records that this man is divorced . . . I am not a criminal judge; I am a family law judge. The *qadi* has no responsibility under the law to report anything to the authorities . . .

Regardless of the Islamic officialdom's rhetoric of independence – which, some argue, is mainly used by *qadis* to obscure the reality of ongoing secularization, or what Abou Ramadan (2005–2006) calls the "Israelization" of *shari'a* courts – it was repeatedly pointed out by both

Muslim and Jewish practitioners and experts whom I interviewed that the real issue here has not been whether *qadis* were reporting alleged violations of law to the civil authorities, but whether the authorities were sincerely interested in prosecuting such seemingly "trivial" matters as the marriage of a juvenile girl, or the repudiation of a Muslim wife against her will within the Arab sector: "The police [usually] does not interfere in personal status issues . . . they very rarely do that . . . [In fact] we face a big problem in enforcing the laws [such as] the age of marriage and polygamy in the community . . . Unfortunately, it is not a priority of the state to deal with these issues among Arabs."[29]

Like the rabbinical courts, jurisdiction of *shariʿa* courts in succession matters is contingent upon the written consent of all interested parties. If matters of succession are brought to civil courts, the deceased's property will be divided according to the ISL of 1965. However, if the matter goes to the *shariʿa* court, then *qadis* will apply the traditional Islamic law of inheritance. Yet, as reported by many observers, the ISL has had little or no impact on the distribution of inheritance among Israeli Muslims (Eisenman 1978, pp. 201–208; Edelman 1994, pp. 84–87; Layish 2006, pp. 307–326). In other words, the Muslim community has ignored the secular legislation and continued to bring its inheritance cases to the Islamic courts,[30] as if these still had exclusive jurisdiction over matters of succession.

The most significant reduction in the subject matter jurisdiction of *shariʿa* courts to date occurred in November 2001 with the passage of the LFCA, which downgraded the jurisdiction of Muslim and Christian courts

---

[29] Personal interview with Nasreen Alemy-Kabha, the former coordinator of the WGEPSI (Nazareth, January 2005). Treitel (1995) makes a similar observation in regard to the Israeli government's unwillingness to prosecute individuals who violate the MAL of 1950. Under the law, the minimum age for marriage is 17. According to a report prepared by the Working Group on the Status of Palestinian Women in Israel, 22 percent of married Muslim women were under the age of 18 in 2007. For the same year the figure was only 0.5 percent among Christian Arab women (Yazbak 2007). I do not have access to information regarding how many underage marriage cases were prosecuted by the Israeli authorities in 2007. However, there is an earlier figure from 1990–1995, according to which only seven cases of underage marriage were prosecuted during the entire period, resulting in just two convictions (Working Group on the Status of Palestinian Women in Israel (1997), p. 63). Given that, in 1995 alone, nearly 1,750 underage marriages were contracted in the Arab community, the dismal number of convictions for the period 1990–1995 evidences the Israeli authorities' lack of interest in upholding secular family laws among its Palestinian citizens.

[30] Although the ISL of 1965 effectively repealed the SO of 1923 and the OLS of 1913, as the latter had already been incorporated into the former, *qadis* still continue issuing succession orders according to the OLS of 1913 (for *miri*) and the *shariʿa* (for *mülk* and movables) as if the ISL never came into effect.

from exclusive to concurrent in such matters as maintenance and custody. However, unlike the earlier interventions into the jurisdiction of Islamic courts, which were unilaterally imposed by the Israeli legislature, this recent intervention was actually initiated by the parliament in response to the demands of some liberal and feminist groups within the Arab sector. According to the new law, both Muslims and Christians are now allowed to submit their cases of maintenance and custody to the secular family courts. However, because there is no secular or territorial law of maintenance or custody in Israel, judges of civil family courts, mostly Jews, are now required by law to interpret and apply Islamic and canonical laws when Muslims or Christians resort to their jurisdiction. In this regard the LFCA of 2001 stands apart from the Knesset's past legislative interventions into jurisdiction of *shari'a* and ecclesiastical courts (e.g., the ISL of 1965), as this time the legislature not only diminished their subject matter jurisdiction, but also broke up their monopoly of interpreting and applying their own religious laws.

Religious courts of Christian communities

[Pointing to the platform where the judges sit in the courtroom of the Roman Catholic Ecclesiastical Tribunal in Jerusalem]

"*Qadi Ahmad Natour, the Chief Islamic Justice, is sitting in front of an Israeli flag and a menorah* [referring to the national emblem of the State of Israel], *but you do not see any of that here.*"[31]

Christian citizens of Israel (about 2.1 percent of the total population) are subject to the jurisdiction of church courts in matters of personal status (Bassok 2004). Although the government had recognized the rights of ten individual Christian communities to establish their own tribunals, some Eastern Catholic churches[32] have delegated their jurisdiction to the ecclesiastical courts of the Roman Catholic Church, mainly due to the sheer size of their populations, and the lack of qualified judges, judicial personnel and resources which they need to run their own independent courts.[33] Like the *shari'a* and rabbinical court systems, the ecclesiastical courts were also incorporated into the Israeli legal system in 1948 and their rulings have since been enforced and executed by the

---

[31] Personal interview with Father Anton Issa, President of the Ecclesiastical Court of Latin Patriarchate (Jerusalem, January 2005).

[32] These are the Greek Catholics, the Armenian Catholics, the Melkites and the Syrian Catholics.

[33] Personal interview with Father Anton Issa (see n. 31 above).

Israeli government (Ben-Ami 1978). However, the Christian courts differ from the courts of other religious communities in an important way. They have never been placed under the supervision of the Ministry of Religious Affairs or the Ministry of Justice. Their operations are not funded by the public budget.[34] Neither are their judges salaried or appointed by the government. Instead, each church is responsible for the funding of its courts, and the training and appointment of its own judicial personnel.

Another aspect in which the Christian courts significantly differ from the rest of the religious courts is their extra-territorial personal jurisdiction (Goadby 1926; Vitta 1947, pp. 112–120; Wardi 1950). While the territorial jurisdiction of the Muslim, Jewish and Druze Courts is limited to the boundaries of Israel proper, the Christian courts' jurisdiction often extends into the West Bank, Gaza and Jordan (Culbertson 1981; Meron 1982; Tsimhoni 1993). The extra-territoriality of their jurisdiction has been recognized by the Israeli High Court of Justice.[35] Most of these courts also have appellate levels located outside the country. For example, the appeals from the Court of the Roman Catholic Church are referred to the Sacra Rota Romana in the Holy See; similarly, appeals from the Court of the Armenian Orthodox Church go to the Court of Appeals in Armenia.[36] As far as their subject matter jurisdiction is concerned, however, the courts have exclusive jurisdiction in matters of marriage and divorce, and concurrent jurisdiction with civil courts in all other issues of personal status (i.e., maintenance and succession). The material law that the courts apply is often the law of their church. In particular, the rules of matrimonial matters are strictly regulated, and are often codified and translated into Arabic (Neuhaus 1983; Abou Ramadan 2000, 2001).[37]

[34] I was told by the Director of the Department of Christian Affairs in the Interior Ministry, Mr. Cesare Marjieh, that his department, which controlled a budget of about NIS 2 million for the year 2005, has given money to churches and Christian cemeteries, provided private cars to the heads of the religious communities and paid the expenses of these cars. Personal interview (Jerusalem, January 2005).

[35] The two important rulings of the High Court of Justice in this regard are: HCJ 171/68 *Avalon Hanzalis* v. *Ecclesiastical Court of the Greek Orthodox Church* [1969] IsrSC 23(1) 260, and HCJ 94/75 *George Nassar* v. *Tribunal of the Gregorian-Armenian Community* [1976] IsrSC 30(2) 44. For details see Guberman (1970) and Goldwater (1977).

[36] Personal interview with Archbishop Aris Shirvanian, Director of the Armenian Orthodox Patriarchate Ecumenical and Foreign Relations Board (Jerusalem, January 2005).

[37] On the other hand, most Christian communities do not have elaborate succession laws. They often resort to a combination of Islamic, Ottoman and Jordanian laws in matters of intestate succession.

Druze courts

> We have an Israeli flag in our courtroom as well as the Druze flag.[38]

The Druze citizens of Israel, roughly 1.7 percent of the entire population,[39] are subject to the jurisdiction of the Druze religious courts for their matters of personal status. At the time of writing there were two courts of first instance as well as a court of appeals serving the Druze population of Israel and the Israeli-occupied Golan Heights. The status of a recognized religious community was not conferred upon the Druzes under Ottoman or British rule. In other words, they never had a system of religious courts or an overt legal code until they were officially recognized by the State of Israel in 1957.[40] In 1962, the Knesset passed the Druze Religious Courts Law (DRCL),[41] "thereby completing the process of legal recognition of the community" (Dana 1980, p. 63). The 1962 law specifically provided for the establishment of a court of first instance and a court of appeals, and declared the judges (*Qadi Madhhab*) of these courts salaried state officials appointed by the President of the State upon the recommendation of a nomination committee (Layish 1982; Edelman 1987; 1994, pp. 89–99).

Also, a year earlier the Druze Religious Council (the Spiritual Leadership) adopted the Law of Personal Status of the Druze Community of Lebanon of 1948 (LPSDCL),[42] with certain modifications, as the personal status law of the Druze community in Israel (the LPSDCI of 1961).[43] Of all the religious courts in the country, the subject matter jurisdiction of the Druze courts is the most limited. They have

---

[38] Personal interview with Mr. Zeidan Atashi (Jerusalem, January 2005).

[39] The figure was provided by Mr. Zeidan Atashi during our conversation (Jerusalem, January 2005). The same figure (1.7 percent) is also confirmed by the Israel Central Bureau of Statistics – see www.cbs.gov.il/www/hodaot2005/01_05_91e.pdf (accessed in May 2012).

[40] Layish (1979, p. 13) notes that under Turkish rule "the Druzes were theoretically amenable to the *shariʿa* courts in matters of personal status and succession, yet not as Muslims (as is usually assumed owing to the custom of *taqiyya*, dissimulation, prevailing among them) but as persons not belonging to a recognized religion." Later the Mandatory regime continued the Ottoman practice of non-recognition towards the Druze community, but at the same time granted it a certain degree of autonomy in matters of marriage while all other matters of personal status of the Druzes were referred to the civil district courts. The British had ended the Druzes' subjection to the jurisdiction of *shariʿa* courts by effectively preventing these courts from exercising any authority over non-Muslim litigants.

[41] A copy of the DRCL can be found in Dana (1980, pp. 221–226).

[42] The original Arabic text of the LPSDCL of 1948 can be found in Dana (2003, pp. 155–184); also for a comprehensive evaluation of the law, see Anderson (1952–1953).

[43] An electronic copy of the LPSDCI of 1961 can be obtained at www.justice.gov.il/NR/rdonlyres/ F27F50BE-11D8-4D54-BF9C-1E3327667286/0/ChokMaamadIsi.doc (accessed in October 2012).

exclusive jurisdiction in matters of marriage and divorce, while their jurisdiction in other matters of personal status, as the Israeli Supreme Court decided in 2004,[44] is contingent upon the consent of all interested parties.

II. WHY DID ISRAEL PRESERVE THE OTTOMAN *MILLET* SYSTEM?

Today, Israel still maintains a pluri-legal personal status system whose structural backbone has remained relatively unchanged since the day the British left the country. In other words, even though there were many territorial laws in such matters as custody, adoption, legal capacity, age of marriage, etc. which were – at least principally – uniformly applied across all communities, the Israeli government has deliberately refrained from introducing any changes into the system that would lead to unification of complex and scattered religious laws under a uniform civil code and the communal courts under an overarching network of civil courts. But what factors led to preservation of the old *millet* system, albeit in its modified form? In this regard, I believe it was not the case that Israel had no choice other than to preserve its centuries-old personal status system.[45] Neither do I think that the continuation of the *millet* system can simply be attributed to the failure of the Israeli state to overcome the resistance of religious groups and reform its judicial system, as is often claimed by scholars who have written on state–religion relations in Israel (Roshwald 1972, pp. 32–33; Avi-Hai 1974, pp. 107–108). On the contrary, Israel was a relatively strong and competent state (Migdal 1988, 1989, 2001). Especially when compared to other postcolonial national movements, the young Jewish state was exceptionally successful in establishing necessary parastatal organizations and legislating in practically every sphere of human activity from property rights, criminal laws, torts and labor laws to territorial waters (Sassoon 1968, p. 411; Segev and Weinstein 1986, pp. 95–116; Kimmerling 2001, pp. 69–70; Sachar 2002).

Right at this point, a group of scholars argue that the initial retention of the *millet* system by the post-independence government was a direct consequence of the so-called "Status Quo" agreement in 1947.

[44] HCJ 9611/00 *Badr (Mar'i) Nabal* v. *Mar'i Nazia* [2004] IsrSC 58(4) 256.
[45] Both Edelman (1994, p. 121) and Kimmerling (2001, p. 183) have argued that the founders of Israel decided to maintain the existing system of personal status and build a *millet*-based citizenry even before the establishment of the state in 1948.

According to proponents of this thought, in order to ensure the support of recalcitrant religious groups in the state-building process, the Zionist leadership allowed them several concessions, which included the recognition of rabbinical courts' jurisdiction over issues of personal status in addition to compromises relating to Jewish dietary laws, the official day of rest and religious schools (Abramov 1976, pp. 157–163; Strum 1989, p. 486; Mittleman 1993). From this point of view, the continuation of *millet* or the Ottoman personal status system in its modified form is simply viewed as a political concession which would not have been made by the so-called "secular" leadership if there had not been an urgent need to appease the ultra-orthodox Jews.

Perhaps in the absence of pressure from the religious sector, Israeli leaders would have neither allowed the establishment of independent religious seminaries, nor readily accepted such a strictly enforced observance of Shabbat as the official day of rest. But I do not agree with an assertion that the continuation of rabbinical courts' jurisdiction over matters of marriage and divorce was only allowed in response to demands of the ultra-orthodox; and if it was solely up to the founding elite, these courts would never have been maintained (Strum 1995, p. 85). This is not to deny the pivotal role the ultra-orthodox played in the negotiations that led to issuance of the infamous Status Quo letter by the Jewish Agency Executive. However, in June 1947, as Friedman eloquently demonstrates, the ultra-orthodox – especially Agudat Yisrael, which at the time was preoccupied with political and economic problems as well as internal schisms – were in no position to command such a strong bargaining position and force the leaders of the fledgling state to concede to their demands (Friedman 1995, pp. 57–61). Moreover, the ultra-orthodox were further weakened by the fact that they were a relatively small minority group mainly concentrated in an area of Jerusalem that was not designated as part of the Jewish State (Harris 2002, p. 42). In fact the leaders of the Jewish Agency Executive, who knew about the challenges that Agudat leaders had to tackle at the time, held the stronger hand in negotiations and eventually delivered an elusively worded letter after backing away from some of their earlier promises (Friedman 1995, p. 65). The language of the letter regarding the jurisdiction of rabbinical courts in marital affairs was particularly ambiguous. It simply stated that the members of the Executive had recognized the seriousness of the problem and would do "all that can be done to satisfy the needs of the religiously observant . . . and to prevent a rift in the Jewish People" (Friedman 1995, p. 79). In other words, as Triger quite convincingly argues, the letter did not include anything that can be construed as an obligation to incorporate religious marriage and divorce laws into the Israeli legal system. Religious courts were retained not because of a compromise reached in 1947 but as a natural consequence of Israel's founding ideology (Triger 2005, p. 175).

Simply put, this was not just a matter of political concession. Israeli leaders had a more genuine interest in who got married to whom rather than in who observed Shabbat or kept *kosher*. In the eyes of the ruling elite at the time, the questions of marriage and divorce were much more central than any other religious issue. As Golda Meir declared once, the survival of Israel and the Jewish people, to a great extent, depended on their connection to their religion (Schnapper 1998, p. 103; Rejwan 1999, p. 106). And the safety and purity of this link between the Jewish people and their faith could only be ensured by the preservation of rabbinical courts' monopoly over the marital affairs of all Israeli Jews (Ben Rafael 2002).

In addition, like Karayanni (2006), I am also of the opinion that the continuation of the *millet* system under Israeli rule cannot be sufficiently understood by solely focusing on the recognition of rabbinical courts' jurisdiction and Jewish law alone – as some scholars of state–religion relations in Israel often do. Instead one needs to look at Israeli policy towards both Jewish and non-Jewish communities and their institutions together, as Israeli policy towards rabbinical courts has not been unconnected to its policy towards Muslim, Christian or Druze institutions. There has been a fairly consistent policy in place in regard to issues of personal status across all communities. In effect, the Israeli regime has utilized the old *millet* system in the nation-building process as an instrument of vertical segmentation and horizontal homogenization. Having said this, however, I do not mean that Israel's initial reception of the *millet* system came as a result of a premeditated grandiose plan or a clandestine program orchestrated by high government officials behind closed doors. Instead, as Treitel, Harris and Peled have quite credibly argued, it was a spontaneous process through which the Ottoman personal status system was gradually transformed, in accordance with the dictates of the founding ideology, into a potent tool of nation-building (Treitel 1995, p. 419; Peled 2001, p. 3; Harris 2002, pp. 21–54). And, as its instrumentality for achieving the regime's twin goals of homogenization and differentiation was increasingly realized, the furtherance and retention of the old *millet* system seems to have eventually become a deliberate government policy even though its initial reception was the result of a bit of spontaneity and a bit of coincidence.

Exclusionary and religious characteristics of the Israeli regime

The founding ideology of Israel was a combination of Ben-Gurion's own brand of etatism, *Mamlachtiyut*, on the one hand, and messianic principles, Zionist political ideals and bitter lessons of the Holocaust on the other (Jones and Murphy 2002, p. 125). One of the main goals of this peculiar ideology was to create a new sense of belonging and national identity by resuscitating the long-forgotten link between Hebrews and their ancient homeland. In the reformulation of this vital link, religion played a pivotal role. Religion was not only the foremost common denominator for hundreds of thousands of Jewish immigrants coming from diverse cultural, political and linguistic backgrounds, but also indispensable for the reassertion of the Jewish people's "god-given" rights to the Promised Land (Kimmerling 1985, pp. 263–264; Yanai 1996, p. 128).

For that matter, the founding elite wanted to subjugate and utilize the religion[46] as a powerful instrument of nation-building by coopting religious institutions and selectively incorporating various religious symbols and narratives into the founding ideology of the new state.[47] And this is why, from the beginning, the American model of separation of religion and state was considered inconceivable and purposefully avoided by the ruling elite. Nonetheless, this still does not mean that the founders of the country desired a full-blown Jewish theocracy. For instance, Ben-Gurion had repeatedly reminded the religious groups that

---

[46] In fact, at one point Ben-Gurion was reported to have announced that he would never accept the separation of state and religion, as he wanted the state to hold religion in its hand (Strum 1995, p. 92).

[47] Starting from the early days of independence, Jewish religious symbols and institutions were zealously nationalized by the Israeli leaders. For example, the basic symbols of the state, its name, flag, anthem, as well as its national emblem depicting the menorah, were all appropriated from Judaic symbols and Jewish history (Cohen 1989, p. 69). In the institutional sphere, the Ministry of Religious Affairs was established, and the Chief Rabbinate was incorporated into the body politic while a variety of religiously inspired legislation – from how to carry out autopsies to pig-raising and consumption of pork products – was ordained both by the local and national authorities (Birnbaum 1970, pp. 83–86, 111–116; Zucker 1973, pp. 76–86; Barak-Erez 2007). Consequently, in this growing environment of ethno-religious zealotry, the Jewishness of the State of Israel was declared by the Supreme Court judges to be the fundamental credo of the political establishment (HCJ 73/53 *Kol Ha'Am* v. *Minister of the Interior* [1953] IsrSC 7(1) 871), and questioning of this credo was later prohibited with an amendment to the Basic Law by the Knesset in 1985 (Kretzmer 1990, pp. 35–39).

Israel was "a state of law and not *halakhah*" (Avi-Hai 1974, p. 103; Segev and Weinstein 1986, p. 258; Susser and Liebman 1999, p. 132). However, even though the founding elite never aimed to establish a full-blown Jewish theocracy, their very concept of "Jewish State" was still paradoxically less grounded in legalistic ideas than in religious and theological considerations (Klein 1978, p. 42; Safran 1981, p. 207; Friedman 1989, pp. 188–203; Shimoni 1995). Thus, from the beginning religion was allowed to play an increasingly central role in the socio-political life of the country. And, in the ensuing years, the built-in theocratic contours and proclivities of the Israeli regime have become only more visible in parallel to the rising power of the religious right (Cantor 1988, pp. 207–215; Shetreet 2002, p. 12).

The primary objective of the founding ideology was to create a uniform and homogeneous Israeli-Jewish collectivity. In this regard, the founding ideology was innately exclusionary as much as it was theocratically inclined. In fact, the ethnocentric and religious contours of the regime entailed the undertaking of two simultaneous processes of nation-building: homogenization among the Jews, and differentiation between the Jews and non-Jews. At the first level, the Zionists aimed to minimize the cultural, linguistic, sectarian and ideological differences among the Jewish immigrants by melding them into a modern Israeli-Jewish identity known as *sabra* (Almog 2000). At the inter-ethnic level, a complementary process of differentiation was undertaken to accentuate cultural, social and religious disparities between the Palestinians and the Jews. That is to say, even though non-Jews were granted full citizenship on paper, in reality Israel has never aimed to create a civic sense of citizenship or Israeli nationality (*leumiut yisrailit*) on equal terms, but rather has opted for a stratified citizenry.[48] In fact, as shown below, the preservation of the old *millet* system has enabled the Israeli regime to simultaneously pursue the goals of homogenization and differentiation

---

[48] For example, the majority of the Palestinians who remained in the country after 1948 were dispossessed of their land and denied full membership in economic organizations and labor unions (Lustick 1980, pp. 58–59; Oppenheimer 1985, p. 270; Shalev 1989; Kretzmer 1990, pp. 50–66; Dumper 1994, pp. 30–35; Hofnung 1996, pp. 109–112). Also, the Israeli nationality laws have been specifically designed to disenfranchise as many non-Jews as possible from Israeli citizenship and permanent residency (Peretz 1954, pp. 146–148; Rubinstein 1976, pp. 76–86; Hofnung 1996). Moreover, Palestinian citizens of Israel are also excluded from the military. While the Arabic-speaking Druzes and Bedouins have been conscripted by the Israeli army, the Muslim and Christian Palestinians have been systematically denied military service even when they were willing to serve, as they have been perceived as a potential security threat to the Jewish State (Pappé 1995, p. 625).

by institutionalizing confessional divisions among the subjects of the Jewish State (Lustick 1980, pp. 58–59; Oppenheimer 1985, p. 270; Kretzmer 1990, pp. 50–66; Shafir and Peled 1998).

Israel's interventions into its personal status system

The *millet* system was further modified by the Israeli government to make it correspond more closely to the latter's ideological and practical needs. The primary purpose of these modifications was to create a monolithic Israeli-Jewish identity by drawing a visible ethnic boundary that would encompass all Jewish inhabitants of Israel who differed along ethnic, sectarian and ideological lines (Woods 2004, p. 236). The first step taken in this direction was the recognition of rabbinical courts' jurisdiction with the so-called Status Quo agreement in 1947. Rabbinical authorities were now put in charge of deciding who could marry whom, who could have a child with whom, and, more importantly, who was entitled to group membership within the Israeli-Jewish community by *halachic* criteria (Woods 2008, p. 61). The Israeli leaders viewed the monopoly of rabbinical courts over marital affairs as the foremost guarantee of the purity of Jewish identity, as the whole system was essentially designed to prevent interreligious unions (Friedman 1995, p. 61; Triger 2005, pp. 205–207). In fact, two years later the Israeli government further fortified its position against exogamy in a letter to Agudat Yisrael, and noted that it would never introduce civil marriage and divorce, which could lead to dehomogenization of the Israeli-Jewish identity by enabling interfaith unions (Abramov 1976, p. 194; Segev and Weinstein 1986, p. 252).

In 1953, the government took a much more conspicuous step towards homogenization of the Jewish national identity with a new law that abandoned the earlier principle of voluntary association and forced the jurisdiction of state-run rabbinical courts, which applied only the orthodox interpretation of *halakhah*, on all Jewish residents of the country (Chigier 1967, p. 159; Strum 1989, p. 488). Now the jurisdiction of non-conformist Jewish communities (e.g., Karaites, Samaritans,[49] and

---

[49] Neither the Samaritans nor the Karaites were ever formally recognized as a religious community under British rule. Neither were they included in the list of recognized communities that was published as an amendment to the Second Schedule of the POC in 1939. However, according to the Marriage and Divorce (Registration) Ordinance (MDRO) of 1919, their religious leaders and tribunals were still regarded as competent authorities to register marriages within their own communities (Corinaldi 1978–1980, pp. 115–116; 1984; Beinin 1998, pp. 182–184; Corinaldi 2000).

followers of the ultra-orthodox Agudat Yisrael[50]), which ran their own separate legal institutions before 1948, was completely terminated. In brief, with the passage of the RCJL of 1953, Israeli authorities aimed to replace the internal plurality of Jewish law with a uniform legal structure which, they hoped, would help create a unified Jewish identity by removing the barriers to mixed marriages between Jews from different ethnic and sectarian backgrounds, while "banning" interfaith marriages (especially between Jews and Arabs) (Eliash 1983, p. 351; Triger 2005, pp. 196–207). For the success of the Zionist nation-building project, a Yemenite and a Polish Jew had to be able to marry one another without wondering whether his or her future spouse was a "proper" Jew (Porat-Martin 1979, p. 214). Hence, to maintain the purity of the nation and prevent the split of the house of Israel into two, all marriages among Jews had to be in consonance with *halakhah*. In fact, as many proponents of the Bill stated during the debates in the Knesset, this was precisely what the Israeli leaders had set out to achieve with the 1953 law (Bentwich 1964, p. 244; Chigier 1967, pp. 156–159; Rubinstein 1967, p. 386; Abramov 1976, pp. 195–196). In the end, the law was passed with the overwhelming support of the secular majority in the Knesset (mostly from the ruling Mapai), while the ultra-orthodox protested as Shlomo Lorentz of Agudat Yisrael had suggested, calling it "the disgracing of religious courts law" (חוק בזיון בית-הדין הרבני) for diminishing the jurisdiction of religious courts in comparison to the Mandate period (Johnson 1987, p. 552; Triger 2005, p. 201).

The process of homogenization among Israeli Jews logically necessitated the invention and conservation of non-Jewish identities. In this regard, Israeli leaders have also exploited the existing *millet* system as an instrument of exclusion and differentiation. In their eyes, differentiation of non-Jewish identities was not only necessary to ensure the homogeneity of the Israeli-Jewish identity by preventing non-*kosher* interfaith marriages, but also highly desirable to further divide the native population of Palestine along sectarian lines for establishment of an effective regime of domination (Lustick 1980, pp. 132–134; Safran 1981, p. 203; Edelman 1994, p. 122; Pappé 1995, p. 643; Shepherd 2000, p. 245;

---

[50] Since Agudat Yisrael's applications to the British authorities for official recognition as a separate community were repeatedly rejected, its leaders decided to form their own religious tribunals independent of the official network of rabbinical courts. These tribunals were later granted the status of a registering authority for purposes of marriages and divorces among Agudat's adherents, in accordance with the stipulations of the MDRO of 1919 (Vitta 1947, pp. 108–112; Likhovski 2006, pp. 39–40).

Kanaaneh 2002, p. 140). In fact, as a result of this deliberate policy, the number of communities which were legally entitled to run their own religious courts rose from eleven to fourteen.

Among the newly recognized groups, the case of the Druze community is particularly indicative of the Israeli government's differentialist objectives in its preservation of the old *millet* system. As Ben-Gurion put it as early as 1948, the main reason for the creation of Druze religious courts was to "foster among the Druze an awareness that they are a separate community vis-à-vis the Muslim community" (Firro 1999, p. 94). Similarly, Haim Hirshberg, the director of the Muslim and Druze Section in the Ministry of Religious Affairs, had repeatedly stated that, "since the government had an interest in separating the Druze community from Muslims it [was] necessary to propose legislation ... which will grant the Druze community independent legal status in religious matters" (Firro 1999, p. 101). In fact, as a top-secret Shin Bet (the domestic intelligence agency) report from 1962 confesses, the government's "divide and conquer" policy that broke down the trust between the Druze and other Arab communities by creating sectarian divisions had been, to a great extent, successful, and prevented "the Arab minority from coalescing into one united body by causing the leaders of each community to be preoccupied largely by sectarian affairs and not by general Arab affairs" (Oppenheimer 1985, p. 268; Segev and Weinstein 1986, p. 66; Firro 1999, pp. 179–180; Quigley 2005, p. 136). Hence, as exemplified by the Druze case, the government has systematically manipulated the old *millet* system to discourage mixed marriages among the members of non-Jewish communities (Lustick 1980, p. 133) and prevent them from forming an overarching Palestinian identity.[51]

In sum, as long as the modified *millet* system served the regime's twin goals of homogenization and differentiation, Israeli leaders have refrained from introducing any normative or institutional changes in its nature. In effect, changes they introduced in the field of familial relations (e.g., minimum age for marriage, prohibition of polygyny, etc.) were mostly limited or symbolic.[52]

---

[51] The most recent example of Israel's exclusionary policies is the CEIL of 2003, which denies spouses of Israeli citizens and permanent residents who are married to Palestinians from the Occupied Territories the opportunity to acquire Israeli citizenship or residency rights, while foreign spouses of Israeli citizens are automatically granted citizenship if they are Jewish – see Human Rights Watch (2006) and Jacobsohn (2010, pp. 271–322).

[52] Right at this point, the question that comes to mind is, was there ever an attempt to abolish the old *millet* system and build a uniform and secular system of family law in its place? The answer, in

III. THE IMPACT OF PERSONAL STATUS LAWS ON THE RIGHTS AND FREEDOMS OF ISRAELI CITIZENS

The 23-year-old Russian immigrant, Sergeant Nikolai Rappaport was a combat soldier in a unit assigned to the Israeli-controlled buffer zone in southern Lebanon. He was killed in a Hezbollah ambush on February 7, 1998. His family expected their son to be honored as a "martyr" and buried in a military ceremony (Schmemann 1998). But Nikolai's funeral was a bit different than those of other Israeli soldiers who fell in combat. "The flag-draped coffin [of Sgt. Rappaport] was laid out before the stone memorial ... There was no open grave for his comrades ... to pass and shovel in clods of earth, but just an IDF command car, waiting to take his body to Ben-Gurion Airport for the journey to Krasnodar [Russia]" where he was eventually buried (O'Sullivan 1998). Religious authorities did not allow Sgt. Rappaport to be interred in a Jewish cemetery in Israel for they did not consider him a Jew under *halakhah* as Nikolai was not born to a Jewish mother, but rather to a Jewish father. Even though he was good enough to make *aliyah*,[53] trustworthy enough to be conscripted, and brave enough to sacrifice his life for the country, he still was not "Jewish" enough in the eyes of the orthodox establishment to be buried in the land this young man loved dearly and died for. As one reporter puts it so poetically, today Nikolai no longer speaks, "but at dusk, when darkness sets on the forlorn post-communist domain where he ended up in spite of himself, those who listen carefully enough to the winds blowing above his tombstone can hear Nikolai whisper: 'If I am not a Jew, who the hell is?'"
(Asa-El 1998)[54]

short, is "No." Still, it is highly possible that some people around Ben-Gurion, who were secularist or concerned with the growing theocratic tendencies of the regime, may have entertained such ideas. At least two of these individuals were probably Pinhas Rosen and Haim H. Cohn, who both served as Ministers of Law in the Ben-Gurion and Sharett governments. As he noted in the introduction to the draft Succession Law of 1952, Rosen hoped that the draft law would one day fit into the framework of a comprehensive Civil Code. Similarly, Cohn once told Prof. Strum in an interview that despite his repeated attempts to raise the subject of civil family courts, Ben-Gurion persistently rebuked them and never contemplated the creation of a system of secular courts in place of the existing *millet* structure as a serious policy alternative. In short, it can be said that even though some bureaucrats and cabinet members may have entertained such ideas, these were never adopted or even considered as viable policy options by the ruling elite (Yadin 1966, p. 120; Eisenman 1978, pp. 196–199; Strum 1995, pp. 85–87; Radzyner and Shuki Friedman 2005, p. 223).

53 Jewish immigration to Israel; plural: *aliyot*.

54 "The orthodox Rabbinate must certify the Jewish heritage of [Israeli citizens] in order for them to receive full Jewish burial rights; however, many Russian immigrants could not obtain approval to be buried in a Jewish cemetery. [As a response to this growing problem], the 1996 Alternative Burial Law [was passed, which] established the individual right to be buried in an alternative civil cemetery and that these cemeteries were to be located throughout the country. Several non-orthodox Jewish and secular groups have complained, however, that the Ministry of Religious

As this saddening anecdote exemplifies, the monopoly of the religious courts and the law over matters of personal status has had far-reaching impacts on the fundamental rights and freedoms of Israeli citizens in every phase of life from cradle to grave. Like Nikolai, hundreds of thousands of Israelis are denied their rights to be buried in Israel, marry and found a family, and obtain a divorce; alternately they are branded by the state as a "*mamzer*" (bastard) or an "*agunah*" (anchored woman) by being forcibly subjected to the purview of religious laws and institutions. In others words, religious courts exercise their jurisdiction upon Israelis whether they consent to it or not. Worse, Israel does not furnish its citizens with an alternative civil law of marriage and divorce – *à la* the SMA of 1954 in India – that would give individuals a secular option and facilitate interfaith marriages among Israeli citizens. Thus, in Israel, personal status-related human rights violations occur as a frequent and widespread phenomenon.

Since the Israeli *millet* system – like many other personal status systems – has often institutionalized restrictive and less egalitarian interpretations of religious laws by granting them formal recognition and state-sanctioned backing, its impact has been particularly harsh on women, religious dissidents and people whose religious identity has been challenged on religious grounds (i.e., non-*halachic* Jews). However, the present section demonstrates that people do not silently accept the limitations placed upon their fundamental rights by state-sanctioned religious laws and authorities, but instead constantly innovate and resort to strategies and tactics of resistance in order to protect and advance their rights under the current system. They travel abroad to contract interreligious marriages and escape other marriage-related disabilities, form hermeneutic communities to offer alternative interpretations of state-enforced religious laws to redefine their rights and entitlements, set up alternative institutions to solemnize marriages and grant divorces independent of the state and religious authorities, build cross-communal alliances by transcending ethno-religious divides, stage demonstrations and lobby for legal change. As they do so, they constantly challenge the legitimacy of state-imposed religious laws, oppose the regime's exclusionary practices, and subvert the boundaries of the political community by offering competing legalities, discourses of rights and alternative interpretations of religious precepts.

Affairs has been slow to implement this law and that there have been an inadequate number of civil cemeteries designated" (US Department of State 2003). After long delays and hesitations, the first Israeli civil cemetery was inaugurated in Be'er Sheva in May 1999 (Acri 1999).

In this respect, the following analysis of emerging human and women's rights discourses and sites where detrimental impacts of state-enforced religious laws become more visible also sheds light upon ongoing state–society contestations, and gives us an idea about the extent to which the Israeli regime has achieved its twin goals of vertical segmentation and horizontal homogenization that some hoped to attain through retention of, and subsequent interventions into, the old *millet* system. In brief, the present section shows that, even though the primary intent for furtherance of the old *millet* system was to homogenize the Jewish population, rabbinical authorities have over time evolved into divisive institutions by breaking up the Israeli-Jewish community into ethno-genealogical camps of "marriageable" and "non-marriageable" Jews. As far as the project of differentiation is concerned, however, it can be said that the *millet* system has served some of its intended goals, but its success is still far from complete, as group boundaries that the *millet* system was relied upon to keep in place have been increasingly challenged and blurred by the cross-communal activities of civil rights and conservative groups in recent years.

"I now pronounce you 'unfit' for marriage and divorce. *Mazel tov!*"
Even though the existing system of personal status carries implications for the rights and freedoms of Israelis from every religious community, the situation is much more serious within the Jewish sector where the monopoly of rabbinical courts has literally spawned a *Kulturkampf* between the secular and religious Jews. This is because in the process of making their decisions the rabbinical courts, like other religious courts, function as gatekeepers of the communal identity and decide who is a "proper" Jew, who is a *mamzer* (bastard), or whether a woman was properly divorced by her husband on the basis of *halachic* norms to which the majority of Israeli Jews do not subscribe but are forcibly subjected. Therefore, the non-religious majority resent their unwillful subjection to the orthodox *halakhah*, and protest the restrictions placed upon their fundamental rights and liberties by the rabbinical authorities (Neuberger 1997, pp. 17–18; 2000, pp. 78–82).

Halakhah forbids a union between a Jew and non-Jew, between a man and a woman who is not properly divorced (by *halachic* criteria), and between a *mamzer* (bastard) and any other Jew except another *mamzer* (Edelman 1994, p. 61). That is to say, prior to wedding, both bride and groom have to be vetted by rabbinical authorities in order for these to determine their Jewishness and ascertain whether either of the spouses is a *mamzer*, or the woman is an *agunah*. For instance, *halakhah* defines a Jew as a person whose mother was Jewish at the time of his birth, or a person converted to Judaism by a recognized rabbinical court (Biale 1984, pp. 70–101). If the person fails the vetting, he or she would be deemed unfit to marry other Jews. In fact, throughout the years, rabbinical courts have disqualified hundreds of thousands of Jews from marriage and have created a new category of "unmarriageable" or "non-*halachic*" Jews.

Although under Israel's Law of Return (1950) and Nationality Law (1952) new immigrants have been immediately granted citizenship upon arrival,[55] the orthodox Rabbinate has systematically refused to marry immigrants from such countries as India, Ethiopia and the Soviet Union unless they undergo a full orthodox conversion. Because there is no civil marriage in Israel, immigrants from these countries have been unable to wed or have their unions recognized as legitimate before the state (Cohen and Susser 2000, pp. 110–121). Worse, when we factor in the people who belong to non-recognized communities (e.g., Karaites, Protestants – other than members of the Evangelical Episcopal community, etc.) and individuals who were converted to Judaism by non-orthodox rabbis,[56] the number of Israelis who are banned from marriage by the rabbinical authorities reportedly exceeds 400,000.[57]

---

[55] In 1970, a monumental amendment of the Law of Return was passed by the Knesset officially defining a "Jew" for immigration purposes. According to the amended law, any Jew – defined as "a person who was born of a Jewish mother or has become converted to Judaism" – may immigrate to Israel. The manner of conversion was not defined in the law, an imprecision that led to contentious court challenges in the coming decades. In addition, the amended law has also created a new class of immigrants who would have the "rights of a Jew" without being one. These individuals (any child or grandchild of a Jew, male or female; the spouse of a Jew; the spouse of a child of a Jew; and the spouse of a grandchild of a Jew) would be able to immigrate under the Law of Return but would not be recognized as Jews by the state. The amendment noted that individuals enjoying the "rights of a Jew" would be eligible as citizens of Israel under the law, but could not be registered as Jews either by "ethnic affiliation or religion if they do not fulfill the definition of Jew." Thus, those individuals who immigrated to Israel under the Law of Return but who are not Jewish could not be registered by the Interior Ministry as Jews. As non-Jews, these individuals would be barred by the religious authorities from marrying Jews or being buried in a Jewish cemetery in Israel (Anti-Defamation League 2002).

[56] Following the Israeli Supreme Court's several favorable rulings (i.e., HCJ 1031/93 *Pesaro (Goldstein) v. Minister of Interior* [1995] IsrSC 49(4) 661; HCJ 5070/95 *Naamat, Working and Volunteer Women's Movement v. Minister of Interior* [2002] IsrSC 56(2) 721; and HCJ 2597/99 *Rodriguez-Toshbaim v. Minister of Interior* [2005] IsrSC 59(6) 721), the Interior Ministry has recently started accepting certain types of non-orthodox conversions for the purpose of registering citizenship under the Law of Return, but the Chief Rabbinate is not obliged to recognize these registrations for matrimonial purposes. For further information, see ACRI (2002); Gross (2003, 2005); Myre (2005).

[57] Personal interview with the former Member of Knesset Ronny Brison of Shinui Party (Jerusalem, February 2005). Mr. Brison sponsored a civil marriage and divorce Bill in the Sixteenth Knesset

A recalcitrant husband who refuses to issue a *get* has to be persuaded to grant a divorce of his own free will. In this game of persuasion women usually buy their way out of deadlocked marriages by paying the husband off or forgoing their claims to future child support and alimony (Bogoch and Halperin-Kaddari 2006). Paying a husband to obtain a *get* has become such a common practice that even the National Insurance Institute regularly allocates funds to help *agunot* pay their husbands off (Weiss 2002).[58] Hence, in response to the growing *agunah* problem,[59] the Israeli Parliament enacted the Rabbinical Courts (Enforcement of Divorce Decrees) Law (RCEDDL) in 1995, which aimed to persuade recalcitrant husbands to grant *get* by imposing sanctions that include suspension of their credit cards, bank accounts, passports and driver's and professional licenses – and even incarceration (Blecher and Shmueli 2009). However, the law is reported to have failed to produce much of its intended effect, as some *dayanim*, who believe that the new law violates the *halachic* principle about not coercing a man to divorce his wife against his own will (Corinaldi 2002, pp. 5–6), have effectively limited its application.[60] A Jewish woman's divorce-related troubles may not be over even after the *get* is properly issued by the husband. For

that eventually failed. As a concession to the religious parties, the draft Bill did not include the words "marriage" (*nissuim*) and "divorce" (*gerushim*) as they were considered religious ceremonies solely conducted by the rabbinical authorities. Instead, the Bill used the words "coupling covenant" (*brit hazugiut*) and "release from the covenant" (*hatarat habrit*) in place of marriage and divorce, respectively.

[58] The cost of recalcitrant husbands to the Israeli national budget was, for instance, reported to be more than US $200 million in 2001 (Weiss 2002).

[59] A woman denied a *get* (divorce writ) by her husband is technically called *mesurevet get* in Jewish law, yet the term *agunah* is much more commonly used. According to Rabbi Eliyahu Ben-Dahan, the former Director of the Rabbinical Courts Administration, as of 2007 there were 69 *agunot* (plural of *agunah*) or chained women, and only 25 of them lived in Israel at the time (Ratzlav-Katz 2007). Israeli women's rights activists, however, argue that rabbinical authorities deliberately reduce the number of *agunot* by using a very narrow and technical definition according to which they only count the women who had waited over two years for the husband's consent, and the women whose husband has disappeared and cannot be located. Despite the deflated figures offered by the rabbinical authorities on the number of *agunot*, a report presented to the Knesset Committee on the Status of Women in 2005 estimated that over the years about 100,000 women in Israel had been either denied a divorce or forced to comply with conditions set by the husband in order to obtain a divorce (Lerner 2011, p. 213, n. 12).

[60] Halperin-Kaddari reports that from 1995 to 1999, only 163 restraining orders were issued against recalcitrant husbands by the rabbinical courts. Of these, 76 came from the same rabbinical court in a single district (2004, p. 239). In 2006, of 942 unresolved *get* cases, only in 41 did judges issue compulsion decrees against recalcitrant husbands (Ratzlav-Katz 2007). Sanctions against husbands were imposed in 44 cases in 2009 and in 73 cases in 2008. "Only 6 of the verdicts handed down in 2009 included arrest warrants for the husbands, as compared to 23 cases in 2008" (Ettinger 2010). The leniency shown by the courts to recalcitrant husbands is mostly due to ultra-orthodox judges' personal and ideological convictions about the superiority of men and unequal gender relations in Jewish law. They view sanctions unfavorably and resort to them only in the most extreme cases, "like those involving a violent, ill, or sterile husband" (Ettinger 2010).

instance, as some activist *dayanim* have decided in recent years, rabbinical courts can retroactively invalidate divorce decrees that they earlier granted, and put women, especially those who remarried and had children, in a legal limbo.[61] In other words, even after divorce the women's rights and status continue to be dominated by the rabbinical authorities (Raz and Neuman 2008). Thus the failure of the Israeli government to offer a tangible solution to the predicament of marriage and divorce has disgruntled hundreds of thousands of Israelis, and forced them to take the matter into their own hands by searching for alternative modes of marriage and divorce.

Competing legalities: alternative modes of marriage and divorce

The search for other modes of marriage and divorce has further fragmented the Israeli personal status system, as various communities from religious right to secular left have begun offering their alternative interpretations of state-enforced religious laws and competing legalities rooted in variant discourses of rights. Among these groups, some (e.g., rule-making communities) have responded by taking more drastic steps, setting up alternative institutions of marriage and divorce to escape restrictive state-sanctioned religious laws and practices; moderate or hermeneutic groups have advocated for change from within, addressing their everyday needs in an aging legal framework by reengaging religious norms, narratives and traditions without necessarily dismantling or replacing the current personal status system.

Individuals who are unable to wed in Israel or resent the orthodox establishment often bypass the rabbinical authorities and opt for alternative modes of marriage. In fact, "about one-fifth of Israeli couples now are marrying outside of the Rabbinate," according to Freedom of Choice in Marriage, a Jerusalem-based civil society organization (Kraft 2004). Since civil ceremonies performed overseas are recognized by Israel under the private international law,[62] couples who can afford it often fly to Cyprus to marry. Those who cannot afford the Cyprus option usually prefer the "Mexican" or "Paraguay" marriages, "in which the couple

---

[61] "Such a scenario can arise when the husband claims that the divorce is contingent on the agreement to certain conditions (such as the size of alimony payments), and the wife tries to change these terms" (Raz and Neuman 2008).

[62] In *Funk-Schlesinger* v. *Minister of Interior* (HCJ 143/62 [1963] IsrSC 17(1) 225), the Supreme Court of Israel held the view that the registration official was not competent to examine the validity of a civil marriage performed abroad, thereby he was required by law to register the applicants' status as "married" upon the presentation of a foreign marriage certificate (Einhorn 2009, p. 181).

receive ... their marriage certificate by mail without having to personally appear in another state" (Shifman 2002, p. 32). However, the recognition of these marriages does not solve the problem entirely. The children of the couple may still not be recognized as Jewish if it is an interfaith marriage (where the wife is a non-Jew) or if the parents' Jewishness is contested; or, in the case of divorce, the marriage still needs to be dissolved according to the religious law (i.e., by issuing a *get*). Moreover, even if they go abroad and obtain a civil divorce, the couple may still be considered married in the eyes of the rabbinical authorities (Shifman 2002, pp. 38–42).[63]

In addition to the foreign-marriage option, an increasing number of Israelis (nearly 180,000 couples) opt for common law unions or de facto marriages (*yeduim betzibur*) without entering into a religious or state-administered marriage contract.[64] The position of the Israeli law on common law marriages can, at best, be described as ambivalent. However, in recent years in a number of cases Israeli courts have awarded common law couples a nearly equal status with married couples in regard to such matters as taxes, national insurance, inheritance, custody and adoption (Halperin-Kaddari 2001).[65] Unlike married couples, however, in order for common law spouses to have access to such benefits they need to prove the status and existence of their relationship with physical evidence and documentation to the satisfaction of the authorities. In this respect, some civil society organizations (e.g., Freedom of Choice in Marriage, the New Family Organization) have recently begun to "solemnize" and register such unions by drawing up secular marital contracts and providing couples with an alternative "marriage certificate" as a legal affidavit and proof of their commitment. However, as Irit Rosenblum, Executive Director of the New Family Organization (which performs about 400 wedding ceremonies and a small number of divorces every year) put it, these unions and divorces are not yet recognized by rabbinical authorities.[66] Similarly, the

---

[63] Divorce of an interfaith couple who married overseas is still subject to Israeli law. The marriage has to be dissolved according to the legal mechanism laid out in the Law of Matters of Dissolution of Marriage (Jurisdiction in Special Cases) (LMDM) of 1969.

[64] Currently the number of common law couples is estimated to be around 180,000 – see www.newfamily.org.il/rec/187-Common-Law-Marriage/ (accessed in May 2009).

[65] For example, see HCJ 2000/97 *Lindorn v. Karnit, Fund for Compensation of Victims of Road Accidents* [1999] IsrSC 55(1) 12, and HCJ 2622/01 *Manager of Land Betterment Tax v. Aliza Lebanon* [2003] IsrSC 37(5) 309.

[66] Personal interview with Irit Rosenblum, Executive Director of the New Family Organization (Tel-Aviv, January 2005).

Conservative and Reform Movements also perform their alternative marriage ceremonies and divorce proceedings for the increasing number of individuals who refuse to get involved with the orthodox Rabbinate. As I was told by Rabbi Michael Boyden,[67] the Director of the Rabbinic Court of the Israel Council of Progressive Rabbis, individuals who prefer the Reform Movement's ceremonies are not necessarily less religious or "impure" Jews: "These are people who want to wed in a religiously meaningful but at the same time a modern and egalitarian ceremony."[68] Besides the secular and non-orthodox Jewish communities who have set up alternative institutions of marriage and divorce, the Haredi community (which on both theological and ideological grounds has long rejected any engagement with the Israeli state and its courts) has also established and operated its own religious courts that adjudicate family and non-family civil matters among the members of the community.

As part of an effort to find a comprehensive solution to the problem of divorce and marriage, some secular groups in recent years have promoted the idea of civil marriage and divorce. However, their attempts to pass a civil marriage and divorce law have been repeatedly defeated in the parliament, even though about 60 percent of Israelis support the introduction of civil marriage and divorce as an alternative which could coexist with the current system (Lynfield 2004). In fact, between 1963 and 2009, as Lerner reports, "nearly one hundred bills concerning the RCJL or the issue of civil marriage have been introduced to the Knesset by representatives of non-religious parties," but "none reached the final stage of legislation" (Lerner 2012). The foremost reason for the rejection of civil marriage has been the failure or the unwillingness of the major center parties (e.g., Likud, Labor, Kadima) to surmount the religious groups' and rabbinical authorities' opposition to the idea.[69]

---

[67] Personal interview with Rabbi Michael Boyden, Director of the Rabbinic Court of the Israel Council of Progressive Rabbis (Tel-Aviv, January 2005).

[68] For example, marriage contracts (ketubot; singular, ketubah) of the Reform Movement are significantly different from their orthodox version. These contracts are written in Hebrew and have to be signed by both bride and groom, unlike the orthodox ketubah, which is in Aramaic and signed only by the groom. The witnesses to the Reform ketubah could be either men or women, whereas the orthodox one only recognizes the testimony of men. Unlike the orthodox contract, the Reform ketubah does not mention or specify a particular amount of cash gift (mohar) to be paid by the groom to the bride. Divorce proceedings and requirements are equally egalitarian, as both man and woman are required to release one another from the marital union, while the orthodox halakhah bestows this right solely upon the husband.

[69] In May 2010 the Knesset passed a law that allows brit hazugiut or couplehood unions. However, in order to register a union (legally not a "marriage") under the new law both spouses have to be lacking a formally recognized religion. As opponents of the law put it, only about 170 couples a year are estimated to be helped by it (Zarchin 2010).

Despite the repeated failure of civil marriage and divorce initiatives, a promising trend which has the potential of easing marriage- and divorce-related difficulties has emerged in recent years. Some religious groups, having recognized the urgency of the situation, engaged in hermeneutics to find *halachically* acceptable solutions to such problems as *mamzerut* and *agunot*. Among those proposed solutions several are worth mentioning: prenuptial agreements, *kiddushei ta'ut* and *hafka'at kiddushin*. Prenuptial agreements use *halachic* rules to set up an automatic mechanism for the payment of alimony and division of property, with possible financial sanctions against the husband who refuses to grant his wife a *get* (Shindler 1996; Herring 2000; Na'amat 2001; Weiss 2009). *Kiddushei ta'ut*, on the other hand, is suggested for relieving *agunot* of their predicament by simply annulling their marriages on grounds of erroneous assumptions or defects hidden from the bride at the time of the wedding. Similarly, through *hafka'at kiddushin* the rabbinical court could relieve an *agunah* by retroactively annulling the betrothal on technical grounds (Riskin 2002; Westreich 2008). Several years ago, Kolech, an Orthodox women's organization, proposed a *hafka'at* Bill that would empower the rabbinical courts to annul the marriage of an anchored women and release her from the bond of marriage without a *get* by declaring that her wedding ring did not originally belong to her husband, and thereby the marriage technically never existed. Eventually, the Bill failed to garner the necessary support in the Knesset as it also did not have the backing of religious authorities.[70] Likewise, neither *kiddushei ta'ut* nor the prenuptial option is yet legally recognized or endorsed by rabbinical authorities, even though they are practised among some Jewish groups across the country.

Although the primary intent for furtherance of the rabbinical courts' control over personal status was to homogenize the Jewish population, rabbinical authorities' entrenched position on matrimonial issues has, on the contrary, engendered serious ideological divisions and undermined the unity of the Jewish people. The divisiveness of state-sanctioned religious institutions has become apparent particularly with the arrival of Indian, Ethiopian and later Russian immigrants whose "Jewishness" has been continuously challenged by the rabbinical authorities on *halachic* grounds, denying them the right to marry other "proper" Jews (Abramov 1976, pp. 275–280; Israel 1984). In other words, rabbinical courts have evolved into divisive institutions which not only

---

[70] Phone interview with Dr. Hannah Kehat, the founder and former chairwoman of Kolech (April 2010).

disqualify individuals from membership in the political community on religious grounds but also break the Israeli-Jewish community into ethno-genealogical camps based on the sole criterion of marriageability.

When the Israeli leaders realized the shortcomings of the rabbinical courts-induced homogenization project, it was too late to try to divest the courts of their monopoly, as the religious groups and parties were already too strong and the major political parties had grown too dependent upon their support in order to stay in power (Sezgin 2003, 2004a). However, the failure of the centrist parties to overcome the opposition of religious groups to civil marriage cannot be solely attributed to their chronic inability or overdependence. The fear of the unknown should also be factored in. Many politicians and decision-makers are unsure of the potential impact of such a "drastic" change in matrimonial laws. In fact, some argue that even a symbolic change could catalyze and radicalize the trends towards division and polarization which are already underway (Shifman 2002, pp. 98–99; Shochetman 2002, pp. 143–146; Fogiel-Bijaoui 2003). Outspoken proponents of civil marriage, such as Ronny Brison of Shinui,[71] however, argue that the paranoia of division (i.e., the house of Israel being split into two as a result of civil marriage) has been intentionally kept alive in the collective consciousness of the Israeli people by representatives of the orthodox establishment.[72]

In sum, what we are recently witnessing in the field of marriage and divorce is a quiet revolution. The struggle between the Israeli state and religious establishment on the one hand, and society on the other, has been over whose word was law and whose interpretation of the Holy Scripture was definitive. As various communities have performed their own

---

[71] Personal interview with the former Member of Knesset Ronny Brison of Shinui Party, who introduced a failed civil marriage Bill in the Sixteenth Knesset (Jerusalem, February 2005).

[72] For instance Rabbi Eliyahu Ben-Dahan, the former Director General of the Rabbinical Courts of Israel, expresses his objection to the introduction of civil marriage and divorce in Israel in the following words:

> When the State of Israel was established, the intention was to establish a new state that would unify [the Jewish people], and turn them into a single body, into one people [Woods 2004, p. 235] ... If we were to behave in Israel such that personal law was not defined by *halakhah*, we would create two peoples [Woods 2004, p. 237].

Along the same lines, in a personal interview in January 2005 Rabbi Shear Yishuv Cohen, the former Chief Rabbi of Haifa, told me:

> If there was no religious monopoly of rabbinical courts, it would have been forbidden for some Jews to marry other Jews ... [And that's why] I do not think that there should be a civil marriage. [But at the same time,] I am not afraid of [it]; I think, even if we have civil marriage in Israel, 99% of the people will still be married by rabbis and rabbinical authorities, and divorce at the rabbinical courts.

alternative marriage ceremonies and established their independent institutions to adjudicate divorce and marital disputes, this struggle has taken an interesting turn and begun contesting not only the legitimacy of the state and religious authorities, but also the *halachically* enforced boundaries of the political community by blurring the line between the so-called "outsiders" and "insiders." Hence, in many regards, recent challenges to the rabbinical authorities' monopoly over marital affairs have been an overt rebellion against the Zionist value system that has long esteemed and upheld the ideals that initially gave rise to this particular system of personal status.

Cross-communal coalitions: a push for change from within

The shared sense of deprivation of their basic rights and freedoms under the current system has led individuals from various communities to form coalitions and collectively voice their demand for reform in personal status laws. This trend has been particularly visible among some Israeli women's organizations, which have often built alliances against gender-unequal practices of state-enforced religious norms and institutions by transcending the established boundaries of gender, class, religion and ethnicity. A quintessential example of these grassroots alliances is the International Coalition for Agunah Rights (ICAR) that brings together twenty-seven women's organizations from North America and Israel to find a solution to the problem of *agunot*. ICAR is a diverse array of Orthodox, Conservative, Reform and secular women's organizations. Some of the members of ICAR have long advocated female representation in the rabbinical system in order to ease the predicament of *agunah*. The first step in this direction was taken in 1990 when Orthodox women's groups succeeded in getting the religious authorities to allow female advocates (*toanot*) to serve in rabbinical courts alongside their male counterparts (Shilo 2006). ICAR members, who have employed various tactics from lobbying wives of *dayanim*[73] to organizing Torah and Talmud

---

[73] Apart from organizing meetings in which both the representatives of women's organizations and *dayanim* participate, Kolech members also approach the wives of *dayanim* in the hope that they will influence the thinking of their husbands and help them adopt a more favorable stance towards the problems of Jewish women. According to Drorit Rosenfeld, a legal adviser with Kolech, the logic behind this back-door approach is as follows:

> *Dayanim* are stubborn men who refuse to talk to women directly. So, when it is the case, the most effective way to reach them is through their wives. When they go to home at night, most *dayanim* tell their wives about their day in the court and the details of each case that they deal with. So, Kolech believes, if the wives of *dayanim* are well-informed, they can influence their husband's opinion and induce a favorable change in their behavior.

Personal interview with Drorit Rosenfeld (Jerusalem, January 2005).

classes in order to empower Jewish women vis-à-vis the rabbinical system, have recently pushed for the idea of appointing female judges to rabbinical courts. Proponents suggest that the current prohibition is of patriarchal interpretation rather than a theological limitation as there is nothing in *halakhah* that bars women from becoming *dayanot* (female rabbinical judges).[74] Although certain ICAR members, such as Kolech and Mavoi Satum,[75] have already taken some modest steps towards realization of this dream, feminist leaders recognize that the time has not yet come for *dayanot* and in the interim have turned their attention to the nomination committee that names rabbinical judges.

In the last decade, ICAR has mainly focused its efforts on influencing the process through which rabbinical court judges are appointed by placing one of its members on the ten-person nomination committee. In fact, in December 2002,[76] after an energetic lobbying campaign, Sharon Shenhav, an ICAR attorney, was successfully elected to the committee as one of two representatives of the Israel Bar Association (Shenhav 2004). As one of the few female voices on the orthodox male-dominated committee, Shenhav soon proved to be a formidable force to reckon with in the appointment process. She played the role of feminist watchdog and carefully scrutinized each candidate by making sure that only the people who were in touch with mainstream Israeli society and sympathetic to women's causes were appointed as *dayanim*:[77]

> In my interviews with the candidates I want to see if they recognize modern ideas on psychology, sociology, anthropology, child development ... Since [rabbinical court judges] have jurisdiction over divorce, custody of children and division of marital property ... I want to make sure that [candidates] know about the modern life. I also want to know if they are aware of the violence against women, and what it means to them ... Because they are all Orthodox men, and there are no female rabbinic judges at the moment ... [I want to see] if they really understand the problems that women face.[78]

If Shenhav's election was a major success for ICAR, the passage of the LFCA of 2001 was an equally important achievement for the Working

---

[74] Phone interviews with Dr. Deborah Weissman (March 2010), Dr. Hannah Kehat (April 2010) and Sharon Shenhav (April 2010).

[75] Kolech is currently planning to establish a new institute that will train both female and male *dayanim*, while Mavoi Satum is undertaking a multi-staged project to set up an independent *Bet Din* (rabbinical court) in the hope that it will help resolve the problem of *agunot* once and for all.

[76] Ms. Shenhav was reelected for a second term in December 2005.

[77] Phone interview with Sharon Shenhav (April 2010).

[78] Personal interview with Sharon Shenhav (Jerusalem, January 2005).

Group for Equality in Personal Status Issues (WGEPSI), a consortium of various civil and women's rights groups representing Muslims, Jews and Christians in Israel.[79] This time women's organizations joined hands with civil rights movements to equalize the legal status of Muslim and Christian women to that of Jewish and Druze women by granting them "the option of recourse in maintenance suits – as well as in all other matters of personal status, except for marriages and divorces – to the new civil family courts" (Shahar 2006, p. 130).

Like Jewish women under rabbinical law, Israeli Muslim women, too, have their fair share of problems under the state-enforced religious laws (Layish 2006). However, for the most part, Muslim women have remained silent on matrimonial issues, which are viewed as pillars of Palestinian autonomy and identity in the Jewish State, and confined their demands for change to procedural aspects of law and such issues as maintenance or child support. For example, as far as the amount of money in maintenance (*nafaqa*) awards is concerned, Israeli *shari'a* courts, like other religious courts in the country, have historically been very conservative. They "never ordered a man to pay child support in an amount higher than 500 shekels per child per month, while this amount was the minimum ordered in civil courts" (El-Taji T. 2008, p. 88). Hence, in order to increase the amount of maintenance Arab women received, feminist activists advocated for a legislative change that would transfer the *shari'a* courts' jurisdiction over maintenance to civil family courts which they believed would be fairer and friendlier to women (Abou Ramadan 2006 p. 32).[80]

To that end, in 1997 the WGEPSI initiated a Bill for amendment of the FCL of 1995 with the support of a Palestinian Member of Knesset, Nawwaf Masalha. Throughout the process, the coalition members successfully publicized the economic inequalities which Palestinian women faced by presenting the National Insurance Institute statistics indicating that alimony and child maintenance payments Muslim women received from *shari'a* courts were significantly lower than the sums awarded to

[79] The following civil society organizations participated in the WGEPSI: Women Against Violence, the Association for Citizen's Rights in Israel, Israel Women's Network, Kayan (a feminist organization), Al-Tufula Pedagogical Center, the Center for Family Development and the Arab Association for Human Rights.

[80] Civil family courts would still need to adjudicate upon maintenance cases according to rules set out in the OLFR of 1917. However, as is the case with laws of other religious communities, *shari'a* applied by secularly trained civil court judges, most of whom are Jews, would not be the same Islamic law as applied by *qadis* at *shari'a* courts. Civil courts, which operate on principles of a different legal culture than those of *shari'a* courts, would employ their own rules of evidence and procedure and abide by standards of private international law while implementing *shari'a* (Abou Ramadan 2006 p. 43).

non-Muslim women by the civil family courts (Shahar 2006, p. 130). After a successful public campaign and four years of horse-trading in the parliament, the amendment was finally passed in November 2001 by a majority vote (51/23).[81]

As expected, the law caused some profound schisms between the pro-reform groups and conservative elements within the Arab community. Even some leftist and liberal members of the community joined conservatives in their opposition to the law because they perceived it as an assault on the national, cultural and institutional autonomy of the Arab minority in Israel (El-Taji T. 2008, pp. 89–90). Nonetheless, what was really unique about the experience was that, throughout the reform process, the coalition of Muslim and Jewish women's organizations was fiercely confronted by an alliance of Muslim and Jewish conservatives both outside and within the Knesset. Outside the parliament, *qadis* formed an alliance with members of the Palestinian Islamic Movement against the pro-reform groups (Abou Ramadan 2006, pp. 42–46), while in the Knesset the Islamist and conservative Palestinian representatives joined their hands with Orthodox Jewish parties to forestall and thwart the legislative process. The conservative front in the parliament was eventually defeated by a counter-alliance of secular and centrist parties. In hindsight, as Nasreen Alemy-Kabha, the former coordinator of the WGEPSI, put it, "Orthodox religious parties saw this initiative as an assault on religion by secularist forces," and joined the Islamists against the reform in the parliament.[82]

Even though the passage of the LFCA of 2001 was an important achievement for Israeli-Arab women, nearly ten years after its coming into force the legislative change has not yet produced many of its intended outcomes due to various structural and political reasons.[83] But there were

---

[81] There were seven Arab MKs present at the vote – three abstained and four voted against the Bill (El-Taji T. 2008, pp. 95–96).

[82] Personal interview with Nasreen Alemy-Kabha (Nazareth, January 2005).

[83] Although Israeli family courts do not provide any statistics regarding ethnic and religious background of their clients, anecdotal evidence suggests that the actual number of Arab women coming to civil courts is far less than envisaged by the architects of the law in 2001. As argued by proponents of the law, this is mostly due to inherent structural problems and limitations of the civil court system. For example, at the time of writing there were only four Muslim judges and less than ten Palestinian social workers in all thirteen family courts in the country. As the current coordinator of the WGEPSI indicates, this situation is still far from sufficient to make civil family courts an attractive and feasible option for Muslim women. Moreover, proceedings at family courts are conducted in Hebrew, and courts do not provide *pro bono* translation services for Arab citizens. In particular, the lack of Arabic-speaking personnel who are familiar with the culturally specific concerns of the Palestinian families reportedly continues to make these courts an alien and unwelcoming environment for many Arab women

some unintended and indirect changes that retrospectively made the WGEPSI's efforts a major success. Under threat of losing their jurisdiction and clients to the civil family courts, in 1995 Israeli *shari'a* courts initiated a reform of their own by reinventing a judicial mechanism that was used a century earlier by the British in the Sudan: legal circular or *marsoum qadai* (Zahalka 2010b, pp. 180–183).[84] The circular, which was issued in the midst of calls for intervention by Knesset, ordered *qadis* to rely upon written evidence (*e.g.*, tax return, insurance documents, etc.) for determining the amount of maintenance instead of *mukhbirun* or informants. In the months following the promulgation of the new circular, sums of maintenance awards made to Muslim women by the *shari'a* court in West Jerusalem had risen by nearly 50 percent (Shahar 2006, p. 132). In fact, some report that *shari'a* courts now award the highest average sums of maintenance in the country (Natour 2009, p. 207; Zahalka 2010a). I could not independently verify whether this claim is true or not; however my analyses of some family court cases from 2006 to 2012, as well as a recent conversation with the *qadi* of West Jerusalem Shari'a Court,[85] indicate that the average sums of maintenance and alimony awards across civil and Islamic courts seem to be in the same range of NIS 1,200–1,500 per month.

Despite this encouraging development, Muslim women continue to face major difficulties and restrictions under the current system. Some women attribute this to the lack of female voices in the *shari'a* courts and advocate appointment of female *qadis*. The current coordinator of the WGEPSI indicates that women's groups have already raised the issue with the nomination committee for *shari'a* judges and received the vocal support of several key members.[86] Muslim feminists remain hopeful that the Israeli authorities will follow the pioneering example set by the Palestinian Authority and appoint female judges to *shari'a* courts.[87] However, Muslim women, like their Jewish counterparts, recognize that the road to such a change will be long and thorny, as the idea of

(phone interview with Heba Yazbak, April 2010). Perhaps the social and national sanctions against the use of Israeli courts for personal status matters that normally fall under *shari'a* can also be said to play a role and discourage many women from resorting to family courts to resolve their maintenance or custody disputes. Personal interview with Prof. Aharon Layish (Jerusalem, June 2004).

[84] For further information on *marsoum qadai*, see Reiter (1997b), Abou Ramadan (2003, 2005, 2006) and Natour (2009).

[85] Personal interview with Qadi Iyad Zahalka (New York, October 2012).

[86] Phone interview with Heba Yazbak (April 2010).

[87] The Palestinian government in the West Bank appointed two female *qadis*, Khuloud Faqih and Asmahan Wuheidi, to Islamic courts in February 2009.

female *qadis* will most likely be opposed not only by Muslim conservatives but also Orthodox Jewish parties which are reportedly wary of the impact of such a major change on the rabbinical system.

The 2001 experience has taught women two invaluable lessons about the limitations of a solely secular approach to the issue of reform of Muslim laws in Israel. First, since public discourse is often shaped by the official *shari'a* establishment and the Islamists, any change brought through collaboration with "enemy" institutions (e.g., the Knesset or Israeli civil courts) or foreigners (e.g., international development and grant-making agencies) is likely to discredit the organizations and individuals who initiated the reform in the eyes of the Palestinian population. Second, the deep distrust among Palestinians of Israeli institutions, inaccessibility of Hebrew-run courts to the Arabic-speaking population and the unwillingness of the Israeli state to uphold its own laws that aim to protect women's rights within the Arab community, could undermine any reform and lessen its applicability and effectiveness. Thus, immediately after the 2001 reform, some despairing women's groups began looking for solutions to the problem of Muslim personal status law within the community by providing women-friendly interpretations of classical sources of *shari'a* such as the Qur'an and *sunna*. The leading representative of this new trend has been Nissa wa Afaq (NwA – Women and Horizons). Modeled on Kolech and inspired by Muslim feminists such as Fatima Mernissi and Farida Bennani, NwA not only advocates rereading of classical Islamic law and history through liberal and feminist lenses and encourages comparative study of personal status reforms in the broader Muslim world to inspire change at home, but is also working on a new personal status law that would replace the OLFR of 1917 to empower women and promote their human rights within the *shari'a* system.[88]

Even though some civil society organizations still prefer more subtle tactics rather than such cross-communal coalitions and direct confrontation with state-sanctioned religious authorities, the examples of ICAR and WGEPSI, as well as the anti-reform coalition between the Orthodox Jews and conservative Muslims formed in the Knesset in order to block passage of the LFCA of 2001, demonstrate that the legitimacy of communal boundaries and the value system that has upheld the current personal status system have been increasingly challenged and discredited in recent years. In short, the activities of these

---

[88] Email correspondence with Nissa wa Afaq (September 2010).

groups, which transcend their ethnic and religious differences and build cross-communal coalitions, somewhat attest to the inadequacy of the system that was originally put in place in order to magnify communal differences and demarcate and enforce ethno-religious boundaries.

CONCLUSION

Israel retained a variant of the Ottoman *millet* system upon independence and made no attempts to institutionally or normatively unify its system – unlike Egypt or India. This is because the founding elite deemed the retention and furtherance of the old *millet* system instrumental for the preservation and homogenization of the Jewish identity on the one hand, and the differentiation of non-Jewish identities on the other. However, as far as the first objective is concerned, the analysis above has shown that the Israeli *millet* system has encountered serious challenges in producing its intended goal of homogenizing and unifying the country's Jewish population. On the contrary, the monopoly granted to rabbinical courts has caused profound ideological and societal divisions within the Jewish sector due to the forcible subjection of the secular majority to state-enforced orthodox laws and restrictive practices of the religious authorities.

As far as the second objective is concerned, however, the *millet* system has served some of its intended goals, but its success is still far from complete. Especially in the backdrop of the examples of ICAR and the WGEPSI, one may argue that if the original intent of retaining the old fragmented confessional system was to segregate groups from one another by fortifying communal boundaries, then the *millet* system has flunked in this respect, too. After all, the system was retained to reinforce the colonial/imperial categories of subjectivity, but the cross-communal activities of civil rights and conservative groups have increasingly challenged the long-established communal boundaries and blurred the imaginary categories of gender, ethnicity and religion. As individuals established cross-communal coalitions and formed hermeneutic and rule-making communities they constantly challenged the interpretive monopoly of state-sanctioned religious institutions, forced them to respond to their demands for reform and continuously made and remade the Israeli *millet* system through their everyday interactions with personal status institutions. For instance, when Jewish women successfully campaigned for the admittance of female pleaders to rabbinical courts in the late 1980s, or when women's and civil rights groups lobbied the Knesset to allow Muslim women to bring their maintenance suits to civil courts in the late 1990s, they not only compelled the state and religious authorities operating under its auspices to self-reform, but also renegotiated with the authorities the rules of personal status and remade the entire system.

In this regard, perhaps, one generalizable lesson to be drawn from the chapter is that regulation of pluri-legal personal status systems is a gigantic and equally challenging task for any government, however strong. First, regardless of the motives that originally led a government to intervene in its personal status system, there might be some unintended consequences which could potentially undermine chances of success for intervening governments. Second, state-enforced religious laws carry serious implications for the rights and liberties of the people who are subject to their jurisdiction. Third, individuals who employ various resistance strategies to respond to limitations imposed upon their rights decisively interfere with governments' attempts to regulate their personal status systems, and through their everyday interactions often force state-sanctioned religious laws and authorities to self-reform and continuously make and remake the overall system. Chapter 5 looks at similar issues in the context of Egypt, identifies the dynamics that contributed to the emergence of a unified confessional personal status system in the country, and analyzes the effects of this particular model on the rights and freedoms of Egyptian citizens.

5

A UNIFIED CONFESSIONAL SYSTEM: STATE-ENFORCED RELIGIOUS FAMILY LAWS AND HUMAN RIGHTS IN EGYPT

As in Israel, the origins of the Egyptian personal status system can be traced back to the Ottoman *millet* system, which the Egyptian government had formally inherited upon the termination of Ottoman suzerainty, and enactment of Law No. 8 of 1915 (Hanna 1995; Abdal-Rehim 1996). The fragmented confessional system under which the government recognized the jurisdiction of fifteen ethno-religious communities[1] was more or less preserved without much change until the Nasserist Revolution in 1952.

The Free Officers abolished the *shari'a* and *milliyah* courts and transferred their jurisdiction to the newly established personal status chambers of national courts (*mahakim ahliyya*) by enacting Law No. 462 in September 1955. However, while the Nasserist regime unified the religious courts of various communities under an overarching network of national courts, it refrained from introducing a uniform civil code that would apply equally to all Egyptian citizens irrespective of religion. As a result, unlike in Israel where state-sanctioned religious courts apply their own communal laws (e.g., rabbinical courts applying Jewish law, *shari'a* courts applying Muslim law, etc.), in Egypt different bodies of religious laws are directly applied by state-appointed and secularly trained judges at civil family courts.[2] In other words, Egyptian family court judges

---

[1] These communities were: Sunni Muslims; Copts, both Orthodox and Catholic; Melkites; Greek Orthodox; Maronites; Armenian Gregorians; Armenian Catholics; Syrian Orthodox; Syrian Catholics; Chaldeans; Roman Catholics; Anglican Protestants; Karaite Jews; and Rabbanite Jews.

[2] Since the enactment of Law No. 10 in March 2004, the personal status chambers of the national courts have been replaced by a specialized network of family courts.

continuously switch between Muslim and Christian laws depending upon the religious and communal affiliation of litigants. That is to say, the same family court judge (most likely a Muslim man) would apply *shari'a* law in the case of a Muslim litigant and Christian law in the case of a Christian litigant.

In this respect, the main question that will be addressed in this chapter is why such an allegedly progressive and revolutionary government contented itself with mere institutional unification, and did not take its project of legal centralization one step further by enacting an accompanying civil code that would be applicable to everyone throughout the national territory. In other words, why did Egypt stop short of normative unification, and not seek to enact a uniform civil code, like India tried in the 1950s? What factors brought about the emergence of its unified confessional system? How has this particular model of personal status system affected the rights and freedoms of Egyptian citizens, and how did Egyptians respond to limitations and disabilities imposed upon their rights by state-enforced religious laws?

In brief, I argue that the Nasserist regime closely resembled what I called in Chapter 2 a "technocratic-authoritarian" regime that preoccupied itself primarily with the consolidation of its power, rationalization of public administration, elimination of the remnants of *ancien régime* and the neutralization of political opposition. Particularly during the early years, the regime lacked a clearly formulated ideology or philosophy. In fact, the revolutionary government's lack of ideological vision and its preoccupation with such mechanical considerations as rationalizing the public administration and accumulating political power in the hands of central government was nowhere more evident than in its abolition of the *shari'a* and *milliyah* courts in 1955. In other words, the Nasserist regime did not aspire to redefine provisions of membership in the political community or the role of religious norms and institutions in public life through its interventions in the old *millet* system. That is why it merely confined itself to institutional unification and refrained from normative interventions, which usually require an unshakable moral and ideological commitment that was simply lacking in the Egyptian case.

The impact of Egypt's personal status laws on its citizens' rights and freedoms has not been very different from that of the Israeli personal status system on the rights and freedoms of Israelis. This is because Egypt, too, forcibly holds people subject to state-enforced religious laws without seeking their consent or furnishing them with an alternative civil code, as India does. Furthermore, as explained in greater detail below,

Egyptian law, under certain circumstances, also holds non-Muslims involuntarily subject to *shari'a* law. As discussed in Chapter 3, the forcible subjection of individuals to state-enforced personal status laws often leads to infringement of such rights and liberties as freedom of religion, equality before the law, marital and familial rights and certain procedural rights. Similarly, under the Egyptian personal status system, like in Israel and India, major human rights concerns are often related to marital rights, particularly the problem of divorce and remarriage within the Coptic Orthodox community, and women's rights to divorce in the Muslim sector – which I analyze below. However, the unique human rights aspect of the Egyptian personal status system concerns the manipulation and exploitation of Muslim marital laws by religious activists (in connection with the *hisba* principle) in order to declare religious dissidents apostates and forcibly break up their families. Such inquisitorial and vindictive lawsuits against secular intellectuals not only encroach upon their basic rights and aim to silence them, but also pose a great danger to their lives. Thus, given the uniqueness of this particular issue – this aspect of personal status systems is not observable in Israel or India – I will, in my discussion below, first turn my attention to it and then look at more commonly observed divorce- and marriage-related concerns.

Like Israelis and Indians, Egyptians, too, have responded to the challenge of living under state-enforced religious laws by adopting various resistance strategies from forum-shopping to forming hermeneutic communities. While engaging in these resistance strategies they have constantly contested the interpretive monopoly of the state and nationalized religious authorities, and continuously made and remade rules and institutions of personal status through their everyday interactions with them. In the same vein, religious activists and Christian clergy have also engaged the system and pressured it to change by constantly challenging the legitimacy and authority of state-enforced religious rules and institutions. In this respect, like everywhere else, the field of human rights in Egypt has, too, become a site of resistance, and functioned as a testing ground of sorts for evaluating the performance of the Egyptian government's interventions into its personal status system. Thus in the following pages I will use the examples of the Abu Zayd case, the crisis of remarriage and forum-shopping within the Coptic Orthodox community, the issue of women's rights to divorce in the Muslim community and the Khul' Law of 2000 as litmus tests to find out whether the Egyptian government has achieved any of its stated objectives in enacting Law No. 462. As explained in the memorandum accompanying Law No. 462, the main objectives of the government were to systematize the justice administration, put an end to the "anarchy" of multiple jurisdictions, divest religious authorities of their juridical powers, break the independent political power of religious institutions and neutralize the Islamic opposition. Thus, through the following analysis of personal status-related human rights concerns and specific tactics and strategies that people adopt in response, I demonstrate that the 1955 reform has only partially succeeded in producing the objectives that the Nasserist government had hoped to attain with the enactment of Law No. 462.

The chapter is comprised of three sections. I first explain the current Egyptian personal status system and its historical origins by specifically focusing on the Muslim and Coptic Orthodox communities. In the second section I delve into the history of the Egyptian Revolution, and identify the main considerations that led the Nasserist regime to undertake only institutional unification without enacting an accompanying civil code that would have been uniformly applied to all Egyptian citizens. In the last section I describe how the post-1955 personal status system has influenced the rights and freedoms of Egyptian citizens, and how individuals have responded to the limitations and disabilities imposed upon their rights, by analyzing apostasy charges brought (in connection with personal status issues) against secular intellectuals, religious conversions (usually undergone out of convenience rather than conviction) and women's demands for expanded rights to divorce. As in the Israeli case, my analysis here of human rights violations, talks and discourses shall serve as a testing ground on which I will analyze the extent to which the 1955 reform achieved its intended goals.

I. THE EGYPTIAN PERSONAL STATUS SYSTEM

Shariʿa and Coptic Orthodox personal law before and after 1955

Up until 1955, Egypt had a very similar personal status system to that of Israel in which religious courts were directly responsible for application of their communal laws within their respective communities. In this regard, shariʿa courts enjoyed exclusive jurisdiction over all personal status matters (e.g., marriage, divorce, maintenance, inheritance, etc.) of Egyptian Muslims (Salim 2000, pp. 371–408). The courts also had residual jurisdiction over personal status matters of non-Muslims where spouses did not belong to the same sect (taʾifa) and rite (milla), or when they belonged to the same sect and rite but at least one of them requested the shariʿa courts to resolve the dispute according to Islamic law (Shaham 1995;

Berger 2001; Shaham 2006). The substantive laws that *qadis* applied were partially codified enactments based on Islamic law, which included Law No. 25 of 1920 and Law No. 25 of 1929 that mainly dealt with issues of marriage, divorce and maintenance, and Laws No. 77 of 1943 and No. 71 of 1946 which respectively dealt with intestate succession and testamentary dispositions. Article 280 of Law No. 78 of 1931 ordered *qadis* to deliver their decisions according to the preponderant *Hanafi* opinion if the subject matter was not covered by statutory law.[3] However, in most cases *qadis* consulted Qadri Pasha's unofficial nineteenth-century compilation of Islamic personal status laws (Qadri 1914).

Personal status matters of Orthodox Copts were, historically, subject to the jurisdiction of ecclesiastical courts of the Coptic Orthodox Church. However, the Ottoman Imperial Decree of May 14, 1883 removed the clergy's judicial authority and reinvested it in the *Maglis Milli*, a council of twelve lay members presided over by the patriarch (Du Rausas 1911, p. 110; Hajjar 1956, p. 12; Seikaly 1970, pp. 251–253; Bestavros 1976; Meinardus 1999, pp. 71–72).[4] Following the 1883 decree, the *Maglis Milli* established a separate court of first instance and a court of appeal for adjudication of personal status matters. Both courts were recognized as courts of law under Egyptian law, and their rulings were directly executed through government offices. According to the 1883 decree and Law No. 8 of 1915, *Maglis Milli* courts had exclusive jurisdiction over matters of marriage, divorce and maintenance if both parties were members of the Coptic Orthodox Church and neither party requested intervention of *shari'a* courts.[5] In matters of succession, however, their jurisdiction was conditional upon the consent of all interested parties under Article 1 of Law No. 25 of 1944.[6] Otherwise, succession matters of Orthodox Copts

---

[3] Although the majority of Muslims in Egypt adhere to either the *Shafi'i* school (in Lower Egypt) or the *Maliki* school (in Upper Egypt), the dominant school in the Egyptian *shari'a* courts was, and still is, the *Hanafi*, a direct legacy of Ottoman rule (Shaham 1997, pp. 12–13).

[4] According to the 1883 decree, the *Maglis Milli* was empowered to handle "all matters pertaining to marriage, divorce, separation, alimony, *mahr* [dower], trousseau, custody, *nasab* [paternity], wills, succession, *awqaf* [religious endowments] and bequests" (Sfeir 1956, p. 250).

[5] The question of whether Islamic law principally allows non-Muslim litigants to opt for the application of *shari'a* at their request is highly controversial in the literature. As Shaham points out, even within the *Hanafi* school there was a disagreement among scholars as to whether the preponderant opinion had allowed the application of Islamic law to non-Muslims who had resorted to the Egyptian *shari'a* courts before 1955 (Shaham 2006, pp. 463–466). However, Berger authoritatively argues that post-1955 Egyptian case law (Court of Cassation, Case No. 182, 35th Judicial Year, March 20, 1969) denied this freedom to non-Muslim couples who shared the same sect and rite (Berger 2001, p. 112).

[6] Shaham argues that state authorities had always shown a special interest in *dhimmi* inheritance cases, especially when they involved real estate. This is because, according to Islamic law, the Public Treasury was to serve as a "residual heir whenever the deceased (Muslim and *dhimmi* alike)

were dealt with by the *shariʿa* courts according to Islamic inheritance laws as codified into Law No. 77 of 1943 and Law No. 71 of 1946.[7]

In response to repeated demands by the Egyptian government to ascertain and publish their procedural and substantive laws, on May 9, 1938 the *Maglis Milli* released the PSOCOC that laid down the rules pertaining to marriage, divorce, maintenance and, to a lesser extent, inheritance (Ziadeh 1968, p. 114; Carter 1986, pp. 230–239; Kramer 1989, p. 73; Shaham 1995, pp. 121–122). The liberal attitude towards divorce adopted in the 1938 ordinance caused profound frictions between the clergy and the liberal-minded *Maglis Milli*, which single-handedly produced the ordinance without much input from the religious leadership. Articles 50–58 listed nine different grounds[8] for divorce that included a wide range of elements from spousal incompatibility to the husband's sexual incompetence (Al-Banna 1984, pp. 28–36; Atiya 1991, p. 1943; Salim 2004, p. 55; Shaham 2010, p. 411). In 1945, Pope Macarius III denounced this liberal attitude on divorce, and later the Holy Synod declared that, as per teachings of the Gospel, the church would allow divorce only in the case of adultery. Similarly, the late Pope, Shenouda III, has also followed in the footsteps of his predecessors and repeatedly voiced his opposition to the 1938 ordinance. In this spirit he issued two papal decrees, in 1971 and 1996, effectively limiting divorce only to cases of adultery (Guindy, Shukrallah *et al.* 1999). As shown below, the normative discrepancy between the church's position on divorce and the 1938 ordinance's liberal attitude has, throughout the years, put thousands of Copts in a legal limbo in which they could not remarry within the church after having been divorced by the courts for any reason other than adultery.

Law No. 462 of September 21, 1955 abolished 123 *shariʿa* courts and 22 *milliyah* courts belonging to 14 different non-Muslim communities

---

died childless or if the shares awarded to the legal heirs did not exhaust the estate" (1995, p. 117). Similarly, Berger also notes that Egyptian non-Muslims had been subject to Islamic intestate succession laws long before the enactment of the 1943 and 1946 inheritance laws (2001, p. 95).

[7] Although Articles 875 and 915 of the Egyptian Civil Code of 1949 declared *shariʿa* and the statutory laws of 1943 and 1946 to be applicable to both Muslim and non-Muslim Egyptians in matters of testate and intestate succession, as some commentators have argued the *Maglis Milli* courts retained their concurrent jurisdiction and continued to adjudicate inheritance cases in accordance with Article 1 of Law No. 25 of 1944 until their termination in 1955 (Al-Gammal 2002, pp. 35–36).

[8] These include: (1) adultery; (2) one of the spouses' conversion to another religion; (3) five-year absence with no news of the spouse's whereabouts; (4) imprisonment for seven years or more; (5) mental illness that has lasted more than three years with no hope of cure; or a contagious disease that threatens the partner's health; or the husband's sexual impotence over a period of three years; (6) domestic violence; (7) "immoral" or "incorrigible" behavior (e.g., homosexuality); (8) spousal incompatibility for over a period of three years; (9) joining a monastic order.

with a single stroke of a pen (*Al-Ahram*, Sep. 23, 1955, p. 1).[9] Effective from January 1, 1956, all cases pending at religious courts were transferred to the National Courts (*mahakim ahliyya*) for further consideration. Article 6 provided that in cases that previously came under the jurisdiction of *shari'a* courts, decisions were to be delivered according to the preponderant *Hanafi* opinion, except where specific statutory legislation had been issued (e.g., Law No. 25 of 1920 and Law No. 25 of 1929).[10] The same Article also stipulated that suits of non-Muslim couples who belonged to the same sect (*ta'ifa*) and rite (*milla*), and who had their own religious courts at the time of the promulgation of Law No. 462, were to be decided according to their own religious laws with due respect to public order (*al-nizam al-amm*) (Hajjar 1955, pp. 316–317; Safran 1958, pp. 20–21; Liebesny 1975, pp. 101–102).

With the enactment of Law No. 462, the Egyptian government undertook a major step towards institutional unification. The new law abolished the institutional plurality of communal courts in the field of personal status and transferred their jurisdiction to the Personal Status Chambers of National Courts. Unlike their Indian counterparts, however, the Egyptian leaders never planned or attempted to take their unification project to the next level by enacting a uniform civil code that would be applicable to all Egyptians regardless of religion. In fact, after 1955, successive Egyptian governments largely neglected the field of personal status, and only occasionally intervened to make limited substantive changes in Muslim personal status laws – often in response to demands for the improvement of women's rights to divorce (e.g., Law No. 44 of 1979 and Law No. 1 of 2000). Although the procedural provisions of some of the legislation on alimony and maintenance that were primarily passed for the benefit of the Muslim community were also

---

[9] The actual number of courts that were suppressed by Law No. 462 is somewhat debated in the literature. For example, De Bellefonds reports that, as of September 1955, there were 125 Courts of Summary Justice, 15 Courts of First Instance and 1 Supreme Court of *shari'a* in the Islamic sector, whereas the Coptic Orthodox community had 18 Courts of First Instance and 1 Court of Appeals throughout the country (1956, pp. 414, 420).

[10] Article 6 of Law No. 462 of 1955 required the application of *Hanafi* law by virtue of Article 280 of Law No. 78 of 1931. However, Article 4 of Law No. 1 of 2000 abolished both Law No. 462 of 1955 and Law No. 78 of 1931, and thereby technically removed the main legal ground which entailed the application of *Hanafi* law in the event of legal lacuna. In order to prevent possible legal vacuum, however, Article 3 of Law No. 1 of 2000 continued requiring the application of the preponderant opinion of the *Hanafi* jurisprudence where no specific provision was prescribed in statutory laws.

made applicable to non-Muslim Egyptians,[11] no direct changes have ever been made in the personal status laws of the Coptic Orthodox community. As a result, today "secularly trained" judges at civil courts – specialized family courts since October 2004 – still continue to apply different bodies of religious law to individuals with different ethno-religious backgrounds. For example, when a Muslim Egyptian comes to the Family Court, the judge will decide the case according to Islamic law (statutory laws and *Hanafi* jurisprudence where the law is silent). Similarly, when an Orthodox Copt resorts to the court, the judge will apply the PSOCOC of 1938 if it is a matrimonial matter, provided that the application of non-Muslim laws will not violate the Egyptian public order (*al-nizam al-amm*) or essential principles of Islamic law that are the general law of the land in matters of personal status for all Egyptians (De Bellefonds 1956, pp. 422–423; Berger 2001). If it is an inheritance-related dispute, however, then the judge will apply not the Christian law but the provisions of both statutory (1943 and 1946 laws) and uncodified Islamic law to the case of Christian litigants.[12]

II. WHY DID EGYPT STOP SHORT OF NORMATIVE UNIFICATION THAT WOULD COMPLEMENT ITS UNIFICATION OF RELIGIOUS COURTS?

With the promulgation of Law No. 462 of 1955, the Egyptian government institutionally unified its personal status system while it continued allowing a considerable amount of normative plurality. In fact, the revolutionary government completely ignored the normative dimension of unification and exclusively focused its energy on the abolition of religious courts and the creation of an overarching system of national courts in their place. In this regard, the question that needs to be addressed is why such an allegedly "progressive" and revolutionary government contented itself with mere institutional unification, and did not further its process of judicial centralization by enacting an accompanying civil code that would be applicable to all Egyptians irrespective of religion; why did the Free Officers not pursue a goal of normative unification like the Indian leaders attempted in the 1950s?

---

[11] The provisions of Law No. 1 of 2000 (and also those of Law No. 62 of 1976 prior to that) which govern procedural aspects of financial support and alimony were declared applicable to non-Muslim Egyptians.

[12] This is because Law No. 462 of 1955 stripped non-Muslim Egyptians of juridical autonomy in matters of inheritance that had been granted them under Law No. 25 of 1944.

Although these are key questions to understanding the motivations of Egyptian reformers, they have often been neglected by scholars, who have instead focused extensively on substantive changes in Egyptian personal status laws (Al-Nowaihi 1979; Hussein 1981; Nasir 1986; Najjar 1988; Badran 1991; Mayer 1995; Afifi 1996; Qassem 2002; Hasan 2003; Fawzy 2004). Nonetheless, while the normative aspect of unification has been marginalized in these circles, a few have drawn their attention to the abrogation of *shari'a* and *milliyah* courts in 1955 and endeavored to offer an explanation for this surprising move by the revolutionary government (Hajjar 1955; De Bellefonds 1956; Sfeir 1956; Safran 1958; Naveh 1997). In effect, the confluence of these accounts seems to be consonant with the contention of the present study that the revolutionary government was mainly motivated by mechanical concerns such as increasing the efficiency of its central administration and reinstating the sovereignty of the Egyptian state over its territory, rather than ideological considerations such as secularizing the public sphere or redefining the provisions of membership in the political community. Thus, in an attempt to identify the motivations that led the Free Officers to undertake the 1955 reform that resulted in the unification of communal jurisdictions, the section below demonstrates the technocratic-authoritarian characteristics of the Egyptian regime in detail.

The technocratic-authoritarian characteristics of the Egyptian regime
The new Egyptian government, which was established after the 1952 revolution, could be characterized as a technocratic-authoritarian regime that primarily preoccupied itself with the consolidation of its power and establishment of effective means of control over society (Rodinson 1968, pp. 94–95; Waterbury 1983, pp. 6–12; Fahmy 2002, pp. 242–247). Especially during the early phases of the revolution (1952–1957), the new government pursued an extensive program of centralization, embracing various forms of corporatist and authoritarian measures (Moore 1974) in its fight against the so-called enemies of the revolution. For instance in January 1953 all political parties were dissolved and thousands of activists, mainly from the Wafd, were arrested and tried by revolutionary tribunals as part of the government's efforts to subdue domestic opposition. The campaign against the *ancien régime* was intensified after the abolition of the monarchy and the subsequent proclamation of the republic in June 1953. The following year, universities were closed down. Then the press and professional associations fell prey to the regime, which

127

staffed their upper echelons with handpicked candidates (Wheelock 1960, p. 39). After a failed assassination attempt on Nasser in October 1954, the government also banned the Muslim Brotherhood (*al-Ikhwan al-Muslimun*), executed its leaders and jailed the majority of its members (Rodinson 1968, p. 99). With the destruction of the Ikhwan's organizational structure and leadership, the Egyptian government not only gained an upper hand vis-à-vis one of its staunchest enemies but also found a new space within which it was able to advance the objectives of the revolution without much social opposition (Wheelock 1960, pp. 27–28, 44–47; Vatikiotis 1969, pp. 374–388; 1978, pp. 126–151; Goldberg 1990; Gordon 1992, pp. 68–108).

The concentration of power in the hands of the central government further continued as the new regime began to create its own political institutions (e.g., the Liberation Rally and National Union) to mobilize the masses behind it and fill in the organizational power vacuum created by its destruction of Egyptian civil society (Rodinson 1968, p. 98; Harik 1973, pp. 85–86; Waterbury 1983, pp. 312–316; Ayubi 1999, pp. 216–218). The centralist and corporatist policies of the new regime also led to an unprecedented expansion of government bureaucracy and the public sector (Vitalis 1995, pp. 206–217; Ayubi 1999, pp. 296–301). In fact, as Ayubi reports, government expenditure, the number of public employees and the number of administrative units increased steadily from 1952 to 1970 (Wheelock 1960, pp. 145–149; Ayubi 1980, pp. 238–253). Yet, the explosion in the size of the public bureaucracy was not inconsistent with the new administrative philosophy that regarded the modernization of the public administration a "magic" remedy for the ills from which Egyptian society had long suffered (Ayubi 1990, p. 140). Hence, as soon as they took over, the Free Officers launched an extensive program of bureaucratic rationalization to create a uniform, coherent and efficient system of public administration which they deemed vital for the success of the revolution and the establishment of a strong developmental state (Rodinson 1968, p. 100). Consequently, the military men in power strongly believed in the value of specialized technical knowledge, professionalization and uniformity in public administration; and that conviction profoundly shaped the new regime's socio-economic policies and Egyptian public life throughout the 1950s (Stephens 1971, p. 110; Perlmutter 1974, pp. 81–106; Baker 1978, pp. 70–87, 175–192; Ayubi 1980, pp. 471–495).

However, apart from these centralist and technocratic proclivities, the regime did not have a clear program or an ideology to mobilize the masses and mediate the transition to a republican order (Rodinson 1968, p. 94; Dekmejian 1971, pp. 64–70; Harik 1973, p. 83; Lacouture 1973, pp. 144–145; Gordon 1992, p. 12; Ginat 1997, p. 13; Ayubi 1999, p. 26). Put this way, if ideology is defined as a system of meanings and symbols that attempt to create a collective consciousness, generate ideals and mobilize masses around these ideals in order to implement policies and maintain power, then, as both Nasser and Sadat have confessed at one point (Aldeeb Abu-Sahlieh 1979, p. 103), the new regime did not possess a well-defined ideology, at least until the emergence of Nasser's own version of socialism in the late 1950s (Wheelock 1960, pp. 69–73; Baker 1978, p. 60; Hopwood 1991, pp. 90–91; Ginat 1997). The Six Principles, published in January 1953 by the Free Officers, listing the eradication of imperialism, abolition of feudalism and achievement of social justice among the objectives of the revolution, were rather vaguely defined guiding principles and inadequate to equip the regime with a tangible administrative philosophy in the long term (Lacouture 1973, p. 222; Ansari 1986, p. 84; Hopwood 1991, p. 88). Hence in the final analysis the Nasserist regime lacked a clear ideological direction, and was instead led by its leaders' intuition and unguided desires to gain full independence from the British; build a strong developmental state; and remove the privileges of the old elite and institutions which they considered remnants of Egypt's colonial past that were still trespassing upon its national sovereignty.

The 1955 reform: the abolition of *shari'a* and *milliyah* courts

The revolutionary regime's lack of ideological vision, and its preoccupation with such mechanical considerations as systematizing public administration and accumulating political power in the hands of central government, was nowhere more evident than in its abolition of the *shari'a* and *milliyah* courts on September 21, 1955. Law No. 462 was published with an accompanying memorandum that explained the official reasons for the removal of *shari'a* and *milliyah* courts in great detail. A close reading of the memorandum shows that the Egyptian leaders were primarily concerned with the inefficiencies and harmful impact of the existing personal status system on Egyptian sovereignty. In fact, it puts so much emphasis on national sovereignty (*siyada*) and the irrationalities caused by the multiplicity of communal jurisdictions that at some point it reads more like a Weberian manifesto than a memorandum prepared by a military government:

> The rules of public law require that the sovereignty of the state be complete and absolute over its territory ... [A]ll persons who are domiciled therein ... should be subject to ... a single judicial authority no matter what ... the law applicable to them [Sfeir 1956, p. 252]. But in Egypt the situation contradicts this principle. The jurisdictions to which the Egyptians themselves submit in matters of personal status are numerous ... This has been the situation despite the fact that the nation has already reassumed its judicial prerogatives with regard to foreigners so that the national courts have become exclusively competent in all their conflicts ... [T]here should not remain in the country any vestige of an exceptional organization which would limit the power and the sovereignty of the state ... The government cannot suffer the existence on the national territory of judiciary autonomies which impose their will upon it, oppose its policy of reform or, lastly, choose their own way of reform ...
>   (Hajjar 1956, pp. 318–322; Safran 1958, pp. 21–23)

The Egyptian leaders believed that the existence of *shari'a* and non-Muslim communal courts had infringed on national sovereignty. As they clearly expressed in the memorandum, they also believed that there had to be a single and unified jurisdiction to which all residents of the country, irrespective of their religious affiliation, had to submit in regard to personal status. Yet, surprisingly, the memorandum only focused on the institutional and procedural aspects of the matter and completely ignored the more substantive issues. It addressed the multiplicity of courts and the lack of uniformity, but said almost nothing about the multiplicity of substantive laws of personal status that these jurisdictions were applying in the first place. That is to say, the government was mainly interested in institutional reform rather than full-scale normative unification.

Moreover, for many reasons, the government chose to liken the existing system of religious courts to the former regime of capitulations and the Mixed Courts that Egypt had recently eliminated in 1949 (Crabites 1927; Brinton 1968; Hoyle 1987, 1991). The memorandum explained how the religious courts were originally recognized and imposed upon Egypt by the imperialist Turkish rulers (Hajjar 1956). From this point of view, the existing system of religious courts was just a legacy of colonialism that had to be eradicated, in the same way that the Mixed Courts and capitulations had been abolished a decade earlier (Cassis Bey 1951; Brown 1997, pp. 61–69). By explicitly portraying religious courts as an alien imposition, the government was probably appealing to nationalist sentiments and aiming to lessen the potential opposition to its actions among the people.

The explanatory memorandum also highlighted what the Free Officers considered to be the main inefficiencies and irrationalities of the old system, which were caused by the existence of conflicting and overlapping jurisdictions that encouraged litigants to shop between courts. In addition to the "problem" of forum-shopping, the memorandum claimed, the incumbent system had also been crippled by the lack of uniform rules of procedure and fixed court fees, and delays and problems of physical inaccessibility which, in turn, not only led to chaos but also undermined citizens' confidence in the system of justice. In this regard, the memorandum asserted that the sole objective of Law No. 462 was to put an end to this ongoing "juridical anarchy" and restore citizens' confidence in the legal system:

> Egypt has retained from the past a multiplicity of judicial organizations in matters of personal status. [For instance,] the non-Muslim communities possess fourteen different jurisdictions, some of which sit only at very long intervals and in localities remote from the homes of the parties. This makes the process of justice very onerous ... and shows signs of tyranny and oppression. The juridical rules which most of these jurisdictions apply are not written ... The explanations and commentaries ... are written in Latin, Greek, Syriac, Hebrew, Armenian, or Coptic – all languages not understood by the majority of the parties ... The rules of forming the courts, of procedure, and of appeal are neither uniform nor stable. The judiciary fees are not unified; some of these courts do not even have any regulation in this matter ... In the face of this abnormal situation, in the face of this anarchy which has become unbearable ... the only victims are the parties and the sovereignty of the nation.
>
> ... Since the Revolution has set for itself the task ... of dealing a deadly blow to evil in all its manifestations, the difficulties mentioned above could not stop the government from fulfilling its duties with regard to the judicial organization by facilitating the paths to justice for all its citizens without distinction ...
>
> (Hajjar 1955, pp. 318–322; Safran 1958, pp. 21–23)

Although, for obvious reasons, it was not explicitly stated in the memorandum, as Crecelius (1966, p. 35) suggests, another objective of Law No. 462 was to bring al-Azhar, the intellectual center of Sunni Islam, and the religious authorities under the firm control of the government. By the time the law was passed in September 1955, the Egyptian government had already been in the midst of a comprehensive process of power-consolidation against the Muslim Brotherhood and Islamic groups. Once the Brotherhood was effectively neutralized, the government next turned its attention to the religious institutions and the *ulama* (Borthwick 1979, p. 156; Zeghal 1999, p. 374). In order to counterbalance the Islamist opposition and legitimize the regime's objectives in the eyes of the conservative population, the revolutionary leadership needed to gain the support and approval of al-Azhar and the Islamic scholars (Barraclough 1998, p. 238; Moustafa 2000, pp. 4–7). However, the subjugation of *ulama* and religious institutions to the will of the revolutionary government was achieved gradually and through several stages, reaching its point of culmination with the nationalization of al-Azhar in 1961 (Zeghal 1999, pp. 371–376; Hatina 2003, p. 60). In this respect, Law No. 462 was the first step in that process, as the government, through the abrogation of Islamic courts, succeeded in stripping the *ulama* of their traditional privileges and breaking "the independent political power of Islamic institutions so it could use them for its own [political] purposes" (Crecelius 1980, p. 65).

The response of the *ulama* to abolition of *shari'a* courts

The decision to abolish *shari'a* courts was made in an atmosphere of extreme revulsion against the "sheikhly" class. At the time, two *qadis* had recently been arrested on charges of delivering propitious verdicts in exchange for sexual favors from female litigants (Hajjar 1955, p. 323; Safran 1958, pp. 25–26; Crecelius 1966, p. 35; Zeghal 1999, p. 375). In this environment, Azharites could not publicly resist the government's abolition of the *shari'a* system. For example, in the months following the enactment of Law No. 462, not a single article dealing with the issue was printed in *Majallat al-Azhar*. On the contrary, as reported by the Egyptian dailies, the *ulama* publicly endorsed the government's unification program (*Al-Ahram*, Sep. 23–28, 1955; *Rose al-Yousef*, Jan. 9, 1956). On September 28, for instance, *Al-Ahram* published an article with a picture of Sheikh Abd al-Rahman Taj, the Rector of al-Azhar, shaking hands with President Nasser and congratulating him for having taken the "liberating step" of abolishing the *shari'a* and *milliyah* courts (Hajjar 1955, p. 325; Safran 1958, p. 26; Abécassis and Le Gall-Kazazian 1992, p. 22).[13]

---

[13] Islamic figures and organizations that were beyond the reach of the Egyptian government, however, burst into a public outcry over the government's move, and protests came from all parts of the Muslim world – Libya, Jordan and particularly from Syria – where the Muslim Brotherhood had a strong presence (Crecelius 1966, p. 35). For example, Safran reports that "the *ulama* of Aleppo ... according to *al-Manar* of October 2nd, 1955, gathered in the great mosque under the presidency of the Mufti of Aleppo and sent protest cables to President Nasser against

Behind the headlines, however, Azharites were extremely unhappy with Law No. 462, which transferred their monopoly over *shari'a* to lay judges and worsened their job prospects, as Islamic courts were a place where Azharites often found employment with relative ease as judges, lawyers and court clerks (Crecelius 1966, p. 36; 1967, pp. 294–295; Reid 1991, pp. 139–156). In an attempt to coopt the disgruntled *'ulama'* and placate their employment-related concerns, the government appointed 190 of the 212 *qadis* who had formerly worked at *shari'a* courts to personal status committees within the Ministry of Justice and the newly established personal status chambers of National Courts, where they continued to sit on the bench next to the civil judges for nearly two decades (Hajjar 1956; Abécassis and Le Gall-Kazazian 1992).

The clergy's response to abolition of *milliyah* courts

On the other hand, Christian minorities were much more outspoken and direct in their critique of the government's abolition of their courts. The clergy were particularly outraged by the fact that *qadis* were absorbed into the civil system and put in charge of applying not only *shari'a* but also the Christian law which they knew nothing about, while the Christian judges were left out and discriminated against by the government. It became even more disturbing for the Christian clerics when they learned that Law No. 462 also provided for the application of *shari'a* to non-Muslims in at least two instances: when the parties were not members of the same Christian sect and rite (Article 6); and when one of the parties converted to Islam, even in the course of litigation (Article 7) (Hajjar 1955, pp. 326–331; Abécassis and Le Gall-Kazazian 1992, pp. 22–24).

In the face of what they perceived to be the most serious attack on their rights in centuries, Egyptian Christians responded to Law No. 462 with an exceptional display of unity. The spiritual heads of all Christian communities in Egypt gathered at the Coptic Orthodox Patriarchate in Cairo on September 27, and unanimously approved a strongly worded resolution that expressed their opposition to the abolition of *milliyah* courts: "the new legislation . . . far from fulfilling its avowed aim (establishing equality among all citizens) destroys in an organized manner the liberty proclaimed by the revolution . . . and threatens the very existence

the new law which was described as a 'blow to divine law and a wound inflicted on the heart of Islam.' In Damascus [on the other hand], the Muslim Brethren distributed pamphlets after the Friday prayers in which Nasser was attacked as one who had 'declared war on Islam.' [Similarly], *al-Ray al-Amm* of September 25th reported that the law had a disastrous effect on the spirit of the Muslims of Syria" (Hajjar 1956, p. 326; Safran 1958, p. 26).

of Christianity in Egypt" (Safran 1958, p. 24). Furthermore, in response to the government's insistence on application of *shari'a* to non-Muslims in the two instances mentioned above, the resolution adopted an unusually controversial approach by asking the government, what would be the position of Palestinian Muslims "if Israel imposed on them the Mosaic law under the pretext of safeguarding her sovereignty? And what would be the position of the Muslims of Ethiopia if the *shari'a* courts were abolished?" (Safran 1958, p. 24). The resolution closed with a note that Christian communities would not accept the erosion of their jurisdiction, and urged the President to reconsider his decision and continue the tradition of "glorious Sultans and Caliphs" by allowing the People of the Book (*ahl al-kitab*, that is Jews and Christians) to reinstate their courts.

In the following weeks, Christian communities continued to pressure the government to reverse its decision to abolish *milliyah* courts. However, the government refused to talk to protestors and remained oblivious to their demands until the Catholic and Orthodox communities threatened to cancel Christmas celebrations throughout the country unless the regime took the necessary steps to ameliorate the situation (Hajjar 1955, pp. 326–331; *The Washington Post* and *Times Herald* 1955). This time, the Free Officers responded with a small concession, passing Law No. 629 on December 21, which reinstated the non-Muslim clergy's notarial powers to register and issue marriage licenses to couples who belonged to the same sect and rite. Catholics found the government's concession insufficient and rejected it outright. In protest, none of the Catholic communities in Egypt celebrated Christmas that year (Abécassis and Le Gall-Kazazian 1992, p. 22). Meanwhile, however, the government broke up the Christian coalition by separately convincing the Holy Synod of the Coptic Orthodox Church to accept the concession, thereby ending its protest. Unlike the Catholics, the Orthodox Copts celebrated Christmas on January 6, 1956. Even though it was the largest Christian community in Egypt, the Coptic Orthodox community gave in quickly to the demands of the government without getting much in return, as the community was in no position to resist due to its weakness caused by severe internal schisms.[14]

---

[14] The Patriarchy of Pope Joseph II was one of the most divisive periods in the history of the Coptic Orthodox Church. The Pope's policies and practices antagonized the radical elements within the community. In July 1954, members of al-Umma al-Qibtiya (The Coptic Nation), a militarist reform movement, kidnapped the Pope and forced him to sign a letter of abdication. The captors subsequently released him, but the event made the mismanagement of the Church highly visible and put it at the top of the national agenda. One year later, just a day before the enactment of Law No. 462, a young Orthodox Copt, encouraged by a local priest, made a failed assassination

In sum, the revolutionary government successfully surmounted the opposition of both Muslim and Christian clergy and assured their acquiescence by resorting to various forms of coercion, cooptation and accommodation. However, as noted above, the revolutionary leadership's abolition of the religious courts was solely motivated by mechanical considerations. As Crecelius (1980) argues, the Nasserist regime considered it necessary in order to restore Egyptian sovereignty, subordinate the religious institutions and turn them into agents of state power, rather than secularize the Egyptian state or redefine the provisions of membership in the political community. In fact, had the goal of the Egyptian government been to secularize its legal system or create an inclusionary regime, it would have at least attempted some sort of normative unification in tandem with Law No. 462. On the contrary, the Egyptian regime did not make even the slightest effort to introduce any normative changes in its system of personal status, as it never had an agenda of inclusionary or secular transformation.[15]

The Egyptian leaders not only neglected the normative reform that would have required their unshakable moral and ideological commitment, but also refrained from making any substantive changes in personal status laws. As far as social policy was concerned, the revolutionaries were quite conservative, even though they were political radicals. As Botman notes, the Free Officers "had no interest in extending their progressive attitudes to the private domain of the family, considering traditional domestic relations inviolable" (1999, p. 52). That is to say, the Egyptian leaders did not pay attention to the issue of personal status or the rights of women in the family despite the fact that they initially expanded women's political and civil rights after the revolution (Badran 1991, pp. 215–217;

attempt on the life of Joseph II. In September 1956, at the request of the *Maglis Milli*, the Egyptian government intervened by deposing and later banishing the Pope to a monastery in the desert. Two months later, the Pope died at a community hospital in Cairo. The death of Joseph II was followed by further chaos and a three-year-long succession crisis. In the end, government had to once again step in and bring order to the community by appointing Cyril VI as the new Pope in 1959 (Pennington 1982, p. 163; Ibrahim 1996, p. 15; Talhami 1996, p. 36; Meinardus 1999, p. 73).

[15] The revolutionary government had a pragmatic and manipulative approach towards religion. They certainly did not wish to secularize Egyptian society the way Atatürk did in Turkey or Bourguiba attempted in Tunisia (Sfeir 1956, p. 256; Borthwick 1979; Philipp 1995, pp. 139–140; Winter 1995, pp. 48–50). Rather, they wanted to coopt religious institutions and use them for their own political purposes (Borthwick 1979, p. 156). They even declared Islam the official religion of the state in the 1956 Constitution. Hence their abolition of the *shari'a* and *milliyah* courts should be solely viewed through the lens of this pragmatic approach. Law No. 462 was not a secular law. On the contrary, as some commentators have pointed out, it further enhanced the position of Islam within the Egyptian legal system by imposing *shari'a* upon non-Muslims (Philipp 1985, pp. 148–149).

Inhorn 1996, p. 28; Botman 1999, p. 54; Bier 2011, pp. 107–120). Egyptian women had to wait until 2000 to see some improvements in the personal status laws that furthered their rights to divorce and maintenance.[16] With this in mind the next section examines the impact of the Egyptian government's abstention from normative reform, and its conservative attitude towards introducing other substantive changes in the laws of personal status, upon rights and freedoms of its Muslim and non-Muslim citizens.

III. THE IMPACT OF PERSONAL STATUS LAWS ON THE RIGHTS AND FREEDOMS OF EGYPTIAN CITIZENS

In this section I analyze the impact of the persistence of state-imposed personal status laws, as well as the effects of the Egyptian government's conservative attitude towards substantive reform in personal status laws, on the rights and freedoms of Egyptian citizens. As indicated in Chapter 3, state-enforced religious laws usually carry negative implications for four groups of rights and liberties in particular: the freedom of religion; equality before the law; marital and familial rights; and procedural rights. The three examples presented below affirm this assertion, and show that state-enforced religious laws in Egypt, like in Israel and India, have often proved detrimental for individuals' rights and liberties. For instance, the first example below, the Abu Zayd case, demonstrates that inherent uncertainties, loopholes and the lack of institutional checks in personal status systems can be effectively exploited by those wishing to intimidate and harm outspoken intellectuals and religious dissidents by forcibly separating them from their families, declaring them apostates and instigating violence against them. When used in this vein, the Egyptian personal status system can be said not only to encroach upon individuals' rights to family integrity and privacy, freedom of religion, equality before the law, fair trial and freedom of expression, but also indirectly to put people's lives in danger.

The second example deals with the so-called crisis of remarriage within the Coptic Orthodox community. As explained in greater detail

---

[16] The only change introduced into Muslim personal status laws during the presidency of Nasser was rather a limited one. "In February 1967 the [M]inister of [J]ustice passed a ministerial decree that discontinued the practice of using the police to implement judgments by the courts requiring a wife to obey her husband and return to the family home. The minister claimed that more ambitious changes of the law were planned but that, according to him, the defeat suffered in the 1967 war had changed the political climate and agendas" (Al-Nowaihi 1981, p. 116; Hatem 2000, pp. 51–52; Cuno 2009).

below, the normative discrepancy between the church's steadfast position on divorce and the PSOCOC of 1938's relatively liberal attitude towards it has put thousands of Orthodox Copts in a legal limbo where they cannot remarry after getting a divorce on grounds other than adultery. The church allows divorce only in case of adultery. The 1938 ordinance, on the other hand, which the courts apply, grants divorce on nine different grounds including adultery. Since there is no civil marriage in Egypt, when an Orthodox Copt who is granted a divorce by the family court on non-adulterous grounds wants to remarry, the only option available to her is to denounce her faith and then embrace a new one that would allow remarriage. In this respect, it can be argued that the forcible imposition of state-enforced personal status laws, and the failure of the Egyptian state to introduce a civil marriage and divorce law (or its disinterest in doing so), has led to infringement of thousands of Egyptians' freedom of religion since they are "compelled" by the state and religious authorities to change their religion in order to enjoy another fundamental right – the right to marry and found a family.

As noted below, with the exception of President Sadat's failed attempt to expand women's right to divorce in 1979, Egyptian marital laws remained more or less unchanged from about the 1920s until 2000 when Law No. 1 was promulgated. In other words, despite drastic family law reforms that took place throughout the Muslim world in the second half of the last century, the Egyptian government actively refrained from undertaking any major substantive reforms in its personal status laws for nearly seven decades. Against this background, the third example below shows that the government's abstention from reform has born serious implications, particularly for Muslim women. The unfavorable treatment and status of women were especially visible in regard to divorce laws and practices. During this time, despite Egypt's historical and intellectual leading role in the Muslim and Arab world, Egyptian women's familial rights considerably lagged behind those of Muslim women in the neighboring North African and Middle Eastern countries. However, like women in Israel and India, Egyptian women did not silently accept the limitations and disabilities imposed upon their rights. Instead, they fiercely resisted the unequal treatment inflicted upon them by the state in the name of so-called "divine laws," and challenged the state and nationalized religious institutions' hermeneutic monopoly by reinterpreting scriptural and prophetic sources of *shari'a* through liberal and feminist lenses.

137

In this respect, like everywhere else, the field of human rights in Egypt has become a site of resistance, and functioned as a testing ground of sorts for evaluating the performance of the government's interventions into its personal status system. In this vein, the following analyses of emerging human rights discourses and violations under the Egyptian personal status laws show that if the original intent of the Nasserist regime, as declared in the memorandum accompanying Law No. 462, was to systematize the justice administration, put an end to the "anarchy" of multiple jurisdictions, divest religious authorities of their juridical powers, break the independent political power of religious institutions and neutralize the Islamic opposition, then the 1955 reform has, to a significant extent, failed to fully achieve any of those objectives. For instance, the example of the Abu Zayd case indicates that even though one of the objectives of the 1955 reform was to subjugate Islamic law and institutions and use them for government purposes, those the government call "extremists" have still been able to exploit the loopholes left by Law No. 462, thereby challenging the regime's Islamic credentials, swaying public opinion against the government and intimidating the secularist forces in Egyptian society by using the very institutions which were designed by the revolutionary government. Likewise, continuing instances of forum-shopping also attest to the failure of another objective of Law No. 462, this being to stop conniving individuals from hopping from one jurisdiction to another, and thus restore the public's confidence in the state's legal system. That is to say, despite institutional unification, the system still suffers from the same "irrationalities" and chronic inconsistencies that the revolutionaries aimed to get rid of by enacting Law No. 462. Lastly, the Coptic clergy's continued exercise of its authority over matters of divorce and remarriage within the Coptic Orthodox community attests to another shortcoming of Law No. 462 in achieving one of its main objectives, which was to divest religious authorities of their juridical powers completely.

The exploitation of personal status laws by Islamists in order to intimidate secular intellectuals and challenge the government's Islamic credentials

> From the moment the text [the Qur'an] was revealed and read by the Prophet [Mohammed], it was transformed from being divine text and became human understanding because it had immediately changed from revelation to interpretation. The Prophet's comprehension of the text represents the initial stage in the text's interaction with the human

mind ... [This view contradicts the traditional] claim that the Prophet's comprehension of the text corresponds to the text itself ... [which is] attributing divine qualities to the Prophet and sanctifying him by concealing his human nature and consequently the fact that he was only a Prophet.

(Sfeir 1998, pp. 410–411)

It is time we [Arabs and Muslims] reexamined our conditions, and liberated ourselves ... from the authority of the religious text.

(Najjar 2000, p. 179)

The author of these lines, Nasr Hamid Abu Zayd, a former professor of Arabic and Islamic studies at Cairo University, was accused of heresy due to his writings and sued by a group of Islamist activists seeking to suspend him from teaching and separate him from his wife, Ibtihal Yunis, on grounds of apostasy (*ridda*). Even though the Personal Status Chamber of the Giza Court of First Instance rejected the apostasy lawsuit against Professor Abu Zayd on procedural grounds, the Personal Status Chamber of the Cairo Court of Appeals reversed the Giza court's decision in June 1995, declared Professor Abu Zayd an apostate (*murtadd*), and separated him from his wife because according to *shari'a*, an apostate's marriage becomes void, and he cannot remain married to his Muslim wife. Later, in August 1996, *Mahkamat al-Naqd* (the Court of Cassation: Case Nos. 475, 478, 481, 65th Judicial Year, August 5, 1996) affirmed the Cairo court's ruling and found Professor Abu Zayd guilty on charges of apostasy:

[Professor Abu Zayd] denounces that the Qur'an is the word of God ... He describes Islam as an Arabic religion, denying its universality and availability to everybody ... He attacks the application of *shari'a* by describing it as backward and reactionary ... He describes the adoption of religious text as slavery ... He goes as far as calling for liberation from *shari'a* texts, claiming that they lack any essential and fixed elements ... He is, therefore, considered an apostate ... He revealed his unbelief ... and he has adopted a stance contrary to Islam.

(Berger 1998; Berger 2003, pp. 731–732)

The court's affirmation of Professor Abu Zayd's alleged heresy led many militant Islamists to view the court's ruling as tantamount to a death sentence waiting for an executioner (El-Magd 2000). Consequently, as radical Islamists intensified their criticism of his work and repeatedly called for his assassination, Professor Abu Zayd and his wife were forced to leave Egypt and go into a self-imposed exile in the Netherlands.

As the case of Professor Abu Zayd shows, the Egyptian personal status system has recently been transformed into an instrument of persecution by Islamist groups against religious dissidents, intellectuals and feminists in the country (Abdo 2000, pp. 163–173). The detrimental effects of state-enforced personal status laws on the rights of women, children and other individuals have been widely documented in the literature (Hamad 1999; Nassar 1999). However, the Abu Zayd case has shown us a very peculiar and unprecedented method of using personal status laws, in connection with Islamic rules of apostasy, against intellectuals in Egypt. The field of Egyptian personal status has long been a battle-ground between so-called "traditionalists" and "liberals" as each group has tried to reshape the foundations of family and redefine gender roles in it by imposing its own values. However, this time the battle was not about personal status laws themselves. They were, rather, the vessels through which Islamists launched a larger battle against secular elements in Egyptian society.

Although under classical *shari'a* law public apostasy was reportedly accepted as a crime punishable by death or banishment, Egyptian positive law does not view it as such (Saeed and Saeed 2004). Egyptian courts are not legally authorized to adjudicate cases of apostasy, or declare whether a person has committed it. However, there is still one back channel. If accusations of apostasy are successfully tied to matrimonial matters, the court will first need to determine whether the defendant has actually committed the crime of apostasy before it can rule over the matter of personal status in question (Johansen 2006). Since there are no statutory laws governing apostasy, the court needs to decide the case according to the most preponderant opinion of the *Hanafi* school[17] that renders an apostate's marriage both null and void (*batil*).

Those who wanted to have someone declared an apostate in con-nection with personal status still had to surmount a procedural limita-tion (CCCP, Article 3) that allowed only people who had a direct and personal interest in the case to bring such a petition to the court (Bälz 1997, p. 138; Najjar 2000, p. 191; Berger 2003, p. 729). This impedi-ment was finally overcome when a group of Islamist lawyers resuscitated a nearly forgotten principle of *shari'a* called *hisba* during the heyday

---

[17] Article 6 of Law No. 462 of 1955 required the application of *Hanafi* jurisprudence by virtue of Article 280 of Law No. 78 of 1931. Similarly, Article 3 of Law No. 1 of 2000, which replaced Law No. 462, still requires judges to deliver their judgments in accordance with preponderant *Hanafi* opinion when statutory laws are silent.

of Islamist legal mobilization in the 1990s (Moustafa 2007, 2010).[18] Resorting to *hisba*, which allows any Muslim to file a case against a person suspected of violating "God's rights" (*huquq Allah*) – that being the direct and personal interest in the case – activist lawyers demanded that the courts allow them to defend Islam against people – like Abu Zayd – who allegedly commit blasphemous crimes (*kufr*), by bringing their apostasy charges in connection with matrimonial matters to personal status courts (Berger 2003). Eventually, the Egyptian Court of Cassation agreed – in its aforementioned ruling in August 1996 – with the Islamists' interpretation of *shari'a* and admitted the apostasy charge against Professor Abu Zayd (Dupret 2003).[19]

Prior to the Abu Zayd case, the place and applicability of *hisba* (the duty of every Muslim to command goodness and condemn evil) under Egyptian positive law was a matter of great political and legal controversy. Even though the Court of Cassation upheld the admissibility of *hisba* in 1966 in a case relating to personal status (Court of Cassation, Case No. 20, 34th Judicial Year, March 30, 1966), this old principle of *shari'a* had remained largely unknown outside the Egyptian personal status field until it was reactivated by Islamist judges and lawyers in the mid-1990s (Bälz 1997, p. 140; Bernard-Maugiron 1999, p. 178). In this respect, the Abu Zayd case was particularly instrumental in reintroducing and popularizing the concept in the Egyptian public discourse. In fact, the Court of Cassation's reaffirmation of the *hisba* principle and declaration of Abu Zayd an apostate in August 1996 soon led to a vindictive wave of litigation targeting both Muslim and non-Muslim intellectuals. The main goal of the Islamist activists who filed *hisba* petitions in connection with both personal status- and non-personal status-related matters was to have these secular authors and thinkers legally declared apostates by the courts, and publicly condemn them for their "heretical" activities.

The Egyptian penal laws do not punish apostasy. However, as Sheikh Mohammad al-Ghazali, a distinguished former member of al-Azhar, put

---

[18] For further information on *hisba* see Ibn Taym'iyah *et al.* (1982), Sfeir (1998), Thielmann (1998) and Olsson (2008).

[19] The question of whether *hisba* is part of Egyptian positive law is highly controversial. Some argue that Law No. 78 of 1931 (Articles 89 and 110) recognized Egyptians' right to *hisba*. Law No. 1 of 2000, however, removed that basis by abolishing Law No. 78. Nonetheless, some suggest that by virtue of Article 3 of Law No. 1, which requires judges to apply *Hanafi fiqh* in the case of statutory lacuna, Article 2 of the Constitution, which defines *shari'a* as the principle source of legislation, and the case law (especially the Court of Cassation rulings), *hisba* remains a part of the Egyptian legal system. Moreover, as explained below, since the enactment of Law No. 3 of 1996 that regulates the use of *hisba* procedure in personal status cases, *hisba* has become an integral part of Egyptian law.

it in 1993 at the trial of the militant who killed Farag Foda – a secularist writer who was accused of blasphemy by al-Azhar – it was often believed that *shari'a* demanded the execution of a *murtadd*. "If the state fails to [carry out the death sentence]" al-Ghazali said in defense of Foda's killer, "and someone takes it upon himself to kill [the] apostate, then he is considered to have done what the government should have done [in the first place]" (Viorst 1998, p. 41). Such views calling for assassination of Egyptian secular intellectuals and glorification of violence against them were broadly circulated and popularized by extremist elements within Egyptian society in the mid-1990s. A *hisba* petition does not have to be presented in connection with personal status issues. However, the activists' exploitation of personal status laws in the *hisba* cases brought against such people as Abu Zayd, and later Nawal al-Sadaawi, should be analyzed against this background of rising extremism and violence. In this respect, the Islamist activists used the personal status system in connection with the principle of *hisba* to intimidate secularist forces and challenge and delegitimize the government by disclosing its alleged failure to fulfill its Islamic obligations – that is, to punish the *murtadd* – towards God and *umma* (the community of believers). As soon as this subversive and disruptive potential of *hisba* was realized, the Egyptian government immediately took action and passed the Law on Regulation of the Procedures of the Hisba in Personal Status Matters (Law No. 3 of 1996) in order to deprive the Islamist activists of such a valuable weapon by limiting their access to courts and ability to file *hisba* cases (Najjar 2000, pp. 191–192). The parliament declared the purpose of the law as being to "combat intellectual terrorism and protect intellectuals from attempts to inflict moral and psychological harm upon them ... [by] extremists" (Bälz 1997, p. 141).

According to the new law, any person who wishes to initiate a *hisba* case must first approach a public prosecutor with a petition. The public prosecutor shall then use his discretion to either forward the file to a personal status court, or deny it if the petitioner's claim is found to be unsubstantiated (Bernard-Maugiron 2004, p. 336). The purpose of Law No. 3 was to limit the number of *hisba* cases by enabling the public prosecutor to determine what constituted an infringement of "God's rights" (*huquq Allah*) (Sfeir 1998, pp. 413–414; Najjar 2000, p. 192). However, the law has not been very effective in limiting the number of *hisba* cases. For example in 2008 alone, more than 600 *hisba* cases were brought against writers, journalists and human rights activists (Mcgrath 2009). In response to the change in the law, Islamist groups have altered their tactics accordingly. For example in 2001 an Islamist lawyer, Nabih El-Wahsh, filed a *hisba* case against the prominent Egyptian feminist Nawal al-Sadaawi[20] and demanded her separation from her husband on grounds of apostasy. El-Wahsh bypassed the Office of the Public Prosecutor and directly filed his case in the personal status court (Dawoud 2001a, 2001b). As expected, however, the case was later rejected on technical grounds. Of course, El-Wahsh knew that his petition would be denied. But he still went ahead and filed the case in the belief that the public accusation of apostasy would give the Islamist movement an opportunity to further imbue the public space with religious narratives and discourses, discredit the "secular" regime and further intimidate secularist elements in society. In other words, Law No. 3 did not slow down or diminish the capacity of Islamist forces to bring apostasy charges. On the contrary, the enactment of Law No. 3 was a great achievement for the Islamist activists, who successfully forced the government to not only recognize the individual Muslim's right to *hisba*, but also incorporate this long forgotten principle of *shari'a* into modern-day Egyptian law (Sfeir 1998, p. 414; Agrama 2011). All in all, *hisba* cases brought against secular intellectuals by Islamic activists in connection with personal status matters have shown that legal ambiguities and loopholes created by Law No. 462 have not only created serious human rights implications, but also provided the Islamist opposition with a potent tool with which to challenge and discredit the government and terrorize secular forces in Egyptian society.

In personal status systems, individuals' religious affiliations single-handedly determine what set of rules should be applied in their case. As a result, changes in religious affiliation[21] are considered not a matter of personal conviction but of public policy. In particular, the renunciation of Islam (*ridda*) – as seen in Egypt – has serious repercussions on individuals' civil rights (Bälz 1997, p. 138; Hamad 1999, p. 224): it renders the marriage of an apostate null and void (*batil*), requires separation (*tafriq*) from his or her spouse, severs blood ties to his or her children and "prevents the apostate from entering into a new marriage, even with a non-Muslim" (Berger 2003, pp. 723–724). Moreover, an apostate will

---

[20] In April 2007, the head of al-Azhar, Sheikh Mohammad Sayyid Tantawi, publicly condemned Saadawi's recent play, *God Resigns at the Summit Meeting*, for allegedly offending Islam, and announced that '*ulama*' of al-Azhar were determined to bring another *hisba* case against Sadaawi (retrieved in April 2007 from www.indexonline.org/en/news/articles/2007/1/egypt-leading-woman-novelist-condemned-for-i.shtml).

[21] People who do not belong to a recognized community are subject to the law of the land, which is Islamic *shari'a*; see Pink (2003).

also relinquish his or her rights to inherit and bequeath (Berger 2003, p. 724). Although apostasy charges are usually brought to courts for political purposes, considering these ramifications on familial relations they may very well be used as a legal stratagem by conniving individuals who seek to separate a person from his or her spouse, deny legitimacy to siblings or offspring in paternity cases, or exclude certain relatives from an inheritance case (Hamad 1999, p. 227; Berger 2003, p. 724).

Escaping the remarriage ban: shopping for a legal forum in the market of faiths

Non-Muslim Egyptians also resort to similar tactics for legal gains in personal status courts. However, the tactic most commonly used by non-Muslim litigants is forum-shopping. For instance, it is not unusual to see a non-Muslim litigant converting from Christianity to Islam or migrating from one Christian denomination to another in pursuit of laws that would tip the scales in her favor in the court (Ziadeh 1968, pp. 106–113; Shaham 1995; Afifi 1996; Shaham 2006). As noted earlier, one of the motives behind Law No. 462 of 1955 was to end the practice of forum-shopping, which revolutionaries believed was responsible for the erosion of people's trust in the system of justice. Ironically, however, the law left the door wide open for forum-shopping by creating a number of incentives for non-Muslims to migrate between different denominations or convert to Islam in pursuit of legal gains.

In this regard, Articles 6 and 7 are particularly worthy of mention. Although these two Articles were abrogated along with Law No. 462 by Law No. 1 of 2000, the principles embodied in the Articles are still part of Egyptian legal culture and the case law. Egyptian Christians had been divided into twelve sects within three major rites.[22] With this in mind, Article 6 stipulated that non-Muslim couples who shared the same sect

---

[22] "(1) The Orthodox rite, divided into: Coptic, Greek, Armenian and Syrian sects; (2) the Catholic rite, divided into: Armenian, Syrian, Coptic (all three seceded from the Orthodox Church), Latin (or Greek-Catholic, from Lebanon), Maronites (from Lebanon), Chaldeans (from Iraq), and Roman sects; (3) the Protestant rite (which was mistakenly recognized as one sect by a governmental decree in 1850, and hence still retains the official status of a single sect, regardless of its subdivisions)" (Berger 2001, p. 97). These three Christian rites and twelve sects have a total of six personal status laws. While each sect within the Orthodox rite has its own personal status law, Catholics and Protestants, regardless of sectarian differences, are subject to a single law of their own rite. For example both a Greek Catholic and a Syriac Catholic would be governed by the same Catholic law, even though they belong to different sects. However under Law No. 462, Article 6, a union between a Greek Catholic and a Syriac Catholic would still be subject to Islamic law because the parties belong to different sects. In short, Law No. 462 did not concern itself with legal communities so much as ethno-religious divisions among the communities.

(*ta'ifa*) and rite (*milla*) would be subject to their own personal status law, provided that the application of non-Muslim law did not violate Egyptian public order (*al-nizam al-amm*).[23] If the parties did not belong to the same sect and rite, then they were subject to Islamic law. For example, a mixed marriage between an Orthodox Copt and a Catholic Copt or a Christian and a Jew would be subject to Islamic law. If the couple ever came before the family court for any reason (i.e., divorce, inheritance or maintenance), the judge would decide the case according to *shari'a*. In this regard, Article 6 was the first loophole created (intentionally or unintentionally) by Law No. 462 encouraging parties to change denominational affiliation whenever they deemed application of *shari'a* advantageous. The only limitation mentioned by the law was in Article 7, which provided that change of religious affiliation by a party during the course of litigation could not affect the proceedings unless the change was done in favor of Islam (Safran 1958, p. 21). Thus, Article 7 was the second loophole created by Law No. 462, actively encouraging non-Muslims to convert to Islam for the sake of legal gains even during the course of litigation.[24]

The most common reason for non-Muslims to change denominations is the difficulty of obtaining divorce under their personal status laws. In this regard, the greater availability of divorce under Islamic law has always offered an attractive option to both Christian men and women. For example, as the Court of Cassation has repeatedly maintained,[25] a Christian husband could exercise the right of unilateral, extrajudicial no-fault divorce (*talaq*), just like a Muslim husband, if he migrates to a denomination other than his wife's (Berger 2001, p. 121).[26] If he

---

[23] Berger argues that "although this practice may seem odd, there is a historical justification for it. Prior to 1956, all Jewish and Christian sects (with the exception of the Latin-Catholics) had their own courts and in order to avoid problems of conflicting jurisdiction, it was standard procedure for these courts to refer non-Muslim couples of different rite or sect to the *shari'a* court, which was competent to apply only Islamic law" (Berger 2001, p. 97). Hence the practice of referring couples of different sects and rites to Islamic law was continued by Law No. 462, even after the abolition of religious courts in 1955.

[24] The conversion of a non-Muslim Egyptian to Islam during the course of litigation might also require the replacement of any non-Muslim judge on the bench. I was repeatedly told by Egyptian lawyers and judges of an "unspoken rule" that non-Muslim judges are never assigned to a Muslim case because *shari'a* does not allow non-Muslims to exercise legal power (*wilaya*) over Muslims. For similar observations, see Berger (2001).

[25] Some of those rulings are: Court of Cassation, Case No. 36, 29th Judicial Year, February 6, 1963; Court of Cassation, Case No. 17, 43rd Judicial Year, November 5, 1975; and Court of Cassation, Case No. 68, 53rd Judicial Year, December 24, 1985. For further information, see Berger (2001, p. 121, n. 125).

[26] This brings another question to mind: whether a non-Muslim man could also be allowed to enter into polygynous marriage under Islamic law when he changes his confessional affiliation.

converts to Islam, his "payoff" will be even larger as he can both exercise *talaq* and contract polygynous marriages. Similarly, conversion to Islam can also be used as a legal stratagem by a non-Muslim wife in order to quickly eject herself from a deadlocked marriage. Since Islamic law prohibits a union between a non-Muslim man and Muslim woman, the marriage of a non-Muslim couple will become instantaneously null and void (*batil*) the moment the wife embraces Islam.

Deceptive conversions, carried out due to convenience rather than conviction, cause frictions among different religious communities and disrupt the stability within individual churches. The latter problem is particularly visible within the Coptic Orthodox community. For instance, a non-negligible number of Copts have converted to Islam or migrated to other Christian denominations due to the church's steadfast doctrinal position on divorce (Nazila 2005, p. 208). As mentioned earlier, the source of the problem is that the 1938 ordinance's liberal attitude towards divorce has been repeatedly denounced by the church, which allows divorce only on grounds of adultery. However, despite the church's refusal, family courts have continued to grant divorce decrees to Coptic Orthodox couples on grounds other than adultery in accordance with the 1938 ordinance. This duality, for instance, has put about 50,000 Coptic Orthodox divorcees in a position in which they could not remarry within the church after having been divorced by courts on grounds other than adultery (Shukri 1990; Ibrahim 2001).[27]

In this respect, as Coptic Orthodox scholar Mariz Tadros suggests, "the problem in the community has not been really about divorce but rather remarriage."[28] As already seen in Chapter 3, the denial of a person's right to remarry by religious authorities has grave consequences. Since there is no civil marriage in Egypt, a person who is denied a right to remarry will be permanently deprived of that right unless he or she converts to Islam or

---

Although the Court of Cassation declared in 1978 that a Christian husband was entitled to multiple wives (Court of Cassation, Case No. 104, 94th Judicial Year, March 21, 1978), the court later took a different approach in a similar case (Court of Cassation, Case Nos. 16 and 26, 48th Judicial Year, January 17, 1979) and announced that allowing a non-Muslim husband to contract polygynous marriages would irreparably damage the essential principles of Christian faith, thereby violating the Egyptian *al-nizam al-amm* (Spuler, 1980, p. 481; Edge, 1990, p. 48; Philipp, 1995, p. 146; Berger, 2001, pp. 118–119; Berger, 2004, pp. 355–357).

[27] In June 2010, an Egyptian court ordered the Coptic Orthodox Church to allow divorced Copts to remarry. Infuriated by the civil court's intervention in their domestic affairs, Pope Shenouda and members of the Holy Synod announced that "the Coptic Church respects the law, but does not accept rulings which are against the Bible ... The recent ruling is not acceptable to our conscience, and we cannot implement it." Moreover, the Pope said: "Let whoever wants to remarry to [sic] do it away from us. There are many ways and churches to marry in ... Whoever wants to remain within the church has to abide by its laws" (Abdelmassih 2010).

[28] Personal interview with Dr. Mariz Tadros (Cairo, April 2004).

migrates to another denomination that would first recognize the divorce granted by the civil court, and then allow him or her to remarry within his or her new faith.

The predicament of remarriage is also acknowledged by some members of the clergy. For example I was told by Father Ishaia Bibawy of St. Mark's Cathedral, the center of the Coptic Orthodox Patriarchate in Cairo,[29] that "people who are unable to remarry in the church could marry in another church ... which could be [for example] a Protestant church ... But once a person marries outside the church he cannot be a member of the communion anymore." Father Bibawy also told me that people who do not want to leave the church usually resort to another tactic:

> [When a person comes to us for permission to remarry] we will study the court's verdict. If the reason for divorce is adultery, we will give the permission to remarry [to the party who is not responsible for the breakdown of marriage due to his or her adulterous relationship]. If it is not adultery, [however,] many times they tell us that "I was shy; I could not say in the court that my wife committed *zina* [adultery] ... Because of that I lied and gave another reason to the judges." If we find the person's story convincing and his evidence credible, then we will [recognize the divorce, and] grant him the permission for remarriage ...

Opportunistic conversions have also caused frictions between different religious communities. The Coptic Orthodox Church is particularly unhappy about the fact that many Copts leave the church to divorce or remarry under the rules of another faith or denomination; thus it often accuses other churches of enticing its members with relaxed marriage and divorce rules. In addition, the leaders of Christian communities are also unhappy about application of *shariʿa* to Christians (Najjar 1992; Bernard-Maugiron 2003, pp. 339–395; Dupret 2003; Shahine 2007). Thus with these considerations in mind, leaders of all Christian communities, united under the leadership of the Coptic Orthodox Church, drafted a unified Christian Personal Status Law in 1978 (Barsoum 1981). The draft law harmonized the positions of different churches and recognized the possibility of divorce for non-Catholic couples only on the grounds of adultery and apostasy (Barsoum 1981). The main purpose of the draft law was to end the practice of applying Islamic law to Christian couples of different sects and rites, and avoid the problems caused by

---

[29] Personal interview with Father Ishaia Bibawy (Cairo, May 2004).

people migrating between churches in pursuit of legal gains. In 1980, the draft law was submitted to the Ministry of Justice to be further studied and eventually brought to the parliament for a vote. However, the Egyptian government constantly ignored the Christian leaders' cries for reform and shelved the draft law indefinitely. Although in the late 1990s the project was revived by the Coptic Orthodox Church and resubmitted to the government for approval, Egyptian authorities once again chose to remain oblivious to the demands of the Christian communities and indefinitely shelved the proposed law (Guindy, Shukrallah *et al.* 1999; Ibrahim 2001). In the words of a former member of the committee that prepared the draft law:

> The government does not want to see the Christians unified. They want us weak and divided. The reason . . . why they refuse to approve the draft law is because they want to impose *shari'a* upon Christians . . . All judges [at the Personal Status Courts] are Muslims. They do not know the Christian law. They are happy to apply *shari'a* [to Christians] and grant divorces [as freely as they wish] to Christians . . .[30]

In sum, despite its intentions, Law No. 462 of 1955 failed to eliminate forum-shopping and divest religious authorities of their juridical powers completely. First, as seen in the context of divorce and remarriage in the Coptic Orthodox Church, individuals have continued to migrate from one community to another in pursuit of legal gains, which has undermined the government's efforts to establish a systematized judicial system free of such structural loopholes as forum-shopping. Second, the clergy have continued to exercise a great degree of authority over marital affairs by determining whose divorce shall be recognized as "valid" and who shall be granted permission to remarry. As shown, this has had dire implications for the rights and liberties of Christian Egyptians. Next, I demonstrate how Muslim Egyptians cope with similar limitations imposed by Muslim law, how they navigate the system, and what tactics they use in order to advance their rights and freedoms under the state-enforced religious laws.

Whose word is law? Women redefine *shari'a* to advance their right to divorce

The Egyptian government's unwillingness or lack of interest in introducing even limited substantive changes to its personal status system has

---

[30] Personal interview (Cairo, May 2004). Informant declined to be identified.

had serious implications for Egyptian women's rights, particularly in the field of divorce. Under the law, a Muslim man has a right to unilateral no-fault extra-judicial divorce known as *talaq*. The husband, who can have up to four wives, can divorce his wife anytime for any reason without a need to appear before the court, by pronouncing *talaq* three times. The Muslim woman, on the other hand, has only been given truncated rights to "judicial" divorce (*tatliq*), through which she can ask the court to dissolve her marriage on grounds of harm or injury (*darar*) (Esposito and Delong-Bas 2001, pp. 27–34, 49–61). For example, under certain conditions (e.g., husband's sexual incompetence, prolonged absence or imprisonment of husband, etc.)[31] in which *darar* to the wife by the husband is satisfactorily established through evidence and at least two witnesses, the judge may dissolve the marriage at the request of the wife. However, unlike *talaq*, *tatliq* is a painful and costly process. It takes on average eight to ten years for a woman to obtain a divorce through the courts (Sachs 2000; Leila 2003b; Singerman 2005, pp. 165–166). Moreover, women also have to tackle bureaucratic hassles[32] through the country's overworked court system and win over the hearts and minds of male judges[33] who are reportedly more sympathetic to the causes and interests of men than those of women (Sachs 2000; Leila 2003b; Singerman 2005, pp. 165–166).

---

[31] Other grounds for divorce are: husband's failure to provide maintenance (*nafaqa*); contagious or dangerous disease of the husband; and the husband's maltreatment of his wife (Karam 1998, p. 148; Nassar 1999, pp. 198–202; Esposito and Delong-Bas 2001, p. 51).

[32] Prior to the establishment of specialized Family Courts in October 2004, women had to shuttle between different types of court where each court was authorized to hear different types of case such as divorce, alimony and child custody. This had been one of the major reasons why the finalization of divorce cases took so long. Hence, in order to remedy the problem, the new Family Courts were designed as "One Stop Centers" that decide all marital disputes in an effective and speedy manner (Leila 2003b, 2003a). However, Al-Sharmani reports that nearly five years after their formation, the performance of Family Courts has been, at best, equivocal. Their effectiveness, she argues, has been diminished by such problems as legislative gaps, procedural shortcomings and lack of effective implementation mechanisms (Al-Sharmani 2010).

[33] All Egyptian judges have been male until recently. In 2003, Dr. Tahani El Gebali was appointed to the Supreme Constitutional Court as Egypt's first ever female judge. In a follow-up move, in March 2007, the government appointed thirty-one new female judges to different courts of first instance in Cairo, Giza and Alexandria. These appointments were fiercely criticized by conservative groups within the Egyptian judiciary and in Egyptian society who wanted to permanently bar women from holding judicial positions. In March 2010, however, the Supreme Constitutional Court, responding to a request by the government to interpret a statutory provision regulating the appointment of judges, ruled that the pertinent legislation had granted both men and women equal rights to assume judicial positions and thereby further opened the door to appointment of female judges across the Egyptian legal system. Despite the court's gender-equalizing interpretation in 2010, however, at the time of writing, of about 12,000 Egyptian judges only 42 were women. For further information, see www.muslimwomennews.com/n.php?nid=5690 (accessed in October 2012).

Improving women's rights to divorce by reforming personal status laws that had been left almost unchanged since the 1920s had long been on the agenda of Egyptian women's organizations (Bibars 1987, pp. 26–41; Howard-Merriam 1988; Badran 1995). The long-awaited change came in 1979 with Law No. 44, which stipulated that taking a second wife without the consent of the first wife constituted an injury (*darar*) to the first wife, and therefore entitled her to seek a divorce from the court within twelve months of her learning of the husband's second marriage. Law No. 44, which was unconstitutionally promulgated by a presidential decree, was a major step for improvement of women's rights to divorce. However, it did not take long for opponents of Law No. 44, who viewed the new law as in violation of *shari'a* for curbing Muslim men's "god-given" right to polygyny, to launch a judicial onslaught to stop its implementation. In May 1985, the efforts of these opponents finally came to fruition when *al-Mahkamah al-Dusturiyyah al-'Ulya*, the Supreme Constitutional Court (Case No. 28, 2nd Judicial Year, May 4, 1985), declared Law No. 44 unconstitutional on technical grounds (Eldin, Hill *et al.* 1985). Two months later, a revised personal status law (Law No. 100) was hastily put together by the parliament as a replacement which eliminated the controversial provision of Law No. 44 that "considered a second marriage by the husband as *ipso facto* a cause of harm to the first wife" (Najjar 1988, p. 341) and thereby grounds for divorce.

The failure of the 1979 law taught two invaluable lessons to Egyptian women's rights groups intent on reforming personal status laws: First, the reform had to be initiated *by* the women themselves through a combination of grassroots mobilization and government support, rather than *for* the women through unpopular top-down processes (Hatem 1992). Second, and more importantly, any change in the law had to be firmly rooted in historical sources and the tradition of *shari'a*. Otherwise, as evidenced in the case of Law No. 44, a solely liberal or secular approach would backfire and do more harm than good to the cause of Egyptian women. As one prominent feminist put it, throughout the 1990s Egyptian women's groups adopted the "strategy of engaging religious discourse, based on the women's reading of their rights under the principles of *shari'a*" (Singerman 2005, p. 161). Hence, the setback experienced in 1985 led some women's groups to engage in Islamic hermeneutics through feminist and liberal lenses, and campaign for equal rights by utilizing a religious framework.

With this in mind, in the next twenty years, women's groups devoted their energy to two major projects: (1) the New Marriage Contract; and

(2) the 2000 Khul' Law. The first project aimed to draft a new marriage contract (*aqd al-zawaj*) that would enable women to stipulate conditions, including the right to seek divorce automatically in the event of a husband's violation of his contractual obligations (*yad al-'isma*) (Karam 1998, pp. 145–146; Shaham 1999). Even though the project was later abrogated by its sponsors, many of its provisions were incorporated into a new marriage contract prepared by the Ministry of Justice in June 2000 (Zulficar 1999; El-Kholy 2002, pp. 119–120; Singerman 2005, p. 175). In practice, *yad al-'isma* is very rarely exercised, as most couples shy away from stipulating such conditions.[34] Due to prevailing patriarchal dispositions and stereotypes, it is usually considered socially unacceptable for a husband to forfeit his exclusive right to divorce by permitting his wife to stipulate such conditions in the marital contract. For example, one Caireen marriage registrar (*maazoun*), who reports to have seen no single marriage contract in which the woman had stipulated her right to divorce during his nearly fifteen years in office, is of the opinion that "no man who deserves to be called a man can accept this: a woman to decide for him or to divorce him" (Ezzat 2000, p. 43).

Another major project that women's organizations devoted their time and energy to was Law No. 1 of 2000, or the so-called Khul' Law (Nagib 2003, pp. 105–116). The new law (Article 20) allows the woman to initiate a no-fault divorce even without the consent of the husband, provided that she returns the "prompt dower" (*mahr al-muajjal*) given by the groom at the time of marriage (*nikah*) and forfeits her claims to maintenance (*nafaqa*), compensation (*mata*),[35] and "deferred dower" (*mu'akhar al-sadaq*) that the husband is required by law to pay his wife at divorce.[36] Throughout the process that culminated in the enactment

---

[34] "Information published by the Central Agency for Mobilization and Statistics (CAMPAS) in 1998 revealed that only 35,000 women out of over 18 million of marriageable age had claimed the right of *yad al-'isma*, and these were mostly highly educated women living in affluent suburbs of Cairo and Alexandria" (Ezzat 2000, p. 43).

[35] "Since 1985 (Article 18 bis 1), the wife is entitled to have financial compensation, the amount of which should not be less than two years of maintenance, and is evaluated according to the husband's financial means, and the length of the marriage. The compensation is only due if the marriage was broken without the wife's consent and without her being responsible for it" (Bernard-Maugiron and Dupret 2008, p. 58, n. 20).

[36] Unlike *talaq*, *khul'* divorces are irrevocable in the sense that the husband cannot reinstate his wife at his own will. Moreover, according to Law No. 1, *khul'* decrees are also final and cannot be appealed. In 2002, the constitutionality of the law was challenged in front of the Supreme Constitutional Court (Case No. 201, 23rd Judicial Year, December 15, 2002) for it did not grant individuals the right to appeal *khul'* decisions. However, the court upheld Law No. 1, arguing that the legislature had a right to promulgate laws whose rulings could not be appealed, if there was a justification for this prohibition (Tadros 2002a; Moussa 2011, pp. 159–160).

of Law No. 1, women's groups worked directly with government officials, lobbied the members of the parliament and consulted with *'ulama'* at al-Azhar. As Professor Zeinab Redwan, a female member of the Egyptian Parliament and one of the architects of Law No. 1 noted, "[during the entire process] women repeatedly resorted to the Islamic rhetoric and built their case around a *hadith* that reported Prophet Muhammad allowing a woman to divorce her husband by returning the orchard that she had received as dower."[37]

Although proponents considered the Khul' Law "a historical achievement for equalizing women's rights to those of men in termination of marital contract,"[38] critics viewed it as a failure for two reasons. First, they argued that the law contradicted *shari'a* by granting the wife a right to unilateral divorce and failing to require the husband's consent to the dissolution of the marital union (Al-Goumhouria 2000; Al-Hayat 2000; Al-Shaab 2000a, 2000b; Al-Wafd 2000a, 2000b, 2000c; Tadros 2000, 2002b). Second, they claimed that the law was only meant for rich women, as the poor could not afford to forgo their right to maintenance, compensation and deferred dower, and neither could they pay back the prompt dower. Right at this point, the opponents of Law No. 1 were joined by Human Rights Watch (HRW), which not only considered Law No. 1 insufficient to end gender discrimination in family laws, but also argued that due to the requirement to forfeit claims to future financial support, *khul'* divorce was only "limited to women with significant financial resources" (Deif 2004, p. 48).[39]

However, recent studies show that a fair number of middle- and lower-class women have since taken advantage of *khul'* divorce, as the actual cost of obtaining *khul'* has not been as high as was claimed by the critics (Sakr and Hakim 2001; Zulficar 2004; Singerman 2005; Sonneveld 2007). For instance, a woman[40] who had obtained a divorce in Alexandria reported

---

[37] Personal interview with Professor Zeinab Radwan (Cairo, May 2004).

[38] Personal interview with Mona Zulficar, a lawyer and a prominent member of the coalition that steered the reform process (Cairo, May 2004).

[39] Professor Diane Singerman, a prominent scholar of Egyptian politics and legal studies, is of the opinion that "the HRW report dismissed the reforms because they used an Islamic framework and due to the obvious leftist/secular/liberal critique of this strategy . . . [At the same time] the HRW report on divorce failed to address the political environment of Egypt where Islamists are quite powerful and many Egyptians consider Islamic precedents important. Frankly, I thought the HRW report was quite unfair and dismissive of the efforts of Egyptian women to make even a small change because it was not what HRW would consider the correct approach, but that approach had failed to make any progress for about a hundred years!" (e-mail correspondence with Professor Singerman, March 28, 2007).

[40] Personal interview (Alexandria, May 2004). Informant declined to be identified.

that the court had required her to pay back only EGP 1 to her husband in order to obtain a divorce, as this is how much her *mahr* was according to the marriage contract. In fact, as Sonneveld (2007) reports, it is a very common practice for Egyptian couples to include a symbolic amount as *mahr* in their marriage contract, while grooms are traditionally expected to furnish their brides with *shabka* (jewelry, gifts of gold) and various other gifts that are not recorded in the contract (Singerman and Ibrahim 2003). Thus, women seeking *khul'* mainly need to forfeit their claims to maintenance or *nafaqa* during the *iddat* period – usually three menstrual cycles or until the end of pregnancy – and *mu'akhar al-sadaq* or deferred dower. As a recent study shows, many lower- and middle-class women make that sacrifice to buy their way out of unhappy marriages (Sonneveld 2007).

On the other hand, most of the problems that women have encountered seem to be of a social or institutional nature. Public opinion surveys point out that most Egyptians consider *khul'* as an option to be taken only by "loose" Westernized women (Bahgory 1999; Hassan 2001; Sakr and Hakim 2001; Fawzy 2004; Halim, Al-Bahth *et al.* 2005). In popular culture (e.g., movies, cartoons, etc.), the women who resort to *khul'* are often depicted as immoral persons in Westernized garments who divorce their husbands for frivolous reasons just to run to the arms of their secret lovers (Sonneveld 2006). In particular, men overwhelmingly view it as a dishonorable and degrading practice. As a male personal status lawyer told me,[41] "an honorable man should never accept to be rejected or divorced unilaterally by his wife ... when a man whose wife filed for a *khul'* comes to me, I only say, 'act like a man, divorce [*talaq*] her yourself'." In the early years of the reform, these negative images were also widespread among personal status court judges (Singerman 2005, pp. 181–182). Judges who were opposed to the *khul'* provision of Law No. 1 have often acted *ultra vires* to derail the application of the law. For instance, Azza Soliman, the Director of the Center for Egyptian Women's Legal Assistance (CEWLA), notes that judges who oppose the law have inflated the figures women need to pay back to their husbands (Tadros 2002b). Similarly, during my field research, I came across personal status judges who not only referred to women who filed for *khul'* as "*sharmoota*" (slang for slut), but also misinterpreted the law and told women that in addition to prompt dower they would need to pay back *shabka* and deferred dower, in order to dissuade women from exercising a right they considered "immoral." In fact, some women's rights activists attribute the discrepancy between the

---

[41] Personal interview (Cairo, June 2004). Informant declined to be identified.

number of *khul*[42] petitions filed and the actual number of *khul*[42] decrees
granted by the courts to the unwillingness and obstructive practices of
the judges and other court officials.[43] Even more than ten years after Law
No. 1 came into force, *khul* divorces represent, on an annual basis, no
more than 3 percent of divorce decrees granted by Egyptian courts.[44]

Lastly, Law No. 1 has also opened the door to no-fault divorce for
Christian women. As mentioned above, a Christian wife can resort to
Muslim personal status laws by simply moving out of her husband's
denomination. In fact, some Christian women have been granted *khul*
divorces by the courts after they migrated to a denomination other
than their husband's. Although the Coptic Orthodox Church has consistently resented the application of *khul* to Christian couples, some
consider it as an opportunity for the empowerment of Christian women
vis-à-vis the traditional and patriarchal institutions within the community (Hasan 2003; Tadros 2009). For example, I was told that some
women now threaten the church and communal institutions by saying, "If
you do not give me a divorce, I will take it through *khul*."[45] Apparently,
the increasing availability of *khul* has also changed the attitude of some
clergy-members and caused schisms in the church (Fouad 2002). A Copt
woman who recently converted to the Syrian Orthodox Church and
filed for *khul* told me that she was actually advised by a Coptic Orthodox
priest, who sympathized with her predicament, to change her sectarian
affiliation and apply for a *khul* divorce.[46]

Although the exact number of Christian women who have obtained
khul remains unknown, it must be noted that *khul* does not always furnish
Christian women with a guaranteed means of exit from an unhappy
marriage. Perhaps the main reason is that the Egyptian judiciary remains

---

[42] For example, it is reported that in the Cairo Governorate, only 4.5 percent of the *khul* applications
filed between March 2000 and March 2001 were actually ruled by the personal status courts. The
same rate in the same period was 6.9 percent for the courts of Giza Governorate (Al-Sawi 2002,
pp. 20, 24).

[43] Regarding court officials' obstructive practices, Al-Sharmani demonstrates that specialists (e.g.,
social workers, psychologists and mediators), who are now part of the arbitration process at new
Family Courts, often advise women against exercising their right to *khul* due to their negative
attitudes towards this type of divorce (Al-Sharmani 2009, pp. 101–103).

[44] Even though the Arab Republic of Egypt, Central Agency for Public Mobilization and Statistics
provides divorce statistics, it does not report any information regarding the number of *khul*'
decrees awarded by the courts (retrieved in April 2012 from www.msrintranet.capmas.gov.
eg/pls/census/spart_all_e?lname=FREE&lang=0). Thus nearly all information on the number
of *khul* divorces is based on anecdotal evidence offered by judges, lawyers and activists; see, for
instance, Mourad (2012).

[45] Personal interview with Dr. Mariz Tadros (Cairo, April 2004).

[46] Personal interview with a Coptic Orthodox woman who declined to be identified (Cairo,
May 2004).

deeply divided over the question of whether non-Muslims should be able to obtain *khul'* divorces by resorting to opportunistic conversions (El-Alami 2001–2002; Fouad 2002). In this regard, the Mona Halim and Hala Sidqi cases (2002) are particularly instructive. While the judge in the Mona Halim case refused to issue a *khul'* on grounds that it contradicted the dogmas and teachings of Christianity, two weeks later another judge saw no problems in granting a *khul'* to Hala Sidqi, a well-known actress who changed her denomination to Syrian Orthodox while her husband remained in the Coptic Orthodox Church (Shehab 2002b, 2002a). When I asked Mohamed Hamed El-Gamal, the former President of *Maglis al-Dawla* (The Council of State), about these two high-profile cases, he said:

> I am with the first judge, because *khul'* is against Christianity. As a judge, I cannot make a ruling against the public order (*al-nizam al-amm*). This is the public order of the Christian community. The judge must respect it. Hence, I believe that the judge in the Hala Sidqi case is wrong. This is both politically and judicially a very dangerous decision. It creates an unnecessary tension between the Muslim and Christian communities . . . Very dangerous . . . [However,] there are some judges who are politically oriented. They are inspired by the ideas of such people as Ibn Taymiyyah [a thirteenth- to fourteenth-century Islamic thinker]. And they are the ones who create this tension . . . [However,] the moment you do that you are a political man, not a judge anymore.[47]

In sum, Egyptian women's groups resenting the male-dominated political and religious institutions' negligence of women's rights under the personal status system have become increasingly vocal after the Supreme Constitutional Court struck down Law No. 44 in 1985. In the next two decades, groups and individuals who were well-versed in international women's rights language and the repertoire of emerging feminist and liberal discourses played a pivotal role in translating women's demands into an Islamic language that resonated with mainstream Egyptian society (Sezgin 2012b). In doing so, they not only reinterpreted the classical sources of *shari'a*, but also reinvented the legal traditions of Islam and directly challenged the hermeneutic authority of the state and nationalized religious institutions (e.g., al-Azhar), as well as the ruling ideology that upheld the current personal status system for decades. As women have increasingly confronted the state and religious

---

[47] Personal interview with Mohamed Hamed El-Gamal, the former President of *Maglis al-Dawla* (The Council of State) (Cairo, May 2004).

authorities, which for many years remained oblivious to their demands, the question has arisen over whose words were law and who was qualified to speak for Islam: the state, the *'ulama'* or the women?

CONCLUSION

Like Israel, Egypt also inherited a fragmented confessional system from the Ottoman Empire. Unlike Israel, however, the Egyptian leaders abolished the religious courts and unified them under a network of national courts in 1955. The 1955 reform did not involve the abolition of communal laws and replacement of them with a uniform civil code that would be applicable to all Egyptians throughout the country. In other words, the Nasserist regime merely confined itself to institutional unification and refrained from making an accompanying normative intervention into its system. As argued, the reason for that was the technocratic-authoritarian nature of the Nasserist regime. Unlike its Israeli and Indian counterparts, the Egyptian government was not motivated by such ideological considerations as creating an exclusionary, inclusionary or secular society and institutions. Rather, it was moved by mechanical considerations such as to subordinate religious groups and institutions to the will of the regime, rationalize the justice administration, divest religious authorities of their juridical powers and reclaim the sovereignty of the nation by terminating "non-state" jurisdictions.

The Egyptian government has not only refrained from normative reform, but also shown a conservative attitude towards substantive reform. As noted above, in particular the Egyptian marital laws were left almost unchanged for nearly seven decades from the late 1920s until 2000 when Law No. 1 was enacted. The government's avoidance of substantive reform in pluri-legal personal status laws, which were now applied by civil court judges, had serious implications for fundamental rights and liberties of Egyptian citizens. As explained through analyses of the so-called remarriage crisis within the Coptic Orthodox community, in which individuals were often compelled to change their religious affiliations to be able to remarry, and the Muslim women's predicament of divorce, Egyptian citizens' personal status-related concerns have borne a striking resemblance to those of Israeli citizens who also often travelled abroad to escape marriage-related disabilities at home, and resorted to hermeneutic means to overcome divorce-related limitations of the state-enforced personal status laws. Though what was unique in Egypt was the innovative use of the personal status system in connection with the *hisba* principle by the Islamist groups, who exploited the procedural loopholes of the Egyptian legal system to intimidate secular intellectuals and discredit the regime. If viewed as a question of "who is a Muslim?" the apostasy issue in Egypt, discussed above, was not very different from the ubiquitous question of "who is a Jew?" in Israel. But unlike in Israel, these very questions in Egypt have carried potentially life-threatening implications for individuals who were accused of heresy (remember that Professor Abu Zayd had to flee Egypt after threats to his life), besides their effects on political, civil and social rights.

As in Israel, Egyptians too have responded to the challenge of living under state-enforced religious laws by adopting various resistance strategies. They forum-shopped, established hermeneutic communities and challenged the state and nationalized religious institutions' hermeneutic monopoly in order to escape limitations and disabilities. Challenges to the system also came from Islamist activists who brought *hisba* petitions to personal status courts, as well as the members of Christian clergy who persistently contested the legitimacy and form of Christian law applied by the state courts. Like in the case of the Israeli *millet* system, forces which constantly challenged and engaged with the Egyptian personal status system played a catalytic role in continuous remaking of the system. In this respect, the field of human rights in Egypt has also become a site of resistance and served as a litmus test for assessing the performance of the 1955 reform. In this regard, the exploitation of the personal status system by Islamist activists in order to discredit the regime, the clergy's continued exercise of de facto juridical authority over matters of divorce and remarriage, the persistence of such practices as forum-shopping, and the struggle of various hermeneutic communities to redefine state-imposed religious laws have indicated that the 1955 reform has only partially succeeded in attaining its intended goals.

As heretofore shown in the cases of Israel and Egypt, both countries inherited the same *millet* system from the Ottomans. Differing regime choices and differing configurations of state–community relations in each country gave rise to two distinct personal status systems: fragmented confessional in Israel and unified confessional in Egypt. Nonetheless, as the preceding chapters have shown, the type of personal status system does not seem to have a considerable effect on the magnitude of human rights violations occurring in either of the two nations. In other words, it is not possible to conclude that one type of personal status system is more or less favorable to human rights than another. On the contrary, despite socio-political and historical differences between the two nations, their

157

personal status systems seem to have affected the rights and liberties of their citizens in a strikingly similar way. In the next chapter, I examine unified semi-confessional personal status systems in regard to India, and call into question whether India, a secular regime, has done a better job than Israel or Egypt in protecting its citizens against the encroachments of state-enforced personal status laws.

6

A UNIFIED SEMI-CONFESSIONAL SYSTEM: STATE-ENFORCED RELIGIOUS FAMILY LAWS AND HUMAN RIGHTS IN INDIA

When India gained its independence in 1947, its leaders found already in place a unified confessional system – like that of Egypt – under which the personal laws of Hindus, Muslims, Christians, Sikhs, Buddhists, Jains and Parsis were directly applied by secularly trained Anglo-Indian judges at civil courts. With the promulgation of the 1950 constitution, this system of personal law was formally acquired and integrated into the legal system of the new state. However, as the framers of the constitution hinted at in Articles 44 and 372, the continuance of colonial institutions and practices of personal law was initially viewed as an interim measure until the enactment of a new civil code that would apply to all Indians irrespective of religion.[1]

The inhabitants of India had historically been divided into various castes, factions and tribal and ethno-religious groups. These communal divisions, which were further institutionalized and reinforced under British colonial rule, reached their climax in 1947 when the country was finally partitioned into two independent states along ethno-religious lines: Pakistan for Muslims, and India for Hindus. Yet the founders of India fiercely resisted the British plans for partition on the basis of religion, and maintained their position even after the undesired partition had been imposed upon them against their will. They strongly believed that independent India, unlike its twin sister Pakistan, had to

---

[1] As noted in the Introduction, Indian personal laws (Hindu, Muslim, etc.) do not apply to the following territories and populations: the State of Jammu and Kashmir, Goa, the enclaves of Daman and Diu on the Arabian Sea coast, and scheduled tribes or indigenous populations.

be a non-communal, secular and democratic nation, in which all citizens were treated equally regardless of their communal or religious identity.[2] In other words, India was not to become a "Hindu" state the way Pakistan was declared an Islamic state. Thus, the founders of India aimed to create a secular and inclusionary regime under which an individual's religion or lack thereof was to play no role in defining his or her membership in the political community.

The Indian leaders, such as Nehru and Ambedkar, who were devout believers in the homogenizing and unifying powers of modern law, considered the colonial institutions of personal law as one of the main factors that nurtured communalist sentiments and prevented the people of India from attaining a common sense of unity. Hence, they believed that, if India had to be one composite nation under the law, then the colonial institutions of personal law had to be abolished and replaced with a secular Uniform Civil Code (UCC) that would be applicable to all persons irrespective of caste or religion. This desire of the founding elite was embodied in Article 44 of the 1950 Constitution: "The state shall endeavor to secure for the citizens a uniform civil code throughout the territory of India."

Today, more than sixty years after Article 44 found its way into the constitution, India still does not have a common code applicable to all of its citizens. In other words, India, a socialist, secular and democratic republic, continues to see its judges administer state-sanctioned religious and customary laws and apply different sets of laws to people with different ethno-religious backgrounds, despite its constitutional obligation to treat everyone equally before the law (Article 14) and not to discriminate on the basis of religion, caste or sex (Article 15). In this respect, the leading questions that the present chapter addresses are: why the Indian leaders allowed the continuation of personal laws despite their earlier desires to do away with them and enact a UCC in their place; how they reconciled the apparent paradox of administering

---

[2] Although there were some differences among early Congress leaders (i.e., Gandhi, Nehru, Patel, Prasad) regarding how the new state should relate to religion, particularly Hinduism, they were predominantly of the opinion that independent India, unlike Pakistan, should be a non-communal, secular and democratic nation in which all citizens would be treated equally regardless of their ethno-religious identities. For instance, Sardar V. Patel, the first Home Minister and Deputy Prime Minister of India said in 1950: "Ours is a secular state. We cannot fashion our politics or shape our conduct in the way Pakistan does it. We must see that our secular ideals are actually realized in practice. Here every Muslim should feel that he is an Indian citizen and has equal rights as an Indian citizen" (Chandra, Mukherjee et al. 1999, p. 78).

religious laws as a secular regime; and how the persistence of state-enforced religious laws has affected the rights and freedoms of Indian citizens.

In the following pages, I assert that the founding elite's decision not to pursue the goal of UCC, embodied in Article 44, can be explained partly by their unwillingness to further alienate the Muslim minority in the aftermath of partition or desire to accommodate its religio-legal and cultural demands, and partly by their inability to overcome the muscular opposition of the Muslim community to the idea of UCC. Instead, the Indian leaders carried out a limited version of the wholesale normative unification that they had originally envisaged by unifying the personal laws of Hindus, Sikhs, Buddhists and Jains through the Hindu Code Bill (HCB) reforms of 1955–1956. This transformed the centralized confessional system inherited from the British into a unified semi-confessional system under which Muslims, Christians and Parsis have continued to be governed by their own communal laws while the rest of the population has been governed by Hindu law, which was codified into four separate laws and, on paper, has been uniformly applied throughout the national territory. Besides the normative unification attempt of 1955–1956, the Indian government, particularly since the 1970s, has also pushed for partial convergence and harmonization of separate communal laws, especially in regard to postnuptial maintenance and divorce.

In terms of the effects of Indian personal laws on the rights and freedoms of individuals who are subject to their jurisdiction, like the state-enforced religious laws in Israel and Egypt they have often imposed marriage, divorce, post-nuptial maintenance and inheritance-related disabilities, particularly upon the rights of Muslim and Hindu women. Despite such similarities with Israel and Egypt, however, India stands apart from the former two countries, because unlike them, it claims to give its citizens an optional secular code of marriage and divorce (the SMA of 1954), and theoretically allows them to opt out of religious laws and use secular laws at their own will, and freely contract interfaith marriages. Principally speaking, the mere existence of the SMA attests to not only the inclusionary and secular characteristics of the Indian regime but also its different vision and notion of family and nation that sets India clearly apart from the Israeli and Egyptian cases. However, at this point, the real question is whether the availability of such secular remedies as the SMA of 1954 or Section 125 of the Cr. PC of 1973 has actually provided Indian citizens with a viable exit option: protecting their rights and freedoms against potential encroachments of state-enforced religious laws and making them better off than their counterparts under the Israeli or Egyptian personal status systems. In order to answer this very question, I analyze the Indian Supreme Court's 1985 *Shah Bano* judgment and the ensuing political and legal developments, as well as the position and responses of various actors (e.g., women's groups, communal organizations, courts, etc.) in respect of the so-called crisis of post-nuptial maintenance in the Muslim community, and utilize them as a litmus test to find out whether the Indian government was able to achieve the political objectives that its rulers had aimed to achieve through their interventions; and if it was, as a secular and democratic regime, able to stand by its secular promises and protect individual citizens against threats and encroachment of their cultural communities when they opted for secular or civil remedies in lieu of personal laws. In brief, I argue the Indian government has fallen short not only of fully achieving the goals that some of its earlier rulers aimed to achieve through their interventions, but also providing Indians with a viable secular option (because these remedies are often ineffective or unavailable to the average citizen) and sufficiently protecting them against threats when they wanted to take advantage of state-guaranteed secular remedies.

The chapter is divided into three sections. First, I briefly summarize the history and current state of the Indian personal law system by specifically looking at the laws of Hindu and Muslim communities. Second, I analyze the inclusionary and secular proclivities of the founding elite and framers of the constitution to understand motivations that led them to insert Article 44 into the 1950 Constitution. In the same section, I also explain why the founding leaders of India, despite their strong initial desire, had not been able to bring about a common civil code, and how they modified their strategies and instead pursued a limited version of their earlier plans for wholesale normative unification. In the last section, I demonstrate how the decision of the Indian government not to pursue the goal of UCC, and its persistent unwillingness (or inability) to undertake substantive reform in the personal laws of the Muslim community, have affected the rights and freedoms of Indian Muslims, especially those of women. The last section also evaluates the Indian state's performance as a "secular" regime in attaining its political objectives, and protecting the rights of its individual citizens who exit from their natal, normative communities and instead opt for secular remedies guaranteed by the state against the potential encroachments and threats of their cultural communities and institutions.

I. THE INDIAN PERSONAL LAW SYSTEM

The personal law system before and after independence

Under British rule, the government courts, staffed with Anglo-Indian common law justices – particularly since the ousting of native law officers in 1864 – directly applied different bodies of religious and customary laws to Indian subjects in matters of marriage, divorce, maintenance and succession, provided that the application of these laws did not contravene "natural justice, equity and good conscience" (Derrett 1963). The material laws courts applied were largely based upon what came to be known as Anglo-Hindu and Anglo-Mohammedan case law – primarily inspired by English common law justices' interpretations of Hindu and Muslim laws – as well as local customs and the statutes[3] enacted by the colonial administration (Derrett 1961; Rocher 1972; Derrett 1999, pp. 311–313; Jain 2003, pp. 580–651; Saxena 2003, pp. 56–57). Hence, when India gained its independence in 1947, it found already in place a system in which different bodies of largely unwritten religious and customary laws were directly applied by an overarching network of civil courts throughout the national territory. For those who desired a uniform system of law, the next logical step was to achieve complete normative unification by abolishing different bodies of communal laws and replacing them with a UCC that would be applicable to all citizens regardless of ethno-religious or caste distinctions.

This desire of the founders of India was embodied in Article 44 of the 1950 Constitution, which directs the state "to secure for the citizens a uniform civil code throughout the territory of India" (Nigam 1966; Raju 2003). For reasons I will elaborate later, to date the Indian state has not introduced a UCC or normatively unified its personal law system. Nonetheless, the Indian leaders significantly reduced the normative plurality of their legal system when the parliament passed what are

---

[3] Officially speaking, the British adopted a policy of "non-intervention" in religious and customary practices and actively refrained from introducing any major changes in the personal laws of their Indian subjects. However, as Cohn (1996, p. 71) and Sturman (2005, p. 614) indicate, this policy was largely a symbolic claim frequently used by the colonial state to gain legitimacy among the local populations; in practice the British regularly adjudicated and legislated on family matters, especially property- and inheritance-related matters. In addition, the colonial administration passed some "corrective" and "ameliorative" legislation in response to strong pressure and calls for reform from various local communities. These statutes include HWRA of 1856, which legalized the remarriage of Hindu widows, and DMMA of 1939, which expanded Muslim women's right to judicial divorce (Derrett 1961; Mahmood 2002, p. 47; Menski 2003, pp. 156–185).

collectively known as the HCB Acts in 1955–1956,[4] which significantly codified and unified the personal laws of Hindus, Sikhs, Jains and Buddhists (Ahmad 1949; Tope and Ursekar 1950; Banningan 1952; Ray 1952). The HCB Acts defined adherents of Hinduism as well as Sikhism, Jainism and Buddhism as "Hindus" for the purposes of personal law (Derrett 1999, pp. 46–55). In other words, with the passage of the HCB Acts, the personal laws of the latter three communities were declared *de jure* nonexistent and inapplicable, as their adherents were, by force of law, now brought under the purview of Hindu law.[5]

Apart from their intent to reduce the normative plurality in the field of personal status, the HCB Acts also secularized and codified the traditional sources of Hindu law to a significant extent. To give an example, even though Hindu marriage had been traditionally described as a *samskara* (sacrament), the HMA of 1955, departing from ancient sources of Hindu law, allowed either spouse to seek dissolution of marriage on certain grounds.[6] Furthermore, the new law also prohibited bigamy for Hindus and permitted inter-caste marriages among the followers of Hindu, Sikh, Jain and Buddhist religions (Derrett 1978; Kishwar 1994; Menski 2001, p. 65; 2003, pp. 209–224). Despite this remarkable codification effort by

---

[4] These Acts were: the Hindu Marriage Act (HMA) of 1955, the Hindu Succession Act (HSA) of 1956, the Hindu Minority and Guardianship Act (HMGA) of 1956, and the Hindu Adoptions and Maintenance Act (HAMA) of 1956.

[5] The issue of whether these communities had their own separate laws before they were brought under the purview of HCB Acts is a matter of debate. It is true that none of these religious groups was ever officially recognized as a legal community with the privilege of having its own personal laws similar to those of Hindus or Muslims. But it must also be remembered that during the colonial period, the laws of Sikhs, Jains and Buddhists were usually applied as part of custom and usage in accordance with the rulings of the Privy Council in London and some high courts in India. Moreover, some of these communities came even closer to being recognized as independent legal communities and were granted certain privileges. In this respect, the Anand Marriage Act (1909) and the Punjab Laws Act IV (1872), which had granted formal recognition to customary laws of Punjabi communities, including those of Sikhs, are particularly worth mentioning. The issue of whether the adherents of these faiths should still be treated as Hindus for purposes of personal law or be recognized as independent communities with separate codes of their own is a matter of great controversy, even among the adherents. For example, although the idea of Sikhs having their own separate code has recently become somewhat popular among Sikhs, there is still not an overarching theological, political or legal consensus within the community regarding, first, whether there is such a thing as Sikh law, and second, if there is, whether it would be worth pursuing the goal of separate Sikh personal law given the long history of their conflictual relations with the Hindu majority. To a lesser extent, there are similar demands within the Jain community (Mitra 1913, pp. 49–82; Goswami 1994; Singh 1995; Kharak 1998; Jain 2004). Furthermore, during my field research in India, I observed that some members of the Baha'i community voiced similar demands even though their laws had never been recognized in the past (personal interview with Mr. Arun Sinha, a representative of the Indian Baha'i Community, May 2005, New Delhi).

[6] Grounds for divorce include mutual consent, adultery, cruelty, desertion lasting two years, conversion to another religion and husband's commitment of rape, sodomy or bestiality among others. For further information see Article 13 of the HMA of 1955 (as amended by Act 68 of 1976).

the legislature, the HCB Acts still recognized local customs and usage as part of Hindu law. Thus, as a result, when a Hindu (meaning any person who is not a Muslim, Christian, Parsi or Jew by religion) comes before the civil or family courts,[7] judges need to decide the case according to both written (e.g., legislation and case law) and unwritten (e.g., customs) sources of Hindu personal law (Menski 2003, p. 218).

The "non-Hindu" groups – Muslims, Christians and Parsis – were, on the other hand, left out of these unification schemes and permitted to maintain their pre-independence communal laws. For example, the Muslim personal law continues to remain largely an uncodified body of law that primarily relies upon the Anglo-Mohammedan case law and traditional sources of *shariat* (Mahmood 1995a, 2002).[8] The only piece of legislation on Muslim law that was introduced after independence was the MWPRDA of 1986. Similarly, the marital laws (i.e., the IDA of 1869 and the ICMA of 1872) of the Christian community were also left untouched for many decades by the Indian government. For example, the IDA of 1869 had remained in force without any significant change until it was finally amended by the Indian Divorce (Amendment) Act (51 of 2001). The new Act, which introduced fairly liberal provisions of divorce into Christian personal law, was initiated primarily in response to the successful mobilization of both secular and religious (especially women's) groups and organizations in the Christian community (Agnes 2001, pp. 141–163; 2011, pp. 71–73). The Parsi community, on the other hand, has the nation's most gender-equitable communal laws. This is, in large part, thanks to exemplary collaboration between the leaders of the community and the Indian parliament. For instance, in March 1988 the parliament unanimously voted for an amendment to the PMDA of 1936 that recognized divorce by mutual consent. Three years later, the parliament provided for complete gender equality in respect to inheritance by abolishing the gender unequal provisions of the PISA of 1865 (Articles 50–60 of the ISA of 1925). A similar change

---

[7] The Family Courts Act was passed in 1984. Although the law required the state governments to establish specialized family courts in cities with populations over a million, as of 2003 there were only about sixty cities which had complied with the requirements of the law and set up such courts within their precincts (Verma 1997; Mathew and Bakshi 2002; Patil 2003).

[8] Muslim law in India remains mostly uncodified. Although there is the 1937 MPLSAA, this was simply a declaratory Act which had restated that *shariat* was the only law to be applied to Indian Muslims in matters of personal status. Otherwise, the Act did not create new rights or codify Islamic law. Nevertheless, the Act was instrumental in extending the jurisdiction of *shariat* over some heterodox Muslim communities (e.g., Isma'ili Khojas, the Bohoras, the Cutchi Memons, etc.) that were traditionally subject to Hindu law in matters of inheritance rather than the Islamic rules of succession.

affecting Parsi wives' right to maintenance was also introduced with the passage of the Marriage Laws (Amendment) Act (49 of 2001) (Irani 1968; Jain 1988; Saharay 1999, pp. 428–450; Agnes 2001, pp. 127–140; Palsetia 2001, pp. 197–276; Venkata Subbarao and Subba Rao 2002, pp. 575–580; Kusum 2003, p. 140; Saxena 2003, pp. 11–12). In brief, in respect of laws of "non-Hindu" communities, the post-independence Indian governments mostly remained (with varying levels of continuity) loyal to the British colonial policy of "non-interference" and, as exemplified by recent changes in Parsi and Christian laws, did not attempt to alter their laws without a strong (and often culturally grounded) demand from the communities in question (Williams 2006, p. 9; Subramanian 2010). By the same token, since the government did not unilaterally impose a unification scheme upon minority laws, Indian family law has remained largely un-unified. As a result, today, whenever a Muslim, Christian or Parsi comes before the court, the judge has to decide the case according to the relevant personal law by considering both its written (e.g., statutes and case law) and unwritten (e.g., customs) sources.

As noted earlier, in the absence of a UCC, the Indian state has willy-nilly allowed the continuation of the old personal law system that was solidified by Warren Hastings, the British Governor-General, in 1772. However, by 1954 the Indian leaders, unlike their Israeli and Egyptian counterparts, had already realized that the persistence of the colonial system of personal law and, more importantly, the forcible subjection of persons to state-enforced religious laws without their explicit or implied consent, and the inability of fellow citizens to freely intermarry without any legal or political impediments (considered essential for realization of the goal of composite national identity), utterly contradicted the secular, democratic and inclusionary principles upon which the Indian state was founded. In an attempt to resolve this apparent paradox and ease the potential effects of state-sanctioned religious laws on the rights and freedoms of individual citizens, the parliament passed the SMA in 1954, and it remains in force today. The SMA was designed as secular legislation that would be uniformly applied to all citizens throughout the territory of India. It provided for a civil marriage and postnuptial remedies for individuals who married under this Act or for persons who had already married according to their communal laws but opted to retroactively register their marriage under the SMA. Also, the property of individuals whose marriages were registered under the Act devolved according to the provisions of the

ISA of 1925, rather than their own personal laws.[9] However, the most important aspect of the 1954 Act was that it authorized interreligious marriages among Indians. Hence, thanks to the SMA of 1954, today in India a Muslim and a Hindu, or a Sikh and a Parsi for that matter, can intermarry without legal limitations that normally exist in countries with similar personal status systems (e.g., Israel and Egypt, which lacked the inclusionary and secular orientations that were prevalent in India, especially during the formative years of the republic).

Lastly, the post-independence Indian government has also embraced a "modernist" agenda and undertaken substantive reforms to eliminate certain customs and practices that cut across all distinctions of creed, caste and religion. As in the Israeli case, the Indian government has

[9] When the SMA of 1872 was amended in 1923, several new provisions were made in regard to Hindu, Sikh, Buddhist and Jain persons' right to succession. For example, it was noted that if a person professing any of these aforementioned religions had married under this Act, his marriage would be deemed to sever his membership from a Hindu joint (undivided) family (Section 22 of the 1872 Act). As suggested by the 59th Report of the Law Commission of India, Section 22 – which imposed compulsory severance from joint family – was introduced at the time as a concession to appease conservative Hindu elements who viewed the clause as a deterrent against interfaith marriages between Hindus and non-Hindus (namely Muslims, Christians, etc.). When the new SMA replaced the 1872 Act in 1954, the aforementioned succession-related provision of the 1923 amendment was retained (as Section 19 of the new Act). In addition, the new Act also provided that succession to property of an individual (including a Hindu) who married under this Act would be governed by the ISA of 1925, rather than the parties' personal laws, simplifying the law of succession in case parties marrying under the Act belonged to different religious communities. The statutory severance from joint family and "forcible" application of the ISA of 1925 instead of the HSA of 1956 were long considered by some Hindu legislators as an undue property-related or economic hardship imposed upon Hindus that undermined their ability to contract interfaith marriages under the SMA of 1954. Thus, with the support of secular and liberal members of the parliament, the Marriage Laws (Amendment) Act (68 of 1976) (MLAA) removed the succession-related "disabilities" of the SMA of 1954, and declared that when two Hindus (including Sikhs, Jains and Buddhists) marry under the SMA, their ties to joint family would not be severed, and their property would devolve according to the HSA of 1956 rather than the ISA of 1925 (Sangari 2000, pp. 285–286). This seemingly "liberal" statutory change, that originally aimed to remove succession-related penalties so that people could freely opt out of their communal marriage laws and marry under civil law, had some unintended consequences. First, as Tahir Mahmood (1978a, p. 21) argues, the 1976 amendment openly discriminated against non-Hindus. It allowed only Hindus who married under the SMA to keep their own succession laws, while denying the same right to Muslims and Parsis. Second, it also had negative implications for Hindu women's (especially daughters of Hindu couples who married under the SMA) right to inheritance. The ISA of 1925, being more gender equal than the HSA of 1956, bestowed upon Hindu daughters greater rights to family property vis-à-vis their brothers than the HSA of 1956, at least until the latter law was amended in 2005. Third, like the Special Marriage (Amendment) Act (32 of 1963) that allowed marriage among individuals within degrees of prohibited relationship (like first cousins) providing that at least one of the parties' customs permitted such a marriage, the MLAA (68 of 1976) also led to decodification of the general law, in Derrett's words, by introducing elements of personal law and customs into what was otherwise a secular and territorial legislation (Derrett 1999, pp. 327–328). In other words, the 1976 amendment further forestalled and even reversed the process towards unification and secularization of personal laws in India (Mahmood 1978b; Sivaramayya 1978; Agnes 2011, pp. 154–155).

often resorted to criminal law measures to induce behavioral change and improve the status of women. For example, with a 1995 amendment to the IPC of 1860, bigamy was made punishable for non-Muslim Indians (Derrett 1976). Similarly, in 1961, the government passed a law that prohibited giving and taking dowry (Goody and Tambiah 1973; Gupta 2003). In 1978, the CMRA of 1929 was amended, making it punishable to contract a marriage with a man under 21 or a woman under 18 (the PCMA of 2006 declared child marriages voidable at the option of the contracting underage party) (Agrawal 2010, p. 110). The Domestic Violence Act of 2005 protects the wife or live-in partner against violence perpetrated by her husband, live-in partner or his relatives; and prohibits her being rendered shelterless without following due process of law (Jaising and Sakhani 2007). Most notable among these laws, for the purposes of the current study, is the Cr. PC of 1973 (Sections 125–128), which commanded all Indian husbands – irrespective of religious affiliation – to provide for their wives and ex-wives who were unable to maintain themselves, or face criminal charges (Kusum 2003, pp. 186–206; Menski 2003, pp. 518–522). Since these Acts are part of territorial or general state law rather than personal law, they are uniformly applied to all persons without any distinctions.

II. WHY DID INDIA SET FOR ITSELF THE GOAL OF SECURING A UNIFORM CIVIL CODE?

As noted above, by the time India gained its independence in 1947, its personal law system was already institutionally unified. The state-appointed secular judges at civil courts were in charge of finding different bodies of religious and customary laws and applying them to citizens in accordance with their religious and caste backgrounds. In the eyes of the founding elite, this state of affairs was socially undesirable as much as it was ideologically inconsistent with the secular and inclusionary principles upon which independent India was being built (Keay 2000, pp. 484–508). Personal laws were considered responsible for the persistence and endurance of communalist sentiments that had long prevented the inhabitants of India from attaining a common sense of unity (Shah 1969; Kumar 1992). Thus, the founding leaders of India believed that in order to do away with communalist sentiments and forge a composite and unified national identity, they had to replace the colonial institutions of personal law with a secular civil code that would be applicable to all citizens irrespective of religion, caste or ethnicity (Deshta 2002; Raju 2003).

However, as noted in Chapter 2, normative unification requires not only a strong ideological commitment on the part of the reforming elite, but also a highly capable central authority with the necessary means to impose its will upon ethno-religious groups that oppose its unification measures. In the Indian case, although the reformers were strongly committed to the idea of a UCC – especially in the beginning – they soon realized that in the post-partition environment, where Muslims had become a disgruntled and alienated minority, it was politically "unwise" and impractical for them to unilaterally impose such a code upon the Muslim opposition. Instead, having realized the impossibility of the task of legal unification, the Indian government carried out a limited version of the wholesale normative unification that the framers of the constitution had originally envisaged, by unifying the personal laws of the majority community whose resistance they thought they could handle with relative ease, and, particularly from the 1970s onwards, pushing for partial convergence and harmonization of separate communal laws through judicial and legislative means (Subramanian 2008, p. 642; Solanki 2011, pp. 91–174; Menski 2012, p. 45). Against this background the present section will, first, identify the ideological considerations that had led the founding elite to initially set for themselves the goal of uniform civil code, and second, explain political factors that brought about a change of course that forced them to adopt a rather limited version of the wholesale normative unification they had originally planned for.

Secular and inclusionary characteristics of the Indian regime

Since the very moment when the idea of partition was first conceived, the leaders of the Congress Party had fiercely resisted the division of the country on the basis of religion (Keay 2000, pp. 484–508). British India was a land already deeply divided along communal, sectarian, tribal, geographical, linguistic and caste lines (Furber 1951; Prasad, Mallik et al. 2001, pp. 108–146). Hence what its people needed, as Gandhi and Nehru consistently held, were not more divisions but national unity, which they believed could be achieved only through the establishment of a secular democratic state. Such a state, they maintained, would treat members of all religious communities equally and gradually plant the seeds of a new "Indian" national identity by replacing people's long-held sectarian and parochial loyalties (Shah 1969; Kumar 1992;

169

Subrahmanyam 1992; Lester 1994; Singh 1994a; Nehru 2000, p. 201; Tyagi 2001).

Despite the Congress leaders' opposition, however, British India was eventually partitioned into two independent states as India and Pakistan on August 15, 1947. In the days following the partition, about twelve million people voluntarily or involuntarily left their homes and moved between the newly created India and Pakistan. Communal violence and disturbances spread all over the country, including in major cities such as Delhi, Mumbai and Calcutta, where thousands of people were massacred. Historians estimate that post-partition violence claimed more than a million lives in both countries (Menon 1957, pp. 417–435; Butalia 2000; Pandey 2001). The Congress leaders' commitment to establishing a secular and inclusionary regime, in which an individual's religion, or lack thereof, would play no role in defining his or her membership in the political community, grew stronger following the partition. Despite mass migrations to Pakistan, there was still a sizable Muslim minority (about 47 million people) left within the borders of independent India (Choudhury 1968, p. 170). Thus the founding elite deemed the establishment of a secular state as a powerful remedy that would heal the wounds of partition, placate the aroused fears of the Muslim community and assure the peaceful coexistence of people of all faiths in a free and democratic society (Hasan 1990; Saiyed 1990; Jha 2002).

"In a country like India," Nehru said, "which has many faiths and religions, no real nationalism can be built up except on the basis of secularity" (Nehru 1989, pp. 163–164). A narrower approach, he argued, would only result in the disunity of the people of India and bring about the emergence of separate Hindu, Muslim, Sikh and Christian nationalisms (Nehru 1989, pp. 163–164). Thus, he continued, "[W]e want to put an end to all those infinite divisions ... build a united nation where individuals do not think so much of their particular group or caste but of the community at large" (Nehru 1963, pp. 518–519). Therefore, with these considerations – unlike its twin sister, Pakistan, which was officially declared an Islamic state in 1956 – India was founded as a secular republic (Cohen 2004).[10]

---

[10] The term "secular" did not originally find a place for itself in the Preamble of the 1950 Constitution; it was only added in 1976 with the 42nd amendment. The reasons for the omission of the term were twofold. First, Nehru and others found secularism, as defined in the English language, very restrictive, as they had a much broader concept in mind. The English term, they thought, also had the negative connotation of being "anti-religious." The secular state they envisaged, on the other hand, was not an anti-religious state. In this regard, the inclusion of the

At the outset, however, the concept of secularism in the Indian context must be clearly defined. First, Indian secularism does not erect a wall of separation between the state and religion. Instead, it is understood as a doctrine of non-preference, which requires that the state grant no special privileges to any one religion but keep a "principled distance" from all religions in the country (Smith 1963, p. 381; Bhargava 2002, pp. 12–27; Mahajan 2002; Bhargava 2005). In this regard, the secular state is a state that is not associated with any particular religion, but protects and helps all religions equally. Moreover, the Indian secular state is a religion-blind state in which – at least theoretically – religion plays no role in defining the obligations, rights and duties of the citizens. In other words it is a homogenizing, inclusionary state that aims to eliminate communal, sectarian and caste distinctions among its inhabitants and create a unified and civic citizenry. Lastly, the Indian secular state is a modernizing, reformist state that does not hesitate to intervene in the affairs of religious communities in order to eliminate "undesired" social and religious practices (e.g., untouchability, *devadasi*, polygamy, child marriages, etc.) so as to cultivate a "scientific temper" and "rational" approach to life that is free of superstitions and customs considered unfit for a modern and democratic society (Smith 1958, pp. 149–153; Baird 1978; Parekh 1991, p. 39; Chatterjee 1994; Bhargava 2002, pp. 26–28; Sathe 2003, pp. 161–165). In this regard, Indian leaders who had viewed the colonial system of personal law as one of the culprits for the lack of national unity, stubborn persistence of communalism and "backward" customs (e.g., polygyny, etc.) that allegedly impeded progress, immediately after independence turned their attention to the issue of a secular civil code in order to replace religion-based personal laws and thereby lay the foundations for a modern nation.

Uniform civil code debates in the Constituent Assembly

Article 44 was adopted by the Constituent Assembly on March 30, 1947. Sponsors of the Article were of the opinion that the UCC was

term "secular" in the constitution, they thought, might have given the wrong impression, i.e., that the Indian state was to seclude religion from the public sphere, as did some of its Western counterparts, which would have created an unnecessary tension with more traditional and conservative groups both within and without the Congress Party. Second, the framers of the constitution also believed that, since such secular principles as the freedom of religion and expression were already included in the constitution, there was no need to separately announce that India was a secular state. It would just have been an unnecessary repetition of what had already been implied (Sheshadri and Acharya 1977; Diwan 1978; Nehru 2000, p. 200; Gopal and Iyengar 2003, pp. 194–195).

needed in order to break down the barriers between various religious communities and attain national unity (Rao 1968, p. 128). For instance, Hansa Mehta, a member of the sub-committee on fundamental rights and one of the leaders of the All India Women's Conference (AIWC), made a speech in the Constituent Assembly to the effect that a UCC was much more important than a national language for generating national unity (Lalithambika and Krishnakutty 1998, p. 194). She further argued that personal laws were dividing the country, and if the goal was to build a unified citizenry, then a UCC was essential (Parashar 1992, p. 233).

This point of view was also widely shared and supported by Minister of Law Dr. Ambedkar and other members of the subcommittee,[11] who strongly believed that religion-based personal laws had long kept India divided and prevented its people from developing a common sense of national identity. They also argued that one of the indicators of being a unified nation was the ability of fellow citizens from different religious or caste backgrounds to marry one another without any legal or political impediments.[12] To that effect, some members also proposed to include a clause based on Article 54 of the 1874 Swiss Constitution that "no impediments to marriage between citizens shall be based merely upon difference of religion." Thus, with these considerations, the UCC was deemed imperative to enable interfaith marriages and allow people from different ethno-religious backgrounds to intermingle in order to generate a sense of common nationhood and solidarity among the citizens of India (Greenwood and Lauterpacht 1956, p. 198; Rao 1968, p. 162; Markandan 1984, p. 78; Dhagamwar 1989, p. 23).

---

[11] These were Alladi Krishnaswami Ayyar, Rajkumari Amrit Kaur, K. M. Munshi and Mino Masani.

[12] Amrit Kaur, Hansa Mehta and M. R. Masani, the members who proposed including this clause, also made the comment quoted below in support of their motion. In their critique, the members of parliament complained about the fact that fellow Indians of different religious backgrounds had to travel abroad to solemnize their unions. As mentioned earlier, this is still one of the few options available to Israeli citizens who want to contract interfaith marriages. It is interesting that the problem that still awaits a solution in Israel was diagnosed more than six decades ago by Indian law-makers: "Unfortunately, such marriages cannot be solemnized in India today. Indians who have desired to marry a fellow-national of another religious faith have had to leave the borders of India in order to get married without being forced to perjure themselves. It is only possible, however, for those with more than average means and facilities to leave the country for such a purpose, and the law [the Special Marriage Act of 1872] has actually prevented several conscientious persons of limited means who were unwilling to comply with its requirements [to make the following declaration: 'I do not profess the Christian, Jewish, Hindu, Mohammedan, Parsi, Buddhist, Sikh or Jain religion'] from marrying fellow nationals of their choice" (Rao 1968, pp. 162–163).

As Article 44 was debated in the Constituent Assembly, representatives of religious minorities as well as right-wing Hindu groups voiced their opposition to the abolition of personal laws, and the imposition of a UCC in their place, without the clear consent of the communities concerned (Deshta 2002, pp. 55–61). Muslim representatives in particular were most adamant in their opposition to a UCC. They proposed several amendments to Article 44 in order to stall the legislative process and save *shariat* from the ambit of such a future enactment.[13] In addition, Muslim members, including Mohammad Ismail Sahib from Madras, warned the government that a UCC would also disrupt the long-prevailing status quo and create unnecessary tension between the majority and minority communities:

> Now why do people want a UCC? Their idea evidently is to secure harmony through uniformity. But I maintain that [the imposition of a UCC] will bring discontent, and harmony will be affected. But if people are allowed to follow their own personal law there will be no discontent or dissatisfaction

(Dhagamwar 1989, p. 118)

Although none of the amendments proposed by the Muslim representatives were adopted during the course of the Constituent Assembly debates on Article 44, the Muslim members' remarks that a UCC could possibly cause more disunity than harmony seem to have fundamentally altered the government's policy and the fate of the UCC in two important ways. First, Article 44 was made part of the Directive Principles, the so-called non-justiciable section of the constitution, rather than the justiciable Fundamental Rights section. The main implication of this placement choice is that, although it is still a duty of the state to comply with Article 44, unlike in the case of fundamental rights individuals cannot demand as a matter of right the enforcement of the UCC clause in a court of law (Markandan 1966, pp. 1–5). This gave the government a certain degree of flexibility. Had Article 44 been in the Fundamental Rights section, it would have been perforce applicable equally to all communities. But now the government was free to take action at its own will against certain communities while leaving the personal laws of others untouched – as happened with the Hindu Code Bill Acts in the 1950s (Austin 2004, p. 80). According to Austin, it was

[13] The Muslim representatives who proposed these amendments were Mahboob Ali Baig Sahib Bahadur, Pocker Sahib Bahadur, Mohammad Ismail Sahib and Hussain Imam.

actually Nehru who had insisted, in deference to Muslims' concerns, that "the framing of the UCC be a goal set out in the Directive Principles" (Austin 2001, pp. 17–18). In other words, Article 44 was designated by the government as a non-justiciable principle in order to calm the fears and concerns of the Muslim minority.

Second, although their amendments to exempt Muslim law from the purview of UCC had been rejected, Muslim leaders were given categorical verbal assurances by Minister of Law and the Chairman of the Constitution Drafting Committee, Dr. Ambedkar, that the government would not do away with the Muslim personal law and impose upon the community a UCC against their will. For instance, in an unprecedented speech, Ambedkar acknowledged that his government had neither the will nor the power to impose a UCC on the Muslim minority against its wishes:

> We must all remember that sovereignty is always limited ... because sovereignty in the exercise of that power must reconcile itself to the sentiments of different communities. No government can exercise its power in such a manner as to provoke the Muslim minority to rise in rebellion. I think it would be a mad government if it did so.
>
> (Raju 2003, p. 69)

Similarly, Prime Minister Nehru concurred with his Minister of Law's remarks and recognized that the time was not yet ripe for the government to unilaterally impose a UCC (Smith 1963, p. 290; Gajendragadkar 1971, p. 124). In fact, in 1950, he publicly announced that despite his government's wishes, in the post-partition environment it was practically impossible for the Hindu majority to push for any changes affecting the personal laws of the Muslim community due to the fear that such a move could further alienate the Muslim minority: "Now we do not dare to touch the Muslims because they are a minority and we do not want the Hindu majority to do it. These are personal laws and so will remain for the Muslims until they want to change them" (Rao and Rao 1974, p. 383).

In conclusion, despite their strong desire for and belief in the instrumental value of a UCC to promote national unity, the Indian leaders found it politically imprudent and impractical to impose such a code on religious minorities against their will, and in particular struck a "tacit bargain" with the Muslim minority by accommodating its cultural and religio-legal demands (Brass 1991, p. 82). In the post-partition environment the relations between Hindus and Muslims were already extremely tense, and the imposition of a UCC under these circumstances would have only made things worse. Thus, with that recognition, the government turned its attention to the pending Hindu Code Bill reform, hoping that when parliament took the first steps towards secularizing and unifying the laws of the majority, it would set in motion a revolutionary movement, and that "in the course of time, as a result of education and propaganda the inevitable next step could be taken and Article 44 would then be fully implemented" (Gajendragadkar 1971, pp. 124–125).

The Hindu Code Bill and the Special Marriage Act: the first step towards a uniform civil code?

By the time the Constituent Assembly was debating Article 44, there was already a draft Hindu Code Bill (HCB) under consideration, submitted by the Nehru government in April 1947. However, the whole project was temporarily suspended as both the government and the legislature were preoccupied with the vital tasks of drafting the constitution and coping with the shocks of partition. As things calmed down, a revised draft was resubmitted by the Ministry of Law to the Constituent Assembly in August 1948 (Parashar 1992, p. 80). The main purpose of the Bill was to codify the scattered sources of Hindu law and partly secularize and modernize it in the process (Chatterjee 1994; Derrett 1999, pp. 321–353). Since the goal of UCC was unattainable due to the resistance of minorities, the supporters of the Bill thought that perhaps if the Hindu majority took the first step towards a UCC it would encourage minorities to follow their example and reform their personal laws on a parallel track, so that one day the entire country could be brought under the purview of a UCC (Ambedkar 1995, p. 620).

The HCB was envisaged as a limited version of the UCC. As the latter was promoted to generate national unity among Indians by transcending their communal identities, the HCB was aimed to generate a similar sense of unity within the "Hindu" segment of the population (Parashar 1992, pp. 101–112; Derrett 1999, pp. 330–333; Williams 2006, p. 103). Hindu law had, historically, been a fragmented legal system that lacked a central authority or binding set of rules applicable to all persons and situations. This was largely due to the fact that customs and caste rules, the primary source of Hindu law, varied greatly not only across regions but also from one community to another within the same region (Menski 2001, 2003). For the sponsors of the Bill, this fragmented state of Hindu law was responsible for the lack of harmony within the Hindu population. Thus, for the sake of unity, all Hindus had to be brought under a common code that would be uniformly applied to every person in the fold, regardless of whether he or she was from the North or South, a Brahmin or an Untouchable. As one of the supporters of the Bill put it, the HCB was also designed to abolish "internal" communalism and end disruptive tendencies within the "Hindu" community by removing the boundaries among Hindus, Sikhs and others (Ambedkar 1995, p. 587). By the same token, supporters, who viewed the HCB as a potent tool of assimilation and homogenization, wanted to include adherents of all "native" religions of India under the Hindu fold and subject them to the purview of Hindu law (Ambedkar 1995, p. 591). For instance, Ambedkar estimated that once passed, about 85 percent of the population would have come under the jurisdiction of the HCB (Smith 1963, p. 290). Thus, the HCB consequently defined persons professing Hinduism, Sikhism, Jainism and Buddhism as "Hindus" for the purpose of personal law.[14] In the consecutive amendments, the definition of "Hindu" was further expanded to include any person who was not a Muslim, Christian, Jew or Parsi by religion (Elst 2002).

Although the categorization of Sikhs, Jains and Buddhists as "Hindus" was seen by supporters of the HCB simply as a measure of unification, representatives of the minority communities opposed it, and demanded the recognition of their customs and religious laws on an equal footing with those of Muslim, Christian and Parsi communities (Bhansali 1992; Kharak 1998; Sangari 2000, p. 287; Raju 2003, pp. 52–60; Jain 2004). Even though they eventually bowed to the power of the majority and came under the Hindu law, Sikh members in particular were among the staunchest opponents of the HCB in parliament:

> We are told in one breath that we have so long been governed by Hindu law – well and good – but in another breath we are told that that was not the proper Hindu law. Hindu law is now rediscovered and a code is being brought and thrust upon us ... If it is progressiveness, we claim that our customs are more progressive than the law which is being proposed now ... If you wish to move forward, we are already [in] advance of you. Come after us ... If it is only for the sake of bringing about unity, then ... I am afraid [it] would not succeed ...
>
> (From a speech by Sardar Hukam Singh,
> quoted in Ambedkar, 1995, p. 1243)

---

[14] The sponsors of the HCB argued that the inclusion of adherents of these religions under the "Hindu" fold was justified because these groups had never developed their own personal laws, instead following local customs, which were largely infused with the precepts and values of Hindu law (Lok Sabha Debates, 1951, Vol. 6 (Part 2), cols. 2462–2471). For further information see n. 5 above.

However, minorities were not alone in their opposition to the draft Bill. The changes proposed by the HCB (e.g., legalization of divorce and intercaste marriages, prohibition of polygyny among Hindus, greater rights for women in joint-family property, etc.) were so disruptive that they also caused frictions within the ruling Congress Party. For example, even the President of the Republic, an influential Congress figure, Rajendra Prasad, opposed the Bill and threatened the government with veto (Everett 1979, pp. 169–171; Nehru 1988, pp. 499–501; 1994, pp. 384–385; Gopal and Iyengar 2003, pp. 111–113). But the greatest opposition was mobilized against the tactics and personality of Minister of Law Dr. Ambedkar, an untouchable Hindu. Even the so-called moderate members of parliament were appalled by the idea that an "untouchable" was in charge of reforming "sacred" Hindu law (Som 1994, p. 186; Jatava 1997). In the face of the strong opposition, the government was forced to withdraw the HCB in September 1951. As if this embarrassing defeat was not enough for Prime Minister Nehru, he also lost an invaluable ally, Minister of Law Ambedkar, who resigned in protest and frustration (Banningan 1952).

Once Ambedkar was out of the picture, the government resubmitted a watered-down version of the HCB to parliament in 1952 (Som 1994, p. 193). The original HCB of 1947 was split into four separate Bills,[15] and some of the controversial elements were left out to make it easier to overcome the opposition and defeat their filibustering tactics that had led to the failure of the original Bill in 1951. Over the next four years, the Nehru government gave further concessions to the conservative elements in order to make sure that its legislation saw the light of day (Saxena 1962; Parashar 1992; Sarkar 1999; Chavan and Kidwai 2006). However, as some members of parliament pointed out, these concessions reached such a level that the Acts, which were finally passed in 1955 and 1956, no longer resembled the original HCB (Lok Sabha Debates, 1954, Vol. 5 (Pt. 2), cols. 7252–7253).[16]

---

[15] These Acts were: the HMA of 1955, the HSA of 1956, the HMGA of 1956 and the HAMA of 1956.

[16] According to Williams (2006, p. 113), the Nehru government made a number of additional substantive concessions, besides the ones already made by Ambedkar in the Constituent Assembly, in order to overcome the opposition to the four Bills brought to the parliament after the elections. Some of these changes, that drastically altered the original Hindu Code Bill drafted by Ambedkar in 1947, included "the re-establishment of customary law, and the reduction of the share of inheritance given to daughters in intestate succession, and in devolution of joint family property." For further information, see Williams (2006, p. 113).

While the HCB was being debated in the parliament, the government was consistently criticized for its failure to enact a UCC as directed by Article 44. Representatives, particularly from the Hindu right, continuously accused the government of unjustly singling out the Hindu community for its reformist agenda, and challenged it rather to propose a UCC if it could "dare" to touch Muslim law (Ambedkar 1995, pp. 406–407). Apart from such frequent critiques, there was also a growing sense of uneasiness within ruling circles that, despite the progress on the HCB, the government had not yet taken a concrete step towards a secular code of marriage and divorce that would enable interfaith marriages among Indians. No matter how progressive or secular it was, the proposed HCB was essentially a piece of communal legislation under which a Hindu could not marry a non-Hindu. Moreover, the government was aware that the goal of the UCC was not to be achieved in the foreseeable future. Therefore, the problem before the Nehru government was that, if India was to be a truly secular, democratic and composite nation, then it had to allow interfaith marriages and provide citizens with an alternative civil family code, at least in the interim. In the end, all these considerations led the government to enact the SMA in May 1954.[17]

As noted earlier, the SMA is uniformly applied to all citizens who opted out of their own communal laws and either originally contracted or retroactively registered their marriages under this Act. In this regard, the passage of the SMA of 1954 was important for two reasons: First, it constituted a "UCC in embryo" or, as Nehru put it, the very "first step toward bringing uniformity in social observance" (Smith 1963, p. 278). And second, despite their manoeuvres to claim immunity from its purview, the SMA was also made available to Indian Muslims on a voluntary basis (Smith 1963, pp. 278–279; Parashar 1992, pp. 161–162). Thus, for the first time ever, all Indians, irrespective of religion, were theoretically brought under the jurisdiction of a single civil family code – notwithstanding its voluntary application.

---

[17] Although there already was a Special Marriage Act in force, enacted by the British in 1872, it was simply an inadequate and non-democratic law, as it required those who wanted to marry under the Act to renounce their respective religions; for further information see n. 12 above.

III. THE IMPACT OF PERSONAL LAWS ON THE RIGHTS AND FREEDOMS OF INDIAN CITIZENS

As I previously demonstrated in the cases of Israel and Egypt, state-enforced personal status laws usually carry negative implications for the rights and freedoms of individuals, and cause systemic inequalities by applying different sets of rules to different sexes and people from different ethno-religious backgrounds. The same is also true for the Indian personal law system. As in Israel and Egypt, women's right to divorce, maintenance and succession, polygyny and religious conversions are among the most urgent and widely debated issues under the Indian personal law system. Despite all these similarities among the three countries, what really sets India apart from the other two is that India claims to offer a "secular" alternative to its citizens who want to opt out of their communal laws: the SMA of 1954. As noted in Chapter 2, theoretically speaking, the very existence of such an alternative civil code of marriage and divorce not only strengthens the Indian government's secular and democratic claims, but also helps ameliorate human rights concerns under its personal law system by allowing individuals to opt for a civil option when they do not consent to the authority of state-enforced religious norms.

As many liberal and communitarian thinkers (Kymlicka 1996; Shachar 2001; Barzilai 2003) point out, the existence of *millet*-like systems in today's modern polities raises several important questions: To what extent should a democratic regime tolerate – let alone integrate and directly apply – religious norms that place certain restrictions and disabilities upon the rights and freedoms of individuals who are subject to their jurisdiction? Put another way, can democracies tolerate *millet*-like personal status systems? Both Barzilai (2003, p. 77) and Benhabib (2002, p. 131) suggest that multicultural pluralist arrangements in the legal sphere can be allowed by democratic regimes only if individual community members are granted a freedom of exit and association along with several other institutional and normative prerequisites they identify. In this regard, some may argue that the existence of the SMA of 1954 and other secular remedies, such as Section 125 of the Cr. PC of 1973, provide Indian citizens with a similar "right of exit" and protection against the limitations and disabilities imposed upon individuals' rights by state-enforced religious laws. Some may even argue that whenever individuals submit themselves to the jurisdiction of state-sanctioned personal laws, they do so voluntarily, because the existence of secular alternatives theoretically enables citizens to freely opt out of the communal track and take advantage of the civil remedies that are uniformly applied to all citizens irrespective of religion. At this point, the question is whether the availability of the SMA of 1954 and other secular remedies has actually furnished Indian citizens with the type of right of exit that Barzilai (2003, pp. 251–253) and others have articulated.

In fact, this very question was answered by the Indian Supreme Court's 1985 *Shah Bano* judgment and the ensuing events. In this regard, the present section shows that the political and legal developments in the aftermath of the Supreme Court's landmark decision not only answered the question above by shedding light on the complexities of the community–individual–state triangle from a human rights perspective, and called into question the central tenets of Indian secularism, but also raised a number of questions about the ability and readiness of the Indian government to deliver on its constitutional promises and protect individual citizens against the encroachments and threats of communal forces when they opt for secular or civil remedies instead of personal laws.

Individual rights vs. communal rights: whose rights are to be sacrificed?

Shah Bano and Mohammad Ahmed Khan were married in 1932. The husband, Mohammad Ahmed Khan, was a wealthy advocate who earned roughly Rs. 5,000 per month, while Shah Bano was a housewife with no independent income. After forty-three years of marriage and five children, Mohammad Ahmed Khan took a second wife in 1975 and later divorced Shah Bano by uttering *talaq* three times. Mohammed Ahmed Khan paid Shah Bano the amount of dower that he promised her at the time of marriage and provided her with three months' maintenance as required by the Muslim personal law. Shah Bano was an old woman who had no independent means to support herself. She sued her former husband for failing to provide her with sufficient maintenance under Section 125 of the Cr. PC of 1973 which required men from all religious communities to provide for their indigent wives and ex-wives who were unable to maintain themselves. The lower court awarded Shah Bano Rs. 25 a month (roughly $2 at the time), although she originally asked for Rs. 500 per month, the maximum amount allowed under Section 125 at the time. Disheartened at the meager award made by the lower court, Shah Bano appealed to the Madhya Pradesh High Court, which later raised the amount of award to Rs. 179 (approximately $14). Mohammad

Ahmed Khan, an advocate by profession, appealed the High Court's decision to the Supreme Court of India arguing that he had already fulfilled all his financial obligations under the Muslim personal law. In April 1985, the Supreme Court ruled in favor of Shah Bano and upheld the Madhya Pradesh High Court's judgment. Supreme Court justices noted that the husband was under obligation to provide further maintenance to his divorced wife according to not only the Cr. PC of 1973, but also the Holy Qur'an, citing its relevant verses in both Arabic and English in their ruling. For many Muslims, the court's interference in Muslim personal law was nothing but a full-frontal attack against *shariat* and Muslim identity in India. As soon as it was made public, the judgment of the Supreme Court unleashed an unprecedented tide of demonstrations and riots throughout the country. Appraising the Muslim mood, an Indian newspaper wrote: "Not since … the great upheaval of 1857 has a single non-political act caused so much trauma, fear and indignation among a community" (Misra 2000, p. 7). As thousands of Muslims stormed the streets and protested the government's inaction in the face of the court's alleged encroachments on Muslim personal law, Prime Minister Rajiv Gandhi, who was initially supportive of the court's ruling, later conceded to demands of conservative elements within the Muslim community and enacted the MWPRDA in May 1986. The main objectives of the Act, as most of its opponents and supporters argued at the time, was to reverse the Supreme Court's 1985 decision in the *Shah Bano* case by excluding Muslim women from the purview of Section 125 and limiting the husband's financial responsibility to the period of *iddat*. According to the new law, if the divorced Muslim woman was unable to maintain herself after the *iddat* period, then she had to be taken care of by her children or paternal relatives; if she had no such relatives or if they were unable to provide for her, then, the State Wakf Board (the board that oversees Islamic endowments) had to step in and make her such maintenance payments at the behest of the magistrate. While all this was going on, under pressure from some elements in her community, Shah Bano wrote an open letter in which she denounced the Supreme Court's judgment: "since this judgment is contrary to the Qur'an and *Hadith* and is an open interference in Muslim personal law, I, Shah Bano, being a Muslim, reject it and dissociate myself from every judgment which is contrary to Islamic *shariat*. I am aware of the agony, and distress this judgment has subjected the Muslims of India [to] today" (Pathak and Rajan 1989, p. 572). A couple of months later, Shah Bano reportedly complained that it was no longer possible for her to continue living in her hometown due to communal pressure and sought the government's assistance to start a new life in Delhi (Jayal 2001, p. 121).

Shah Bano was not the first Muslim woman who was awarded maintenance under Section 125 of the Cr. PC of 1973. In fact in two earlier judgments,[18] the Supreme Court had ruled that a Muslim man was under obligation to provide for his divorced wife even after the completion of her *iddat* (three menstrual cycles, or until the end of pregnancy if the wife is pregnant) if she was unable to maintain herself (Singh 1994b; Menski 2007). Although both judgments had had the exact same conclusion as the 1985 ruling, they did not evoke as much controversy as did the *Shah Bano* case (Engineer 1987, pp. 35–41; Hasan 2002, p. 386). The reason why the *Shah Bano* case caused so much anger among Muslims is that, in an effort to justify their rulings in Islamic terms, an all-Hindu bench of the Supreme Court took it upon itself to ascertain the true meaning of religious concepts (as it had earlier done in relation to Hinduism – see Galanter, 1989, pp. 243–244), and exercised neo-*ijtihad* (independent legal reasoning) to reinterpret Islamic law of maintenance by ornamenting its decision with quotes from an English translation of the Qur'an (Mitra and Fischer 2002; Williams 2006, p. 141). In short, the Hindu justices literally told Muslims that they had been misreading provision- and maintenance-related verses of the Qur'an, and that according to their "correct" interpretation, verses 2:241–242[19] had enjoined Muslim men to make additional provision (*mata*)[20] to their divorced wives.

As if the all-Hindu bench had not sufficiently offended the Muslim community by inviting them to read the Qur'an more carefully, it also called upon the government to take the necessary steps to overcome Muslim opposition and immediately start framing a UCC. In an *obiter dictum*, the five-justice bench of the court argued that a UCC would not only help the cause of national unity by removing disparate loyalties, but also dispense with injustices caused by the application of personal laws in a much more comprehensive way. Moreover, they also noted that, since the government lacked the "political courage" to use its legislative competence to enact such a code, "[i]nevitably, the role of the reformer ha[d] to be assumed by the courts because, it [was] beyond the endurance of sensitive minds to allow injustice to be suffered when it [was] so palpable."[21]

---

[18] *Bai Tahira* v. *Ali Hussain Chothia* (1979) and *Fuzlunbi* v. *K. Khadir Vali* (1980).

[19] "(241) For divorced women maintenance (*mata*) should be provided on a reasonable scale. This is a duty on the righteous. (242) Thus doth Allah Make clear His Signs to you: In order that ye may understand" (*The Holy Quran*, trans. Yusuf Ali).

[20] For more information on *mata* in Islamic law, see Masud (2006) and Singh (1994b).

[21] *Mohammad Ahmed Khan* v. *Shah Bano Begum* (1985), retrieved in October 2012 from http://indiankanoon.org/doc/823221/.

In the words of Muslim leaders, the Supreme Court's *Shah Bano* judgment, which interfered with the "sacred" laws of Islam and called for their abolition by way of enacting a UCC, was one of the most serious threats ever posed to Muslim identity in India (Hasan 1994, p. 65). As expected, Muslims, who were also upset about Prime Minister Rajiv Gandhi's decision to open the gates of Babri Masjid to Hindu worshippers, responded harshly and called upon him to take legislative action in order to undo the damages caused by the Supreme Court's judgment (Noorani 2004 pp. 216–220).[22] Demonstrations and riots lasted for weeks. In a tide of protests, the Muslim minority overwhelmingly supported opposition candidates and punished the ruling Congress Party in several provincial assembly elections in 1985–1986 (Hasan 1994, p. 67; Noorani 2004, pp. 216–239). Thus, in fear of losing the Muslim "vote bank" forever, Prime Minister Gandhi reportedly conceded to the demands of Muslim organizations and agreed to take legislative action in order to overturn the *Shah Bano* ruling (Hasan 1989, pp. 48–49; Jayal 2001, pp. 112–143; Williams 2006, pp. 133–147).

Throughout the legislative process, the government almost exclusively consulted with conservative groups, which were known for their opposition to the Supreme Court judgment and their interpretation of *shariat*, and usually neglected the views of relatively secular and liberal groups, particularly those of women's organizations within the Muslim community (Hasan 1994).[23] In particular, the All India Muslim Personal Law Board (AIMPLB) – a non-elected communal organization claiming to defend Muslim personal law and identity in India – was instrumental in drafting the MWPRDA of 1986. As mentioned earlier, the new Act was primarily aimed to exclude Muslim women from the purview of Section 125. In this vein, many supporters and opponents of the Act, which obliged the Muslim husband to make and pay his former wife "within the *iddat* period a reasonable and fair provision and

---

[22] The site of the Babri Masjid in Ayodhya is important for the followers of both faiths, as the masjid was allegedly built on the ruins of a Hindu temple that was demolished by the Mughals in 1528. In order to avenge the 1528 demolition of the temple, the Hindu fundamentalists destroyed the Babri Masjid in December 1992.

[23] The government's collaboration with conservative groups during the legislative process angered and disappointed liberal elements within the Muslim community (Gani 1988, pp. 85–116; Singh 1994b, pp. 101–105). For example, Arif Mohammad Khan, the Muslim Minister of State for Home Affairs in the Gandhi cabinet, resigned from his post and the Congress Party in order to protest against the passage of the law and the Prime Minister's alliance with the AIMPLB (Noorani 2004, p. 225). Among the Muslim members of the parliament the Prime Minister consulted with there were only two female members, who both opposed the Supreme Court judgment (Williams 2006, p. 138).

maintenance," understood it at the time to limit the husband's financial obligations to his ex-wife to just three months (Subramanian 2008, p. 646).

Even though the MWPRDA later proved to be largely supportive (more so than Section 125) of Muslim women's right to maintenance – thanks to the mobilization of various women's and civil rights groups, and activism of state High Courts and the Supreme Court of India – its initial passage, as one may argue, symbolized the Indian state's inability and unwillingness to protect the interests of an individual, who opted out of her own communal laws and took advantage of secular remedies, against the threats and intimidation of male-dominated conservative forces within her cultural community (Shachar 2001, pp. 81–83; Mahajan 2002; Perez 2002; Sunder Rajan 2003, pp. 146–173). In fact, in collaboration with conservative communal forces the so-called secular government stripped Shah Bano of the rights conferred upon her by the constitution and secular legislation, and forcibly brought her back to her community's sphere of influence (Jayal 2001, pp. 148–149). By doing so, the government not only diminished Shah Bano's agency and declared her dependent upon her paternal relatives and the State Wakf Board (Noorani 2004, pp. 216–239), but also, as Solanki (2011) convincingly argues, reneged on its constitutional promise (Article 38 of the 1950 Constitution) to care for its needy citizens by delegating its welfare responsibilities to families and communal institutions.

Post-*Shah Bano* Indian politics: ideological transformation and the communalization of UCC debates

Section 125 of the Cr. PC of 1973 was a territorial provision uniformly applied to all citizens irrespective of religion. The section was also consistently applied to Muslims from 1973 to 1986 without exception. However, with the passage of the MWPRDA, the government took its third[24] most important step to date suggesting that it was formally

---

[24] The first step that contradicted the long-stated policy of replacing personal laws with general laws and provisions was taken with the enactment of the Special Marriage (Amendment) Act (32 of 1963) that allowed marriage among individuals within degrees of prohibited relationship (like first cousins), providing that at least one of the parties' customs permitted such a marriage. The 1963 amendment introduced customs and religious laws into the otherwise secular SMA of 1954 that was supposed to apply to all Indians equally irrespective of religion. The second time the government reintroduced personal laws and customs into otherwise territorial family laws was with the passage of the MLAA in 1976 (Act 68) which declared that when two Hindus married under the SMA of 1954, their ties to joint family would not be severed, and their property would devolve according to the HSA of 1956 – a communal legislation – rather than the ISA of 1925 – a general law. For further information, see n. 9 above.

backtracking from its long-declared policy of replacing personal laws with uniform secular enactments, by introducing communal legislation in lieu of the secular territorial provisions of the Cr. PC (Mahmood 1995b, p. 101). By doing so, the government explicitly acknowledged that it had neither the desire nor the power to enact a UCC and impose it unilaterally against the will of the Muslim minority.

The Congress Party in the post-Nehruvian era had persistently depicted itself as the guardian of Muslim personal law, occasionally accommodating certain needs and demands of the minority in exchange for political support (Sathe 2003, pp. 174–175). Against this background, the enactment of the MWPRDA was seen, particularly by the opposition, as another instance of Congress's traditional appeasement policy towards the Muslim minority (Upadhyaya 1992, pp. 844–848; Hasan 1994, pp. 68–70; Desouza 1999). The public perception of the Congress Party as the "appeaser of Islamists" was reinforced throughout the 1990s, as each time[25] the Supreme Court reminded the government of its obligation under Article 44 the government chose not to act. Naturally, this presented right-wing Hindu groups, particularly the Bharatiya Janata Party (BJP), with a unique opportunity to exploit the resentment and anger felt by some Hindus against the Congress Party, which, they claimed, had deprived them of their religious laws in the name of secularism while leaving the Muslim law untouched to "appease" the minority (Hasan 2001, p. 264; Kishwar 2001, pp. 206–224; Sathe 2003, pp. 191–193). In the years following the *Shah Bano* case, BJP leaders consistently portrayed themselves as positive secularists in contrast to the "pseudo-secularism" of the Congress Party (which allegedly sacrificed national unity for the sake of the Muslim vote), became the foremost advocates of the idea of "one nation under one law" and thereby demanded the immediate enactment of a UCC in the interest of national unity (Pantham 1997, pp. 528–529; Cossman and Kapur 2001, pp. 53–80; Ganguly 2003).

In such an environment, where secularism and the very concept of UCC were appropriated by right-wing politicians, the judiciary's politicized decisions, uncalled *obiter dicta* and insistence upon the government to adopt a UCC in the name of national unity have only served the interests of the Hindu nationalist parties like the BJP and its allies.

---

[25] Some of the cases in which justices of the Supreme Court invited the government to take action on Article 44 include: *National Textile Mazdur Union* v. *P. R. Ramkrishnan* (1983); *Mohammad Ahmed Khan* v. *Shah Bano Begum* (1985); *Jordam Diengdeh* v. *S. S. Chopra* (1985); *Sarla Mudgal* v. *Union of India* (1995); *Lily Thomas* v. *Union of India* (2000); *John Vallamattom* v. *Union of India* (2003).

For example, the Supreme Court's *Sarla Mudgal* judgment in 1995 became a particular favorite of the BJP (Narain 2001, pp. 62–63; Jacobsohn 2003, pp. 112–119). In a case concerning four Hindu men who contracted bigamous marriages after converting to Islam, the bench, adopting an accusatory tone, argued that while Hindus, Sikhs, Buddhists and Jains had forsaken their sentiments in the cause of national unity and integration, Muslims had stubbornly refused to make a similar sacrifice and forgo their communalism. "Those who preferred to remain in India after the partition," the justices declared, "fully knew that the Indian leaders did not believe in a two-nation or three-nation theory," and that in India there was to be only one composite nation.[26] In this respect, they argued, no community had the right to oppose the introduction of a UCC and remain a separate entity on the basis of religion. As soon as the judgment was made public, the BJP leaders adopted it as the party's main platform for the 1996 general elections (Mahmood 1995b, p. 136).

In the aftermath of the 1996 elections, the BJP emerged as a new champion of secularism and its name came to be monopolistically associated with the concept of UCC (Hansen and Jaffrelot 1998; Zavos 2002). However, many have since questioned the credibility of the BJP's commitment to secular principles and UCC (Mahmood 1995b, pp. 135–143; Menski 2001, p. 399). Frankly, critics have not been unjustified in their skepticism. After all, the BJP and its supporters were found responsible for agitating events that had led to the demolition of the Babri Masjid in Ayodhya in 1992, and the 2002 massacre in Gujarat (Hasan 2001, pp. 298–327; Setalva 2003). In fact, many supporters of the BJP have viewed UCC as a "weapon" to strip Muslim men of their patriarchal privileges that were denied to Hindu men in the name of "pseudo-secularism." For instance, Mr. Bachi Singh Shri Rawat, a former BJP Member of Parliament who introduced a failed Uniform Marriage and Divorce Bill in 2004, told me that demographic concerns had motivated him to introduce the Bill. Mr. Rawat first insisted that he had introduced the Bill for the social uplifting of Muslim women. But after our conversation had gone on for a little while and we had drunk our teas, he turned his face to four other people who were sitting in the same room with us, apparently his constituents visiting from Uttar Pradesh, and said to me:

[26] *Sarla Mudgal* v. *Union of India* (1995), retrieved in October 2012 from http://www.indian kanoon.org/doc/733037/.

> You know, the HMA [of 1955] prohibited bigamy for Hindu men, even though our religion allows it. On the other hand, a Muslim can still take up to four wives. There is no ban for them. This is not fair. If this continues, we, the Hindus, will soon become a minority in our own country and the Muslims will be the majority . . .[27]

Although the myths of Muslim polygyny and demographic time-bomb scenarios have been very popular among supporters of the BJP, they are far from reflecting reality. In truth, even though it was banned by the HMA of 1955, polygyny continues to be more commonly practiced among Hindus than Muslims (Muradabadi 2010). Thus, in sum, it can be said that the BJP's communalized rhetoric on UCC has suffered from a lack of sincere commitment to the constitutional principles of secularism and a belief in gender equality. Rather, it has been a vindictive discourse that essentially sought to avenge the loss of Hindu male privileges by inflicting a similar "pain" on Muslim men and subduing the Muslim minority to the will of the Hindu majority by abolishing their communal laws (Jacobsohn 2003, p. 115).

In conclusion, the *Shah Bano* controversy, the demolition of Babri Masjid, the pogroms of Gujarat and the rise of the BJP and its allies have profoundly transformed the Indian political landscape in the 1990s and early 2000s, and inseparably tied the UCC debates to right-wing politics. The politicization of personal law issues has led to rigidification of communal boundaries and reassertion of ethno-religious loyalties and belongings (Narain 2001, p. 97). The politics of religious self-assertion, particularly in minority communities, has suppressed divergent interests and the rights of individuals (especially women) and subordinated them to those of communities. Under such circumstances, where the Hindu fundamentalists cynically took upon themselves the task of elevating Muslim women by introducing a UCC, all actors, from political parties to the judiciary, women's organizations to Islamists, have felt a pressing need to realign their policies and strategies in line with the ideological changes that have shaken Indian politics since 1986.

"Restrained" judicial activism: women's groups push for a change in Muslim personal law

"The absence of a UCC in the last quarter of the twentieth century," declared the 1974 report of the National Committee on the Status of Women, "is an incongruity that cannot be justified with all the emphasis

---

[27] Personal interview with Mr. Bachi Singh Shri Rawat (New Delhi, March 2005).

that is placed on secularism, science and modernism. The continuation of various personal laws which accept discrimination between men and women violates the fundamental rights" (Menon 1998, p. 244). From the 1950s to the mid-1980s, there was a general consensus among Indian women's organizations that the social uplifting of women could only be achieved through the replacement of religious laws with a gender-equitable UCC (Menon 1998, p. 251). However, as Professor Zoya Hasan,[28] a leading member of the Indian feminist movement, puts it, the ideological transformations that have taken place since the mid-1980s, the rise of communal violence and the monopolization of the UCC debate by right-wing ideologues have compelled women's organizations to relinquish the idea of a common civil code as the central platform of gender equality. In fact, claims by Ritu Menon,[29] a prominent feminist publisher, that no women's organization would ever support a UCC Bill sponsored by the BJP due to justified suspicions of the party's actual motives, are indicative of the extent to which women's groups have changed their attitude towards UCC since 1974. However, as the President of the Muslim Women's Forum, Dr. Syeda Hamid, points out, exploitation of personal law issues by "racist" and "sexist" forces and the rising communalism of the 1990s have posed the most difficult ideological and ethical dilemmas for Muslim feminists:

> The bottom line is that there should be a uniform law for all citizens ... But, of course, we changed our attitude and policy ... We had to. ... When the community is battered you keep your silence. How you can talk about reform when you are being killed ...? How you can use the same language [UCC] with the people who are battering you [right-wing Hindus] ...? You know what happened in Ayodhya, you know about the pogroms and genocide of Gujarat ... When the state becomes a predator ... you keep your silence, you do not talk about reforming the Islamic law, because everything is about identity and everything is about religion ...[30]

Against this background, most women's organizations have been forced to modify their strategies and programs in the last two decades. Although in the past they primarily relied upon top-down legislative measures for reform, nowadays they seem to have instead come to articulate alternative positions based on gender equality (Hasan 1999, p. 131). First, since the second half of the 1980s, we have observed a

[28] Personal interview with Prof. Zoya Hasan (New Delhi, March 2005).
[29] Personal interview with Ritu Menon (New Delhi, February 2005).
[30] Personal interview with Dr. Syeda Hamid (New Delhi, April 2005).

widespread effort to reform personal laws from within, particularly across the Christian and Parsi communities. In fact, this new strategy proved successful in the 1990s, when the Parsi and Christian personal laws were amended by the parliament to make them more gender equitable at the request of communal forces. Another strategy which seems to have gained currency among women's activists is legal mobilization, or targeted use of the courts to challenge the legitimacy of gender-unequal norms, raise awareness within the community and lay the groundwork for long-term institutional change from within using the threat of external intervention, as seen in the example of the Muslim maintenance issue in Israel.

In the post-emergency era the Indian Supreme Court and state High Courts have emerged as champions of progressive judicial activism, as access to justice was widened by increasing availability of such remedies as public interest litigation (Desai and Muralidhar 2000; Iyer 2002; Sathe 2003; Johari 2004, pp. 176–185). The courts' new activism was also felt in the field of personal law. A close reading of court rulings in the post-emergency era demonstrates that courts have often tried to advance the rights of women by narrowing the gap between the provisions of general law and the personal laws (Sarkar 2001; Deshta 2002, p. 125; Nussbaum 2005). The same trend reverberated across the Supreme Court and state High Courts, which in several landmark cases have signaled relaxation of their longstanding opposition to challenging the constitutionality of personal laws,[31] particularly in reference to the equal protection (Article 14), gender equality (Article 15) and personal liberty (Article 21) clauses of the constitution (Narain 2001, pp. 67–74; Desai 2004). The courts' increasing activism was paralleled by the birth of a vibrant support structure that included women's and civil rights groups, intellectuals, academics and individual lawyers who spearheaded the feminist legal movement and took advantage of the liberal opening in the court system to promote gender equality (Epp 1998, pp. 71–110; Subramanian 2008).

As noted earlier the Indian Muslim laws, with their traditional gender-unequal practices such as triple *talaq* and polygyny, have failed to keep pace not only with recent changes in Hindu, Christian and Parsi laws in India but also with changes in Muslim family laws in Pakistan

---

[31] *Anil Kumar Mhasi* v. *Union of India* (1994); *Madhu Kishwar* v. *State of Bihar* (1996); *Githa Hariharan* v. *Reserve Bank of India* (1999); *Danial Latifi* v. *Union of India* (2001); *John Vallamattom* v. *Union of India* (2003).

and Bangladesh (Hayat 2001; Fyzee and Mahmood 2005; Shah 2005). In other words, there was a pressing need for reform in order to ease the predicament of Muslim women under marital laws. However, in the aftermath of the Shah Bano debacle, chances of reforming Muslim law through top-down legislative means grew even slimmer. In this respect, the increasing activism of the Indian judiciary presented Muslim women with an invaluable opportunity to mobilize the courts for long-needed remedies that would improve their rights and status. The MWRPDA of 1986, enacted, as feminists believed, with the purpose of restricting the Muslim husband's financial obligations towards his ex-wife to the *iddat* period by removing the Muslim wife from the purview of Section 125 of the Cr. PC of 1973, had been on the radar of women's rights activists for some time (Hameed 2003, pp. 24–26; Kusum 2003, pp. 216–217). Thus, as soon as the 1986 Act came into force, Muslim activists filed petitions to challenge its constitutionality on grounds that it violated fundamental rights enshrined in Articles 14, 15 and 21 of the constitution (Hasan 1993; Desai 2004; Subramanian 2008, p. 646; Serajuddin 2011, p. 64).

While writ petitions challenging the 1986 Act lay dormant in the Supreme Court for nearly fifteen years, the Act itself unfolded in the lower courts (Agnes 2004, p. 8). The intriguing phenomenon that was revealed in the decisions of the lower courts was that, despite the lawmakers' ambiguous intentions, "a seemingly innocuous clause which had missed the attention of protesters and defenders alike" had been invoked by some activist judges to pronounce judgments which practically expanded Muslim women's right to maintenance (Agnes 2004, p. 8).[32] The relevant text in Article 3(1)(a) – "a reasonable and fair provision and maintenance to be made and paid her within the *iddat* period by her former husband" – was interpreted by judges in a way that required the husband to make a lump-sum payment to his ex-wife during the *iddat* period, which included not only the maintenance (*nafaqa*) and the deferred part of her dower (*mahr*), but also a "fair provision" that would financially secure her well beyond the *iddat* period (Serajuddin 2011, pp. 66–67). In fact, the lump-sum amounts awarded by expansionist courts to Muslim wives under the 1986 Act were reported to be significantly higher than what they would otherwise have been under Section 125 of the Cr. PC (Menski 2006, 2007).

---

[32] For example, A. A. *Abdulla* v. A. B. *Mohmuna Saiyadbhai* (1988); *Ahmed* v. *Ayasha* (1990); *Jaitunbi Mubarak Shaikh* v. *Mubarak Shaikh* (1993). For further information, see Subramanian (2008, p. 647, n. 19) and Uma (2004, p. 31, n. xvi).

Apart from such expansionist rulings issued by activist courts, there were also opposing judgments issued by minimalist courts, which interpreted Article 3(1)(a) in a way that limited the husband's responsibility to the *iddat* period alone.[33] As the favorable rulings of the lower courts accumulated, the women's organizations gradually changed their stance towards the MWPRDA and concentrated their efforts on upholding its expansionist interpretations. Hence, they decided to take the battle to the Supreme Court to defeat the minimalist interpretations (Subramanian 2008).

Women argued that construing the provisions of the 1986 Act as less beneficial than the provisions of the Cr. PC and holding the husband liable to pay maintenance only for the *iddat* period would result in discrimination against divorced Muslim wives under Articles 14, 15 and 21 of the constitution. In defense of the minimalist interpretations of Article 3(1)(a), the AIMPLB and Islamic Shariat Board (ISB) argued that, under Islamic law, a Muslim man could not be obliged to pay maintenance to his ex-wife beyond the *iddat* period. In the end, the court upheld the 1986 Act as constitutional, but it struck down its restrictive interpretations as unconstitutional. It also declared that a Muslim husband was liable to make reasonable and fair payment to his divorced wife that would include maintenance as well as a generous provision extending well beyond *iddat*.[34]

The case that has come to be known as *Danial Latifi* v. *Union of India* (2001) was an important symbolic victory for the women's rights activists. But it was also remarkable because it taught women's rights groups what they needed to know for successful legal mobilization. Even though the court in the *Danial Latifi* case arrived at practically the same conclusion as that of the bench in the *Shah Bano* case and extended the Muslim husband's responsibility towards his ex-wife, the decision did not evoke as much opposition among Muslims as did the latter case. There were certainly no violent demonstrations or riots on the streets. Apart from the fact that it was announced only seventeen days after the 9/11 attacks at a time when Indian Muslims may have been particularly averse to going out and protesting (Menski 2009, p. 42), one of the main reasons for the rather quiet acceptance of the judgment in the *Danial Latifi* case was that the court exercised extreme restraint, limiting the

---

[33] For example, *Mohammed Yunus* v. *Bibi Phenkani, alias Tasrun Nisa* (1987); *Abid Ali* v. *Mst. Rasia Begum* (1988); *Usman Khan Bahamani* v. *Fathimunnisa Begum* (1990). For further information, see Subramanian (2008, p. 646, n.18) and Uma (2004, p. 31, n. XVII).

[34] *Danial Latifi* v. *Union of India* (2001), retrieved in October 2012 from http://indiankanoon.org/doc/1751784/.

scope of its inquiry to immediate questions of rights without provoking
reactions from religious conservatives by making assertions about the
desirability of a UCC, the allegedly "misogynistic" nature of Islam or
engaging in Qur'anic exegesis (Subramanian 2008, p. 648; Sen 2010,
pp. 146–148):

> In this case to find out the personal law of Muslims with regard
> to divorced women's rights, the starting point should be Shah Bano's
> case and not the original texts or any other material – all the more so
> when varying versions as to the authenticity of the source are shown to
> exist. Hence, we have refrained from referring to them in detail. That
> declaration was made after considering the Holy *Qur'an*, and other
> commentaries or other texts. *When a Constitution Bench of this Court
> analyzed Suras* [sic] *241–242 of Chapter II of the Holy Qur'an and other
> relevant textual material, we do not think, it is open for us to re-examine that
> position and delve into a research to reach another conclusion* [emphasis
> added]. We respectfully abide by what has been stated therein. All that
> needs to be considered is whether in the Act specific deviation has been
> made from the personal laws as declared by this Court in Shah Bano's
> case without mutilating its underlying rationale. We have carefully
> analyzed the same and come to the conclusion that *the Act actually and
> in reality codifies what was stated in Shah Bano's case* [emphasis added].[35]

In this regard, the first lesson the women's rights activists learned from
the experience of *Danial Latifi* was that, for successful legal mobilization,
they needed the collaboration of "prudent" judges who would exercise
restraint and shy away from politicized decisions and writing unsolicited
obiter dicta that did more harm than good to the cause of women's rights
in both the short and long term. *Danial Latifi* was not the only case where
women's rights activists sought judicial intervention to bring about
changes in Muslim personal law. In two earlier cases (*Ahmedabad
Women's Action Group [AWAG]* v. *Union of India* in 1997 and *Lily
Thomas* v. *Union of India* in 2000), women's rights groups challenged
the constitutionality of Islamic inheritance laws as well as triple *talaq*
and polygyny on grounds that they discriminated against women and
violated the relevant provisions of the constitution (Kusum 2003,
pp. 312–314; Uma 2004, p. 31). The Supreme Court dismissed both
petitions and instead advised the claimants to approach the government
with a note that it was up to the parliament to make and amend laws, not
the judges, who were by law required to exercise judicial restraint.

[35] *Ibid.*

Hence, the second lesson for women's rights activists was that courts were hesitant to usurp the powers of the legislature and introduce significant changes in personal laws. They were only willing to make piecemeal changes without causing a disruption in the system. In other words, there were limits to legal mobilization and judicial intervention. The desired change in the Muslim personal laws had to come from within the Muslim community. The question was, however, whether the communal institutions were ready and willing to allow such a change and grant women greater freedoms.

The women's response to *shariat* courts and rising conservatism of communal institutions

Notwithstanding the landmark decision of the Supreme Court in the *Danial Latifi* case, in which the justices provided a binding interpretation of Section 3(1)(a) of the MWPRDA,[36] some confusion regarding its application continued to exist in the following decade (Serajuddin 2011, p. 67). Some lower- as well as state-level High Courts continued to limit divorced Muslim women's right to maintenance to the *iddat* period alone. For instance, in *Sabra Shamim* v. *Maqsood Ansari* (2004), *Iqbal Bano* v. *State of UP* (2007) and *Shabana Bano* v. *Imran Khan* (2009), the Supreme Court had to intervene in order to strike down the rulings of lower courts that contradicted the court's decision in the *Danial Latifi* case, and reminded them of the binding nature of the interpretation of Section 3(1)(a) it provided therein. What seem to be the main reasons for such contradictory decisions of the lower courts and provincial High Courts are the lack of coordination between the Supreme Court and lower courts, and the lower court judges' and lawyers' misunderstanding and lack of knowledge of the Supreme Court rulings and their wider implications. In fact, in explaining the reasons why lower court judges often disregard the Supreme Court's landmark decisions on triple *talaq* (i.e., *Shamim Ara* v. *State of UP* (2002)),[37] which laid down criteria to regulate it and prevent its misuse, Solanki arrives at a similar conclusion:

---

[36] "A reasonable and fair provision and maintenance to be made and paid to her within the *iddat* period by her former husband."

[37] In *Shamim Ara* v. *State of UP* (2002), the Supreme Court laid down the following criteria for the validity of triple *talaq*: An oral *talaq*, if contested by the wife, will need to be proved in court (witnesses, documentation, etc.). Moreover, to be legally valid, *talaq* must be given for a reasonable cause. And there have to be attempts at reconciliation between the husband and the wife by two arbiters before the husband can legally grant a divorce.

> ... state-led attempts at reforms from above are diffused due to lack of coordination between higher and lower courts in India. Communal outlook of the judges ... fear of reversal and lack of knowledge about the Muslim personal law, and a desire to avoid controversy (especially in the matter of Muslim personal law) are some reasons why judges in the Family Court do not push for strict criteria to validate triple *talaq* ... I also found that ... a majority of lawyers were unaware of this judgment and its implications.
>
> (Solanki 2011, pp. 136–137)

In other words, however important or revolutionary they may have been, changes introduced through judicial means have been rather equivocal and have had limited effects on the ground. The limitation has not only been due to the aforementioned resistance of the lower courts in complying with the Supreme Court's rulings, and the lack of coordination between the two, but also to the fact that state courts (both family and magistrates' courts) have continued to remain largely inaccessible (and even irrelevant) to the majority of Indian women (Muslim and non-Muslim alike). Most Indian Muslims have instead used non-state dispute resolution mechanisms that include community-run *shariat* courts, plus other informal legal sites that Solanki (2011) refers to as "doorstep law courts." Against this background, therefore, in order for any change in the Muslim personal law to be meaningful – that is, to have immediate impact on the rights and livelihoods of average men and women from whom the parliamentary Acts, state courts and judicial precedents have long remained distant – it has to come from within the community with the support and blessing of the communal forces concerned.

Yet, in order for this option to work, as seen in both the Christian and Parsi examples above, the community in question has to first reach an internal consensus regarding the nature of the problem and the desired changes. However, communal institutions (e.g., AIMPLB) that were supposed to spearhead reform processes in the Muslim community, have long been controlled by conservative groups which have opposed almost any possibility of change in the name of "protecting" the Muslim identity against the Hindu majority. Moreover, these very same groups have been recognized as the only representatives of the Muslim community by the government, and exclusively consulted by authorities on questions of Muslim personal law (e.g., the amendment of the Cr. PC of 1973 and drafting of the MWPRDA of 1986) (Williams 2006, p. 138). Thus, the conservative groups have established firm control over the Muslim community and its institutions, successfully forestalling nearly all attempts at external or internal reform in its laws.

The All India Muslim Personal Law Board (AIMPLB) has been the leading institution shaping the development of Indian Muslim personal law in the last three decades. It was founded in 1972 in order to ensure continued application of Muslim personal law and subvert legislative attempts to introduce a UCC. The Board rose to political prominence during the *Shah Bano* controversy as a member of the group with whom Rajiv Gandhi negotiated the terms of the 1986 Act (Noorani 2004, pp. 216–239). Apart from its role in the legislative process, one of the very first responses of the Board to the *Shah Bano* case was to adopt a resolution for setting up an independent network of *shariat* courts or *Dar-ul Qazas*. The Board has since set up about two dozen such courts throughout India, which have so far decided about 6,400 personal status cases (Hussain 2007, p. 6).[38] An executive committee member of the AIMPLB, Dr. Qasim Rasool Ilyas,[39] explained the reasons why the formation of a parallel judicial system reserved exclusively for Muslims became, in the view of the Board, a necessity:

> [First] the Indian courts are not qualified to interpret the *shariat* – especially when the judges are non-Muslims. How can a Hindu judge interpret the Holy *Qur'an*? According to *shariat*, non-Muslims cannot legislate or administer the Islamic law . . . only the members of *'ulama'* can do that. [Second], Islam requires the believers to approach *shariat* courts and resolve their differences according to the customs and rules of Islam. [Third], the 1937 Shariat Application Act [MPLSAA] provided the legal legitimation for setting up such courts . . . So, these courts are not illegal or harmful bodies . . . This is a system of *Lok Adalat* . . . We are only trying to help the Indian judicial system.

The members of *'ulama'* appointed by the AIMPLB are employed as *qazis* in the *shariat* courts. Most of these judges are well versed in Arabic, Urdu and Islamic jurisprudence. They decide all sorts of matrimonial and succession-related disputes among Muslims. They also occasionally issue *fatwas* (legal opinions) in regard to such legal questions as whether

---

[38] In addition to *Dar-ul Qazas* set up by the AIMPLB, there are several other organizations which also run their own courts. For instance, the Imarat-e Shariah Bihar and Orissa has operated its own network of *shariat* courts in several states since the 1920s (Mahmood 2001). Apart from these hierarchically structured networks, there are also a number of autonomous *shariat* courts throughout India which primarily arbitrate personal law-related disputes among Muslims (Kozlowski 2005, pp. 110–112; Hussain 2007, p. 7).

[39] Personal interview with Dr. Qasim Rasool Ilyas (New Delhi, March 2005).

pronouncement of *talaq* through internet or video conferencing will be religiously sound and valid (Islamic Fiqh Academy 2001). All cases brought to *Dar-ul Qazas* are decided according to the *Compendium of Islamic Law* – a Board-authorized compilation of Muslim personal laws (All India Muslim Personal Law Board 2001). *Shariat* courts are essentially voluntary arbitration councils, which cannot require individual Muslims to accept their jurisdiction or force anyone to abide by their decisions. The implementation issue is often cited as a serious concern by the people who use these courts. In some instances, as Hussain reports, individuals who initially came to *shariat* courts found themselves needing to subsequently refile their cases with civil courts to recover their matrimonial rights (maintenance, etc.) because *shariat* courts lacked the authority to implement their decisions (Hussain 2007, p. 24). Nonetheless, as I observed during my interviews with both *qazis* and clients who resorted to *shariat* courts, most people, in spite of this implementation-related drawback, seem to come to *Dar-ul Qazas* as a result of a confluence of factors such as cost, speed, religious conviction, cultural familiarity and social and familial pressure.

The *qazi* of the Delhi *shariat* court, located in a relatively poor neighborhood in South Delhi, was a soft-spoken young man with a long beard and a white turban on his head. After he learned that I was from Turkey, he warmly welcomed me and said:

> It is the obligation of a Muslim to live according to rules of *shariat*. When there is a *shariat* court, if one goes to state courts and wins a case according to rules applied by non-Muslims it will be *haram* or a sin in the eyes of Allah ... Muslims have to come to *shariat* courts; even if they lose, they will [still] be winners in the eyes of Allah.[40]

In effect, *Qazi* Qasmi was only expressing the official position of the AIMPLB, which has actively sought to discourage Muslims from resorting to civil courts, particularly in the aftermath of the *Danial Latifi* case where it failed to influence the Supreme Court's interpretation of the 1986 Act. Members of the Board widely popularized the view that it was Islamically forbidden for Muslim women to demand maintenance from their husbands after completion of their *iddat*. In fact, as both Vatuk (2001, 2005) and Uma (2004, p. 31) demonstrate, the Board's conservative views on maintenance have effectively discouraged Muslim women from asserting their rights to post-nuptial maintenance under

---

[40] Personal interview with Qazi Mohammad Kamil Qasmi (New Delhi, March 2005).

the 1986 Act. That the Board has promoted its own informal legal institutions at the expense of state courts has caused friction both within and without the community. For example, in 2005 a public interest petition (*Vishwa Lochan Madan* v. *Union of India*) was submitted to the Supreme Court of India asking the bench to declare *Dar-ul Qazas* established by the AIMPLB and other similar organizations absolutely "illegal" and "unconstitutional." The petition also asked the court to issue a clear direction to the union and state governments to forthwith take effective steps to disband all *Dar-ul Qazas* set up throughout the country. However, in its reply to the petition, the central government noted that:

> [the] freedom guaranteed by Article 26 to every religious denomination or every section thereof to establish and maintain institutions for religious and charitable purposes and to manage its own affairs in matters of religion would include the freedom to establish *Dar-ul Qazas* to settle disputes between two persons professing Islam, according to the *shariat*. [Seeking dismissal of the petition, the government further argued that] the *Dar-ul Qazas* do not prevent Muslims from reporting matters to the judicial machinery set up under the law of the land. Those who do not want to resort to the *Dar-ul Qazas* are at liberty to resort to courts of law. The *Dar-ul Qazas* are just a form of alternative dispute redressal forum without any enforcement power.
>
> (Negi 2006; Wunrn 2007)

With regard to the government's reply to the Supreme Court, it is highly possible that the government did not want to upset the feelings of conservative Muslims by directly challenging the legitimacy of the Islamic institutions and *'ulama'*.[41] However, the government's assertions seem to be in agreement with the prevailing position of the Indian judiciary. In interviews that I conducted with Indian justices who served in various capacities at civil courts,[42] I was told that the decisions of the *shariat* courts can be upheld by the state courts under the provisions of the 1996 Arbitration and Conciliation Act. In a number of cases, in fact, the courts actually recognized the decisions of the Islamic courts, accepted their records as part of evidence, and allowed the *qazis* to stand as witnesses to testify the validity of these records (Khan 2005; Thomas 2006).

---

[41] For a detailed analysis of the Indian government's response to the petition, see Redding (2010).
[42] Personal interviews with the former Chief Justice of the High Court of Delhi, Japal Singh, and the former Chief Justice of the High Court of Punjab and Haryana, P. C. Jain (New Delhi, April 2005).

The political and legal recognition granted to the Board and its *shariat* courts has boosted its domineering control over the community and given it the support to subordinate groups within the community who promote non-orthodox interpretations of Islamic law. From the beginning, realizing the increasing control of the AIMPLB over religious law and institutions, many Muslim women activists joined the Board and its decision-making bodies in order to draw attention to and resolve women's issues under the Muslim personal law (Manjul 2005). For example, like the Egyptian Muslim women who wanted to put an end to the predicament of triple *talaq*, some female members prepared a model *nikahnama* (marriage contract), which allowed women to stipulate conditions in the contract such as an option for delegated divorce (*talaq-e tawfiz*), through which the husband permits his wife to divorce at her own will, and presented it to the Board for approval. However, the male-dominated Board rejected it on the claim that it was an "un-Islamic" proposal, and swiftly silenced non-compliant women's voices throughout the organization (Niaz 2004, p. 28).

In response, some female members of the Board split from it and set up the All India Muslim Women Personal Law Board (AIMWPLB) in 2005 in Lucknow. As with several other women's organizations (e.g., the Muslim Women's Rights Network (MWRN), the Bharatiya Muslim Mahila Andolan (BMMA), etc.), one of the first things the women-led Board did was to release a women-friendly model *nikahnama* in March 2008 (Solanki 2011, pp. 316–320). That laywomen who read and reinterpreted scriptural and prophetic sources of Islamic law through "feminist" lenses had drafted a women-friendly *nikahnama* sparked a new controversy within the community and raised some eyebrows, particularly among the AIMPLB-affiliated clergy (Ramakrishnan 2008). The main strategy the AIMWPLB adopted, as explained by the president of the new Board, Shaista Amber, was to advance women's rights within an Islamic framework without publicly discussing the status of women under Islam or radically disrupting existing power relations and institutions in the community.[43] With this in mind, the new *nikahnama* prohibited *talaq* through text messaging, email, video-conferencing or phone, and recognized women's right to delegated (*talaq-e tawfiz*) and no-fault divorce (*khulʿ*) (Ramakrishnan 2008). Moreover, the model *nikahnama*, which allowed women to seek dissolution of the marriage if the husband had had an illicit relationship

---

[43] Phone interview with Shaista Amber (May 2010).

with another woman or refused to disclose his HIV/AIDS status before or after marriage, also stipulated, in consonance with Qur'anic injunctions and the Supreme Court's recent decisions, that in order for *talaq* to be legally valid it has to be preceded by arbitration or reconciliation attempts.

Shaista Amber reports that the new *nikahnama* has steadily gained acceptance in the community and about fifty couples have so far married under the relatively gender-balanced contract.[44] Even though the number of marriages contracted under women-friendly *nikahnamas* (including those of AIMWPLB, BMMA, MWRN, etc.) remains relatively small for various social and structural reasons, they have reportedly played an instrumental role in raising the awareness of both brides and grooms about the status and rights of women conferred by Islam but currently denied under the state- or community-enforced Muslim personal laws (Kirmani 2011, p. 61). Besides the model *nikahnama*, the women's Board has also set up its own court (*mahila adalat*) and has begun deciding cases according to a woman-friendly interpretation of *shariat* (Awasthi 2006). The women's court is located in Lucknow and convenes every Friday at a local mosque built by Shaista Amber. It currently decides about two hundred divorce cases per year. Both male and female *qazis* sit together at the *mahila adalat*. The law they apply, according to Ms. Amber, is not substantively different from the Muslim personal law applied by AIMPLB courts, but *qazis* at the *mahila adalat* implement it with an eye on "universal standards of human and women's rights."[45]

A few months before the departure of the women's groups from the AIMPLB, the Barelvi and Shiʿa Muslims had also left the Board and set up their own independent platforms: All India Muslim Personal Law Board-Jadeed (AIMPLB-J) and the All India Shiʿa Personal Law Board (AISPLB) respectively (Mukerjee 2005). The rising power of the right-wing Hindu groups, the demolition of the Babri Masjid and the massacres of Gujarat may have, understandably, put the communal institutions on high alert and made them more defensive about external interventions in Muslim personal laws. But it is worth noting that besides external interventions and demands for change, the AIMPLB has also rejected relatively modest reform demands coming from within the community, all in the name of protecting the Muslim identity. The Board's conservative stance towards non-orthodox representations of

---

[44] *Ibid.*   [45] *Ibid.*

Muslim laws has not only caused Muslim personal laws to lag behind those in neighboring Pakistan and Bangladesh (i.e., in terms of women's rights to divorce, etc.), but also disunity among Indian Muslims, as evidenced by recent break-ups of personal law boards. In this respect, one may conclude that as long as the AIMPLB and similar organizations maintain a domineering control over the community, one cannot expect to see a tangible change in Muslim personal law in the short term. This may be a grim picture. But, as exemplified by the growing number of Muslim women's organizations (i.e., AIMWPLB, Aawaaz-e-Niswaan, BMMA, MWRN, etc.) in recent years, there is equally a hope for change through hermeneutic means (Vatuk 2008; Schneider 2009). In fact, what we are witnessing is a slow but steady revolution spearheaded by Muslim women who could rely on neither the secular state nor the male-dominated communal institutions to recover their matrimonial rights, but only on their own initiative in reinterpreting *shariat* through feminist and liberal lenses.

CONCLUSION

Before independence, India had long been divided along ethno-religious and caste lines. If the country was to become a unified and composite nation, the founders of the Indian Republic believed it had to welcome all, and make differences based on caste, religion and ethnicity irrelevant in defining the rights and duties of its citizens. To that end, religion- and caste-based personal laws that were believed to nurture communalist sentiments had to be abolished and replaced with a secular UCC that would inculcate a spirit of national unity among the inhabitants of the country. However, even though more than six decades have passed since Article 44 found its way into the constitution, the Indian government has not yet enacted such a common civil code – partly due to its leaders' unwillingness to further alienate the already estranged Muslim minority, and partly due to their inability to overcome the opposition of minority groups to the idea of UCC.

In the absence of a UCC, the Indian government instead turned its attention to the unification and codification of the personal laws of the "Hindu" majority, in the hope that in the course of time the minorities would follow the example set by the majority community so that one day the entire country could be brought under the purview of a UCC. However, 1955–1956 HCB reforms never set in motion a revolutionary change, as some hoped for, in the laws of minority communities. Thus, the country was never brought under a single civil code. Instead, having increasingly realized the impossibility of the task of legal unification, the Indian government, particularly from the 1970s onwards, undertook partial convergence and harmonization of separate communal laws through judicial and legislative means. For instance, two days after the Supreme Court upheld the expansionist interpretations of Article 3(1)(a) of the 1986 Act in the *Danial Latifi* case, the Indian Parliament removed the Rs. 500 per month upper limit under Section 125 of the Cr. PC of 1973, and thereby brought non-Muslim women's post-nuptial maintenance rights on a par with those of Muslim women (Subramanian 2008, p. 648). In other words, as Menski puts it, with the removal of the aforesaid limit, "the post-divorce maintenance law for all Indians was restored to an equitable level" (Menski 2012, p. 45). "Only a few minutes later, parliament proceeded to harmonize India's divorce laws further, introducing long-demanded additional grounds for Christian divorce [Act No. 51 of 2001]" so that Indian divorce laws were now made virtually uniform, particularly across the Hindu, Parsee and Christian communities (Menski 2012, p. 45). In this respect, as Solanki demonstrates, after 1984 some Family Courts also pushed for routinization and centralization of family laws across different religious communities through adjudicative means. However, the trend towards harmonization, as she argues, was simultaneously accompanied by a decentralizing tendency within the state law that further fragmented and led to "societalization" of the law which, in turn, offset some of the gains made (especially in respect to gender equality) through convergence and harmonization of communal laws during the last several decades (Solanki 2011, pp. 91–174).

The impacts of state-enforced religious personal laws on the fundamental rights and liberties of Indian citizens have been, in many regards, similar to those of state-enforced religious laws on the citizens of Israel and Egypt. The detrimental impacts of state-enforced religious laws were particularly visible in respect of women's rights to inheritance and property (despite recent legislative changes) in the Hindu community, and in relation to women's rights to divorce and post-nuptial maintenance – at least until the Supreme Court's landmark decision in 2001 – in the Muslim community. Like the Egyptian and Israeli governments, which have long refrained from undertaking substantive reforms in Muslim personal laws (with certain exceptions, as explained in Chapters 3 and 4), the Indian state has systematically shied away from interfering with Muslim marital laws for fear of further antagonizing the Muslim minority, especially conservative male elements within it.

The government's unwillingness to undertake substantive reform in Muslim personal laws has put an extra burden on Indian Muslim women, whose rights, particularly in respect of marriage and divorce, have lagged behind those of not only Hindu, Christian and Parsi women in India but also Muslim women in Pakistan and Bangladesh. However, like their counterparts in Israel and Egypt, Indian Muslim women have responded to the limitations and disabilities imposed upon their rights under state-enforced religious laws by employing various resistance strategies. The first strategy they used was legal mobilization. The common law tradition, the availability of public interest litigation, the increasing judicial activism of Indian courts after 1977 and the near closure of the door of legislative intervention after 1986, have all made legal mobilization an appealing strategy for Muslim women who wanted to reform their personal laws. However, as seen in the example of the *Danial Latifi* case, changes introduced through judicial means have had rather equivocal and limited effects on the ground. As explained above, the reason is twofold: First, due to lack of coordination between lower and higher courts, and lower courts judges' and lawyers' lack of knowledge of relevant judicial precedents, spoils of the judicial gains have often not trickled down and had an immediate impact on the ground. Second, state courts where precedent-setting victories were won have continued to remain inaccessible to the majority of women, especially outside of cities. Moreover, as discussed above, some of those who wanted to use legal and judicial remedies made available to women were effectively discouraged by such groups as the AIMPLB from using state courts, and instead channeled to communal institutions (e.g., *Dar-ul Qazas*). Thus, against this background, as judicial and legislative remedies became increasingly unavailable or ineffective, Indian Muslim women's groups, like those in Israel and Egypt, have in recent years begun to use hermeneutic means in order to solve their personal status-related problems and advance their rights to divorce and maintenance within an Islamic framework.

Unlike Israel or Egypt, India claims to provide its citizens with a civil marriage and divorce law – the SMA of 1954. In other words, Indian citizens who do not want to be subject to state-enforced religious laws can, at least theoretically, opt for the secular law instead of their communal laws. In this respect, the question was, as stated earlier, whether the availability of such secular remedies as the SMA of 1954 or Section 125 of the Cr. PC of 1973 had indeed provided Indians with a viable exit option and made them better off than their counterparts in

Israel and Egypt who lacked a similar optional civil code. The existing evidence suggests that the availability of such secular remedies as the SMA of 1954 has not really furnished Indians with a practicable secular option. For example, as both Mahmood (1978a, pp. 51–55) and Mody (2008, pp. 129–138) demonstrate, most Indians have been either unaware of the existence of the SMA of 1954 or hesitant to use it due to prevailing socio-cultural sanctions against the use of secular state law for family matters, and obstructive practices of authorities who openly discouraged people from registering their marriages under the Act.[46] Similarly, the events which took place in the aftermath of the *Shah Bano* case in 1985 raised an important question about the ability and readiness of the Indian government to deliver on its constitutional promises and protect individual citizens who wanted to step out of their communal boundaries and take advantage of civil remedies guaranteed by the state against the encroachments and threats of communal forces.

In this respect, like in Israel and Egypt, the examination of human rights-related concerns and local rights discourses under the Indian personal law system provides us with a unique insight into the Indian government's performance and ability to achieve the objectives that some of its rulers aimed to achieve through their interventions into the personal law system. The main considerations that led the framers of the constitution to insert Article 44 into it were said to be the desire to secularize and unify the legal system, and to do away with communalism and forge a composite national identity. Some of these concerns were also discernible in respect of other normative and substantive interventions undertaken by the government. Thus, given the ideological polarization and monopolization of UCC debates by pro-Hindutva groups since the 1990s, the recent prevalence of *Dar-ul Qazas* that explicitly aim to demobilize the law and water down women's rights, the political, judicial and legal recognition granted to these informal courts in recent years (which, in some respects, brought about further confessionalization of the Indian personal law system – despite ongoing convergence attempts through legislative and judicial means), as well as the limited resources and the questionable commitment of the Indian

---

[46] As Solanki (2011, p. 111) reports, "in many cases, runaway couples find it easier to opt for religious personal laws through conversion of one of the parties, usually women, because the process is swift and private." Even though the SMA of 1954 remains a rarely utilized law, the Family Courts frequently deal with "interreligious" marriages, undertaken usually after the conversion of the bride-to-be to the religion of her future husband, particularly in cases involving claims for nullity, annulments and maintenance (Solanki 2011, pp. 111–114).

state to protect individual citizens who wanted to take advantage of state-guaranteed secular remedies, one may argue that the Indian state has fallen short of achieving the goals that some of its earlier rulers aimed to achieve through their interventions into the personal law system.

Lastly, the chapter has demonstrated that normative unification is a colossally difficult task for any government. It requires unshakable political and ideological commitment on the part of the reforming elite, and the mobilization of an enormous amount of government resources. In this respect, the example of India offers invaluable insights about the complexity of challenges postcolonial governments encounter in the process of normative unification. The Nehru government not only encountered opposition to its process of normative unification from religious minorities (notably the Muslims), but it also failed to pass the HCB at the first attempt because of its failure to overcome internal opposition within the Congress Party. It was an embarrassing defeat for the Prime Minister, as he was forced to let go of his Minister of Law and to trim some of the more egalitarian and liberal provisions of the original Bill in order to secure the support of conservative Hindus. In the end, the government's failure to overcome the opposition of conservative forces within the Hindu and Muslim communities has undermined its reforms and proved detrimental to the rights and liberties of Indian citizens, particularly women. If even a secular, democratic, socialist regime like India could not shield its citizens against the encroachments of state-sanctioned religious norms and authorities, then how can fundamental rights and liberties be upheld and protected under religious legal systems? The next chapter answers this very important question.

7

CONCLUSION

UPHOLDING HUMAN RIGHTS UNDER RELIGIOUS
LEGAL SYSTEMS

Governments' differing regime choices and varying levels of ability to impress a particular ideological vision and form of subjectivity upon the society on the one hand, and ethno-religious groups' varying capacity to resist the government meddling in communal norms and institutions on the other, have given rise to a different type of personal status system in each of the three countries under scrutiny. However, regardless of which ideal type they resemble, each of these personal status systems is shown to be similarly restrictive of certain constitutional rights and liberties. Perhaps the news that "state-enforced religious family laws in Egypt negatively affect fundamental rights" does not come quite as a surprise given the country's dismal record of human rights violations and its authoritarian form of government (the long-term effects of the so-called "Arab Spring" on the form of government are yet to be seen, as at the time of writing Egypt was undertaking its first-ever freely contested presidential elections) (Human Rights Watch 2012). But it is quite a surprise and shock for many people who hear for the first time that women are held "hostage" (*agunot* or "chained" women) by their recalcitrant husbands who refuse to issue them a *get* under the state-sanctioned Jewish law in "democratic" Israel; or that Muslim men can marry up to four wives and divorce them by texting *talaq* three times on their cellphones in "secular democratic" India. In other words, it is both noteworthy and astonishing for many to observe that even the so-called "free" democratic regimes repeatedly fail to protect the fundamental rights and liberties of their citizens,[1] which they are constitutionally obliged to uphold, due to their strict adherence to state-enforced personal status systems that entail the application of different sets of laws to people from different ethno-religious backgrounds, and the subjection of men and women to different legal standards.

In this respect, the main question that guides the analysis below is, if even a democratic regime cannot sufficiently shield its citizens against the restrictive practices of state-sanctioned religious norms and authorities, is there any hope at all for upholding fundamental human and women's rights principles under personal status systems or state-sanctioned religio-legal systems? Stated differently, what are the best practices and methods for integration and defense of human and women's rights norms and principles under religious laws? These are not just hypothetical questions but policy-relevant questions that require policy-relevant answers. In fact, these are the very questions that I was preoccupied with as an adviser on two separate projects dealing with protection of human and women's rights under pluri-legal systems. The first study was conducted by the Geneva-based International Council on Human Rights Policy (ICHRP), and the second by the United Nations Entity for Gender Equality and the Empowerment of Women (UN Women). In these capacities I have been asked to reflect on my work in Israel, Egypt and India, and identify key lessons and best practices that could prove helpful for policy-makers and human rights defenders who operate under similar religio-legal systems elsewhere. During these assignments I engaged in discussions and conversations with practitioners, policy-makers, activists, donors and members of programmatic communities (UN, World Bank, etc.) who have experience in tackling questions of human rights on the ground in different parts of the world. Moreover, I have recently conducted field research in Sierra Leone as part of a new project dealing with access to justice under customary laws. During this time I had an opportunity to closely observe the impact of Muslim personal laws on Sierra Leonean women, and to study the strategies they have adopted in order to escape disabilities imposed upon their rights and liberties by religious and customary laws.

Thus, in this concluding chapter, I would like first to summarize policy-relevant lessons from the three case studies examined in the preceding chapters, and then make some policy recommendations based on my experiences in these three countries as well as global

---

[1] India and Israel are categorized as "free" regimes by Freedom House; see Puddington (2011).

exposure that I gained through my involvement with the aforementioned projects and the recent fieldwork in Sierra Leone. Besides academics, the following recommendations are primarily intended for policy-makers and human rights defenders (i.e., national governments and human rights agencies, activists, donors, NGOs and international organizations, etc.) who need to design and implement programs to protect and uphold human and women's rights under personal status or similar religio-legal systems elsewhere.

Policy-relevant lessons learned from the Israeli, Egyptian and Indian personal status systems

The first lesson that can be drawn from the preceding chapters is that state-enforced personal status laws are not "sacrosanct" norms in their own right but socio-political constructions which are often built through appropriation of rather restrictive interpretations of sacred texts, traditions and narratives that usually deny women and religious dissidents equal rights in familial matters. Despite the contrary claims of political and state-sanctioned religious authorities, these laws are not mandated by a "heavenly" authority but are man-made laws based on human interpretation of what "God" may have meant by a particular verse, word or phrase in the scriptural and prophetic sources of any given tradition. That is to say, there is nothing inviolable about them as they are open to constant reinterpretation and amendment by human agency. By implication, as shown, personal status-related human or women's rights concerns occur in all three countries not as a result of divine intervention, but as a result of political choice on the part of those who oversee the process of etatization through which less liberal or enlightened interpretations of religious family laws that entrench existing socio-economic disparities and prejudices are codified and transposed into the formal legal system.

A law, whether it is good or bad, can always be manipulated to produce certain outcomes that are not necessarily intended or foreseen by its architects. This depends completely upon who is allowed to interpret and mobilize the law. The same can be said for personal status laws. As shown above, competing interpretations of state-enforced religious family laws often give rise to competing legalities or definitions of what rights, entitlements, protections, liabilities or disabilities people should have under the law (Sezgin 2012b). In this respect, hermeneutic and rule-making communities in particular challenge the legitimacy and interpretive authority of state-sanctified religious norms and institutions, and render emancipatory, feminist and enlightened versions of those state-enforced religious laws. For instance, while the representatives of Kolech – an orthodox Jewish women's organization in Israel – argue that there is nothing in *halakhah* that bans or disqualifies women from becoming rabbinical court judges (*dayanot*), the official version of *halakhah* sanctified by the Israeli state completely denies this right to women and only allows men to serve as rabbinical judges. Thus, another lesson to be drawn from the present study is that personal status laws are multivocal, intersubjective and dynamic. There is no single version of *shari'a* or *halakhah*, but rather multiple versions of each competing to become "the" *shari'a* or *halakhah* which authorities rely upon in deciding questions of personal status.

A close reading of the preceding chapters also warns us against such simplistic conclusions that human or women's rights can be better protected if state-enforced religious family laws are abolished and replaced with secular laws. For instance, as shown by Halperin-Kaddari (2004) and many others, secular family and non-family legislation, from healthcare laws to labor laws, can be equally restrictive of individual rights and liberties. Therefore, a "secular law is good, religious law is bad" sort of dichotomy should be avoided at all costs in order to better understand the multivocality and intersubjectivity of human rights discourses in personal status and other religio-legal systems. In fact, as repeatedly shown throughout the book, alternative interpretations of religious norms and narratives can be successfully harnessed to protect and advance individual rights and liberties. Although this is not something that I personally observed in Israel, Egypt or India, in some pluri-legal settings state- or community-enforced religious laws may provide an even more effective protection to individual rights and liberties than alternative norms in force (i.e., customary, tribal laws, etc.). For instance, as mentioned earlier, during a recent field trip to Sierra Leone I was repeatedly told by Muslim women that they prefer Islamic inheritance laws over customary laws because the latter do not confer upon them a right to spousal maintenance or entitle them to a share of a deceased husband's estate, while the former both recognize their right to maintenance and give them a fixed share in the deceased husband's estate. In the same vein, Ezeilo (2000) makes a similar observation in respect of women's right to inheritance under Islamic and customary laws in Nigeria.

Moreover, in some cases religious laws can serve as an agent of, or a force for, social change that advances individual rights and liberties while prevailing social norms, prejudices, customs, patriarchal attitudes and institutional practices deny people their rights. In this respect, the *khul‘* example in Egypt is particularly instructive. As argued in Chapter 5, thanks to the emancipatory and enlightened interpretations of the Islamic tradition and narratives, in 2000 Egyptian women acquired a new right to no-fault divorce known as *khul‘*, which gave the Muslim wife a religiously acceptable and sound ground on which she could divorce her husband, even without his consent. However, in practice, judges and court officials who internalized widespread societal prejudices and negative patriarchal attitudes against this particular type of divorce have reportedly discouraged women from exercising their right to *khul‘* – which was bestowed upon women by Prophet Mohammad in the first place – through their *ultra vires* interpretations and obstructive practices. In other words, in this particular case the religious law gave women the right they demanded while the patriarchal attitudes and practices of judicial authorities deterred women from exercising their "prophet-given" right. The same observation can also be made in respect of Muslim women's right to delegated divorce or self-divorce by inclusion of a specific provision to that effect in their marriage contracts. However, even though this is another type of divorce women are entitled to under Muslim personal status laws from Egypt to India, most are either unaware of its existence or actively discouraged from exercising it due to prevailing patriarchal dispositions and stereotypes. The man's delegation of his exclusive right to divorce by permitting his wife to stipulate such conditions in the marital contract (*al-'isma* or *talaq-e tawfiz*) is often considered a demasculating practice and popularly frowned upon, as the following statement of a Caireen marriage registrar (*maazoun*) exemplifies: "No man who deserves to be called a man can accept this [*al-'isma*]: a woman to decide for him or to divorce him" (Ezzat 2000a, p. 43).

Moreover, state or community-sanctioned religious laws and institutions may be capable of self-reform provided that the "right" conditions exist (i.e., the "right" amount of external pressure is exerted, a reformist leadership takes over religious institutions, presence of a vibrant hermeneutic community, etc.). A good example in this regard is the so-called maintenance reform by Israeli *qadis* initiated under the leadership of Qadi Ahmad Natour, the incumbent President of the Shari‘a Court of Appeals. As may be recalled from Chapter 4, moved by the fear of losing their clients and jurisdiction to civil family courts, Israeli *qadis* under the directives of Qadi Natour reinvented an old judicial mechanism – *marsoum qadai* or legal circular – that was used a century earlier by the

British in the Sudan. The new circular ordered *qadis* to stop relying upon informants for determining the amount of postnuptial maintenance but instead base their decisions on written evidence such as tax and insurance documents. This procedural change initiated by *qadis* themselves has brought about a nearly 50 percent increase in the amount of maintenance awards made to Muslim women by the Israeli *shari'a* courts (Shahar 2006, p. 132). In retrospect, the WGEPSI's efforts, the threat posed by the pending amendment Bill in the parliament – which later evolved into the LFCA of 2001 – and the critical role played in the process by Qadi Natour seem to have made this limited opening possible and set an example for future change in Muslim personal status laws in Israel.

Another important observation drawn from the preceding chapters is that material laws of marriage and divorce in personal status systems are very difficult to reform. As argued in Chapter 3, even though marital laws implemented under personal status systems are not "sacred" laws, most governments, however, successfully frame them as such, and the majority of people subscribing to the official propaganda often view these laws as the pillar of their ethno-religious identity, genealogical purity and the guarantee of their cultural autonomy (Pateman 1989; Yuval-Davis, Anthias *et al.* 1989; Kandiyoti 1991). This emphasis is especially true for Muslim minorities living in Israel and India, and the Coptic Orthodox minority in Egypt, which throughout the decades have grown extremely protective of their marital laws. For example, Israeli and Indian governments have largely refrained from directly interfering with substantive Muslim family laws of marriage and divorce because of their fear of further antagonizing various nationalist and conservative elements within minority communities. In minority settings, where issues of marriage and divorce are intricately entangled with identity politics, human and women's rights groups have encountered similar constraints and usually dealt with procedural and less controversial issues (e.g., maintenance, custody, etc.) through legislative (e.g., LFCA of 2001 in Israel) and judicial (e.g., *Danial Latifi* case, 2001, in India) channels, while mostly shying away from addressing substantive issues of marriage and divorce. If controversial issues of marriage and divorce were ever addressed, they were usually addressed within the community through hermeneutic means (e.g., new marriage contracts or *nikahnamas* issued by various Muslim women's organizations in India).

Chapters 3 and 5 have also shown that interventions into minority institutions and laws by majority-dominated institutions (e.g., the parliament or judiciary) are often perceived as hostile acts and are fiercely resisted by some communal forces, usually producing limited impact. In fact, more often than not, they have had the reverse effect of solidifying conservative masculine forces' resolve and making them less receptive to calls for change in communal laws. For example, the Indian Supreme Court's judgments (especially in the *Shah Bano* case) that aimed to expand Muslim women's right to maintenance have further antagonized conservative groups within the Muslim community, and motivated them to drift away from mainstream state-run institutions of personal law to alternative Islamic courts (*Dar-ul Qazas*), which, in turn, have increasingly discouraged Muslim women from resorting to civil courts and claiming their expanded rights to maintenance. Similarly, the LFCA of 2001 that aimed to empower Muslim women in Israel by granting them the option of recourse in maintenance suits to civil family courts has brought about only a limited impact, due to inaccessibility of these courts to Arabic-speaking populations and sanctions among Palestinians nationally against the use of civil courts for personal status matters that normally fall under the purview of *shariʿa* courts. However this does not necessarily mean that secular interventions are always doomed to fail. As exemplified by recent changes in Christian and Parsi laws in India, in some rare instances, where the community in question first reaches an internal consensus regarding the nature of the problem and the desired changes, and then successfully communicates its demands to judicial and legislative authorities, secular interventions carried out in collaboration with communal authorities usually have a higher chance of success and acceptance. Nonetheless, as evidenced by the example of LFCA of 2001, which induced Israeli *shariʿa* courts to undertake an internal reform as a way of stopping women from going to civil courts, in most cases the impact of secular top-down interventions tends to be rather symbolic, limited and indirect, as they rarely offer a viable option to members of ethno-religious minorities (e.g., women), especially in places where the relations between the majority and minority communities are already tense.

Reforming marital laws has not been any easier for majority governments, either. Even though majority governments are believed to possess the necessary moral authority and legitimacy to reform material laws of matrimony within majority communities, their top-down interventions have usually encountered serious opposition and failed to fully implement their reformist objectives. In this respect, the Nehru government's campaign to reform Hindu law between 1948 and 1951, which resulted in an embarrassing defeat for the government, and President Sadat's attempt to expand Egyptian women's right to divorce by means of Law No. 44, which he unconstitutionally promulgated in 1979 with a presidential decree while the Egyptian parliament was on a recess, are particularly didactic examples. In fact, the Egyptian example has also shown us that top-down interventions into personal status systems can potentially be harmful to the cause of human and women's rights in the long term by galvanizing anti-reform conservative forces into action and fortifying their ranks and demands. As it may be recalled, conservative groups, which were discontented with Law No. 44 and launched a campaign to repeal it, finally succeeded in getting the Supreme Constitutional Court to declare the law unconstitutional on technical grounds in 1985. Law No. 100 of 1985, which was hastily put together by the Egyptian government as a replacement, reverted women's rights to divorce back to their pre-1979 state.

As noted in Chapter 5, the setback experienced in 1985 taught the Egyptian women's rights groups two invaluable lessons: First, the reform has to be initiated *by* women themselves through a combination of grassroots mobilization and government support, rather than *for* women through unpopular top-down processes. Second, and more importantly, any change in the law needs to be firmly grounded in the historical sources and traditions of *shari'a* to gain the approval and support of conservative groups and the religious establishment. In the next two decades, Egyptian women's organizations increasingly engaged in Islamic hermeneutics and advocated for gender-egalitarian personal status laws by using a religious framework. In fact, this new strategy proved unprecedentedly successful when the Egyptian parliament finally enacted Law No. 1 of 2000, or the so-called Khul' Law.[2] Similarly, human and women's rights defenders in other majority settings have also used hermeneutic approaches to contest the legitimacy of religious

---

[2] At the time of writing (May 2012), Egypt was going through a number of political and ideological transformations as a result of the toppling of President Hosni Mubarak in February 2011. The parliamentary elections, held in three stages in 2011–2012, produced an Islamist-dominated parliament – nearly 70 percent of the seats were controlled by the Islamist groups and factions (notably the Muslim Brotherhood and the so-called Salafis). Shortly after the elections, some of the Islamist members of parliament reportedly drafted a Bill to abrogate Law No. 1 of 2000 (the so-called Khul' Law) on grounds that it had violated the *shari'a*. It was also reported that some Salafi members of parliament had called for Egypt's withdrawal from CEDAW and the removal of "anti-Islamic" minimum age of marriage – currently set at 18. Against this background, it remained to be seen whether the modest gains Egyptian women made in the last decade, such as the right to no-fault divorce (*khul'*), would be reversed or maintained by the new regime (Mourad 2012).

norms and institutions, and voice their demands for change in a language resonating with prevailing cultural references and narratives (e.g., orthodox women's groups in Israel which advocate for *agunah* rights by employing *halachic* references and solutions).

As noted earlier, interventions into minority laws by majority institutions are usually viewed as hostile attempts to take over the community and are fiercely resisted by communal forces, and therefore rarely produce significant changes. Moreover, as the experiences of Israeli and Indian Muslim women's organizations evidence, whenever human and women's rights defenders from minority communities collaborate with like-minded majority groups or seek the assistance of majority institutions (e.g., courts, the parliament, etc.) to induce change in communal laws, they are usually accused of "treachery" and attacked by conservative elements and institutions claiming to protect the cultural heritage and national identity of the community. For instance, in an interview I conducted in January 2005, Qadi Ahmad Natour repeatedly accused Arab and Muslim members of WGEPSI of collaborating with the Zionist authorities and foreign institutions such as "the European Union, and the Fulbright and Adenauer Foundations" during the campaign for LFCA that "usurped and conquered the jurisdiction of Muslim courts."[3] Thus, as experiences of Palestinian and Indian Muslim women's groups demonstrate, as well as in majority settings, hermeneutics has emerged as a major choice of reform in minority settings, as reform through external or secular means in recent years has become increasingly less reliable, less effective and less available to groups seeking to alter minority laws and institutions.

As argued throughout the book, state-appropriated personal status laws are socio-political constructions built through selective (often androcentric and ethnocentric) interpretations of sacred texts and traditions that come to deny women and subaltern groups equal representation in the construction of secular and religious legality. However, the preceding analyses of Israeli, Egyptian and Indian personal status systems have shown that hermeneutic groups in all three countries constantly alter the way we understand the legality of state-enforced religious laws that dictate the role and place of individuals, particularly women, in familial and public space, by deconstructing the meaning of texts, historical narratives and traditions. Thus, perhaps the most important observation of the present study is that both in majority and minority settings the hermeneutic approach seems to have emerged as the most

---

[3] Personal interview with Qadi Ahmad Natour (Jerusalem, January 2005).

promising approach (at least in the short and medium term) to reform in pluri-legal personal status systems.

Recommendations for human rights defenders: how to uphold fundamental rights and liberties under state-enforced religious laws

In all three countries under examination, state-enforced personal status laws have imposed certain limitations and disabilities on fundamental rights and liberties. And none of the countries seems to have yet found an answer to the question of how to best protect the rights of individuals under personal status systems; or to that of the extent to which they should allow application of non-human-rights-compliant religious laws that impose certain sanctions and restrictions upon the rights and freedoms of their citizens. In search of a solution to this apparent dilemma, some scholars have emphasized the importance of individuals' freedom of association and right of exit from their cultural and normative communities. In plain words, they have argued that if international and constitutional human and women's rights standards are to prevail, then people must be completely free to leave the communal track and transfer their disputes to civil institutions at their own will (Kymlicka 1995, 1996; Rawls 1999; Young 2000; Shachar 2001; Benhabib 2002; Barzilai 2003; Gutmann 2003).

However, as my analyses of the *Shah Bano* case and ensuing developments in India have shown, an individual's right of exit from her cultural and normative community is usually a hollow right which exists solely on paper. Like Kukathas (1992), I am of the opinion that the right of exit can be meaningful only if the community in question grants such a freedom willingly to its individual members, and if there is a larger society outside that embraces liberal values and is ready to welcome and protect the person after she has deserted her own normative community.[4] Put more concretely, the question before us is, for instance, whether the Jewish majority in Israel would stand by and protect a Palestinian Muslim woman if she were persecuted by radical elements in her community wishing to punish her for her decision to renounce *shari'a* courts and seek justice from Jewish-dominated civil family courts

---

[4] Moreover, exercising the right to exit should not deprive the individual of her legitimate claims on communal resources, otherwise property- or resource-related implications may prevent the individual from making a meaningful choice. In addition, the individual should also be free to reverse her decision and return to her cultural community at any point in the future. For further information on the cost of exercising the right of exit, and the right of re-entry, see Parekh (2000, pp. 218–219), Barry (2001, pp. 149–150), Shachar (2001, p. 124), Phillips (2007, pp. 133–157) and Song (2007, pp. 132–134).

instead. It is not really difficult to guess the answer, for we very well know what happened to seventy-five-year-old Shah Bano when she stepped out of her communal boundaries and tried to take advantage of civil remedies made available to her by the Indian state.

This is perhaps a dire picture, but there is still much to be hopeful about. There is a silent but steady revolution unfolding in the personal status systems of many nations, from Malaysia to Morocco. The revolution is spearheaded by rule-making and hermeneutic communities that offer alternative interpretations of officially sanctioned religious norms and precepts to induce change from within. Granted, the change introduced through hermeneutic means may fall short of the so-called international and secular standards of human and women's rights. Or, sometimes, the pace of change and the outcome may be criticized for being too slow or insufficient. In fact this is exactly what Human Rights Watch (HRW), in its critique of Law No. 1 of 2000 in Egypt, pointed out. For HRW, the Khul‘ Law was simply insufficient to remedy the existing inequalities between men and women in respect of divorce. HRW found nothing revolutionary about the new law. On the contrary, it argued, the 2000 law simply perpetuated the oppression and subjugation of women under state-enforced religious laws (Deif 2004). Despite HRW's quick dismissal of Law No. 1, however, I was constantly told by the feminist leaders who had spearheaded the *khul‘* initiative in the 1990s that the passage of Law No. 1 of 2000 was the greatest achievement of the Egyptian women's movement in history. They were proud and hopeful that they could make even greater changes happen in Egypt. In fact, some of these women, whom I personally know, were among the demonstrators in Tahrir Square, Cairo, who brought down Hosni Mubarak's three-decade-old regime in February 2011. I sensed the same feeling of pride and empowerment when I talked to lower- and middle-class women in Cairo and Alexandria who had obtained their divorces through *khul‘*. A woman told me how the Khul‘ Law had enabled her to obtain a divorce, which she had repeatedly failed to receive in the past: "The judge asked me to return my dower, which was only one Egyptian pound (EGP), according to my marriage contract. I gave him [her husband] ten pounds and told him to 'keep the change, and never bother me again' [laughing]."[5]

HRW dismissed the Egyptian women's efforts as "insignificant" because they employed a religious framework, which was not considered

---

[5] Personal interview (Alexandria, May 2004). Informant declined to be identified.

the "correct" approach from the standpoint of HRW's secular and liberal prism of rights. Unfortunately, HRW failed to appreciate the symbolic meaning of the change for the Egyptian women, who successfully adopted a bottom-up approach to challenge the male-dominated religious and political institutions by rendering woman-friendly interpretations of scriptural and prophetic sources of Islam. That small step for HRW was in fact a giant leap for the Egyptian women. Thus, in order to escape the trap HRW fell into, we have to filter out secular and liberal biases of international human rights law, and instead focus on emerging hermeneutic and rule-making communities to better understand the evolving intersubjective nature of human rights talks and discourses under religious legal systems. The "reform from within" approach of hermeneutic communities usually stands a better chance of acceptance and success than the traditional "top-down secular" approach of international human rights law, especially under state-enforced religious legal systems, as the former approach may better reflect the socio-legal, cultural and political constraints and realities on the ground (Sezgin 2010a).

Partnering with hermeneutic communities: The main recommendation of this study, for policy-makers and human rights defenders who need to design and implement programs to protect and uphold fundamental rights and liberties under similar religious legal systems elsewhere, is to identify hermeneutic communities and help them build the necessary capacity to induce internal reform. Conditions vary from country to country, and even from one community to another within the same country. Therefore, there are no generic templates to be adopted. But a good entry point is always a detailed differential diagnosis through which existing human and women's rights concerns and their underlying causes can be identified in each and every communal system. Then, the next step should involve identification and mapping of major actors and their stake in the existing socio-legal and political arrangements. At this stage, a well-defined set of rapid-assessment tools should be utilized by practitioners to identify hermeneutic communities and determine their level of expertise, genealogies, allies, resources, strengths, weaknesses and needs. Once the due diligence process is complete, then potential partners should be shortlisted and offered customized solutions and capacity-building opportunities. These should include legal, technical and financial assistance to help hermeneutic groups build and strengthen their capacity for advocacy, lobbying and impact litigation. However, the level of engagement with hermeneutic communities is of critical importance. Excessive engagement or association with international agencies or foreign NGOs might tarnish the reputation of hermeneutic communities and alienate them in the eyes of their constituency. What makes these groups relatively successful and acceptable in their societies is the cultural authenticity and familiarity of their message and organization. Among the groups analyzed in the book, this seems to be a problem particularly for the WGEPSI in Israel, which some people within the Palestinian community have viewed as "unauthentic" due to its alleged ties to Israeli-Jewish organizations and foreign donors. Thus, international agencies and donors should be especially careful not to harm the social standing of hermeneutic groups by causing them to appear like "agents" or "proxies" of foreign organizations and interests.

Adopting a multipronged strategy: Identification and support of hermeneutic communities is the most important step in the process of upholding fundamental rights and liberties under religious legal systems. But this needs to be sequenced into a multipronged strategy in order to be successful. As noted, hermeneutic groups are not just agents who solely engage in internal scriptural activity, but also "knowledge brokers" (Merry 2006b) who locate and construct cultural references and narratives that promote a particular vision and set of rights by translating global human and women's rights norms and discourses into a culturally resonant vernacular. However, as demonstrated by some of the examples above, there is a limit to what one can achieve by reinterpreting sacred texts, narratives or traditions through liberal or feminist lenses. In other words, one has to recognize that there may be some inherent inequalities under the religious or customary system in question that cannot be simply washed away through hermeneutic activity. Moreover, the hermeneutic activity, as Merry eloquently suggests in the context of vernacularization, will succeed only to the extent that it creates a new set of rights within the tradition by redefining current ways of thinking and cultural practices, and challenging existing gender and power relations (Merry 2006a, p. 136). A remedy can be effective only if its side-effects or shortcomings are known. The same is true for hermeneutics. It can be employed by human rights defenders as a powerful tool only if its limitations are recognized. For instance, in her critique of the recent *nikahnama* campaigns led by Muslim women's organizations in India, Kirmani argues that "Islamically framed approaches [to reform] . . . tend to privilege what is outlined in religious texts as the only legitimate framework for claiming rights . . ." (Kirmani 2011, p. 63). In this respect, it is suggested that overreliance upon hermeneutic approaches might be self-defeating in the long term by limiting human rights defenders' options and strategies to religious means alone, and inadvertently reinforcing the notion that people's lives must be solely governed by religious precepts (*ibid.*). Moreover, as noted in Chapter 3, hermeneutic communities or the strategies of adopting a more liberal interpretation of religious texts, narratives and traditional practices tend to be more prevalent and successful in places where there already exist other civil rights groups that advocate and push for such principles as gender equality through means of non-religious or secular references and frameworks. Hence, with this recognition, hermeneutic means and groups should be employed as part of a multipronged and holistic strategy that views interpretative activities as an interim strategy on the long and thorny road to full integration of international human rights norms and standards into religio-legal systems. Thus, while supporting hermeneutic communities, international development agencies, donors and policy-makers must still continue supporting civil society organizations employing non-religious strategies, lobbying national governments to domesticate international law, comply with their treaty obligations, remove reservations they entered to human and women's rights conventions (e.g., CEDAW),[6] and lay out well-defined procedures and hierarchies of norms to ensure the compliance of state-enforced religious and customary laws with fundamental rights and liberties enshrined in their constitutions (e.g., Articles 15 and 39 of the 1996 Constitution of the Republic of South Africa).

Raising awareness and holding religious authorities accountable: Human rights defenders and policy-makers should also educate individuals about their rights and liberties under the secular and religious law through various legal-literacy and awareness-raising campaigns. Like Israel, many countries have secular laws that set a minimum age for marriage, prohibit bigamy or prevent divorce against the consent of the wife. But, as seen in the case of Israeli *shari'a* courts, religious authorities often tend to ignore such restrictions set upon their jurisdiction by the secular law. In order to hold religious authorities accountable, people within ethno-religious communities should first be made aware of their rights, and then encouraged to get involved in programs that monitor traditional and religious authorities and pressure them to abide by

---

[6] For instance, Israel, Egypt and India entered reservations to CEDAW on the ground that "religious" laws they applied in matters of personal status were not congruent with convention principles. For country-specific reservations and declarations placed on CEDAW, see Appendix.

statutory restrictions placed upon them by the secular legislation. For instance, BRAC and ASK in Bangladesh run very successful monitoring and human rights compliance programs. Because these programs pressure and encourage traditional authorities to adhere to basic human rights principles and due process, traditional *shalish* councils in recent years are reported to have adopted a more egalitarian attitude towards the poor and women (Siddiqi 2006).

Educating individuals about their "god-given" rights: During these awareness-raising campaigns, individuals should be educated by human rights defenders particularly about their rights that already exist under the state-enforced religious laws presently in force. In other words, all in all, before inventing "new" rights, human rights defenders should first make sure that the rights that already exist under the religious or secular law are fully utilized. For example, Muslim women can legally prohibit their husbands from taking a second wife or exercise a right to self-divorce by inserting provisions to those effects into their marital contracts. But, as seen particularly in the Egyptian example, under societal and patriarchal pressure most are discouraged from exercising their rights. For instance, Egyptian women have often been reported to fear that they would be stigmatized as "loose" women if they exercised their "god-given" rights, just as husbands fear that their peers would question their "manhood" if they allowed wives to insert such provisions into marital contracts. In order to defeat these stereotypes, various legal-literacy and awareness-raising campaigns can be organized through the media or by talking directly to religious and traditional leaders, marriage registrars, lawyers and judges. As the USAID-sponsored Women's Legal Rights Initiative successfully demonstrated in Rwanda and Benin, in order to challenge socially embedded negative gender roles and biases, various means of popular culture that people consume everyday – such as radio programs, films, social drama, jingles, folk songs and tales – can be effectively adapted and mobilized.[7]

Targeting men and young boys: Programs focusing on women's rights must target not only women but also men and young boys in order to promote a healthy discussion on women's rights among the local population. The message that has to be unequivocally conveyed is that women's and men's rights are not in contestation, and the former's rights do not come at the expense of the rights of the latter. On the contrary, they are fully compatible and complementary. In this process of

---

[7] Phone interview with Lyn Beth Neylon (March 2010).

redefining societal norms and values about gender roles, religious and traditional leaders should also be targeted and sensitized as they may play a very strategic role in encouraging behavioral change through their writings and sermons.

Tying legal empowerment to socio-economic development: When I asked a Muslim women's rights activist in New Delhi in 2005 what the top five problems the women suffered most from were, she said, *"Poverty, poverty, poverty, poverty and then unequal personal laws which discriminate against women."* In this regard, even though the issue of poverty – due to its complexity and grandiosity – cannot be properly addressed in the present study, human rights defenders should be constantly reminded that in order for individuals to fully enjoy their fundamental rights and liberties, first and foremost their essential needs for food, clothing, housing and medical care must be satisfied. In other words, people need to be free from destitution in order to utilize their rights and actualize their full potential. Hence, the aforementioned legal-literacy and awareness-raising programs can always be integrated into various poverty-eradication, public-health, education and micro-lending programs. Socio-economic empowerment programs bolster their clients' dignity, cultivate their agency and enable them to stand up for themselves and solve their justice problems on their own by successfully navigating through pluri-legal systems. In fact, it has been repeatedly shown that women who participate in the micro-lending programs run by such organizations as BRAC and Grameen Bank over time become more aware of their rights and more assertive in their dealings with traditional, religious and secular authorities (Shehabuddin 2008).

Placing women on the bench: Lastly, human rights defenders should advocate for inclusion and equal representation of women and marginalized populations in religious courts and other decision-making mechanisms. As many women's rights activists indicate, neither Islam nor Judaism necessarily bans women from becoming judges at religious courts. In fact, in recent years, some Muslim governments (i.e., Indonesia, Malaysia and the Palestinian Authority in the West Bank) have begun appointing female *qadis* to *shari'a* courts. However, despite this encouraging development, in most places, due to patriarchal attitudes and prejudices, women are still forbidden from serving as judges not only at religious tribunals but also in secular courts. As we have seen in the case of Israeli rabbinical courts, in places where women are banned from becoming judges they can still play an influential role as members of committees that nominate religious judges (e.g., election of

Sharon Shenhav to the committee that names *dayanim*), or as pleaders and advocates in the courtrooms. Moreover, women should be equally represented in civil family courts where religious personal status laws are applied by civil judges. As frequently observed, female judges tend to interpret and apply the same personal status laws in a more liberal way than male judges. Thus, human rights defenders must pressure governments to appoint more female (and minority) judges to family courts. In fact, this may be a better route to overhauling some of the shortcomings of personal status systems without engaging in lengthy legislative or judicial battles to reform religious family laws.

In the final analysis, personal status systems' lack of compliance with domestic and international human rights law is not an excuse in itself for international organizations, donors and other human rights defenders not to engage with these systems. Well-calculated intervention mechanisms and strategies should be implemented by partnering with hermeneutic communities as well as continuing to lobby national governments to meet their obligations under international law. Engagement with hermeneutic communities, however, requires a paradigm shift by the international community about the attainment and delivery of so-called "universal" rights and liberties around the globe. This is not a plea for "cultural relativism." It is the position of the present study that universal rights are not products of a particular civilization or culture but belong to the entire human family. By the same token, rights and liberties should be equally enjoyed by every human being regardless of race, gender, religion, ethnicity, age, culture or any other consideration. However, this does not mean that international human rights law should be unilaterally and forcibly imposed upon every society around the world. Instead, we have to recognize that each society (especially where religious laws prevail) will adopt so-called international human rights principles at its own pace and to its own liking, and that how individuals will attain these rights may vary widely from one society to another. Thus, with this recognition, human rights defenders must adapt and embrace all possible means without prejudice and work until every single human being – no matter where they are – gets a chance to fully enjoy their fundamental rights and liberties under the law.

COUNTRY-SPECIFIC DECLARATIONS AND RESERVATIONS TO THE CONVENTION ON THE ELIMINATION OF ALL FORMS OF DISCRIMINATION AGAINST WOMEN (CEDAW)[1]

Israel

Reservations:

"1. The State of Israel hereby expresses its reservation with regard to article 7 (b)[2] of the Convention concerning the appointment of women to serve as judges of religious courts where this is prohibited by the laws of any of the religious communities in Israel. Otherwise, the said article is fully implemented in Israel, in view of the fact that women take a prominent part in all aspects of public life.

2. The State of Israel hereby expresses its reservation with regard to article 16[3] of the Convention, to the extent that the laws on personal

---

[1] The information was obtained from the CEDAW website at www.un.org/womenwatch/daw/cedaw/ (accessed in May 2012). For further and up-to-date information on country-specific reservations please refer to the website above.

[2] Author's note. Article 7 of CEDAW: "States Parties shall take all appropriate measures to eliminate discrimination against women in the political and public life of the country and, in particular, shall ensure to women, on equal terms with men, the right: (a) To vote in all elections and public referenda and to be eligible for election to all publicly elected bodies; (b) To participate in the formulation of government policy and the implementation thereof and to hold public office and perform all public functions at all levels of government; (c) To participate in non-governmental organizations and associations concerned with the public and political life of the country."

[3] Author's note. Article 16 of CEDAW: "(1) States Parties shall take all appropriate measures to eliminate discrimination against women in all matters relating to marriage and family relations and in particular shall ensure, on a basis of equality of men and women: (a) The same right to enter into marriage; (b) The same right freely to choose a spouse and to enter into marriage only with their free and full consent; (c) The same rights and responsibilities during marriage and at its dissolution; (d) The same rights and responsibilities as parents, irrespective of their marital status, in matters relating to their children; in all cases the interests of the children shall be paramount;

status which are binding on the various religious communities in Israel do not conform with the provisions of that article."

Declaration:

"3. In accordance with paragraph 2 of article 29[4] of the Convention, the State of Israel hereby declares that it does not consider itself bound by paragraph 1 of that article."

Egypt
Reservations made upon signature and confirmed upon ratification:
In respect of article 9[5]

> "Reservation to the text of article 9, paragraph 2, concerning the granting to women of equal rights with men with respect to the nationality of their children, without prejudice to the acquisition by a child born of a marriage of the nationality of his father. This is in order to prevent a child's acquisition of two nationalities where his parents are of different nationalities, since this may be prejudicial to his future. It is clear that the child's acquisition of his father's nationality is the procedure most suitable for the child and

(e) The same rights to decide freely and responsibly on the number and spacing of their children and to have access to the information, education and means to enable them to exercise these rights; (f) The same rights and responsibilities with regard to guardianship, wardship, trusteeship and adoption of children, or similar institutions where these concepts exist in national legislation; in all cases the interests of the children shall be paramount; (g) The same personal rights as husband and wife, including the right to choose a family name, a profession and an occupation; (h) The same rights for both spouses in respect of the ownership, acquisition, management, administration, enjoyment and disposition of property, whether free of charge or for a valuable consideration. (2) The betrothal and the marriage of a child shall have no legal effect, and all necessary action, including legislation, shall be taken to specify a minimum age for marriage and to make the registration of marriages in an official registry compulsory."

[4] Author's note. Article 29 of CEDAW: "(1) Any dispute between two or more States Parties concerning the interpretation or application of the present Convention which is not settled by negotiation shall, at the request of one of them, be submitted to arbitration. If within six months from the date of the request for arbitration the parties are unable to agree on the organization of the arbitration, any one of those parties may refer the dispute to the International Court of Justice by request in conformity with the Statute of the Court. (2) Each State Party may at the time of signature or ratification of the present Convention or accession thereto declare that it does not consider itself bound by paragraph 1 of this article. The other States Parties shall not be bound by that paragraph with respect to any State Party which has made such a reservation. (3) Any State Party which has made a reservation in accordance with paragraph 2 of this article may at any time withdraw that reservation by notification to the Secretary-General of the United Nations."

[5] Author's note. Article 9 of CEDAW: "(1) States Parties shall grant women equal rights with men to acquire, change or retain their nationality. They shall ensure in particular that neither marriage to an alien nor change of nationality by the husband during marriage shall automatically change the nationality of the wife, render her stateless or force upon her the nationality of the husband. (2) States Parties shall grant women equal rights with men with respect to the nationality of their children."

that this does not infringe upon the principle of equality between men and women, since it is customary for a woman to agree, upon marrying an alien, that her children shall be of the father's nationality."

In respect of article 16[6]

"Reservation to the text of article 16 concerning the equality of men and women in all matters relating to marriage and family relations during the marriage and upon its dissolution, without prejudice to the Islamic *shari'a*'s provisions whereby women are accorded rights equivalent to those of their spouses so as to ensure a just balance between them. This is out of respect for the sacrosanct nature of the firm religious beliefs which govern marital relations in Egypt and which may not be called in question and in view of the fact that one of the most important bases of these relations is an equivalency of rights and duties so as to ensure complementarity which guarantees true equality between the spouses. The provisions of the *shari'a* lay down that the husband shall pay bridal money to the wife and maintain her fully and shall also make a payment to her upon divorce, whereas the wife retains full rights over her property and is not obliged to spend anything on her keep. The *shari'a* therefore restricts the wife's rights to divorce by making it contingent on a judge's ruling, whereas no such restriction is laid down in the case of the husband."

In respect of article 29[7]

"The Egyptian delegation also maintains the reservation contained in article 29, paragraph 2, concerning the right of a State signatory to the Convention to declare that it does not consider itself bound by paragraph 1 of that article concerning the submission to an arbitral body of any dispute which may arise between States concerning the interpretation or application of the Convention. This is in order to avoid being bound by the system of arbitration in this field."

---

[6] Author's note. Article 16 of CEDAW – see n. 2 above.
[7] Author's note. Article 29 of CEDAW – see n. 3 above.

Reservation made upon ratification:
General reservation on article 2:[8]

> "The Arab Republic of Egypt is willing to comply with the content of this article, provided that such compliance does not run counter to the Islamic *shari'a*."

India

Declarations and reservations made upon signature and confirmed upon ratification:

Declarations:

"i) With regard to articles 5[9] (a) and 16[10] (1) of the Convention on the Elimination of All Forms of Discrimination Against Women, the Government of the Republic of India declares that it shall abide by and ensure these provisions in conformity with its policy of non-interference in the personal affairs of any community without its initiative and consent.

ii) With regard to article 16 (2) of the Convention on the Elimination of All Forms of Discrimination Against Women, the Government of the Republic of India declares that though in principle it fully supports the principle of compulsory registration of marriages, it is

---

[8] Author's note. Article 2 of CEDAW: "States Parties condemn discrimination against women in all its forms, agree to pursue by all appropriate means and without delay a policy of eliminating discrimination against women and, to this end, undertake: (a) To embody the principle of the equality of men and women in their national constitutions or other appropriate legislation if not yet incorporated therein and to ensure, through law and other appropriate means, the practical realization of this principle; (b) To adopt appropriate legislative and other measures, including sanctions where appropriate, prohibiting all discrimination against women; (c) To establish legal protection of the rights of women on an equal basis with men and to ensure through competent national tribunals and other public institutions the effective protection of women against any act of discrimination; (d) To refrain from engaging in any act or practice of discrimination against women and to ensure that public authorities and institutions shall act in conformity with this obligation; (e) To take all appropriate measures to eliminate discrimination against women by any person, organization or enterprise; (f) To take all appropriate measures, including legislation, to modify or abolish existing laws, regulations, customs and practices which constitute discrimination against women; (g) To repeal all national penal provisions which constitute discrimination against women."

[9] Author's note. Article 5 of CEDAW: "States Parties shall take all appropriate measures: (a) To modify the social and cultural patterns of conduct of men and women, with a view to achieving the elimination of prejudices and customary and all other practices which are based on the idea of the inferiority or the superiority of either of the sexes or on stereotyped roles for men and women; (b) To ensure that family education includes a proper understanding of maternity as a social function and the recognition of the common responsibility of men and women in the upbringing and development of their children, it being understood that the interest of the children is the primordial consideration in all cases."

[10] Author's note. Article 16 of CEDAW – see n. 2 above.

not practical in a vast country like India with its variety of customs, religions and level of literacy."

Reservation:

"With regard to article 29[11] of the Convention on the Elimination of All Forms of Discrimination Against Women, the Government of the Republic of India declares that it does not consider itself bound by paragraph 1 of this article."

---

[11] Author's note. Article 29 of CEDAW – see n. 3 above.

GLOSSARY OF FOREIGN TERMS

Adat courts	Customary law courts in Indonesia
Agunah	Technically a woman whose husband has disappeared and cannot be located, thus she remains "anchored" to her husband and is not allowed to remarry. Yet the term is commonly used as a synonym for *mesurevet get* (see below) to refer to a woman who is denied a *get* or divorce writ. Plural: *agunot* (Jewish law)
Ahl al-kitab	People of the Book – Jews and Christians (Islamic law)
Al-Azhar	The premier institution of Sunni Islamic learning, located in Cairo, Egypt
Al-Ikhwan al-Muslimun	Muslim Brotherhood (Egypt)
Aliyah	"Heavenly ascent," Jewish immigration to Israel
Al-Mahkamah al-Dusturiyyah al-'Ulya	The Supreme Constitutional Court (Egypt)
Aqd al-zawaj	Contractual marriage certificate (Egypt)
Awqaf	Religious endowments; singular: waqf (Islamic law)
Batil	Null and void (Islamic law)
Bet Din	Rabbinical court
Bet Din ha-Gadol	The Rabbinical Court of Appeals (Israel)

Brit hazugiut	Coupling covenant, civil marriage (Israel)
Chador	Loose black robe worn by Muslim women (especially in Iran)
Chalitza	The ceremony by which both a childless widow and her brother-in-law are released from the duty of contracting a levirate marriage (Jewish law)
Darar	Injury, harm (Islamic law)
Dar-ul Qaza	Informal Islamic (*shariat*) court in India
Dayan	Rabbinical court judge in Israel; plural: *dayanim* (masculine), *dayanot* (feminine)
Dhimmi	Tax-paying (*jizya*) Jews and Christians under Muslim rule
Fatwa	Non-binding legal opinion (Islamic law)
Fiqh	Islamic jurisprudence
Gerushim	Divorce (Jewish law)
Get	Jewish divorce writ issued by husband to wife
Hadith	Reported utterances of Prophet Mohammad
Hafka'at kiddushin	Annulment of marriage on technical grounds (Jewish law)
Halakhah	Jewish law (*halachic*, adjective)
Hanafi	One of the four schools of Sunni Islamic jurisprudence
Haram	Prohibited, unlawful (Islamic law)
Hatarat habrit	Release from covenant or civil marriage (Israel)
Hindutva	Ideology of Hindu nationalism
Hisba	Duty of every believer to promote good and discourage evil (Islamic law)

Homam	Offering made to the fire-god Agni (Hindu law)
Huquq Allah	God's rights (Islamic law)
Iddat	The waiting period that a Muslim woman must observe following the divorce or death of her husband
Ijtihad	Independent legal reasoning (Islamic law)
Imam	The one who leads in prayer in Islam
Iqaron ha-krikhah	Connection principle under Israeli/Jewish law
Ketubah	Marriage contract; plural: *ketubot* (Jewish law)
Khul'	No-fault divorce initiated by wife (Islamic law)
Kiddushei ta'ut	Annulment of marriage on grounds of erroneous assumptions (Jewish law)
Knesset	Israeli Parliament
Knesset Yisrael	Jewish community in Palestine prior to 1948
Kufr	Blasphemy or disbelief (Islamic law)
Leumiut Yisrailit	Israeli nationality
Lok Adalat	People's court (India)
Maazoun	Marriage registrar (Egypt)
Maglis al-Dawla	The Council of State (Egypt)
Maglis Milli	Coptic Community Council
Mahakim Ahliyya	National Courts (Egypt)
Mahila Adalat	Women's court (India)
Mahkamah al-Isti'naf al-Shar'iyya	The Shari'a Court of Appeals (Israel)
Mahkamat al-Naqd	The Court of Cassation (Egypt)
Mahr	Dower, a requirement of Islamic marriage

Mahr al-muajjal	Prompt dower, given by the groom at the time of marriage (Islamic law)
Majallat al-Azhar	Official journal of al-Azhar (Egypt)
Maliki	One of the four schools of Sunni Islamic jurisprudence
Mamlachtiyut	Ben-Gurion's own brand of etatism (Israel)
Mamzer	Bastard; plural: *mamzerim* (Jewish law)
Mamzerut	Bastardy (Jewish law)
Mangalasuthram	Necklace considered as a symbol of marriage among Hindus
Marabout	A *sufi* teacher, living saint in Senegal
Marsoum Qadai	Legal circular issued by Israeli *shari'a* courts
Mata	Additional provision, compensation (Islamic law)
Mesurevet get	Woman whose husband refuses to issue a *get*, or divorce writ. The term *agunah* is also commonly used to refer to a woman who is denied a *get* (Jewish law)
Metlu	Toe rings worn by (mostly) Hindu women
Metruk land	Lands left for general public use (Islamic/Ottoman law)
Mevat land	Unoccupied desert lands, woodlands and grazing spots (Islamic/Ottoman law)
Milla	Religious rite (Egypt)
Millet system	The Ottoman personal status system
Milliyah courts	Communal, religious courts in Egypt prior to 1956

Minhag	Custom (Jewish law)
Miri land	State lands leased to the individuals who held the land by usufruct rather than by title deed (Islamic/Ottoman law)
Mishneh Torah	Maimonides' compilations of Talmudic Law from the twelfth century (Jewish law)
Mitakshara system	It constitutes the backbone of Hindu inheritance law. Under the *Mitakshara* system sons become joint owners of ancestral property upon birth
Mohar	Bride price specified in Jewish marriage contract, similar to Islamic *mahr*
Mu'akhar al-sadaq	Deferred dower, paid by husband at the time of divorce (Islamic law)
Mukhbirun	Informants whom *qadis* relied upon for determining the amount of a maintenance award before 1995 (Israel)
Mülk land	Land held in complete private ownership and exempt from tithe (Islamic/Ottoman law)
Murtadd	Apostate (Islamic law)
Nafaqa	Maintenance of wife and children (Islamic law)
Nasab	Paternity (Islamic law)
Nikah	Muslim marriage
Nikahnama	Islamic marriage contract (India)
Nissuim	Marriage (Jewish law)
Qadi or *Qazi*	Islamic court judge
Qadi Madhhab	Druze religious court judge (Israel)
Ridda	Apostasy (Islamic law)
Sabra	Israeli Jews born after 1948

Samskara	Sacrament (Hindu law)
Saptapadi	The taking of seven steps by the bridegroom and the bride jointly before the sacred fire (Hindu law)
Shabka	Wedding gift (gold jewelry) to bride (Egypt)
Shafiʻi	One of the four schools of Sunni Islamic jurisprudence
Shalish	Traditional dispute resolution mechanism (Bangladesh)
Shariʻa or shariat	Islamic law
Sharmoota	Arabic slang for "slut"
She'elot u-teshuvot	Questions and answers, guidance on ritual and moral questions (Jewish law)
Shin Bet	Domestic intelligence agency (Israel)
Shulchan Aruch	Rabbi Joseph Karo's commentary on *halakhah* from the sixteenth century (Jewish law)
Siyada	Sovereignty (Egypt)
Sunna	Sayings and deeds of Prophet Mohammed
Sura	Chapter in Holy Qur'an
Tafriq	Separation (Islamic law)
Taʻifa	Sect (Egypt)
Takkanot	Rabbinical enactments (Jewish law)
Talaq	Repudiation, unilateral divorce exercised by husband (Islamic law)
Talaq-e tawfiz	Delegated divorce (Islamic law)
Taqiyya	The custom of dissimulation among the Druze
Tatliq	Judicial divorce (Islamic law)
Tilakam	Mark on the forehead, worn by Hindu women

Toanot	Female rabbinical pleaders (Israel)
'Ulama'	Islamic scholars
Umma	The community of believers in Islam
Vakıf land	Land belonging to religious foundations, used for pious purposes (Islamic/Ottoman law)
Wilaya	Private legal power (Islamic law)
Yad al-'isma	Muslim woman's right to insert a self-divorce clause into marriage contract (Egypt)
Yeduim betzibur	Common law unions or de facto marriages (Israel)
Zina	Adultery, fornication (Islamic law)

BIBLIOGRAPHY

Government records consulted
Israel
  Divrei HaKnesset (Minutes of the Knesset)
  Israel Law Reports
  Laws of the State of Israel
  Piskei Din Rabbaniyim (Reports of the Rabbinical Courts)
  Qararat Shariʿa min Al-Mahkama Al-istinafiyya (Decisions of the
    Shariʿa Court of Appeals)
  Selected Judgments of the Supreme Court of Israel

Egypt
  al-Jaridah al-Rasmiyah (Official Gazette)
  al-Mahkama al-Dusturiyya al-ʿUliya (select decisions of the Supreme
    Constitutional Court)

India
  Acts of India (via http://indiacode.nic.in)
  All India Reporter (via http://manupatra.com)
  Constituent Assembly Debates
  Lok Sabha Debates
  Rajya Sabha Debates
  Supreme Court Cases (SCC) (via http://manupatra.com)

Periodicals consulted
Israel
  Haaretz
  The Jerusalem Post
  The Jerusalem Report

Egypt
  Akhbar al-Yowm
  Akher Saʿa
  al-Ahram

al-Ahram Weekly Online Edition
al-Keraza
al-Muhamah
Arab Press Review
Bint el-Nil
Egyptian Gazette
Majallat al-Azhar
Rose al-Youssef
Sabah al-Khair
Watani

India

Combat Law
The Hindu Online Edition
The Milli Gazette Online Edition
The Times of India Online Edition
The Tribune Online Edition

International

The Christian Science Monitor
Los Angeles Times
Middle East Report
New York Times
San Francisco Chronicle

Interviews

Israel

All interviews were conducted in Jerusalem and Tel-Aviv in June 2004 and January to February 2005, unless otherwise noted.

Alisa Peled, the Interdisciplinary Center, Herzliya
Archbishop Aris Shirvanian, Director of the Armenian Orthodox Patriarchate Ecumenical and Foreign Relations Board
Archbishop Constantinis Aristarhos Peristeris, Greek Orthodox Patriarchate
Aviad Hacohen, Hebrew University
Ayelet Blecher-Prigat, Sha'arei Mishpat College
Cesare Marjieh, Director, the Department for Christian Affairs
Chana Pasternak, Director, Kolech
Dafna Barak-Erez, Tel-Aviv University
Daniel Rossing, former Director, the Department for Christian Affairs

Deborah Weissman, orthodox feminist activist, founder of the Kehillat Yedidya Synagogue (phone interview, March 2010)

Diana Diaconeasa, Rabbis for Human Rights

Dov Frimer, Attorney

Drorit Rosenfeld, Rabbinical Court Pleader, Kolech

Elimelech Westreich, Tel-Aviv University

Father Anton Issa, Latin Catholic Patriarchate

Hannah Kehat, founder and former Director, Kolech (phone interview, April 2010)

Heba Yazbak, Coordinator, the WGEPSI, Nazareth (phone interview, April 2010)

Irit Rosenblum, Director, the New Family Organization, Tel-Aviv

Judge Moshe Drori, Jerusalem District Court

Maha Abu Dayyeh, Director, the Women's Center for Legal Aid and Counseling (New York, October 2010)

Menny Mautner, Tel-Aviv University

Michael Corinaldi, Attorney

Michael Karayanni, Hebrew University

Mithkal Natour, Shari'a Advocate, former Lecturer, Baqa Al-Gharbiyya Islamic College

Moshe Ben Haim, former Director, the Department for Muslim Affairs

Moussa Abu-Ramadan, University of Haifa

Nasreen Alemy-Kabha, former Coordinator, the WGEPSI, Nazareth

Pinhas Shifman, Hebrew University

Qadi Ahmad Natour, President, the Shari'a Court of Appeals, Jerusalem

Qadi Iyad Zahalka, West Jerusalem Shari'a Court (New York, October 2012)

Rabbi Edward Rettig, Rabbis for Human Rights

Rabbi Michael Boyden, Director of the *Beit Din* of the Israel Council of Progressive Rabbis

Rabbi Rafael Feuerstein, Tzohar

Rabbi Shear-Yashuv Cohen, former Chief Rabbi of Haifa

Ron Shaham, Hebrew University

Ronny Brison, former Member of Knesset, Shinui

Ruth Halperin-Kaddari, Bar-Ilan University

Sharon Shenhav, Attorney, former Member, Dayan Nomination Committee

Sonia Bouluf, Attorney, Association for Civil Rights in Israel

Tagreed Jahshan, Attorney, Israel Women's Network

Tziona Koenigh, Attorney, Israel Women's Network

Valerie Zilka, Family Courts Advocate, Israel Religious Action Center

Yitzhak Reiter, Hebrew University

Zeidan Atashe, former Consul General, a leading member of the Druze community

(Twenty-two interviewees declined to be identified.)

Egypt

All interviews were conducted in Cairo and Alexandria, April to June 2004, unless otherwise noted.

Abdul Hadi Ghozi, Advocate

Ali El-Sawi, Cairo University

Ashraf Mohtadi, Family Courts Advocate

Bernard Botiveau, CEDEJ

Enid Hill, American University

Father Ishara Bibawy, Coptic Orthodox Patriarchate, St. Mark's Cathedral

Geralyn Busnardo, Chief of Party, USAID/Egypt Family Justice Project (phone interview, April 2010)

Guirgis Michail, Head of the Anglican Protestant Community Council

Ibrahim Dessouky Abaza, Wafd Party

Judge Edward Ghalib, Member of the Council of State, Member of the Coptic Orthodox Community Council (Maglis Milli)

Judge Mohamed Hamed el-Gamal, former President, the Council of State

Judge Mustafa El-Bedwehi, Cairo Personal Status Court

Judge Nabil Mirhum, Member of the Council of State, Member of the Coptic Orthodox Community Council (Maglis Milli)

Mariz Tadros, American University

Michel Arslanidis, the Greek Orthodox Community, Alexandria

Mohamed Ibrahim Dowidar, Advocate, the Greek Orthodox Community, Alexandria

Mona Zulfiqar, Advocate, National Council for Women

Mostafa Kamil Al-Sayyid, American University, Cairo

Nathalie Bernard-Maugiron, CEDEJ

Omayma Abdel Latif, Correspondent, al-Ahram Weekly

Reem Leila, Correspondent, al-Ahram Weekly
Thanaa El Shamy, Advocate, National Council for Women
Yunan Labib Rizk, Historian, Columnist, al-Ahram Weekly
Zeinab Radwan, Member of Legislative Council, Shura Council
(Thirty-one interviewees declined to be identified.)

India
All interviews were conducted in New Delhi and Mumbai, February to
May 2005, unless otherwise noted.

Amin Usmani, Islamic Fiqh Academy of India
Arun Sinha, Baha'i House
Bachi Singh Shri Rawat, BJP, former Member of Lok Sabha
Bina Agarwal, Delhi University (phone interview, April 2010)
Fali Nariman, Member of Rajya Sabha, President of the Bar
    Association of India
Flavia Agnes, lawyer, feminist activist; Director, Majlis
General Adi Sethna, President, Delhi Parsi Anjuman
Justice Janpal Singh, former Chief Justice of the High Court of Delhi
Justice P. C. Jain, former Chief Justice of the High Court of Punjab
    and Haryana
Kiran Gupta, Delhi University
Lama Lobzang, Buddhist monk, Member of the National Commission
    for Minorities
Ludo Rocher, the American Institute of Indian Studies
M. P. Raju, Senior Supreme Court Advocate
Nivedita Menon, Delhi University
Nomita Aggarwal, Delhi University
Poonam Saxena, Delhi University
Dr. Qasim Rasool Ilyas, Excecutive Committee Member, AIMPLB
Qazi Mohammad Kamil Qasmi, New Delhi *Dar-ul Qaza* (Shariat
    Court)
Rajeev Bhargava, Jawaharlal Nehru University
Rajeev Dhavan, Senior Supreme Court Advocate
Rani Jethmalani, Director, Women's Action Research and Legal
    Action for Women
Ritu Menon, feminist activist, publisher, Women Unlimited
S. J. Mathew, Supreme Court Advocate, Indian Social Institute
Sayeed Saif Mahmood, Advocate
Shaista Amber, Director, AIMWPLB (phone interview, May 2010)

Soli Sorebjee, former Attorney General of India
Syed Shahabuddin, President, All India Muslim Majlis-e-Mushawarat
Syeda Hameed, Director, Muslim Women's Forum
Tahir Mahmood, Amity Law College
Tehmina Arora, Christian Legal Association of India
Yogesh Mehta, National Commission for Women
Zoya Hasan, Jawaharlal Nehru University
(Thirty-three interviewees declined to be identified.)

Non-location-specific interviews
Lyn Beth Neylon, the Women's Legal Rights Initiative, March 2010

Electronic correspondence
Batya Cahana-Dror, Attorney, Director of Mavoi Satum
Bernard Jackson, University of Manchester
Diane Singerman, the American University, Washington, DC
Enid Hill, American University in Cairo
Gordon Woodman, University of Birmingham
Hanna Lerner, Tel-Aviv University
Ido Shahar, Ben-Gurion University of the Negev
Jeff A. Redding, Saint Louis University School of Law
Madhu Kishwar, founder and Editor, Manushi
Maha El Taji-Daghash, Abraham Fund Initiatives
Maurits Berger, Netherlands Institute of International Relations
Mengia Hong Tschalaer, University of Zurich
Moussa Abu-Ramadan, Faculty of Law, University of Haifa
Mulki Al-Sharmani, American University in Cairo
Nadia Sonneveld, International Institute for the Study of Islam, Leiden
Nathan Brown, George Washington University
Nissa wa Afaq, Kafr Kara
Nivedita Menon, Delhi University
Parveen Abdi, AIMPLB
Perveez Mody, Cambridge University
Qadi Iyad Zahalka, West Jerusalem Shari'a Court
Rishabh Sancheti, Advocate
Ron Shaham, Hebrew University of Jerusalem
Sharada Sugirtharajah, University of Birmingham
Shyama Prasad Rout, Jawaharlal Nehru University

Tamir Moustafa, Simon Fraser University
Werner Menski, SOAS, University of London

Cases cited
(In chronological order.)

Israel

HCJ 73/53 *Kol Ha'Am* v. *Minister of the Interior* [1953] IsrSC 7(1) 871

HCJ 143/62 *Funk-Schlesinger* v. *Minister of Interior* [1963] IsrSC 17(1) 225

HCJ 301/63 *Schtreit* v. *The Chief Rabbi of Israel* [1964] IsrSC 18(1) 598

HCJ 171/68 *Avalon Hanzalis* v. *Ecclesiastical Court of the Greek Orthodox Church* [1969] IsrSC 23(1) 260

HCJ 94/75 *George Nassar* v. *Tribunal of the Gregorian-Armenian Community* [1976] IsrSC 30(2) 44

HCJ 1842/92 *Naomi Blaugrund* v. *The Rabbinical Court of Appeals* [1992] IsrSC 46(3) 423

HCJ 5182/93 *Levy* v. *The Rabbinical Court of Tel Aviv-Jaffa* [1994] IsrSC 48(3) 1

CA 3077/90 *Plonit* v. *Ploni* [1995] IsrSC 49(3) 578

HCJ 1031/93 *Pesaro (Goldstein)* v. *Minister of Interior* [1995] IsrSC 49(4) 661

HCJ 3269/95 *Katz* v. *The Rabbinical Court of Jerusalem* [1996] IsrSC 50(4) 590

CA 2000/97 *Lindorn* v. *Karnit, Fund for Compensation of Victims of Road Accidents* [1999] IsrSC 55(1) 12

HCJ 9347/99 *Ali Hamza* v. *Shari'a Court of Appeals and Others* [2001] IsrSC 55(2) 54

HCJ 5070/95 *Naamat, Working and Volunteer Women's Movement* v. *Minister of Interior* [2002] IsrSC 56(2) 721

CA 2622/01 *Manager of Land Betterment Tax* v. *Aliza Lebanon* [2003] IsrSC 37(5) 309

HCJ 9611/00 *Badr (Mar'i) Nabal* v. *Mar'i Nazia* [2004] IsrSC 58(4) 256

HCJ 6751/04 *Sabbag* v. *The Rabbinical Court of Appeals* [2004] IsrSC 59(4) 817

HCJ 2597/99 *Rodriguez-Toshbaim* v. *Minister of Interior* [2005] IsrSC 59(6) 721

HCJ 9740/05 *Plonit* v. *Shari'a Court of Appeals* [2006] IsrSC 60(1) 1541

HCJ 1129/06 *Plonit and Another v. Shari'a Court of Appeals* [2006] IsrSC 60(2) 3313

HCJ 8638/03 *Sima Amir v. The Rabbinical Court of Appeals* [2006] IsrSC 61(1) 259

Egypt

Court of Cassation, Case No. 36, 29th Judicial Year, February 6, 1963

Court of Cassation, Case No. 20, 34th Judicial Year, March 30, 1966

Court of Cassation, Case No. 182, 35th Judicial Year, March 20, 1969

Court of Cassation, Case No. 17, 43rd Judicial Year, November 5, 1975

Court of Cassation, Case No. 104, 94th Judicial Year, March 21, 1978

Court of Cassation, Case Nos. 16 and 26, 48th Judicial Year, January 17, 1979

Supreme Constitutional Court, Case No. 28, 2nd Judicial Year, May 4, 1985

Court of Cassation, Case No. 68, 53rd Judicial Year, December 24, 1985

Court of Cassation, Case Nos. 475, 478, 481, 65th Judicial Year, August 5, 1996

Supreme Constitutional Court, Case No. 201, 23rd Judicial Year, December 15, 2002

India
(In alphabetical order.)

A. A. Abdulla v. *A. B. Mohmuna Saiyadbhai* (AIR 1988 Guj 141)

Abid Ali v. *Mst. Rasia Begum* (1988 RCC 51)

Ahmed v. *Ayasha* (1990 (2) DMC 110)

Ahmedabad Women's Action Group [AWAG] v. *Union of India* (AIR 1997 SC 3614)

Anil Kumar Mhasi v. *Union of India* (1994 (5) SCC 704)

B. Chandra Manikyamma, v. *B. Sudarsana Rao* (1988 Cri LJ 1849)

Bai Tahira v. *Ali Hussain Chothia* (1979 (2) SCC 316)

Danial Latifi v. *Union of India* (2001 (7) SCC 740)

Fuzlunbi v. *K. Khadir Vali* (1980 (4) SCC 125)

Githa Hariharan v. *Reserve Bank of India* (AIR 1999 SC 1149)

Iqbal Bano v. *State of UP* (2007 (8) SC 648)

Jaitunbi Mubarak Shaikh v. *Mubarak Shaikh* (1993 (3) Mh LJ 694)

John Vallamattom v. *Union of India* (2003 (6) SCC 611)

Jordam Diengdeh v. *S. S. Chopra* (AIR 1985 SC 935)

Lily Thomas v. *Union of India* (AIR 2000 SC 1650)

Madhu Kishwar v. *State of Bihar* (1996 AIR 1864)

Mohammad Ahmed Khan v. *Shah Bano Begum* (1985 (3) SCR 844)

Mohammed Yunus v. *Bibi Phenkani alias Tasrun Nisa* (1987 MLR 214)

National Textile Mazdur Union v. *P. R. Ramkrishnan* (1983 (1) SCC 224)

Sabra Shamim v. *Maqsood Ansari* (2004 (9) SCC 616)

Sarla Mudgal v. *Union of India* (AIR 1995 SC 1531)

Shabana Bano v. *Imran Khan* (2010 (1) SCC 666)

Shamim Ara v. *State of UP* (AIR 2002 SC 3551)

Usman Khan Bahamani v. *Fathimunnisa Begum* (1990 Cri LJ 1364)

Vishwa Lochan Madan v. *Union of India*, Writ Petition (Civil) No. 386/2005

European Court of Human Rights

Refah Partisi (The Welfare Party) and Others v. *Turkey* (2003) 37 EHRR 1

United States

Hosanna-Tabor Evangelical Lutheran Church and School v. *Equal Employment Opportunity Commission*, 565 US (2012) – (Docket No. 10–553)

Legislation cited

(In chronological order.)

Israel

Ottoman Land Law, 1858

Ottoman Law of Succession, 1913

Ottoman Law of Family Rights, 1917

Ottoman Law of Procedure for Shariʿa Courts, 1917

Marriage and Divorce (Registration) Ordinance, 1919

Palestine Order in Council, 1922

Succession Ordinance, 1923

Law and Administration Ordinance, 1948

Law of Personal Status of the Druze Community of Lebanon, 1948

Law of Return, 1950

Marriage Age Law, 1950

Women's Equal Rights Law, 1951

Nationality Law, 1952

Rabbinical Courts Jurisdiction (Marriage and Divorce) Law, 1953

Shari'a Courts (Validation of Appointments) Law, 1953
Dayanim Law, 1955
Courts Law, 1957
Family Law Amendment (Maintenance) Law, 1959
Penal Law Amendment (Bigamy) Law, 1959
Law of Personal Status of the Druze Community of Israel, 1961
Qadis Law, 1961
Druze Religious Courts Law, 1962
Israel Succession Law, 1965
Arbitration Law, 1968
Israel Land Law, 1969
Law of Matters of Dissolution of Marriage (Jurisdiction in Special
    Cases), 1969
Basic Law: the Judiciary, 1984
Family Courts Law, 1995
Rabbinical Courts (Enforcement of Divorce Decrees) Law, 1995
Alternative Burial Law, 1996
Law of Family Courts (Amendment No. 5), 2001
Qadis Law (Amendment No. 10), 2002
Citizenship and Entry into Israel Law, 2003

Egypt
The Ottoman Imperial Decree (May 14, 1883)
Law No. 8, 1915
Law No. 25, 1920
Law No. 25, 1929
Law No. 78, 1931
The Personal Status Ordinance of the Coptic Orthodox Community,
    1938
Law No. 77, 1943
Law No. 25, 1944
Law No. 71, 1946
The Egyptian Civil Code, 1949
Law No. 462, 1955
Law No. 629, 1955
The Code of Civil and Commercial Procedure, 1968
Law No. 62, 1976
Law No. 44, 1979
Law No. 100, 1985
Law No. 3, 1996

Law No. 1, 2000
Law No. 10, 2004

India

The Hindu Widows' Remarriage Act, 1856
The Indian Penal Code, 1860
The Parsee Intestate Succession Act, 1865
The Indian Divorce Act, 1869
The Indian Christian Marriage Act, 1872
The Punjab Laws Act IV, 1872
The Special Marriage Act, 1872
The Anand Marriage Act, 1909
The Indian Succession Act, 1925
The Child Marriage Restraint Act, 1929
The Parsee Marriage and Divorce Act, 1936
The Hindu Women's Rights to Property Act, 1937
The Muslim Personal Law (Shariat) Application Act, 1937
The Dissolution of Muslim Marriages Act, 1939
The Hindu Marriage Disabilities Removal Act, 1946
The Hindu Married Women's Right to Separate Residence and
    Maintenance Act, 1946
The Hindu Marriage Act, 1955
The Hindu Adoptions and Maintenance Act, 1956
The Hindu Minority and Guardianship Act, 1956
The Hindu Succession Act, 1956
The Dowry Prohibition Act, 1961
The Special Marriage (Amendment) Act (32 of 1963)
The Criminal Procedure Code, 1973
The Marriage Laws (Amendment) Act (68 of 1976)
The Family Courts Act, 1984
The Muslim Women (Protection of Rights on Divorce) Act, 1986
The Arbitration and Conciliation Act, 1996
The Marriage Laws (Amendment) Act (49 of 2001)
The Indian Divorce (Amendment) Act (51 of 2001)
The Domestic Violence Act, 2005
The Prohibition of Child Marriage Act, 2006

Books and articles

Abdal-Rehim, Adbal-Rahman Abdal-Rehim (1996). The Family and Gender
    Laws in Egypt during the Ottoman Period. *Women, the Family, and Divorce*

Laws in Islamic History. A. E. A. Sonbol. Syracuse University Press: 96–111.

Abdelmassih, Mary (2010). "Coptic Pope Rejects Egyptian Court Ruling on Remarriage of Divorcees." Accessed in June, 2010, from www.pakistan christianpost.com/headlinenewsd.php?hnewsid=2035.

Abdo, Geneive (2000). *No God but God: Egypt and the Triumph of Islam*. Oxford University Press.

Abécassis, Frédéric and Le Gall-Kazazian, Anne (1992). "L'identité au miroir du droit. Le statut des personnes en Égypte (fin XIXe–début XXe siècle)." *Égypte-Monde Arabe* 11: 11–38.

Abghari, Adineh (2008). *Introduction to the Iranian Legal System and the Protection of Human Rights in Iran*. London, British Institute of International and Comparative Law.

Abou Ramadan, Moussa (2000). "La loi applicable à la communauté roum-orthodoxe de l'Etat d'Israël." *Proche-Orient Chrétien* 50: 105–141.

(2001). "La protection de la liberté religieuse des minorités en Israël." *Mediterranean Human Rights Law Journal* 5: 39–80.

(2003). "Judicial Activism of the Shari'ah Appeals Court in Israel (1994–2001): Rise and Crisis." *Fordham International Law Journal* 27: 254–298.

(2005). "Divorce Reform in the Shari'a Court of Appeals in Israel (1992–2003)." *Islamic Law and Society* 13(2): 242–274.

(2005–2006). "The Shari'a in Israel: Islamicization, Israelization and the Invented Islamic Law." *UCLA Journal of Islamic and Near Eastern Law* 5: 81–129.

(2006). "Islamic Legal Reform: *Shari'a* Court of Appeals and Maintenance for Muslim Wives in Israel." *Hawwa: Journal of Women in the Middle East and the Islamic World* 4(1): 29–75.

(2008). "Recent Developments in Child Custody in Shari'a Courts: Notes on HCJ 9740/05 Plonit v. Shari'a Court of Appeals and HCJ 1129/06 Plonit and Another v. Shari'a Court of Appeals." *Mishpakha ve Mishpat* 2: 69–105 [in Hebrew].

Abramov, S. Zalman (1976). *Perpetual Dilemma: Jewish Religion in the Jewish State*. Rutherford, NJ, Fairleigh Dickinson University Press.

Abu-Gosh, Subhi (1991). The Sharia Courts from the Perspective of Israeli Pluralism. *Perspectives on Israeli Pluralism: Proceedings of a Conference on Pluralism in Israel*. K. O. Cohen and J. S. Gerber. New York, The Israel Colloquium: 45–52.

Ackerly, Brooke A. (2008). *Universal Human Rights in a World of Difference*. Cambridge, UK; New York, Cambridge University Press.

ACRI (1999). "First Alternative Civil Cemetery in Israel Opens in Beer Sheva." Accessed in December, 2006, from www.acri.org.il/english-acri/engine/story.asp?id=72.

(2002). "Supreme Court Rules: Non-Orthodox Conversions are Valid." Accessed in December, 2006, from www.acri.org.il/english-acri/engine/story.asp?id=96.

Afifi, Mohamed (1996). Reflections on the Personal Status Laws of Egyptian Copts. *Women, the Family, and Divorce Laws in Islamic History.* A. S. E. Azhary. Syracuse University Press: 202–215.

Afshari, Reza (2001). *Human Rights in Iran: The Abuse of Cultural Relativism.* Philadelphia, PA, University of Pennsylvania Press.

Agarwal, Bina (2005). "Landmark Step to Gender Equality." *The Hindu Online Edition*, Sep 25. Accessed in June, 2012, from www.hindu.com/thehindu/mag/2005/09/25/stories/2005092500050100.htm.

Agnes, Flavia (2001). *Law and Gender Inequality: The Politics of Women's Rights in India.* New Delhi, Oxford University Press.

(2004). "Constitutional Challenges, Communal Hues and Reforms within Personal Laws." *Combat Law* 3(4): 4–10.

(2011). *Family Law* vol. I: *Family Laws and Constitutional Claims.* New Delhi, Oxford University Press.

Agrama, Hussein Ali (2011). Sovereign Power and Secular Indeterminacy: Is Egypt a Secular or a Religious State? *After Secular Law.* W. F. Sullivan, R. A. Yelle and M. Taussig-Rubbo. Stanford University Press: 181–199.

Agrawal, K. B. (2010). *Family Law in India.* Alphen aan den Rijn, The Netherlands, Kluwer Law International.

Ahluwalia, D. Pal (2001). *Politics and Post-Colonial Theory: African Inflections.* London, Routledge.

Ahmad, Naziruddin (1949). *Fallacy of Hindu Code Bill Exposed in the Indian Parliament.* Delhi, All India Anti-Hindu Code Bill Committee.

Ahmed, Ishtiaq (2010). The Pakistan State Project: A Secular Critique. *State and Secularism: Perspectives from Asia.* M. H. Siam-Heng and T. C. Liew. Hackensack, NJ, World Scientific: 185–211.

Al-Banna, Kamal Salih (1984). *The Personal Status of Orthodox Copts in the Light of Jurisprudence and the Court of Cassation.* Al-Qahira, Alam al-Kotob [in Arabic].

Al-Gammal, Moustafa (2002). *The Personal Status of Non-Muslims.* Al-Qahira, Manshurat Al-Halaby [in Arabic].

Al-Goumhouria (2000). "Azhar Scholars Ask for 3-Month Grace to Review Personal Status Bill." *Economic Press Review*: 6.

Al-Hayat (2000). "Azhar Scholars Lash Out at Personal Status Bill." *Economic Press Review*: 5.

Al-Nowaihi, Mohamed (1979). Changing the Law on Personal Status in Egypt within a Liberal Interpretation of the Shari'a. *Law and Social Change: Problems and Challenges in Contemporary Egypt.* C. Nelson and K.-F. Koch. American University in Cairo: 97–115.

(1981). Changing the Law on Personal Status in Egypt within a Liberal Interpretation of the Shari'a. *Religion and Politics in the Middle East*. M. Curtis. Boulder, CO, Westview Press: 109–123.

Al-Sawi, Ahmad, ed. (2002). *The Harvest: Two Years after Khul'*. Al-Qahira, Markaz Qadaia al-Mara al-Masriyya (CEWLA) [in Arabic].

Al-Shaab (2000a, Jan. 14). "Pa to Fingerprint Government's Amendments to 'Personal Status' Bill." *Arab Press Review*, p. 1.

(2000b, Jan. 18). "Zionist Scheme to Destroy Family More Dangerous Than Personal Status Bill Amendments." *Arab Press Review*, pp. 2–3.

Al-Sharmani, Mulki (2009). "Egyptian Family Courts: A Pathway of Women's Empowerment?" *Hawwa: Journal of Women in the Middle East and the Islamic World* 7(2): 89–110.

(2010). "Legal Reform, Women's Empowerment and Social Change: The Case of Egypt." *IDS Bulletin* 41(2): 10–17.

Al-Wafd (2000a, Jan. 24–25). "Azhar Scholars Front Demand *Khula'* Bill Postponed." *Arab Press Review*, p. 3.

(2000b, Jan. 17). "Heated Discussion in Pa over Personal Status Bill Amendments." *Arab Press Review*, p. 1.

(2000c, Jan. 25–26). "Wafd Deputies Withdraw in Protest against Personal Status Bill Being Cooked." *Arab Press Review*, pp. 6–7.

Aldeeb Abu-Sahlieh, Sami Awad (1979). *L'impact de la religion sur l'ordre juridique: Cas de l'Égypte – non-Musulmans en pays d'Islam*. Fribourg, Éditions Universitaires.

All India Muslim Personal Law Board (2001). *Compendium of Islamic Laws: A Section-Wise Compilation of Rules of Shari'at Relating to Muslim Personal Law*. New Delhi, All India Muslim Personal Law Board.

Allott, Anthony (1980). *The Limits of Law*. London, Butterworths.

Almog, Oz (2000). *The Sabra: The Creation of the New Jew*. Berkeley, University of California Press.

Ambedkar, Babasaheb (1995). *Dr. Babasaheb Ambedkar – Writings and Speeches*. Bombay, Govt. of Maharashtra.

An-Naim, Abdullahi Ahmed (1992). Toward a Cross-Cultural Approach to Defining International Standards of Human Rights: The Meaning of Cruel, Inhuman or Degrading Treatment or Punishment. *Rights in Cross-Cultural Perspectives: A Quest for Consensus*. A. A. An-Naim. Philadelphia, University of Pennsylvania Press: 19–43.

(2008). *Islam and the Secular State: Negotiating the Future of Shari'a*. Cambridge, Mass., Harvard University Press.

(2011). "Religious Norms and Family Law: Is it Legal or Normative Pluralism?" *Emory International Law Review* 25: 785–809.

(2012). Islam and Human Rights: Framing and Reframing the Discourse. *Religion and Human Rights: An Introduction*. J. Witte and M. C. Green. Oxford; New York, Oxford University Press: 56–70.

and Gort, Jeral D., *et al.*, eds. (1995). *Human Rights and Religious Values: An Uneasy Relationship?* Amsterdam, Editions Rodopi.

and Hammond, Jeffrey (2002). Cultural Transformation and Human Rights in African Societies. *Cultural Transformation and Human Rights in Africa.* A. A. An-Naim, ed. London, Zed Books: 15–37.

Anderson, Benedict R. (1991). *Imagined Communities: Reflections on the Origin and Spread of Nationalism.* London; New York, Verso.

Anderson, J. N. D. (1952–1953). "The Personal Law of the Druze Community." *Die Welt des Islams* 2: 1–9; 83–94.

(1958). "The Tunisian Law of Personal Status." *International and Comparative Law Quarterly* 7: 262–279.

(1969). "Comments with Reference to the Muslim Community." *East African Law Journal* 5: 5–20.

Anderson, Perry (1974). *Lineages of the Absolutist State.* London, NLB.

Ansari, Hamied (1986). *Egypt: The Stalled Society.* Albany, SUNY Press.

Anti-Defamation League (2002). "The Conversion Crisis: The Current Debate on Religion, State and Conversion in Israel." Accessed in December, 2006, from www.adl.org/Israel/Conversion/testing-principles.asp#3.

Arthurs, H. W. (1985). *Without the Law – Administrative Justice and Legal Pluralism in Nineteenth-Century England.* University of Toronto Press.

Asa-El, Amotz (1998, Sep. 25). "Man of the Year." *The Jerusalem Post*, p. 9.

Atiya, Aziz Suryal (1991). *The Coptic Encyclopedia.* New York, Macmillan.

Austin, Granville (2001). Religion, Personal Law, and Identity in India. *Religion and Personal Law in Secular India: A Call to Judgment.* G. J. Larson. Bloomington, Indiana University Press: 15–23.

(2004). *The Indian Constitution: Cornerstone of a Nation.* New Delhi, Oxford University Press.

Avi-Hai, Avraham (1974). *Ben Gurion, State-Builder: Principles and Pragmatism 1948–1963.* New York, John Wiley & Sons.

Awasthi, Puja (2006). "Our Own Personal Law Board." Accessed in June, 2007, from www.indiatogether.org/2006/sep/wom-aimwplb.htm.

Aydın, M. Akif (1985). *İslam-Osmanlı Aile Hukuku.* Istanbul, Marmara Üniversitesi İlahiyat Fakültesi Yayınları /Anka Ofset.

(2000). The Codification of the Islamic-Ottoman Family Law and the Decree of "Hukuk-I Aile." *The Great Ottoman-Turkish Civilisation.* K. Cicek. Ankara, Yeni Turkiye. Vol. III (Philosophy, Science and Institutions): 705–713.

Ayubi, Nazih N. M. (1980). *Bureaucracy & Politics in Contemporary Egypt.* London, Ithaca Press.

Arab Bureaucracies: Expanding Size, Changing Roles. *The Arab State.* G. Luciani. Berkeley, University of California Press: 129–149.

Over-Stating the Arab State: Politics and Society in the Middle East. New York, IB Tauris.

Badran, Margot (1991). Competing Agenda: Feminists, Islam and the State in 19th and 20th Century Egypt. *Women, Islam, and the State*. D. Kandiyoti. Basingstoke, Macmillan: 201–236.

(1995). *Feminists, Islam, and Nation: Gender and the Making of Modern Egypt*. Princeton University Press.

Bahgory, George (1999, Aug. 12–18). "Train of Thought." *Al-Ahram Weekly Online*: 442. Accessed in May, 2006, from http://weekly.ahram.org.eg/1999/442/feature.htm.

Baird, Robert D. (1978). Religion and the Legitimation of Nehru's Concept of the Secular State. *Religion and the Legitimation of Power in South Asia*. B. L. Smith. Leiden, Brill: 73–87.

Baker, John Hamilton (2002). *An Introduction to English Legal History*. London, Butterworths.

Baker, Raymond William (1978). *Egypt's Uncertain Revolution under Nasser and Sadat*. Cambridge, MA, Harvard University Press.

Balchin, Cassandra (2009). Family Law in Contemporary Muslim Contexts: Triggers and Strategies for Change. *Wanted: Equality and Justice in the Muslim Family*. A. Zainah. Selangor, Musawah: 209–234.

Bälz, Kilian (1997). "Submitting Faith to Judicial Scrutiny through the Family Trial: The Abu Zayd Case." *Die Welt des Islams* 37(2): 135–155.

Banningan, John A. (1952). "The Hindu Code Bill." *Far Eastern Survey* 21(17): 173–176.

Barak-Erez, Daphne (2007). *Outlawed Pigs: Law, Religion, and Culture in Israel*. Madison, The University of Wisconsin Press.

Barka, Amiram. (2006, April 20). "Chief Rabbis Plan Legislation that would Bypass High Court Ruling." *Ha'aretz*, p. n.a.

Barkey, Karen (1994). *Bandits and Bureaucrats: The Ottoman Route to State Centralization*. Ithaca, NY, Cornell University Press.

Barraclough, Steven (1998). "Al-Azhar: Between the Government and the Islamists." *Middle East Journal* 52(2): 236–249.

Barry, Brian M. (2001). *Culture and Equality: An Egalitarian Critique of Multiculturalism*. Cambridge, MA, Harvard University Press.

Barsoum, Gamil (1981). "Vers une unifee du statut personnel en Égypte." *Bulletin du CEDEJ* 10(13): 173–185.

Barzilai, Gad (2003). *Communities and Law: Politics and Cultures of Legal Identities*. Ann Arbor, University of Michigan Press.

Bassok, Moti (2004). "Christians Made Up of 2.1% of Israel's Population in 2003." *Ha'aretz*, p. n.a.

Basson, Lauren (2004). Challenging Boundaries and Belongings: "Mixed Blood" Allotment Disputes at the Turn of the Twentieth Century. *Boundaries and Belonging: States and Societies in the Struggle to Shape Identities and Local Practices*. J. S. Migdal. Cambridge University Press: 151–176.

Baumgartner, Frederic J. (1995). *France in the Sixteenth Century*. New York, St. Martin's Press.

Beinin, Joel (1998). *The Dispersion of Egyptian Jewry: Culture, Politics, and the Formation of a Modern Diaspora*. Berkeley, University of California Press.

Bell, Derrick A. (2004). *Race, Racism, and American Law*. New York, Aspen Publishers.

Ben-Ami, Maimon H. (1978). "Christian Courts in Israel." *Christian News from Israel* 26: 128–131.

Ben Rafael, Eliezer (2002). *Jewish Identities: Fifty Intellectuals Answer Ben Gurion*. Leiden, Brill.

Benda-Beckmann, Franz and Keebet Von, *et al.* (2006). *Changing Properties of Property*. New York, Berghahn Books.

Benda-Beckmann, Keebet Von (1981). "Forum Shopping and Shopping Forums: Dispute Processing in a Minangkabau Village in West Sumatra." *Journal of Legal Pluralism* 19: 117–159.

Benhabib, Seyla (2002a). *The Claims of Culture: Equality and Diversity in the Global Era*. Princeton University Press.

Benjamin, Braude (1982). Foundation Myth of the Millet System. *Christians and Jews in the Ottoman Empire: The Functioning of a Plural Society*. B. Braude and B. Lewis. New York, Holmes & Meier Publishers, Inc.: 69–88.

Bennett, T. W. (2011). "Legal Pluralism and the Family in South Africa: Lessons from Customary Law Reform." *Emory International Law Review* 25: 1029–1059.

and Peart, N. S. (1983). The Dualism of Marriage Laws in Africa. *Family Law in the Last Two Decades of the Twentieth Century*. T. W. Bennett, ed. Cape Town, Juta: 145–170.

and Vermeulen, T. (1979). "Codification of Customary Law." *Journal of African Law* 23(1): 206–219.

Bennigsen, Alexandre and Lemercier-Quelquejay, Chantal (1979). "'Official' Islam in the Soviet Union." *Religion in Communist Lands* 7(3): 149–159.

Benton, Lauren A. (2002). *Law and Colonial Cultures: Legal Regimes in World History, 1400–1900*. Cambridge University Press.

Bentwich, Norman (1964). "The Legal System of Israel." *International and Comparative Law Quarterly* 13: 236–255.

Bentzon, Agnete Weis and Brøndsted, Henning (1983). Recognition, Repression and Transformation of Customary Law in Greenland During the Last Forty Years of Transition to Capitalism. *Papers of the Symposia on Folk Law and Legal Pluralism, 11th Icaes*. H. W. Finkler, ed. Vancouver, Commission on Folk Law and Legal Pluralism: 598–620.

Berger, Maurits (1998). "Jurisprudence Abû Zayd." *Droits d'Égypte: Histoire et sociologie* (34): 193–201.

(2001). "Public Policy and Islamic Law: The Modern *Dhimmi* in Contemporary Egyptian Family Law." *Islamic Law and Society* 8(1): 88–134.

(2003). "Apostasy and Public Policy in Contemporary Egypt: An Evaluation of Recent Cases from Egypt's Highest Courts." *Human Rights Quarterly* 25(3): 720–740.

(2004). Regulating Tolerance: Protecting Egypt's Minorities? *Standing Trial: Law and Person in the Modern Middle East.* B. Dupret, ed. London, IB Tauris: 345–371.

Berkes, Niyazi (1998). *The Development of Secularism in Turkey.* London, Hurst Co.

Berman, Harold Joseph (1983). *Law and Revolution: The Formation of the Western Legal Tradition.* Cambridge, MA, Harvard University Press.

(2000). *Faith and Order: The Reconciliation of Law and Religion.* Grand Rapids, MI, Williams B. Eerdmans Pub. Co.

Bernard-Maugiron, Nathalie (1999). Legal Pluralism and the Closure of the Legal Field: The Al-Muhajir Case. *Legal Pluralism in the Arab World.* B. Dupret, M. Berger and L. Al-Zwaini, eds. The Hague, Kluwer Law International: 173–189.

(2003). *Le politique à l'épreuve du judiciaire: La justice constitutionnelle en Égypte.* Brussels, Bruylant/Cedej.

(2004). Can Hisba be "Modernised"? The Individual and the Protection of the General Interest before Egyptian Courts. *Standing Trial: Law and Person in the Modern Middle East.* B. Dupret, ed. London, IB Tauris: 318–344.

and Dupret, Baudouin (2008). "Breaking up the Family: Divorce in Egyptian Law and Practice." *Hawwa: Journal of Women in the Middle East and the Islamic World* 6(1): 52–74.

Bestavros, Adel (1976). "The Organization and History of the Patriarchal Laical Councils in the Coptic Orthodox Church of Egypt." *Society of the Law of the Oriental Churches,* Vienna: 7–18.

Bhansali, S. R. (1992). *Legal System in India.* Jaipur, Universal Book House.

Bhargava, Rajeev (2002). "What is Indian Secularism and What is it For?" *Indian Review* 1(1): 1–32.

(2005). India's Secular Constitution. *India's Living Constitution: Ideas, Practices, Controversies.* Z. Hasan, E. Sridharan and R. Sudarshan, eds. London, Anthem: 105–133.

Biale, Rachel (1984). *Women and Jewish Law: An Exploration of Women's Issues in Halakhic Sources.* New York, Schocken Books.

(1995). *Women and Jewish Law: The Essential Texts, Their History, and Their Relevance for Today.* New York, Schocken Books.

Bibars, Iman M. Diaa El Din (1987). *Women's Political Interest Groups in Egypt: An Analysis of Women's Political Interest Groups in Egypt and an Evaluation of Their Effectiveness in the Establishment of Personal Status Law No. 100 of 1985.* M.A. thesis, American University in Cairo.

Bier, Laura (2011). *Revolutionary Womanhood: Feminisms, Modernity, and the State in Nasser's Egypt.* Stanford University Press.

Binder, Leonard (1963). *Religion and Politics in Pakistan.* Berkeley, University of California Press.

Birnbaum, Ervin (1970). *The Politics of Compromise: State and Religion in Israel.* Rutherford, Fairleigh Dickinson University Press.

Blecher, Ayelet and Shmueli, Benjamin (2009). "The Interplay between Tort Law and Religious Family Law: The Israeli Case." *Arizona Journal of International and Comparative Law* 26(2): 279–301.

Bogdan, Michael (2000). "Legal Pluralism in the Comoros and Djibouti." *Nordic Journal of International Law* 69(2): 195–208.

Bogoch, Bryna and Halperin-Kaddari, Ruth (2006). "Divorce Israeli Style: Professional Perceptions of Gender and Power in Mediated and Lawyer-Negotiated Divorces." *Law & Policy* 28(2): 137–163.

Bonfield, Lloyd (2001). The History of the European Family, vol. I: *Family Life in Early Modern Times 1500–1789.* D. I. Kertzer and M. Barbagli, eds. New Haven, Yale University Press: 87–124.

    (2002). The History of the European Family, vol. II: *Family Life in the Long Nineteenth Century 1789–1913.* D. I. Kertzer and M. Barbagli, eds. New Haven, Yale University Press: 109–154.

Boogert, Maurits H. van den (2012). Millets: Past and Present. *Religious Minorities in the Middle East: Domination, Self-Empowerment, Accommodation.* A. N. Longva and A. S. Roald, eds. Leiden, Brill: 25–45.

Boone, Catherine (2003a). "Decentralization as Political Strategy in West Africa." *Comparative Political Studies* 36(4): 355–380.

    (2003b). *Political Topographies of the African State: Territorial Authority and Institutional Choice.* Cambridge University Press.

Borrmans, Maurice (1977). *Statut personnel et famille au Maghreb: De 1940 à nos jours.* Paris, Mouton.

Borthwick, Bruce M. (1979). "Religion and Politics in Israel and Egypt." *The Middle East Journal* 33(2): 145–163.

Botman, Selma (1999). *Engendering Citizenship in Egypt.* New York, Columbia University Press.

Boyle, Kevin (2004). "Human Rights, Religion and Democracy: The Refah Party Case." *Essex Human Rights Review* 1(1): 1–16.

Brackman, Nicole (1999). "Who is Jew? The American Jewish Community in Conflict with Israel." *Journal of Church and State* 41: 795–824.

Bradley, David (1996). *Family Law and Political Culture: Scandinavian Laws in Comparative Perspective.* London, Sweet & Maxwell.

Brass, Paul R. (1991). *Ethnicity and Nationalism: Theory and Comparison.* New Delhi; Newbury Park, CA, Sage Publications.

Brinton, Jasper Yeates (1968). *The Mixed Courts of Egypt.* New Haven, Yale University Press.

Brissaud, Jean (1912). *A History of French Private Law.* Boston, Little, Brown & Co.

Brown, Beverly (1994). "Islamic Law, Qadhis' Courts and Muslim Women's Legal Status: The Case of Kenya." *Journal of the Institute of Muslim Minority Affairs* 14(12): 94–101.

Brown, Nathan J. (1997). *The Rule of Law in the Arab World: Courts in Egypt and the Gulf.* Cambridge University Press.

Brubaker, Rogers (1996). *Nationalism Reframed: Nationhood and the National Question in the New Europe.* Cambridge University Press.

Bunce, Valerie (1999). *Subversive Institutions: The Design and the Destruction of Socialism and the State.* Cambridge University Press.

Buskens, Leon (2010). Sharia and National Law in Morocco. *Sharia Incorporated: A Comparative Overview of the Legal Systems of Twelve Muslim Countries in Past and Present.* J. M. Otto, ed. Leiden University Press: 89–138.

Butalia, Urvashi (2000). *The Other Side of Silence: Voices from the Partition of India.* Durham, NC, Duke University Press.

Butenschøn, Nils A. (2000). State, Power and Citizenship in the Middle East: A Theoretical Introduction. *Citizenship and the State in the Middle East: Approaches and Applications.* N. A. Butenschøn, U. Davis and M. S. Hassassian, eds. Syracuse, NY, Syracuse University Press: 3–27.

Butt, Liaqat Ali (2008). *Comprehensive and Exhaustive Commentary on Manual of Family Laws in Pakistan: Amendments and Case Law up-to-Date.* Lahore Eastern Law Book House.

Caenegem, R. C. van (1992). *An Historical Introduction to Private Law.* Cambridge, UK; New York, Cambridge University Press.

Caldwell, Lesley (1991). *Italian Family Matters: Women, Politics, and Legal Reform.* Houndmills, Macmillan Academic & Professional.

Canning, Kathleen and Rose, Sonya O. (2002). Gender, Citizenships and Subjectivities: Some Historical and Theoretical Considerations. *Gender, Citizenships and Subjectivities.* K. Canning and S. O. Rose, eds. Oxford, Blackwell: 1–17.

Cantor, Norman L. (1988). "Religion and State in Israel and the United States." *Tel Aviv Studies in Law* 8: 185–218.

Carson, J. B. (1958). "Further Notes on the African Court System in Kenya." *Journal of African Administration* 10(1): 34–38.

Carter, B. L. (1986). *The Copts in Egyptian Politics, 1918–1952.* London, Croom Helm.

Cassin, René (1956). Codification and National Unity. *The Code Napoleon and the Common-Law World*. B. Schwartz, ed. New York University Press: 46–54.

Cassis Bey, Joseph (1951). "Les tribunaux Égyptiens de statut personnel." *Le Lien: Revue Mensuelle Grecque-Catholique* 16(5–6): 153–162.

Chandra, Bipan, Mukherjee, Aditya, *et al.* (1999). *India after Independence*. New Delhi; London, Penguin Books.

Chanock, Martin (2000). "Culture" and Human Rights: Orientalising, Occidentalising and Authenticity. *Beyond Rights Talk and Culture Talk: Comparative Essays on the Politics of Rights and Culture*. M. Mamdani, ed. New York, St. Martin's Press: 15–36.

Charrad, Mounira M. (2001). *States and Women's Rights: The Making of Postcolonial Tunisia, Algeria, and Morocco*. Berkeley, University of California Press.

Chartier, Roger, ed. (1989). *A History of Private Life*, vol III: *Passions of the Renaissance*. Cambridge, MA, Harvard University Press.

Chatterjee, Partha (1994). "Secularism and Toleration." *Economic and Political Weekly* 29(28): 1768–1777.

Chavan, Nandini and Kidwai, Qutub Jehan (2006). *Personal Law Reforms and Gender Empowerment: A Debate on Uniform Civil Code*. Gurgaon, Hope India.

Chesterman, John and Galligan, Brian (1997). *Citizens Without Rights: Aborigines and Australian Citizenship*. Cambridge University Press.

Chiba, Masaji (1998). "Other Phases of Legal Pluralism in the Contemporary World." *Ratio Juris* 11(3): 228–245.

Chigier, M. (1967). "The Rabbinical Courts in the State of Israel." *Israel Law Review* 2(2): 147–181.

(1979). "Codification of Jewish Law." *The Jewish Law Annual* 2: 3–32.

Choudhury, Golam Wahed (1968). *Pakistan's Relations with India 1947–1966*. London, Pall Mall Press.

Cohen, Asher and Susser, Bernard (2000). *Israel and the Politics of Jewish Identity: The Secular-Religious Impasse*. Baltimore, The Johns Hopkins University Press.

Cohen, Erik (1989). Citizenship, Nationality and Religion in Israel and Thailand. *The Israeli State and Society: Boundaries and Frontiers*. B. Kimmerling, ed. Albany, NY, SUNY Press: 66–92.

Cohen, Lenard J. (1985). "Judicial Elites in Yugoslavia: The Professionalization of Political Justice." *Review of Socialist Law* 11: 313–344.

Cohen, Stephen P. (2004). *The Idea of Pakistan*. Washington, DC, Brookings Institution Press.

Cohn, Bernard S. (1996). *Colonialism and its Forms of Knowledge*. Princeton University Press.

Corinaldi, Michael (1978–1980). "The Problem of Divorce by Judicial Decree in Karaite Halakhah." *Diné Israel* 9: 101–144.

(1984). *The Personal Status of the Karaites*. Yerushalayim, R. Mas [in Hebrew].

(2000). The Personal Status of the Samaritans in Israel. *Samaritan Researches*, vol. v. V. Morabito, A. D. Crown and L. Davey, eds. Sydney, Mandelbaum Publishing: 85–96.

(2002). "A Halakhic Solution for Women whose Husbands Refuse to Grant a Divorce: The Shunning Measure of Rabbeinu Tam." *Jewish Law Watch* 5: 5–16.

Cossman, Brenda and Kapur, Ratna (2001). *Secularism's Last Sigh? Hindutva and the (Mis)Rule of Law*. Delhi, Oxford University Press.

Cotran, Eugene (1965). "Integration of Courts and Application of Customary Law in Tanganyika." *East African Law Journal* 1(2): 108–123.

(1996). "Marriage, Divorce and Succession Laws in Kenya: Is Integration or Unification Possible?" *Journal of African Law* 40(2): 194–204.

Coulson, N. J. (1957). "Reform of Family Law in Pakistan." *Studia Islamica* 7: 135–155.

Crabites, Pierre (1927). "The Golden Jubilee of the Mixed Tribunals of Egypt." *Loyola Law Journal* 8(1): 1–15.

Crecelius, Daniel Neil (1966). "Al-Azhar in the Revolution." *The Middle East Journal* 20(1): 31–49.

(1967). *The Ulama and the State in Modern Egypt*. Ph.D. thesis, Princeton University.

(1980). The Course of Secularization in Modern Egypt. *Islam and Development: Religion and Sociopolitical Change*. J. L. Esposito and H. Askari, eds. Syracuse University Press: 49–70.

Cretney, Stephen Michael (2005). *Family Law in the Twentieth Century: A History*. Oxford University Press.

Crook, Richard C. (2004). "Access to Justice and Land Disputes in Ghana's State Courts: The Litigants' Perspective." *Journal of Legal Pluralism* 50: 1–28.

Crubaugh, Anthony (2001). *Balancing the Scales of Justice: Local Courts and Rural Society in Southwest France, 1750–1800*. University Park, PA, Pennsylvania State University Press.

Culbertson, Philip L. (1981). "The Anglican Family Court in Israel and the West Bank." *Journal of Church and State* 23: 285–308.

Cuno, Kenneth M. (2009). Disobedient Wives and Neglectful Husbands: Marital Relations and the First Phase of Family Law Reform in Egypt. *Family, Gender, and Law in a Globalizing Middle East and South Asia*. K. M. Cuno and M. Desai, eds. Syracuse University Press: 3–18.

Cutler, A. Claire (2003). *Private Power and Global Authority: Transnational Merchant Law in the Global Political Economy*. Cambridge University Press.

d'Encausse, Hélène Carrère (1974). "Islam in the Soviet Union: Attempts at Modernization." *Religion in Communist Lands* 2(4–5): 12–17.

Dalacoura, Katerina (2002). "A Critique of Communitarianism with Reference to Post-Revolutionary Iran." *Review of International Studies* 28(1): 75–92.

Daloz, Jean-Pascal and Chabal, Patrick (1999). *Africa Works: Disorder as Political Instrument.* Oxford, International African Institute.

Dana, Nissim (1980). *The Druse: A Religious Community in Transition.* Jerusalem, Turtledove Publishing.

    (2003). *The Druze in the Middle East: Their Faith, Leadership, Identity and Status.* Brighton, Sussex Academic Press.

Dane, Perry (1991). "Maps of Sovereignty: A Meditation." *Cardozo Law Review* 12(3–4): 959–1006.

David, René (1962). "Civil Code for Ethiopia: Considerations on the Codification of the Civil Law in African Countries." *Tulane Law Review* 37: 187–204.

Dawoud, Khaled (2001a, June 21–27). "Did *Hisba* Ever Go Away?" *Al-Ahram Weekly Online*: 539. Accessed in Oct., 2006, from http://weekly.ahram. org.eg/2001/539/eg7.htm.

    (2001b, June 14–20). "Mobilising for Saadawi." *Al-Ahram Weekly Online*: 538. Accessed in June, 2007, from http://weekly.ahram.org.eg/2001/538/ eg7.htm.

De Bellefonds, Linant Y. (1956). "La suppression des jurisdictions de statut personnel en Égypte." *Revue Internationale de Droit Comparé* 8(1): 412–425.

Deif, Farida (2004). "Divorced from Justice: Women's Unequal Access to Divorce in Egypt." New York, Human Rights Watch. Accessed in June, 2007, from http://hrw.org/reports/2004/egypt1204/egypt1204.pdf.

Dekmejian, R. Hrair (1971). *Egypt under Nasir: A Study in Political Dynamics.* Albany, SUNY Press.

Derrett, J. D. M. (1961). "The Administration of Hindu Law by the British." *Comparative Studies in Society and History* 4(1): 10–52.

    (1963). Justice, Equity and Good Conscience. *Changing Law in Developing Countries.* J. N. D. Anderson, ed. London, Allen & Unwin: 114–153.

    (1969). "Comments with Reference to Hindu Law." *East African Law Journal* 5: 21–53.

    (1976). A Round-up of Bigamous Marriages. *Essays in Classical and Modern Hindu Law*, vol. IV. D. J. Derrett, ed. Leiden, Brill: 85–95.

    (1978). *The Death of a Marriage Law: Epitaph for the Rishis.* New Delhi, Vikas Pub. House.

    (1999). *Religion, Law and the State in India.* Delhi, Oxford University Press.

Desai, Ashok H. and Muralidhar, S. (2000). Public Interest Litigation: Potential and Problems. *Supreme But Not Infallible: Essays in Honour of the Supreme Court of India.* B. N. Kirpal, A. H. Desai and G. Subramanium, eds. New Delhi, Oxford University Press: 159–192.

Desai, Mihir (2004). "The Flip Flop." *Combat Law* 3(4): 15–19.

Deshta, Kiran (2002). *Uniform Civil Code in Retrospect and Prospect*. New Delhi, Deep & Deep.

Desouza, Peter Ronald (1999). Appeasement of Minorities and Multiculturalism: The Indian Debate. *Minority Identities and the Nation-State*. D. L. Sheth and G. Mahajan, eds. New Delhi, Oxford University Press: 206–219.

Dewar, John and Parker, Stephen (1992). *Law and the Family*. London, Butterworths.

Dhagamwar, Vasudha (1989). *Towards the Uniform Civil Code*. Bombay, N. M. Tripathi Private Ltd.

Diamant, Neil J. (2000). *Revolutionizing the Family*. Berkeley, University of California Press.

Diwan, Paras (1978). *Abrogation of Forty-Second Amendment: Does Our Constitution Need a Second Look*. New Delhi, Sterling Publishers.

Don-Yehiya, Eliezer (1999). *Religion and Political Accommodation in Israel*. Jerusalem, The Floersheimer Institute for Policy Studies.

Donnelly, Jack (2002). *Universal Human Rights in Theory and Practice*. Ithaca, Cornell University Press.

Donzelot, Jacques (1997). *The Policing of Families*. Baltimore, Johns Hopkins University Press.

Du Rausas, Pélissié M. G. (1911). "L'organisation judiciaire indigène en Égypte." *L'Égypte Contemporaine* 2: 95–122.

Dumper, Michael (1994). *Islam and Israel: Muslim Religious Endowments and the Jewish State*. Washington, DC, Institute for Palestine Studies.

Dupret, Baudouin (2003). A Return to the Shariah? Egyptian Judges and Referring to Islam. *Modernizing Islam: Religion in the Public Sphere in the Middle East and Europe*. J. L. Esposito and F. Burgat, eds. New Brunswick, NJ, Rutgers University Press: 125–143.

Durkheim, Emile (1984). *The Division of Labor in Society*. New York, The Free Press.

Edelman, Martin (1987). "The Druze Courts in the Political System of Israel." *Middle East Review* 19(4): 54–61.

(1994). *Courts, Politics, and Culture in Israel*. Charlottesville, University Press of Virginia.

(1998). "Who is an Israeli? Halakhah and Citizenship in the Jewish State." *Jewish Political Studies Review* 10(3–4): 87–115.

Edge, Ian (1990). A Comparative Approach to the Treatment of Non-Muslim Minorities in the Middle East with Special Reference to Egypt. *Islamic Family Law*. C. Mallat and J. F. Connors, eds. London; Boston, Graham & Trotman: 31–54.

Einhorn, Talia (2009). *Private International Law in Israel*. Austin, Wolters Kluwer.

Eisenman, Robert H. (1978). *Islamic Law in Palestine and Israel: A History of the Survival of Tanzimat and Shari'a in the British Mandate and the Jewish State*. Leiden, Brill.

El-Alami, Dawoud S. (2001–2002). "Can Islamic Device of *Khul* Provide a Remedy for Non-Muslim Women in Egypt?" *Yearbook of Islamic and Middle Eastern Law* 8: 122–125.

El-Gemayel, Antoine Elias (1985). *The Lebanese Legal System*. Washington, DC, International Law Institute in cooperation with Georgetown University.

El-Kholy, Heba Aziz (2002). *Defiance and Compliance: Negotiating Gender in Low-Income Cairo*. New York, Berghahn Books.

El-Magd, Nadia Abou (2000, June 15–21). "When the Professor Can't Teach." *Al-Ahram Weekly Online*: 486. from http://weekly.ahram.org.eg/2000/486/eg6.htm.

El-Taji, Maha T. (2008). *Arab Local Authorities in Israel: Hamulas, Nationalism and Dilemmas of Social Change*. Ph.D. thesis, University of Washington, Seattle.

Eldin, Kamal Amany, Hill, Enid, *et al.* (1985). "After Jihan's Law: A New Battle over Women's Rights." *The Middle East Magazine* 129: 17–20.

Eliash, Ben Zion (1981–1983). "The Limited Influence of Israeli Rabbinical Enactments on the Israeli Rabbinical Courts." *Diné Israel* 10–11: 177–215 [in Hebrew].

  (1983). "Ethnic Pluralism or Melting Pot? The Dilemma of Rabbinical Adjudication in Israeli Family Law." *Israel Law Review* 11(3–4): 348–380.

Elon, Menachem (1967). "The Sources and Nature of Jewish Law and its Application in the State of Israel – 1." *Israel Law Review* 2(4): 515–565.

  (1968a). "The Sources and Nature of Jewish Law and its Application in the State of Israel – 2." *Israel Law Review* 3(1): 88–126.

  (1968b). "The Sources and Nature of Jewish Law and its Application in the State of Israel – 3." *Israel Law Review* 3(3): 416–457.

  (1969). "The Sources and Nature of Jewish Law and its Application in the State of Israel – 4." *Israel Law Review* 4(1): 80–140.

Elst, Koenraad (2002). *Who is a Hindu? Hindu Revivalist Views of Animism, Buddhism, Sikhism and Other Offshoots of Hinduism*. New Delhi, Voice of India.

Engineer, Asgharali (1987). *The Shah Bano Controversy*. Bombay, Orient Longman.

Epp, Charles R. (1998). *The Rights Revolution: Lawyers, Activists, and Supreme Courts in Comparative Perspective*. Chicago, University of Chicago Press.

Esposito, John L. and Delong-Bas, Natana J. (2001a). *Women in Muslim Family Law*. Syracuse University Press.

Estin, Ann Laquer (2011). "Family Law, Pluralism, and Human Rights." *Emory International Law Review* 25: 811–828.

Ettinger, Yair (2010). "Rabbinical Courts Softened Stance on Husbands Refusing their Wives Divorce." Accessed in March, 2010, from www.haaretz.com/hasen/spages/1145446.html.

Everett, Jana Matson (1979). *Women and Social Change in India*. New Delhi, Heritage Publishers.

Ezeilo, Joy Ngozi (2000). "Laws and Practices Relating to Women's Inheritance Rights in Nigeria." Enugu, Nigeria, Women's Aid Collective.

Ezzat, Dina (2000a). Sacred Knots and Unholy Deals: The Road towards Pro-Women Legal Reform in Egypt. *No Paradise Yet: The World's Women Face the New Century*. J. Mirsky and M. Radlett, eds. London, PANOS/Zed: 39–60.

Ezzat, Heba Raouf (2000b). Secularism, the State and the Social Bond: The Withering Away of the Family. *Islam and Secularism in the Middle East*. A. Tamimi and J. L. Esposito, eds. London, C. Hurst: 124–138.

Fahmy, Ninette S. (2002). *The Politics of Egypt: State-Society Relationship*. London, Routledge Curzon.

Fawzy, Essam (2004). Muslim Personal Status Law in Egypt: The Current Situation and Possibilities of Reform through Internal Initiatives. *Women's Rights and Islamic Family Law: Perspectives on Reform*. L. Welchman, ed. London, Zed Books: 15–94.

Firro, Kais (1999). *The Druzes in the Jewish State: A Brief History*. Leiden, Brill.

Fitzpatrick, Peter (1983). Law, Plurality and Underdevelopment. *Legality, Ideology and the State*. D. Sugarman, ed. London, Academic Press: 159–182.

(1984). "Law and Societies." *Osgoode Hall Law Journal* 22(1): 115–138.

Fogiel-Bijaoui, Silvie (2003). "Why won't there be Civil Marriage Any Time Soon in Israel? Or: Personal Law – The Silenced Issue of the Israeli-Palestinian Conflict." *Nashim: A Journal of Jewish Women's Studies & Gender Issues* 6: 28–34.

Fouad, Hala (2002). "Khulʿ for Copts ... An Issue Open for Debate." *Akher Saʿa*: 38–39.

Freeman, Michael D. A. (1984). *The State, the Law, and the Family: Critical Perspectives*. London, Tavistock Publications.

Friedman, Menachem (1989). The State of Israel as a Theological Dilemma. *The Israeli State and Society: Boundaries and Frontiers*. B. Kimmerling, ed. Albany, NY, SUNY Press: 165–215.

(1995). The Structural Foundation for Religio-Political Accommodation in Israel: Fallacy and Reality. *Israel: The First Decade of Independence*. S. I. Troen and N. Lucas, eds. Albany, SUNY Press: 51–82.

Furber, Holden (1951). "The Unification of India, 1947–1951." *Pacific Affairs* 24(4): 352–371.

Fyzee, Asaf Ali Asghar and Mahmood, Syed Tahir (2005). *Cases in the Muhammadan Law of India and Pakistan*. New Delhi, Oxford University Press.

Gaay Fortman, Bastiaan De, Martens, Kurt, *et al.* (2010). *Hermeneutics, Scriptural Politics, and Human Rights: Between Text and Context*. Basingstoke, Palgrave Macmillan.

259

Gabriel, Theodore (2007). *Christian Citizens in an Islamic State: The Pakistan Experience*. Aldershot, Ashgate.

Gajendragadkar, P. B. (1971). *Secularism and the Constitution of India*. Bombay, University of Bombay.

Galanter, Marc (1966). The Modernization of Law. *Modernization: The Dynamics of Growth*. M. Weiner, ed. New York, Basic Books Inc.: 153–165.

(1981). "Justice in Many Rooms: Courts, Private Ordering, and Indigenous Law." *Journal of Legal Pluralism* 19: 1–47.

(1989). *Law and Society in Modern India*. Delhi, Oxford University Press.

Ganguly, Sumit (2003). "The Crisis of Indian Secularism." *Journal of Democracy* 14(4): 11–25.

Gani, H. A. (1988). *Reform of Muslim Personal Law: The Shah Bano Controversy and the Muslim Women (Protection of Rights on Divorce) Act, 1986*. New Delhi, Deep & Deep Publications.

Gardbaum, Stephen (2003). "The 'Horizontal Effect' of Constitutional Rights." *Michigan Law Review* 102: 388–459.

Garvey, John H. (1993). Introduction: Fundamentalism and Politics. *Fundamentalisms and the State: Remaking Polities, Economies and Militance*. M. E. Marty and S. R. Appleby. Chicago University Press: 13–27.

Gearon, Liam (2002). *Human Rights and Religion: A Reader*. Brighton; Portland, OR, Sussex Academic Press.

Geddes, Barbara (1990). "How the Cases You Choose Affect the Answers You Get: Selection Bias in Comparative Politics." *Political Analysis* 2: 131–150.

George, Alexander L. and Bennett, Andrew (2005). *Case Studies and Theory Development in the Social Sciences*. Cambridge, MA, MIT Press.

Gerber, Haim (1987). *The Social Origins of the Modern Middle East*. Boulder, CO, L. Rienner.

Ghai, Yash P. (1975). "Notes towards a Theory of Law and Ideology: Tanzanian Perspectives." *East African Law Journal* 11(2): 143–207.

Ghandour, Zeina (1990). "Religious Law in a Secular State: The Jurisdiction of the Shari'a Courts of Palestine and Israel." *Arab Law Quarterly* 5(1): 25–48.

Ghanem, As'ad (2001). *The Palestinian-Arab Minority in Israel, 1948–2000*. New York, SUNY Press.

Giddens, Anthony (1985). *The Nation-State and Violence*. Berkeley, University of California Press.

Ginat, Rami (1997). *Egypt's Incomplete Revolution: Lutfi Al-Khuli and Nasser's Socialism in the 1960s*. London, Frank Cass.

Gittins, Diana (1985). *The Family in Question: Changing Households and Familiar Ideologies*. Basingstoke, Macmillan.

Glendon, Mary Ann (1989). *The Transformation of Family Law: State, Law, and Family in the United States and Western Europe*. University of Chicago Press.

Gordon, Michael W., *et al.* (1999). *Comparative Legal Traditions in a Nutshell.* St. Paul, MN, West Group.

Goadby, Frederic Maurice (1926). *International and Inter-Religious Private Law in Palestine.* Jerusalem, "Hamadpis" Press.

Goffman, Daniel (1994). "Ottoman Millets in the Early Seventeenth Century." *New Perspectives on Turkey* 11: 135–158.

Goldberg, Ellis J. (1990). Jamal Abdul Nasser. *Political Leaders of the Contemporary Middle East and North Africa: A Biographical Dictionary.* B. Reich, ed. New York, Greenwood Press: 379–387.

Goldstein, Stephen (1992). "Israel: A Secular or a Religious State?" *Saint Louis University Law Journal* 36(1): 143–162.

Goldstone, Jack A. (2003). Comparative Historical Analysis and Knowledge Accumulation in the Study of Revolutions. *Comparative Historical Analysis in the Social Sciences.* J. Mahoney and D. Rueschemeyer, eds. Cambridge University Press: 41–90.

Goldwater, Chaim (1977). "Religious Tribunals with a Dual Capacity." *Israel Law Review* 12(1): 114–119.

Goodale, Mark and Merry, Sally Engle (2007). *The Practice of Human Rights: Tracking Law between the Global and the Local.* Cambridge University Press.

Goody, Jack (1983). *The Development of the Family and Marriage in Europe.* Cambridge University Press.

and Tambiah, Stanley Jeyaraja (1973). *Bridewealth and Dowry.* Cambridge University Press.

Gopal, S. and Iyengar, Uma, eds. (2003). *The Essential Writings of Jawaharlal Nehru.* New Delhi, Oxford University Press.

Gordon, Joel (1992). *Nasser's Blessed Movement: Egypt's Free Officers and the July Revolution.* New York, Oxford University Press.

Goswami, Samanrendra Nath (1994). *The Principles of Baha'i Personal Law.* Dhaka, The Bangladesh Law Times.

Greenhouse, Carol J. (1982). "Nature is to Culture as Praying is to Suing: Legal Pluralism in an American Suburb." *Journal of Legal Pluralism* 20: 17–35.

and Strijbosch, Fons (1993). "Legal Pluralism in Industrialized Societies." *Journal of Legal Pluralism* 33: 1–9.

Greenwood, Christopher J. and Lauterpacht, Elihu (1956). *International Law Reports.* Cambridge, Grotius Pub. Ltd.

Griffiths, John (1986). "What is Legal Pluralism?" *Journal of Legal Pluralism* 24: 1–55.

Gross, C. Netty (2003). "When Luciano Met Kayu." *The Jerusalem Report:* 15–16.

(2005). "Local Non-Orthodox Conversions Possible." *The Jerusalem Report:* 6.

Grubbs, Judith Evans (1995). *Law and Family in Late Antiquity: The Emperor Constantine's Marriage Legislation.* Oxford, Clarendon Press.

Guberman, Shlomo (1970). "Christian Religious Courts and the Unification of Jerusalem." *Israel Law Review* 5(1): 120–137.

Guillet, David (1998). "Rethinking Legal Pluralism: Local Law and State Law in the Evolution of Water Property Rights in Northwestern Spain." *Comparative Studies in Society and History* 40(1): 42–70.

Guindy, Hosny, Shukrallah, Hani, et al. (1999, April 1–7). "Marriage, Politics and Jerusalem." *Al-Ahram Weekly Online*: 423. Accessed in July, 2010, from http://weekly.ahram.org.eg/1999/423/intrview.htm.

Gupta, Nidhi (2003). "Women's Human Rights and the Practice of Dowry in India: Adapting a Global Discourse to Local Demands." *Journal of Legal Pluralism and Unofficial Law* 48: 85–123.

Gutmann, Amy (2003). *Identity in Democracy*. Princeton University Press.

Hajjar, Joseph P. (1955). "Questions d'actualité: La suppression des tribunaux confessionnels en Égypte." *Proche-Orient Chrétien* 5: 316–331.

(1956). "La suppression des tribunaux confessionnels en Égypte." *Proche-Orient Chrétien* 6: 11–27.

Halim, Nadia, Al-Bahth, Hay'at, et al. (2005). *The Social Effects of Khul': A Comparative Study of Khul' and Tatliq*. Al-Qahira, Markaz Qadaia al-Mara al-Masriyya (CEWLA) [in Arabic].

Halperin-Kaddari, Ruth (1993). *The Interaction between Religious Systems of Adjudication and the Secular Legal System in the United States*. J.S.D. thesis, Yale Law School, New Haven.

(2001). "Towards Concluding Civil Family Law – Israel Style." *Mehkarei Mishpat (Bar-Ilan Law Studies)* 17: 105–157 [in Hebrew].

(2002). Expressions of Legal Pluralism in Israel: The Interaction between the High Court of Justice and Rabbinical Courts in Family Matters and Beyond. *Jewish Family Law in the State of Israel*. M. D. A. Freeman, ed. Binghamton, NY, Global Publications/SUNY: 185–244.

(2004). *Women in Israel: A State of Their Own*. Philadelphia, University of Pennsylvania Press.

Hamad, Ahmed Seif Al-Islam (1999). Legal Plurality and Legitimation of Human Rights Abuses: A Case Study of State Council Rulings Concerning the Rights of Apostates. *Legal Pluralism in the Arab World*. B. Dupret, M. Berger and L. Al-Zwaini, eds. The Hague, Kluwer Law International: 219 228.

Hameed, Syeda Saiyidain (2003). *My Voice Shall be Heard: Muslim Women in India, 2003*. New Delhi, Muslim Women's Forum.

Hanna, Nelly (1995). The Administration of Courts in Ottoman Cairo. *The State and its Servants: Administration in Egypt from Ottoman Times to the Present*. Cairo, American University in Cairo Press: 44–59.

Hansen, Thomas Blom and Jaffrelot, Christophe (1998). *The BJP and the Compulsions of Politics in India*. Delhi, Oxford University Press.

Harik, Iliya (1973). "The Single Party as a Subordinate Movement: The Case of Egypt." *World Politics* 26(1): 80–105.

Harring, Sidney L. (1994). *Crow Dog's Case: American Indian Sovereignty, Tribal Law, and United States Law in the Nineteenth Century*. Cambridge University Press.

Harris, Ron (2002). Historical Opportunities and Absent-Minded Omissions: On the Incorporation of Jewish Law. *Nascent Israeli Law, in Both Sides of the Bridge: Church and State in Early Israel*. M. Bar-On and Z. Zameret, eds. Jerusalem, Yad Izhak Ben-Zvi Press 21–54 [in Hebrew].

Hasan, Amir (1990). Secularism Versus State: Communalism in India. *Secularism in Retreat: The Communal-Secular Paradox in India*. B. Chakrabarty, ed. New Delhi, Segment Book Distributors: 115–123.

Hasan, Aznan (2003). "Granting Khul' for a Non-Muslim Couple in Egyptian Personal Status Law: Generosity or Laxity?" *Arab Law Quarterly* 18(1): 81–89.

Hasan, Mushirul (2001). *Legacy of a Divided Nation: India's Muslims Since Independence*. New Delhi, Oxford University Press.

(2002). *Islam in the Subcontinent: Muslims in a Plural Society*. New Delhi, Manohar.

Hasan, Zoya (1989). "Minority Identity, Muslim Women Bill Campaign and the Political Process." *Economic and Political Weekly* 24(1): 44–50.

(1993). "Communalism, State Policy and the Question of Women's Rights in Contemporary India." *Bulletin of Concerned Asian Scholars* 25(4): 5–15.

(1994). Minority Identity, State Policy and the Political Process. *Forging Identities: Gender, Communities and the State*. Z. Hasan, ed. New Delhi, Kali for Women: 59–73.

(1999). Muslim Women and the Debate on Legal Reforms. *From Independence towards Freedom: Indian Women since 1947*. B. Ray and A. Basu, eds. New Delhi, Oxford University Press: 120–134.

Hassan, Fayza (2001, Mar. 1–7). "The Meaning of Emancipation." *Al-Ahram Weekly Online*: 523. Accessed in Oct., 2010, from http://weekly.ahram.org.eg/2001/523/sc1.htm.

Hatem, Mervat F. (1992). "Economic and Political Liberation in Egypt and the Demise of State Feminism." *International Journal of Middle East Studies* 24(2): 231–251.

(2000). Nationalist Discourses on Citizenship in Egypt. *Gender and Citizenship in the Middle East*. S. Joseph, ed. Syracuse University Press: 33–57.

Hatina, Meir (2003). "Historical Legacy and the Challenge of Modernity in the Middle East: The Case of Al-Azhar in Egypt." *The Muslim World* 93: 51–68.

Hayat, Muhammad Aslam (2001). *The Manual of Family Laws in Pakistan*. Lahore, Khyber Laws Publishers.

Hazard, John N. (1939). "Law and the Soviet Family." *Wisconsin Law Review*: 224–253.

Hecht, Neil S., Jackson, B. S., *et al.* (1996). *An Introduction to the History and Sources of Jewish Law*. Oxford, Clarendon Press.

Hegel, Georg Wilhelm Friedrich (1991). *Elements of the Philosophy of Right*. Cambridge University Press.

Herbst, Jeffrey Ira (2000). *States and Power in Africa: Comparative Lessons in Authority and Control*. Princeton University Press.

Herring, Basil (2000). "Help for Agunot: Prenuptial Agreements." *Canadian Jewish News* 30(14): 9.

Hessbruegge, Jan Arno (2005). "Human Rights Violations Arising from Conduct of Non-State Actors." *Buffalo Human Rights Law Review* 11: 21–88.

Higgins, Patricia J. (1984). "Minority-State Relations in Contemporary Iran." *Iranian Studies* 17(1): 37–71.

Hofnung, Menachem (1996). *Democracy, Law, and National Security in Israel*. Aldershot, Dartmouth.

Hofri-Winogradow, Adam S. (2010). "A Plurality of Discontent: Legal Pluralism, Religious Adjudication and the State." *Journal of Law and Religion* 26(1): 101–133.

Holdsworth, William Searle (1944). *A History of English Law*. London, Methuen & Co. Ltd.

Hooker, M. B. (1975). *Legal Pluralism: An Introduction to Colonial and Neo-Colonial Laws*. Oxford, Clarendon Press.

Hopwood, Derek (1991). *Egypt, Politics and Society, 1945–1990*. London, HarperCollins Academic.

Howard-Merriam, Kathleen (1988). "Egytian Islamism and the Law: Connecting the 'Private' and the 'Public'." *International Journal of Islamic and Arabic Studies* 5(1): 77–96.

Hoyle, Mark S. W. (1987). "The Mixed Courts of Egypt 1926–1937." *Arab Law Quarterly* 2(4): 357–389.

(1991). *Mixed Courts of Egypt*. London, Graham & Trotman.

Htun, Mala (2003). *Sex and the State: Abortion, Divorce, and the Family under Latin American Dictatorships and Democracies*. Cambridge University Press.

Huebner, Rudolf (1918). *A History of Germanic Private Law*. Boston, Little, Brown and Co.

Human Rights Watch (2006). "Israel: Family Reunification Ruling is Discriminatory." Accessed in December, 2006, from http://hrw.org/english/docs/2006/05/18/isrlpa13403.htm.

(2007). "Egypt – Prohibited Identities: State Interference with Religious Freedom." *EIPR* 19(7): 1–102.

(2012). "The Road Ahead: A Human Rights Agenda for Egypt's New Parliament." New York, Human Rights Watch.

Hunt, Lynn Avery (1992). *The Family Romance of the French Revolution*. Berkeley, University of California Press.

Hussain, Sabiha (2007). *Shariat Courts and Women's Rights in India*. New Delhi, Centre for Women's Development Studies.

Hussein, Aziza (1981). Recently Approved Amendments to Egypt's Law on Personal Status. *Religion and Politics in the Middle East*. M. Curtis, ed. Boulder, CO, Westview Press: 125–128.

Ibn Taym'iyah, Ahmad Ibn Abd Al-Halim, Holland, Muhtar, *et al.* (1982). *Public Duties in Islam: The Institution of the Hisba*. Leicester, Islamic Foundation.

Ibrahim, Amira (2001, Mar. 11–17). "Hope on the Horizon?" *Al-Ahram Weekly Online*: 420. Accessed in July, 2007, from http://weekly.ahram.org.eg/2002/610/fo1.htm.

Ibrahim, Saad Eddin (1996). *The Copts of Egypt*. London, Minority Rights Group International.

ICHRP (2009). *When Legal Worlds Overlap: Human Rights, State and Non-State Law*. Versoix, International Council on Human Rights Policy.

Idris, Ibrahim (1994). Freedom of Religion and Secularization of State: The Legal Status of Islamic Law and Sharia Courts in Ethiopia. *New Trends in Ethiopian Studies. Papers of the 12th International Conference of Ethiopian Studies*, vol. II. H. Marcus, ed. Lawrenceville, Red Sea Press: 151–156.

Ignatieff, Michael and Gutmann, Amy (2001). *Human Rights as Politics and Idolatry*. Princeton University Press.

Inhorn, Marcia Claire (1996). *Infertility and Patriarchy: The Cultural Politics of Gender and Family Life in Egypt*. Philadelphia, University of Pennsylvania Press.

Irani, Phiroze K. (1968). The Personal Law of the Parsis of India. *Family Law in Asia and Africa*. J. N. D. Anderson, ed. New York, Praeger: 273–300.

Islamic Fiqh Academy (2001). *Important Fiqh Decisions*. New Delhi, Islamic Fiqh Academy.

Israel, Benjamin J. (1984). *The Bene Israel of India: Some Studies*. New York, APT Books.

Iyer, V. R. K. (2002, Jun. 11). "Judicial Review in a Democracy." *The Hindu Online Edition*. Accessed from www.hindu.com/thehindu/br/2002/06/11/stories/2002061100090300.htm, June 2007.

Jackson, Robert H. (1990). *Quasi-States: Sovereignty, International Relations, and the Third World*. Cambridge University Press.

Jacobsohn, Gary J. (2003). *The Wheel of Law: India's Secularism in Comparative Constitutional Context*. New Delhi, Oxford University Press.

    (2010). *Constitutional Identity*. Cambridge, MA, Harvard University Press.

Jain, Champat Rai (2004). *Selections from the Jaina Law*. Jaipur, Jaina Vidya Samsthana.

Jain, Kiran B. (1988). "The [Indian] Parsi Marriage and Divorce (Amendment) Act 1988: A Study in Retrospect." *Islamic and Comparative Law Quarterly* 8(4): 337–350.

Jain, Mahabir Prashad (2003). *Outlines of Indian Legal History*. Agra, Wadhwa & Co.

Jaising, Indira and Sakhani, Monica (2007). *Law of Domestic Violence*. Delhi, Universal Law Publishing Co.

Jatava, D. R. (1997). *The Critics of Dr. Ambedkar*. Jaipur, Surabhi Publications.

Jayal, Niraja Gopal (2001). *Democracy and the State: Welfare, Secularism and Development in Contemporary India*. New Delhi, Oxford University Press.

Jeppie, Shamil, Moosa, Ebrahim, *et al.* (2010). *Muslim Family Law in Sub-Saharan Africa: Colonial Legacies and Post-Colonial Challenges*. Amsterdam University Press.

Jha, Shefali (2002). "Secularism in the Constituent Assembly Debates, 1946–1950." *Economic and Political Weekly* 37(30): 3175–3180.

Johansen, Baber (2006). The Constitution and the Principles of Islamic Normativity Against the Rules of Fiqh: A Judgment of the Supreme Constitutional Court of Egypt. *Dispensing Justice in Islam: Qadis and their Judgements*. M. K. Masud, R. Peters and D. S. Powers, eds. Leiden, Brill: 169–193.

Johari, J. C. (2004). *Indian Polity: A Concise Study of Indian Constitution, Government and Politics*. New Delhi, Lotus Press.

Johnson, Paul (1987). *A History of the Jews*. London, Weidenfeld and Nicolson.

Jones, Clive and Murphy, Emma (2002). *Israel: Challenges to Identity, Democracy and the State*. London, Routledge.

Joseph, Suad (1999). "Descent of the Nation: Kinship and Citizenship in Lebanon." *Citizenship Studies* 3(3): 295–318.

    (2000). Civic Myths, Citizenship and Gender in Lebanon. *Gender and Citizenship in the Middle East*. S. Joseph, ed. Syracuse University Press: 107–136.

    (2005). The Kin Contract and Citizenship in the Middle East. *Women and Citizenship*. M. Friedman, ed. Oxford; New York, Oxford University Press: 149–169.

Kaeuper, Richard W. (1988). *War, Justice, and Public Order: England and France in the Later Middle Ages*. Oxford, Clarendon Press.

Kanaaneh, Rhoda Ann (2002). *Birthing the Nation: Strategies of Palestinian Women in Israel*. Berkeley, University of California Press.

Kandiyoti, Deniz (1991). "Identity and its Discontents: Women and the Nation." *Millenium* 20(3): 429–443.

Karam, Azza M. (1998). *Women, Islamisms, and the State: Contemporary Feminisms in Egypt*. New York, St. Martin's Press.

Karayanni, Michael M. (2006). "The Separate Nature of Religious Accommodations for the Palestinian-Arab Minority in Israel." *Northwestern Journal of International Human Rights* 5(1): 41–71.

Karpat, Kemal H. (1982). Millets and Nationality: The Roots of the Incongruity of Nation and State in the Post-Ottoman Era. *Christians and*

Jews in the Ottoman Empire: The Functioning of a Plural Society. B. Braude and B. Lewis, eds. New York, Holmes & Meier Publishers Inc.: 141–169.

Katz, Alan N. (1986a). France. *Legal Traditions and Systems: An International Handbook.* A. N. Katz, ed. New York, Greenwood Press: 105–123.

(1986b). Germany. *Legal Traditions and Systems: An International Handbook.* A. N. Katz, ed. New York, Greenwood Press: 85–103.

Kayaoglu, Turan (2010). *Legal Imperialism: Sovereignty and Extraterritoriality in Japan, the Ottoman Empire, and China.* Cambridge University Press.

Keay, John (2000). *India: A History.* New York, Atlantic Monthly Press.

Kelly, J. M. (1992). *A Short History of Western Legal Theory.* Oxford, Clarendon Press.

Kelsen, Hans (1945). *General Theory of Law and State.* Cambridge, MA, Harvard University Press.

Kempster, Norman (1997, Feb. 13). "Divorced? Jewish Tourists can Face Perilous Times in Israel." *Los Angeles Times,* p. 5.

Khan, Zafarul-Islam (2005). "Petition Against 'Shariat Courts' is Misguided." *The Milli Gazette.*

Kharak, Singh (1998). *On Sikh Personal Law.* Chandigarh, Institute of Sikh Studies.

Kimmerling, Baruch (1985). Between the Primordial and Civil Definitions of the Collective Identity: *Eretz Israel* or the State of Israel? *Comparative Social Dynamics: Essays in Honor of S. N. Eisenstadt.* E. Cohen, M. Lissak and U. Almagor, eds. Boulder, Westview Press: 262–283.

(2001). *The Invention and Decline of Israeliness: State, Society, and the Military.* Berkeley, University of California Press.

King, Gary, Keohane, Robert O., et al. (1994). *Designing Social Inquiry: Scientific Inference in Qualitative Research.* Princeton University Press.

Kirmani, Nida (2011). "Re-thinking the Promotion of Women's Rights through Islam in India." *IDS Bulletin* 42(1): 56–66.

Kishwar, Madhu (1994). "Codified Hindu Law: Myth and Reality." *Economic and Political Weekly* 29(33): 2145–2161.

(2001). *Religion at the Service of Nationalism and Other Essays.* Delhi; Oxford, Oxford University Press.

Klein, Claude (1978). "A Jewish State or a State for Jews?" *The Jerusalem Quarterly* 7: 36–47.

Knox, John H. (2008). "Horizontal Human Rights Law." *American Journal of International Law* 102(1): 1–47.

Kohli, Atul (1994). Centralization and Powerlessness: India's Democracy in a Comparative Perspective. *State Power and Social Forces: Domination and Transformation in the Third World.* J. S. Migdal, A. Kohli and V. Shue, eds. Cambridge University Press: 89–107.

Kosambi, Meera (2007). *Crossing Thresholds: Feminist Essays in Social History.* New Delhi, Permanent Black.

Kozlowski, Gregory C. (2005). Muslim Personal Law and Political Identity in Independent India. *Religion and Law in Independent India*. R. D. Baird, ed. New Delhi, Manohar: 102–120.

Kraft, Dina (2004). "In Israel, Pressure Builds to Find Alternatives to Orthodox Marriage." Accessed in December, 2006, from www.interfaithfamily.com/site/apps/nl/content2.asp?c=ekLSK5MLIrG b=297411 ct=375135.

Kramer, Gudrun (1989). *The Jews in Modern Egypt, 1914–1952*. Seattle, University of Washington Press.

Kretzmer, David (1990). *The Legal Status of the Arabs in Israel*. Boulder, CO, Westview Press.

Kukathas, Chandran (1992). "Are There Any Cultural Rights?" *Political Theory* 20(1): 105–139.

  (1998). "Liberalism and Multiculturalism: The Politics of Indifference." *Political Theory* 26(5): 686–699.

  (2003). *The Liberal Archipelago: A Theory of Diversity and Freedom*. Oxford University Press.

Kumar, Ravinder (1992). Gandhi, Nehru and Communalism. *Towards Understanding Communalism*. P. Kumar, ed. Chandigarh, Centre for Research in Rural and Industrial Development: 131–139.

Kuper, Hilda and Kuper, Leo (1965). Introduction. *African Law: Adaptation and Development*. H. Kuper and L. Kuper, eds. Berkeley, University of California Press.

Kupferschmidt, Uri M. (1987). *The Supreme Muslim Council: Islam under the British Mandate for Palestine*. Leiden, EJ Brill.

Kuru, Ahmet T. (2009). *Secularism and State Policies toward Religion: The United States, France, and Turkey*. Cambridge; New York, Cambridge University Press.

Kusum (2003). *Family Law Lectures – Family Law I*. New Delhi, LexisNexis.

Kymlicka, Will (1995). *The Rights of Minority Cultures*. Oxford; New York, Oxford University Press.

  (1996). Two Models of Pluralism and Tolerance. *Toleration: An Elusive Virtue*. D. Heyd, ed. Princeton University Press: 81–113.

  and Norman, W. J. (2000). *Citizenship in Diverse Societies*. Oxford University Press.

Lacouture, Jean (1973). *Nasser: A Biography*. New York, Alfred A. Knopf.

Lalithambika, Antharjanam and Krishnakutty, Gita (1998). *Cast Me Out if You Will: Stories and Memoir*. New York, Feminist Press.

Larson, Gerald James (2001). *Religion and Personal Law in Secular India: A Call to Judgment*. Bloomington, Indiana University Press.

Layish, Aharon (1971). "Qadis and Shari'a in Israel." *Asian and African Studies* 7: 237–272.

  (1979). "Islam as a Source of Law in Druze Religious Courts." *Israel Law Review* 14(1): 13–30.

(1982). *Marriage, Divorce and Succession in the Druze Family*. Leiden, Brill.

(1993). "The Status of the Shari'a in a Non-Muslim State: The Case of Israel." *Asian and African Studies* 27(1–2): 171–187.

(2006). *Women and Islamic Law in a Non-Muslim State: A Study Based on Decisions of the Shari'a Courts in Israel*. New Brunswick, NJ, Transaction Publishers.

Leacock, Eleanor Burke (1977). On Engel's Origin of the Family, Private Property and the State. *The Family: Functions, Conflicts, and Symbols*. P. J. Stein, ed. Reading, MA, Addison-Wesley: 59–67.

Leila, Reem (2003a, Dec. 4–10). "The Comfort Zone." *Al-Ahram Weekly Online*: 667. Accessed from http://weekly.ahram.org.eg/2003/621/fe1.htm.

(2003b, Jan. 16–22). "A Family Affair." *Al-Ahram Weekly Online*: 621. Accessed from http://weekly.ahram.org.eg/2003/621/fe1.htm.

Lerner, Hanna (2011). *Making Constitutions in Deeply Divided Societies*. Cambridge; New York, Cambridge University Press.

(2012). Constitutional Ambiguity as a Critical Juncture in the Evolution of Religion–State Relations: Evidence from Israel and India [unpublished paper, on file with author].

Lester, Robert C. (1994). Towards Unity with Diversity: Gandhi on Equal Respect for All Religions. *Facets of Mahatma Gandhi*. S. Mukherjee and S. Ramaswamy, eds. New Delhi, Deep & Deep: 262–285.

Lev, Daniel S. (2000). *Legal Evolution and Political Authority in Indonesia: Selected Essays*. The Hague, Kluwer Law International.

Levitt, Peggy and Merry, Sally Engle (2009). "*Unpacking the Vernacularization Process: The Transnational Circulation of Women's Human Rights.*" Paper presented at the ISA 50th Annual Convention, New York.

Lewis, Bernard (1968). *The Emergence of Modern Turkey*. Oxford University Press.

Lieberson, Stanley (1991). "Small N's and Big Conclusions: An Examination of the Reasoning in Comparative Studies Based on a Small Number of Cases." *Social Forces* 70(2): 307–320.

(1994). "More on the Uneasy Case for Using Mill-Type Methods in Small-N Comparative Studies." *Social Forces* 72(4): 1225–1237.

Liebesny, Herbert J. (1975). *The Laws of the Near and Middle East: Readings, Cases, and Materials*. Albany, SUNY Press.

Likhovski, Assaf (2006). *Law and Identity in Mandate Palestine*. Chapel Hill, University of North Carolina Press.

Linz, Juan J. (2000). *Totalitarian and Authoritarian Regimes*. Boulder, CO, Lynne Rienner Publishers.

Loimeier, Roman (1996). The Secular State and Islam in Senegal. *Questioning the Secular State: The Worldwide Resurgence of Religion in Politics*. D. Westerlund, ed. London, Hurst Co.: 183–197.

Lombardi, Clark B. and Brown, Nathan J. (2006). "Do Constitutions Requiring Adherence to Shari'a Threaten Human Rights? How Egypt's Constitutional Court Reconciles Islamic Law with the Liberal Rule of Law." *American University International Law Review* 21(3): 379–435.

Lopez-Alves, Fernando (2000). *State Formation and Democracy in Latin America, 1810–1900.* Durham, NC, Duke University Press.

Louër, Laurence (2003). *Les citoyens Arabes d'Israël.* Paris, Balland.

Lukito, Ratno (2003). Law and Politics in Post-Independence Indonesia: A Case Study of Religious and *Adat* Courts. *Shari'a and Politics in Modern Indonesia.* A. Salim and A. Azra, eds. Singapore, ISEAS: 17–32.

Lustick, Ian (1980). *Arabs in the Jewish State: Israel's Control of a National Minority.* Austin, University of Texas Press.

Lynfield, Ben (2004, Sep. 30). "Israel's Religious Split Over the Time of Day." *The Christian Science Monitor*: 7.

Macklem, Patrick (2006). "Militant Democracy, Legal Pluralism, and the Paradox of Self-Determination." *International Journal of Constitutional Law* 4(3): 488–516.

Mahajan, Gurpreet (2002). "Secularism as Religious Non-Discrimination: The Universal and the Particular in the Indian Context." *Indian Review* 1(1): 33–51.

Mahmood, Syed Tahir (1978a). *Civil Marriage Law: Perspectives and Prospects.* Bombay, NM Tripathi.

(1978b). Religious Elements in a Secular Marriage Law: A Critique. *Studies in the Hindu Marriage and the Special Marriage Acts.* V. Bagga, ed. Bombay, NM Tripathi: 295–309.

(1995a). *Statute-Law Relating to Muslims in India: A Study in Constitutional and Islamic Perspectives.* New Delhi, Institute of Objective Studies.

(1995b). *Uniform Civil Code: Fictions and Facts.* New Delhi, India and Islam Research Council.

(2001). "The Shariat Courts in Modern India." New Delhi, Amity Institute of Advanced Legal Studies [unpublished paper, on file with author].

(2002). *The Muslim Law of India.* New Delhi, LexisNexis.

Mahoney, James (2003). *Strategies of Causal Assessment in Comparative Historical Analysis.* J. Mahoney and D. Rueschemeyer, eds. Cambridge University Press: 337–372.

Maktabi, Rania (2000). State Formation and Citizenship in Lebanon. *Citizenship and the State in the Middle East: Approaches and Applications.* N. A. Butenschon, U. Davis and M. S. Hassassian, eds. Syracuse University Press: 146–178.

Mamdani, Mahmood (1996). *Citizen and Subject: Contemporary Africa and the Legacy of Late Colonialism.* Princeton University Press.

Manjul, T. (2005). "Four Law Boards: Will Muslim Women Find a 'Masiha'?" Accessed in June, 2007, from www.sawf.org/newedit/edit02072005/index.asp.

Markandan, K. C. (1966). *Directive Principles in the Indian Constitution*. Bombay, Allied Publishers.

(1984). *The Preamble: Key to the Minds of the Indian Constitution*. New Delhi, National Pub. House.

Marx, Anthony W. (1996). Contested Citizenship: The Dynamics of Racial Identity and Social Movements. *Citizenship, Identity and Social History*. C. Tilly, ed. Cambridge University Press: 159–184.

Masud, Muhammad Khalid (2006). The Award of *Mata* in the Early Muslim Courts. *Dispensing Justice in Islam: Qadis and their Judgements* M. K. Masud, R. Peters and D. S. Powers, eds. Leiden, Brill: 347–380.

Mathew, S. J. and Bakshi, P. M. (2002). *Family Courts*. New Delhi, Indian Social Institute.

Mautner, Menachem (2011). *Law and the Culture of Israel*. Oxford University Press.

Maxwell, Nancy G. (2003). Unification and Harmonization of Family Law Principles: The United States Experience. *Perspectives for the Unification and Harmonisation of Family Law in Europe*. K. Boele-Woelki, ed. Antwerp, Intersentia: 249–267.

Mayer, Ann Elizabeth (1995). "Reform of Personal Status Laws in North Africa: A Problem of Islamic or Mediterranean Laws?" *Middle East Journal* 49(3): 432–446.

(2012). The Dubious Foundations of the Refah Decision. *Islam, Europe and Emerging Legal Issues*. W. C. Durham, ed. Farnham, Ashgate: 209–234.

McAleavy, Henry (1968). Some Aspects of Marriage and Divorce in Communist China. *Family Law in Asia and Africa*. J. N. D. Anderson, ed. New York, Praeger: 73–89.

Mcgrath, Cam (2009). "Invoking Religion Against Liberals." Accessed in April, 2010, from http://ipsnews.net/news.asp?idnews=48916.

Meinardus, Otto Friedrich August (1999). *Two Thousand Years of Coptic Christianity*. American University in Cairo Press.

Meinzen-Dick, Ruth S. and Pradhan, Rajendra (2002). Legal Pluralism in Natural Resources Management: Implications for Water Rights. *Institutional Reform for Irrigation and Drainage*. F. J. Gonzalez and S. M. A. Salman. eds. Washington, DC, World Bank: 83–99.

Menon, Nivedita (1998). Women and Citizenship. *Wages of Freedom: Fifty Years of the Indian Nation-State*. P. Chatterjee, ed. Delhi, Oxford University Press: 241–266.

Menon, V. P. (1957). *The Transfer of Power in India*. Princeton University Press.

Menski, Werner (2000). *Comparative Law in a Global Context: The Legal Systems of Asia and Africa*. London, Platinium.

(2001). *Modern Indian Family Law*. Surrey, Curzon Press.

(2003). *Hindu Law: Beyond Tradition and Modernity*. New Delhi, Oxford University Press.

(2006). "Asking for the Moon: Legal Uniformity in India from a Kerala Perspective." *Kerala Law Times* (2): 52–78.

(2007). "Double Benefits and Muslim Women's Postnuptial Rights." *Kerala Law Times* (2): 21–34.

(2009). Indian Secular Pluralism and its Relevance for Europe. *Legal Practice and Cultural Diversity.* R. Grillo, R. Ballard, A. Ferrariet, *et al.*, eds. Aldershot, Ashgate: 31–48.

(2012). Ancient Boundary Crossings and Defective Memories: Lessons from Pluralistic Interactions between Personal Laws and Civil Law in Composite India. *Marriage and Divorce in a Multicultural Context: Multi-tiered Marriage and the Boundaries of Civil Law and Religion.* J. A. Nichols, ed. New York, Cambridge University Press: 219–252.

Meron, Ya'akov (1982). The Religious Courts in the Administered Territories. *Military Government in the Territories Administered by Israel, 1967–1980: The Legal Aspects.* M. Shamgar, ed. Hebrew University Jerusalem, Faculty of Law, Harry Sacher Institute for Legislature Research and Comparative Law. Vol. I: 353–367.

Merry, Sally Engle (1988). "Legal Pluralism." *Law & Society Review* 22(5): 869–896.

(2006a). *Human Rights and Gender Violence: Translating International Law into Local Justice.* University of Chicago Press.

(2006b). "Transnational Human Rights and Local Activism: Mapping the Middle." *American Anthropologist* 108(1): 38–51.

Meydani, Assaf (2011). *The Israeli Supreme Court and the Human Rights Revolution: Courts as Agenda Setters.* Cambridge University Press.

Migdal, Joel S. (1988). *Strong Societies and Weak States: State–Society Relations and State Capabilities in the Third World.* Princeton University Press.

(1989). The Crystallization of the State and the Struggles over Rulemaking: Israel in Comparative Perspective. *The Israeli State and Society: Boundaries and Frontiers.* B. Kimmerling, ed. Albany, NY, SUNY Press: 1–27.

(2001). *Through the Lens of Israel: Explorations in State and Society.* Albany, State University of New York Press.

Mir-Hosseini, Ziba (1993). *Marriage on Trial: A Study of Islamic Family Law – Iran and Morocco Compared.* London, IB Tauris.

(2009). Towards Gender Equality: Muslim Family Laws and the Shari'ah. *Wanted: Equality and Justice in the Muslim Family.* A. Zainah, ed. Selangor, Musawah: 23–63.

Mirow, Matthew C. (2004). *Latin American Law: A History of Private Law and Institutions in Spanish America.* Austin, University of Texas Press.

Mishra, Ravikant (2009). "Hindu Jurisprudence on Succession and Gender Equality: The Indian Scenario." Accessed in May, 2010, from www.scribd.com/doc/20313081/Hindu-Jurisprudence-on-Succession-and-Gender-Equality-The-Indian-Scenario.

Misra, Amalendu (2000). "Hindu Nationalism and Muslim Minority Rights in India." *International Journal on Minority and Group Rights* 7(1): 1–18.

Mitra, Siddha Mohana (1913). *Anglo-Indian Studies*. New York, Longmans, Green & Co.

Mitra, Subrata K. and Fischer, Alexander (2002). "Sacred Laws and the Secular State: An Analytical Narrative of the Controversy over Personal Laws in India." *Indian Review* 1(3): 99–130.

Mitter, Dwarka Nath (2006). *The Position of Women in Hindu Law*. New Delhi, Cosmo Publications.

Mittleman, Alan L. (1993). Fundamentalism and Political Development: The Case of Agudat Yisrael. *Jewish Fundamentalism in Comparative Perspective: Religion, Ideology, and the Crisis of Modernity*. L. J. Silberstein, ed. New York, NYU Press: 216–237.

Mody, Perveez (2008). *The Intimate State: Love-Marriage and the Law in Delhi*. New Delhi; London, Routledge.

Moe, Christian (2012). Refah Revisited: Strasbourg's Construction of Islam. *Islam, Europe and Emerging Legal Issues*. W. C. Durham, ed. Farnham, Ashgate: 235–272.

Molyneux, Maxine (1991). The Law, the State and Socialist Policies with Regard to Women: The Case of the People's Democratic Republic of Yemen 1967–1990. *Women, Islam, and the State*. D. Kandiyoti, ed. Basingstoke, Macmillan: 237–271.

Moore, Clement Henry (1974). "Authoritarian Politics in Unincorporated Society: The Case of Nasser's Egypt." *Comparative Politics* 6(2): 193–218.

Moore, Sally F. (1978). *Law as Process: An Anthropological Approach*. London, Routledge & Kegan Paul.

Morse, Bradford W. (2004). "The Scope of Human Rights Law Concerning Indigenous and Minority Peoples." Paper presented at the International Course on Legal Pluralism – Commission on Folk Law and Legal Pluralism 14th International Congress, Fredericton, NB.

Mourad, Sarah (2012). "Changes in Egypt's Family Law: A Step Backwards?". Accessed April 6, 2012, from http://english.ahram.org.eg/News/38053.aspx.

Moussa, Jasmine (2011). *Competing Fundamentalisms and Egyptian Women's Family Rights: International Law and the Reform of Shari'a-Derived Legislation*. Leiden, Brill.

Moustafa, Tamir (2000). "Conflict and Cooperation between the State and Religious Institutions in Contemporary Egypt." *International Journal of Middle East Studies* 32: 3–22.

(2007). *The Struggle for Constitutional Power: Law, Politics, and Economic Development in Egypt*. Cambridge University Press.

(2010). "The Islamist Trend in Egyptian Law." *Politics and Religion* 3: 610–630.

Mukerjee, Sutapa (2005). "India's Muslims Face Up to Rifts." Accessed in June, 2007, from http://news.bbc.co.uk/2/hi/south_asia/4235999.stm.

Munck, Gerardo L. (2004). Tools for Qualitative Research. *Rethinking Social Inquiry: Diverse Tools, Shared Standards.* H. E. Brady and D. Collier, eds. Lanham, MD, Rowman & Littlefield: 105–122.

Muradabadi, Masoom (2010, Aug. 4). "Practice of Bigamy is Prevalent More Among Hindus." *The Milli Gazette,* www.milligazette.com/news/0046-practice-of-bigamy-is-prevalent-more-among-hindus.

Mutua, Makau (2002). *Human Rights: A Political and Cultural Critique.* Philadelphia, University of Pennsylvania.

Myre, Greg (2005, April 1). "Israeli Court Eases Rules on Converting to Judaism." *The New York Times,* p. A6.

Na'amat (2001). "Get Real with a Pre-Nup." *Na'amat* 16(2): 21.

Nagib, Mohamed Fathi (2003). *The Organization of Justice in Egypt.* Al-Qahira, Dar Al-Shorouq [in Arabic].

Najjar, Fauzi M. (1988). "Egypt's Laws of Personal Status." *Arab Studies Quarterly* 10(3): 319–344.

    (1992). "The Application of Sharia Laws in Egypt." *Middle East Policy* 1(3): 62–73.

    (2000). "Islamic Fundamentalism and the Intellectuals: The Case of Nasr Hamid Abu Zayd." *British Journal of Middle Eastern Studies* 20(2): 177–200.

Narain, Vrinda (2001). *Gender and Community: Muslim Women's Rights in India.* University of Toronto Press.

Nasir, Jamal J. (1986). *The Islamic Law of Personal Status.* London, Graham & Trotman.

Nassar, Nagla (1999). Legal Plurality: Reflection on the Status of Women in Egypt. *Legal Pluralism in the Arab World.* B. Dupret, M. Berger and L. Al-Zwaini, eds. The Hague, Kluwer Law International: 191–204.

Natour, Ahmad (2009). "The Role of the Shari'a Court of Appeals in Promoting the Status of Women in Islamic Law in a Non-Muslim State (Israel)." J.S.D. thesis, American University, Washington College of Law, Washington DC.

Natour, Mithkal (1997). *The Field of Islamic Law.* Ramallah, Matba't Al-Wahda [in Arabic].

    (2000). Muslims in Israel. *Israel and Ishmael: Studies in Muslim-Jewish Relations.* T. Parfitt, ed. New York, St. Martin's Press: 239–249.

Naveh, Immanuel (1997). *Application of the Shari'a in Civil Courts in the Twentieth Century: A Comparative Study Based on Decisions of Civil Courts in Matters of Personal Status and Waqf of Muslims in a Muslim State (Egypt) and in a Non-Muslim State (Israel).* Ph.D. thesis [in Hebrew], Hebrew University of Jerusalem.

Nazila, Ghanea (2005). Repressing Minorities and Getting Away with it? A Consideration of Economic, Social and Cultural Rights. *Minorities,*

Peoples, and Self-Determination: Essays in Honour of Patrick Thornberry. N. Ghanea-Hercock, A. Xanthaki and P. Thornberry, eds. Leiden, Martinus Nijhoff Publishers: 193–210.

Negi, S. S. (2005, 17 Aug.). "SC Issues Notice on Fatwas – PIL on Parallel Islamic Courts." *The Tribune Online Edition*, www.tribuneindia.com/2005/20050817/main1.htm.

Nehru, Jawaharlal (1963). *Jawaharlal Nehru's Speeches.* New Delhi, Ministry of Information and Broadcasting, Govt. of India.

(1988). *Selected Works of Jawaharlal Nehru.* New Delhi, Jawaharlal Nehru Memorial Fund.

(1989). *Jawaharlal Nehru on Minorities and Secularism.* Trivandrum, Institute of Management in Government.

(1994). *Selected Works of Jawaharlal Nehru.* New Delhi, Jawaharlal Nehru Memorial Fund.

(2000). *Selected Works of Jawaharlal Nehru.* New Delhi, Jawaharlal Nehru Memorial Fund.

Nettl, J. P. (1968). "The State as a Conceptual Variable." *World Politics* 20(4): 559–592.

Neuberger, Benyamin (1997). *Religion and Democracy in Israel.* Jerusalem, The Floersheimer Institute for Policy Studies.

(2000). Religion and State in Europe and Israel. *Parties, Elections and Cleavages: Israel in Comparative and Theoretical Perspective.* R. Y. Hazan and M. Maor, eds. London, Frank Cass: 65–84.

Neuhaus, David Mark (1991). "Between Quiescence and Arousal: The Political Functions of Religion – a Case Study of the Arab Minority in Israel: 1948–1990." Ph.D. thesis, Hebrew University of Jerusalem.

Neuhaus, Paul Heinrich (1983). Christian Family Law. *International Encyclopedia of Comparative Law.* Tübingen, JCB Mohr. Vol. IV: 3–27.

Niaz, Noorjehan Safia (2004). "Marriage in Islam." *Combat Law* 3(4): 25–28.

Nigam, S. S. (1966). Uniform Civil Code and Secularism. *Secularism: Its Implications for Law and Life in India.* G. S. Sharma, ed. Bombay, NM Tripathi.

Nimkoff, Meyer Francis, ed. (1965). *Comparative Family Systems.* Boston, Houghton Mifflin.

Noorani, Abdul Gafoor Abdul Majeed (2004). *The Muslims of India: A Documentary Record.* New Delhi, Oxford University Press.

North, Douglass (1981). *Structure and Change in Economic History.* New York, Norton.

(1990). *Institutions, Institutional Change and Economic Performance.* Cambridge University Press.

Nussbaum, Martha C. (2005). India, Sex Equality, and Constitutional Law. *The Gender of Constitutional Jurisprudence.* B. Baines and R. Rubio-Marín, eds. Cambridge University Press: 174–204.

Nwogogu, E. I. (1976). "Abolition of Customary Courts – the Nigerian Experiment." *Journal of African Law* 20(1): 1–19.

O'Donnell, Guillermo (1973). *Modernization and Bureaucratic-Authoritarianism: Studies in South American Politics.* Berkeley, Institute of International Studies.

(1979). Tensions in the Bureaucratic-Authoritarian State and the Question of Democracy. *The New Authoritarianism in Latin America.* D. Collier and F. H. Cardoso, eds. Princeton University Press: 285–318.

O'Sullivan, Arieh (1998, Feb. 10). "He was Very Happy to be in Your Army." *The Jerusalem Post*, p. 3.

Obilade, A. O. (1969). "Reform of Customary Court Systems in Nigeria under the Military Government." *Journal of African Law* 13(1): 28–44.

Olsson, Susanne (2008). "Apostasy in Egypt: Contemporary Cases of Hisbah." *The Muslim World* 98(1): 95–115.

Opoku, K. T. (1970). "Reform of Marriage and Divorce Laws in Francophone West Africa." *University of Ghana Law Journal* 7(1): 107–124.

Oppenheimer, Jonathan (1985). The Druze in Israel, as Arabs and Non-Arabs: An Essay on the Manipulation of Categories of Identity in a Non-Civil State. *Studies in Israeli Ethnicity: After the Ingathering.* A. Weingrod, ed. New York, Gordon and Breach Science Publishers: 259–279.

Osanloo, Arzoo (2009). *The Politics of Women's Rights in Iran.* Princeton University Press.

Palsetia, Jesse S. (2001). *The Parsis of India: Preservation of Identity in Bombay City.* Leiden, Brill.

Pandey, Gyanendra (2001). *Remembering Partition: Violence, Nationalism, and History in India.* Cambridge University Press.

Pantham, Thomas (1997). "Indian Secularism and its Critics: Some Reflections." *The Review of Politics* 59(3): 523–540.

Pappé, Ilan (1995). An Uneasy Coexistence: Arabs and Jews in the First Decade of Statehood. *Israel: The First Decade of Independence.* S. I. Troen and N. Lucas, eds. Albany, SUNY Press: 658–659.

Parashar, Archana (1992). *Women and Family Law Reform in India.* New Delhi, Sage.

Parekh, Bhikhu (1991). "Nehru and the National Philosophy of India." *Economic and Political Weekly* 26(1–2): 35–48.

(2000). *Rethinking Multiculturalism: Cultural Diversity and Political Theory.* Cambridge, MA, Harvard University Press.

Patel, Reena (2007). *Hindu Women's Property Rights in Rural India: Law, Labour and Culture in Action.* Aldershot, Ashgate.

Pateman, Carole (1989). *The Disorder of Women: Democracy, Feminism, and Political Theory.* Stanford University Press.

Pathak, Zakia and Rajan, Rajeswari Sunder (1989). "Shahbano." *Signs* 14(3): 558–582.

Patil, Vimla (2003, Apr. 6). "When the Court Steps in to Save Family." *The Tribune Online Edition*, www.tribuneindia.com/2003/20030406/herworld. htm.

Peled, Alisa Rubin (2001). *Debating Islam in the Jewish State: The Development of Policy Toward Islamic Institutions in Israel*. Albany, SUNY Press.

Pennington, J. D. (1982). "The Copts of Modern Egypt." *Middle Eastern Studies* 18(2): 158–179.

Peretz, Don (1954). "The Arab Minority of Israel." *The Middle East Journal* 8(2): 139–154.

Perez, Nahshon (2002). "Should Multiculturalists Oppress the Oppressed? On Religion, Culture, and the Individual and Cultural Rights of Unliberal Communities." *Critical Review of International Social and Political Philosophy* 5(3): 51–79.

Perkins, Kenneth J. (2004). *A History of Modern Tunisia*. New York, Cambridge University Press.

Perlmutter, Amos (1974). *Egypt, the Praetorian State*. New Brunswick, NJ, Transaction Books.

Perrot, Michelle (1990). *A History of Private Life*, vol. IV: *From the Fires of Revolution to the Great War*. Cambridge, MA, Harvard University Press.

Peters, Julie and Wolper, Andrea (1995). *Women's Rights, Human Rights: International Feminist Perspectives*. New York, Routledge.

Peters, Rudolph (2002). "From Jurists' Law to Statute Law or What Happens when the Sharia is Codified." *Mediterranean Politics* 7(3): 82–95.

Philipp, Thomas (1985). *The Syrians in Egypt, 1725–1975*. Stuttgart, Steiner.

(1995). Copts and Other Minorities in the Development of the Egyptian Nation-State. *Egypt from Monarchy to Republic: A Reassessment of Revolution and Change*. S. Shamir, ed. Boulder, Westview Press: 131–150.

Phillips, Anne (2007). *Multiculturalism without Culture*. Princeton University Press.

Pierson, Paul (2004). *Politics in Time: History, Institutions, and Social Analysis*. Princeton University Press.

Pink, Johanna (2003). "A Post-Quranic Religion between Apostasy and Public Order: Egyptian Muftis and Courts on the Legal Status of the Bahai Faith." *Islamic Law and Society* 10(3): 409–434.

Poggi, Gianfranco (1978). *The Development of the Modern State: A Sociological Introduction*. Stanford University Press.

(1990). *The State: Its Nature, Development, and Prospects*. Stanford University Press.

Pollock, Frederick and Maitland, Frederic William (1898). *The History of English Law before the Time of Edward I*. Cambridge University Press.

Porat-Martin, Hedva (1977). "Israeli Rabbinical Courts – Aspects of a More 'Responsive' Legal System." *Diné Israel* 8: 49–76.

(1979). "Rabbinical and Civil Courts in Israel: A Dual Legal System in Action." Ph.D. thesis, University of California, Berkeley.

(1981–1983). "Representation and its Role in Concurrent Jurisdiction (in the Rabbinical and District Courts of Israel)." *Diné Israel* 10–11: 7–42.

Pospisil, Leopold (1967). "Legal Levels and Multiplicity of Legal Systems in Human Societies." *Journal of Conflict Resolution* 2(1): 2–26.

(1978). The Structure of Society and its Multiple Legal Systems. *Cross-Examinations: Essays in Memory of Max Gluckman*. P. H. Gulliver, ed. Leiden, EJ Brill: 96–109.

Prasad, Bimal, Mallik, Sangita, *et al*. (2001). *The Ideas and Men Behind the Indian Constitution: Selections from the Constituent Assembly Debates, 1946–49*. Delhi, Konark Publishers.

Preis, Ann-Belinda S. (1996). "Human Rights as Cultural Practice: An Anthropological Critique." *Human Rights Quarterly* 18(2): 286–315.

Prinsloo, M. W. (1990). "Pluralism or Unification in Family Law in South Africa." *The International and Comparative Law Journal of Southern Africa* 23(3): 324–336.

Puddington, Arch (2011). *Freedom in the World 2011: The Authoritarian Challenge to Democracy*. Washington, DC, Freedom House.

Qadri, Muhammad (1914). *Code of Mohammedan Personal Law According to the Hanafite School*. London, printed for the Sudan Government by Spottiswoode.

Qassem, Y. (2002). Law of the Family (Personal Status Law). *Egypt and its Laws*. N. Bernard-Maugiron and B. Dupret, eds. London, Kluwer Law International: 19–36.

Quigley, John B. (2005). *The Case for Palestine: An International Law Perspective*. Durham, NC, Duke University Press.

Rabe, Johan (2001). *Equality, Affirmative Action, and Justice*. Norderstedt, Demand GmbH.

Radzyner, Amichai and Friedman, Shuki (2005). "The Israeli Legislator and Jewish Law – Haim Cohn between Tomorrow and Yesterday." *Tel-Aviv Studies in Law* 29: 167–256.

Ragin, Charles C. (1987). *The Comparative Method: Moving Beyond Qualitative and Quantitative Strategies*. Berkeley, University of California Press.

Raju, M. P. (2003). *Uniform Civil Code: A Mirage?* Delhi, Media House.

Ramakrishnan, Venkitesh (2008, 29 Mar.–11 Apr.). "Women's Charter." *Frontline* 25(7): 28–30.

Rao, Amiya and Rao, B. G. (1974). *Six Thousand Days: Jawaharlal Nehru, Prime Minister*. New Delhi, Sterling Publishers.

Rao, Shiva B. (1968). *Framing of India's Constitution*. Bombay, The Indian Institute of Public Administration.

Ratzlav-Katz, Nissan (2007). "Statistics Dispel Claims of 'Thousands of Israeli Agunot'." Accessed in March, 2010, from www.israelnationalnews.com/News/News.aspx/122884.

Rautenbach, Christa (2010). "Deep Legal Pluralism in South Africa: Judicial Accommodation of Non-State Law." *Journal of Legal Pluralism* 60: 143–177.

Rawls, John (1999). *A Theory of Justice*. Cambridge, MA, Harvard University Press.

Ray, Renuka (1952). "The Background of the Hindu Code Bill." *Pacific Affairs* 25(3): 268–277.

Raz, Hila and Neuman, Efrat (2008). "Two Steps Backward." Accessed in April, 2010, from www.haaretz.com/hasen/spages/964122.html.

Redding, Jeff (2010). "Institutional v. Liberal Contexts for Contemporary Non-State, Muslim Civil Dispute Resolution Systems." *Journal of Islamic State Practices in International Law* 6(1): 2–26.

Reid, Donald M. (1991). *Cairo University and the Making of Modern Egypt*. American University in Cairo Press.

Reinkowski, Maurus and Saadeh, Sofia (2006). A Nation Divided: Lebanese Confessionalism. *Citizenship and Ethnic Conflict: Challenging the Nation-State*. H. Gülalp, ed. New York, Routledge: 99–116.

Reiter, Yitzhak (1996). *Islamic Endowments in Jerusalem under British Mandate*. London, Frank Cass.

(1997a). *Islamic Institutions in Jerusalem: Palestinian Muslim Organization under Jordanian and Israeli Rule*. The Hague, Kluwer Law International.

(1997b). Qadis and the Implementation of Islamic Law in Present Day Israel. *Islamic Law: Theory and Practice*. R. Gleave and E. Kermeli, eds. London, IB Tauris: 205–231.

Rejwan, Nissim (1999). *Israel in Search of Identity*. Gainesville, University Press of Florida.

Resnik, Judith (1989). "Dependent Sovereigns: Indian Tribes, States, and the Federal Courts." *University of Chicago Law Review* 56(2): 671–759.

Richland, Justin B. and Deer, Sarah (2004). *Introduction to Tribal Legal Studies*. Walnut Creek, CA, Altamira Press.

Riskin, Shlomo (2002). "Hafka'at Kiddushin: Towards Solving the Aguna Problem in Our Time." *Tradition* 36(4): 1–36.

Robbers, Gerhard (2010). *Religion and Law in Germany*. Alphen aan den Rijn, Wolters Kluwer Law & Business.

Roberts, Richard L. and Mann, Kristin (1991). Law in Colonial Africa. *Law in Colonial Africa*. R. L. Roberts and K. Mann, eds. Portsmouth, NH, Heinemann: 3–58.

Rocher, Ludo (1972). "Indian Response to Anglo-Hindu Law." *Journal of the American Oriental Society* 92(3): 419–424.

Rodinson, Maxime (1968). The Political System. *Egypt Since the Revolution.* P. J. Vatikiotis, ed. New York, Praeger: 87–113.

Rose, Nikolas S. (1999). *Powers of Freedom: Reframing Political Thought.* Cambridge University Press.

Rosen, Lawrence (1978). "Law and Social Change in the New Nations." *Comparative Studies in Society and History* 20(1): 3–28.

Rosen-Zvi, Ariel (1989). "The Jurisdictional Race in Matters Connected with Divorce Suits and its Impact on Family Law." *Iyunei Mishpat (Tel Aviv University Law Review)* 14(1): 67–100 [in Hebrew].

Roshwald, Mordecai (1972). "Theocracy in Israel in Antiquity and Today." *The Jewish Journal of Sociology* 14(2): 5–42.

Rubinstein, Amnon (1967). "Law and Religion in Israel." *Israel Law Review* 2(3): 380–414.

(1976). "Israel Nationality." *Tel Aviv Studies in Law* 2: 159–189.

Runzo, Joseph, Martin, Nancy M., *et al.* (2003). *Human Rights and Responsibilities in the World Religions.* Oxford, Oneworld.

Rwezaura, Barthazar A. and Wanitzek, Ulrike (1988). "Family Law Reform in Tanzania: A Socio-Legal Report." *International Journal of Law and the Family* 2: 1–26.

Saadeh, Sofia (2002). Basic Issues Concerning the Personal Status Laws in Lebanon. *Religion between Violence and Reconciliation.* T. Cheffler, ed. Beirut, Orient-Institut der DMG Beirut: 449–456.

Sachar, Howard Morley (2002). *A History of Israel: From the Rise of Zionism to Our Time.* New York, A. A. Knopf.

Sachs, Albie and Welch, Gita Honwana (1990). *Liberating the Law: Creating Popular Justice in Mozambique.* London, Zed Books.

Sachs, Susan (2000, Mar. 1). "Egypt's Women Win Equal Rights to Divorce." *The New York Times*, p. A1.

Saeed, Abdullah and Saeed, Hassan (2004). *Freedom of Religion, Apostasy, and Islam.* Aldershot, Ashgate.

Safran, Nadav (1958). "The Abolition of the Shar'i Courts in Egypt – 1." *The Muslim World* 48(1): 20–28.

(1981). *Israel – The Embattled Ally.* Cambridge, MA, Harvard University Press.

Saharay, H. K. (1999). *Laws of Marriage and Divorce.* Calcutta, Eastern Law House.

Saiyed, A. R. (1990). Secularism and Indian Polity. *Secularism in Retreat – The Communal-Secular Paradox in India.* B. Chakrabarty, ed. New Delhi, Segment Book Distributors: 143–154.

Sakr, Hala and Hakim, Mohamed (2001, Mar. 1–7). "One Law for All." *Al-Ahram Weekly Online*: 523. Accessed from http://weekly.ahram.org.eg/2003/621/fe1.htm.

Salim, A'sam A. (2004). *Principles of Non-Muslims' Personal Status.* Iskandariya, Dar al-Matba'at al-Jamia [in Arabic].

Salim, Latifah Muhammad (2000). *The Modern Egyptian Judicial System*. Al-Qahira, Al-Hay'ah al-Misriyah al-'Ammah lil-Kitab [in Arabic].

Salime, Zakia (2011). *Between Feminism and Islam: Human Rights and Sharia Law in Morocco*. Minneapolis, University of Minnesota Press.

Sanasarian, Eliz (2000). *Religious Minorities in Iran*. Cambridge University Press.

Sangari, Kumkum (2000). Gender Lines: Personal Laws, Uniform Laws, Conversion. *Pluralism and Equality: Values in Indian Society and Politics*. A. Imtiaz, P. S. Gosh and H. Reifeld, eds. New Delhi, Sage: 271–319.

Santos, Boaventura de Sousa (1980). "Law and Community: The Changing Nature of State Power in Late Capitalism." *International Journal of the Sociology of Law* 8(4): 379–397.

  (2002). "Toward a Multicultural Conception of Human Rights." *Beyond Law* 9(25): 9–32.

Sapir, Gidon (2001). "Law or Politics: Israeli Constitutional Adjudication as a Case Study." *UCLA Journal of International Law and Foreign Affairs* 6: 169–206.

Sarkar, Lotika (1999). Reform of Hindu Marriage and Succession Laws: Still the Unequal Sex. *From Independence towards Freedom: Indian Women since 1947*. B. Ray and A. Basu, eds. New Delhi, Oxford University Press: 100–119.

Sarkar, U. K. (2001). *Supreme Court on Women's Law*. Allahabad, Malhotra Law House.

Sartori, Giovanni (1970). "Concept Misformation in Comparative Politics." *The American Political Science Review* 64(4): 1033–1053.

  (1984). Guidelines for Concept Analysis. *Social Science Concepts: A Systematic Analysis*. G. Sartori, ed. Beverly Hills, Sage: 15–88.

Sassoon, David M. (1968). "The Israel Legal System." *American Journal of Comparative Law* 16: 405–415.

Sathe, S. P. (2003). *Judicial Activism in India*. Delhi, Oxford University Press.

Saxena, J. N. (1962). "Widow's Right of Succession in India." *The American Journal of Comparative Law* 11(4): 574–585.

Saxena, Poonam Pradhan (2003). *Family Law Lectures: Family Law II*. New Delhi, LexisNexis.

Schacht, Joseph and Layish, Aharon (1991). Mahkama. *The Encyclopaedia of Islam*, vol. VI. C. E. Bosworth, E. V. Donzel and C. Pellat, eds. Leiden, Brill: 1–42.

Scharf, Wilfried and Nina, Daniel (2001). *The Other Law: Non-State Ordering in South Africa*. Lansdowne, Juta.

Schiller, A. Arthur (1958). "Jurists' Law." *Columbia Law Review* 58(8): 1226–1238.

Schmemann, Serge (1998, Feb. 9). "Tel Hashomer Journal; A Soldier Dies, and a Forlorn Family Shames Israel." *The New York Times*, p. A4.

Schnapper, Dominique (1998). *Community of Citizens: On the Modern Idea of Nationality*. New Brunswick, Transaction Publishers.

Schneider, Nadja-Christina (2009). "Islamic Feminism and Muslim Women's Rights Activism in India: From Transnational Discourse to Local Movement – or Vice Versa?" *Journal of International Women's Studies* 11(1): 57–71.

Schwab, Peter and Pollis, Adamantia (1982). *Toward a Human Rights Framework*. New York, Praeger.

Segev, Tom and Weinstein, Arlen Neal (1986). *1949, the First Israelis*. New York, Free Press; London, Collier Macmillan.

Seidman, Robert B. (1978). *The State, Law and Development*. London, Croom Helm.

Seikaly, Samir (1970). "Coptic Communal Reform: 1860–1914." *Middle Eastern Studies* 6(3): 247–275.

Semidyorkin, N. A. (1988). "Family Law Reform in Russia after the October Revolution (1917)." *The Journal of Legal History* 9(1): 87–97.

Sen, Ronojoy (2010). *Articles of Faith: Religion, Secularism, and the Indian Supreme Court*. New Delhi, Oxford University Press.

Serajuddin, Alamgir Muhammad (2011). *Muslim Family Law, Secular Courts and Muslim Women of South Asia: A Study in Judicial Activism*. Karachi, Oxford University Press.

Setalvad, Teesta (2003). "After the Gujarat Pogrom." *South Asian Journal* 2: 123–134.

Sezgin, Yüksel (2003). "Can the Israeli Status Quo Model Help the Post-February 28 Turkey Solve its Problems?" *Turkish Studies* 4(3): 47–70.

  (2004a). "A Political Account for Legal Confrontation between State and Society: The Case of Israeli Legal Pluralism." *Studies in Law, Politics and Society* 32: 199–235.

  (2004b). "Theorizing Formal Pluralism: Quantification of Legal Pluralism for Spatio-Temporal Analysis." *Journal of Legal Pluralism* 50: 101–118

  (2009). "Legal Unification and Nation Building in the Post-Colonial World: A Comparison of Israel and India." *The Journal of Comparative Asian Development* 8(2): 273–297.

  (2010a). "How to Integrate Universal Human Rights into Customary and Religious Legal Systems?" *Journal of Legal Pluralism* 60: 5–40.

  (2010b). "The Israeli Millet System: Examining Legal Pluralism through Lenses of Nation-Building and Human Rights." *The Israel Law Review* 43(3): 1–24.

  (2011). "Women's Rights in the Triangle of State, Law and Religion: A Comparison of Egypt and India." *Emory International Law Review* 25: 1007–1028.

  (2012a). The Promise and Pitfalls of Women Challenging Muslim Family Laws in India and Israel. *Sexuality in Muslim Contexts: Restrictions and Resistance*. A. Hélie and H. Hoodfar, eds. London, Zed Books: 98–123.

(2012b). The Role of Alternative Legalities in Bringing About Socio-Legal Change in Religious Systems. *Using Legal Culture*. D. Nelken, ed. London, Wildy, Simmonds and Hill: 344–362.

(2012c). Triangulating Reform in Family Law: State, Religion and Women's Rights in Comparative Perspective. *Self-Determination and Women's Rights in Muslim Societies*. C. Raghavan and J. P. Levine, eds. Waltham, MA, Brandeis University Press: 243–272.

Sfeir, George N. (1956). "The Abolition of Confessional Jurisdiction in Egypt – The Non-Muslim Courts." *The Middle East Journal* 10(3): 248–256.

(1998). "Basic Freedoms in a Fractured Legal Culture: Egypt and the Case of Nasr Hamid Abu Zayd." *The Middle East Journal* 52(3): 402–414.

Shachar, Ayelet (2001). *Multicultural Jurisdictions: Cultural Differences and Women's Rights*. Cambridge University Press.

Shafir, Gershon and Peled, Yoav (1998). "Citizenship and Stratification in an Ethnic Democracy." *Ethnic and Racial Studies* 21(3): 408–427.

(2002). *Being Israeli: The Dynamics of Multiple Citizenship*. Cambridge University Press.

Shah, A. B. (1969). Gandhi, Communalism and National Unity. *Gandhi: Theory and Practice – Social Impact and Contemporary Relevance*. S. C. Biswas, ed. Simla, Indian Institute of Advanced Study. Part Two: 169–173.

Shah, Prakash (2005). *Legal Pluralism in Conflict: Coping with Cultural Diversity in Law*. London, Glass House Press.

Shaham, Ron (1995). "Jews and the Shari'a Courts in Modern Egypt." *Studia Islamica* 82(2): 113–136.

(1997). *Family and the Courts in Modern Egypt: A Study Based on Decisions by the Sharia Courts, 1900–1955*. Leiden, Brill.

(1999). "State, Feminists and Islamists – the Debate over Stipulations in Marriage Contracts in Egypt." *Bulletin of the School of Oriental and African Studies* 62(3): 462–483.

(2006). Shopping for Legal Forums: Christians and Family Law in Modern Egypt. *Dispensing Justice in Islam: Qadis and their Judgements*. M. K. Masud, R. Peters and D. S. Powers, eds. Leiden, Brill: 451–469.

(2010). "Communal Identity, Political Islam and Family Law: Copts and the Debate over the Grounds for Dissolution of Marriage in Twentieth-Century Egypt." *Islam and Christian–Muslim Relations* 21(4): 409–422.

Shahar, Ido (2006). *Practicing Islamic Law in a Legal Pluralistic Environment: The Changing Face of a Muslim Court in Present-Day Jerusalem*. Ph.D. thesis, Ben-Gurion University of the Negev, Beer-Sheva.

Shahine, Gihan (2007, Jan. 25–31). "More than Semantics." *Al-Ahram Weekly Online*: 829. Accessed in July, 2008, from http://weekly.ahram.org.eg/2007/829/eg7.htm.

Shalev, Michael (1989). Jewish Organized Labor and the Palestinians: A Study of State/Society Relations in Israel. *The Israeli State and Society: Boundaries and Frontiers*. B. Kimmerling, ed. Albany, NY, SUNY Press: 93–133.

Shapiro, Martin (1981). *Courts: A Comparative and Political Analysis*. University of Chicago Press.

Sharma, Arvind (2006). *Are Human Rights Western? A Contribution to the Dialogue of Civilizations*. New Delhi, Oxford University Press.

Shava, Menashe (1973). "Legal Aspects of Change of Religious Community in Israel." *Israel Yearbook on Human Rights* 3: 256–269.

　(1981). "Matters of Personal Status of Israeli Citizens Not Belonging to a Recognized Religious Community." *Israel Yearbook on Human Rights* 11: 238–255.

　(1985). "The Nature and Scope of Jewish Law in Israel as Applied in the Civil Courts as Compared with its Application in the Rabbinical Courts." *The Jewish Law Annual* 5: 3–24.

　(1998). "The Relationship between Jurisdiction of Family Court and Rabbinical Court." *Hapraklit* 44(1): 44–71 [in Hebrew].

Shehab, Shaden (2002a, April 4–10). "Finally Divorced." *Al-Ahram Weekly Online*: 580. Accessed in July, 2004, from http://weekly.ahram.org.eg/2002/580/eg3.htm.

Shehab, Shaden (2002b, Mar. 21–27). "No Khul' for Copts." *Al-Ahram Weekly Online*: 578. Accessed in June, 2007, from http://weekly.ahram.org.eg/2002/578/eg7.htm.

Shehabuddin, Elora (2008). *Reshaping the Holy: Democracy, Development, and Muslim Women in Bangladesh*. New York, Columbia University Press.

Shenhav, Sharon (2004, Dec. 1). "Busting the Old Boys' Club." *The Jerusalem Post*, p. 15.

Shepherd, Naomi (2000). *Ploughing Sand: British Rule in Palestine, 1917–1948*. New Brunswick, NJ, Rutgers University Press.

Sheshadri, P. and Acharya, K. R. (1977). *Constitution Forty-Second Amendment Act, 1976: A Critical Study*. Hyderabad, Osmania University.

Shetreet, Shimon (2002). *Law and Social Pluralism*. New Delhi, LexisNexis.

Shifman, Pinhas (2002). Civil Marriage in Israel: The Case for Reform. *Jewish Family Law in the State of Israel*. M. D. A. Freeman, ed. Binghamton, NY, Global Publications/SUNY: 9–129.

Shilo, Margalit (2006). "A Religious Orthodox Women's Revolution: The Case of Kolech (1998–2005)." *Israel Studies Forum* 21(1): 81–95.

Shimoni, Gideon (1995). *The Zionist Ideology*. Hanover, Brandeis University Press.

Shindler, Julian (1996). "The Cure before the Malady? Pre-Nuptial Agreements and Jewish Divorce." *Le'ela*. 42: 35–38.

Shochetman, Eliav (2002). Civil Marriage in the State of Israel. *Jewish Family Law in the State of Israel*. M. D. A. Freeman, ed. Binghamton, NY, Global Publications/SUNY: 130–184.

Shukri, Ghali (1990). *The Copts in a Changing Land.* Al-Qahira, Jaridat al-Ahali, Hizb al-Tajammu al-Watani al-Taqaddumi al-Wahdawi [in Arabic].

Siddiqi, Dina Mahnaz (2006). *Ain o Salish Kendra: Twenty Years on the Frontline.* Dhaka, Ain o Salish Kendra.

Singerman, Diane (2005). Rewriting Divorce in Egypt: Reclaiming Islam, Legal Activism, and Coalition Politics. *Remaking Muslim Politics: Pluralism, Contestation, Democratization.* R. W. Hefner, ed. Princeton University Press: 161–188.

and Ibrahim, Barbara (2003). The Costs of Marriage in Egypt: A Hidden Dimension in the New Arab Demography. *The New Arab Family.* N. S. Hopkins, ed. American University in Cairo Press: 80–116.

Singh, Birinder Pal (1994a). Gandhi and the Question of National Identity. *Facets of Mahatma Gandhi,* vol. II. S. Mukherjee and S. Ramaswamy, eds. New Delhi, Deep & Deep: 68–80.

Singh, Harbinder Pal (1995). "Indian Constitution and the Sikh Personal Law." *The Sikh Review* 43(10): 25–30.

Singh, Kirti (1994b). The Constitution and Muslim Personal Law. *Forging Identities: Gender, Communities and the State.* Z. Hasan. New Delhi, Kali for Women: 96–107.

Sivaramayya, B. (1978). The Special Marriage Act, 1954 Goes Awry. *Studies in the Hindu Marriage and the Special Marriage Acts* V. Bagga, ed. Bombay, NM Tripathi: 310–318.

Smith, Anthony D. (1987). *The Ethnic Origins of Nations.* Oxford, Blackwell.

Smith, Donald Eugene (1958). *Nehru and Democracy: The Political Thought of an Asian Democrat.* Bombay, Orient Longmans.

(1963). *India as a Secular State.* Princeton University Press.

Smith, Munroe (1979). *The Development of European Law.* Westport, CT, Hyperion Press.

Smith, Rogers M. (1997). *Civic Ideals: Conflicting Visions of Citizenship in US History.* New Haven, CT, Yale University Press.

Smooha, Sammy and Jarve, Priit (2005). *The Fate of Ethnic Democracy in Post-Communist Europe.* Budapest, Open Society Institute.

Solanki, Gopika (2011). *Adjudication in Religious Family Laws: Cultural Accommodation, Legal Pluralism, and Gender Equality in India.* Cambridge; New York, Cambridge University Press.

Som, Reba (1994). "Jawaharlal Nehru and the Hindu Code: A Victory of Symbol over Substance?" *Modern Asian Studies* 28(1): 165–194.

Sonbol, Amira El-Azhary (2009). The Genesis of Family Law: How Shari'ah, Custom and Colonial Laws Influenced the Development of Personal Status Codes. *Wanted: Equality and Justice in the Muslim Family.* A. Zainah, ed. Selangor, Musawah: 179–207.

Song, Sarah (2007). *Justice, Gender, and the Politics of Multiculturalism.* Cambridge; New York, Cambridge University Press.

Sonneveld, Nadia (2006). "If Only there was *Khul'* . . ." *ISIM Review* 17: 50–51.
  (2007). *"Reinterpretation of Khul' in Egypt: Intellectual Disputes, the Practice of the Courts, and Everyday Life*." Ph.D. thesis, Leiden University.

Soto, Hernando de (2000). *The Mystery of Capital: Why Capitalism Triumphs in the West and Fails Everywhere Else*. New York, Basic Books.

Sow, Fatou (2003). "Fundamentalisms, Globalisation and Women's Human Rights in Senegal." *Gender and Development* 11(1): 69–76.

Rennick, Anne C., *et al.* (1989). "Senegal: The Decade and its Consequences." *Issue: A Journal of Opinion* 17(2): 32–36.

Spruyt, Hendrik (1994). *The Sovereign State and its Competitors: An Analysis of Systems Change*. Princeton University Press.

Spuler, Bernard (1980). "Ein Witz – Oder: Die Koptische Kirche Heute." *Orient* 21(4): 479–485.

Stein, Kenneth W. (1984). *The Land Question in Palestine, 1917–1939*. Chapel Hill, University of North Carolina Press.

Stephens, Robert Henry (1971). *Nasser: A Political Biography*. New York, Simon and Schuster.

Stevens, Jacqueline (1999). *Reproducing the State*. Princeton University Press.

Strayer, Joseph Reese (1970). *On the Medieval Origins of the Modern State*. Princeton University Press.

Strum, Philippa (1989). "Women and the Politics of Religion in Israel." *Human Rights Quarterly* 11(4): 483–503
  (1995). The Road Not Taken: Constitutional Non-Decision Making in 1948–1950 and its Impact on Civil Liberties in the Israeli Political Culture. *Israel: The First Decade of Independence*. S. I. Troen and N. Lucas, eds. Albany, State University of New York Press: 83–104.

Sturman, Rachel (2005). "Property and Attachments: Defining Autonomy and the Claims of Family in Nineteenth-Century Western India." *Comparative Studies in Society and History* 47(3): 611–637.

Subrahmanyam, K. (1992). Communalism and Nation-State Building. *Towards Understanding Communalism*. P. Kumar, ed. Chandigarh, Centre for Research in Rural and Industrial Development: 31–43.

Subramanian, Narendra (2008). "Legal Change and Gender Inequality: Changes in Muslim Family Law in India." *Law & Social Inquiry* 33(3): 631–672.
  (2010). "Making Family and Nation: Hindu Marriage Law in Early Postcolonial India." *The Journal of Asian Studies* 69(3): 771–798.

Sunder, Madhavi (2001). "Cultural Dissent." *Stanford Law Review* 54: 495–567.
  (2003). "Piercing the Veil." *Yale Law Journal* 112: 1399–1472.

Sunder Rajan, Rajeswari (2003). *The Scandal of the State: Women, Law, Citizenship in Postcolonial India*. Durham, NC, Duke University Press.

Susser, Bernard and Liebman, Charles S. (1999). *Choosing Survival: Strategies for a Jewish Future*. Oxford University Press.

Tadros, Mariz (2000, Feb. 3–9). "Who Won the Tug-of-War?" *Al-Ahram Weekly Online*: 467. Accessed in June, 2006, from http://weekly.ahram. org.eg/2000/467/li1.htm.

(2002a, Dec. 19–25). "Khul' Law Passes Major Test." *Al-Ahram Weekly Online*: 617. Accessed in July, 2009, from http://weekly.ahram.org.eg/ 2002/617/eg11.htm.

(2002b, Jan. 13–19). "One Step Forward, a Hundred to Go." *Al-Ahram Weekly Online*: 464. Accessed from http://weekly.ahram.org.eg/2003/ 621/fe1.htm.

(2009). "The Non-Muslim 'Other': Gender and Contestations of Hierarchy of Rights." *Hawwa: Journal of Women of the Middle East and the Islamic World* 7(2): 111–143.

Talhami, Ghada Hashem (1996). *The Mobilization of Muslim Women in Egypt*. Gainesville, University Press of Florida.

Tamanaha, Brian Z. (1993). "The Folly of the 'Social Scientific' Concept of Legal Pluralism." *Journal of Law and Society* 20(2): 192–217.

Taylor, Charles and Gutmann, Amy (1994). *Multiculturalism: Examining the Politics of Recognition*. Princeton University Press.

Temperman, Jeroen (2010). *State-Religion Relationships and Human Rights Law: Towards a Right to Religiously Neutral Governance*. Leiden, Martinus Nijhoff Publishers.

Thelen, Kathleen Ann (2004). *How Institutions Evolve: The Political Economy of Skills in Germany, Britain, the United States, and Japan*. Cambridge; New York, Cambridge University Press.

Thielmann, Jorn (1998). "La jurisprudence Égyptienne sur la requête en Hisba." *Egypte/Monde Arabe* 34: 81–97.

Thomas, Abraham (2006, Nov. 11) "Centre, Muslim Board in Sync on Shariat Courts." *The Pioneer*, accessed from www.hvk.org/2006/1106/64.html.

Tilly, Charles (1975a). Reflections on the History of European State-Making. *The Formation of National States in Western Europe*. C. Tilly, ed. Princeton University Press: 3–83.

(1975b). Western State-Making and Theories of Political Transformation. *The Formation of National States in Western Europe*. C. Tilly, ed. Princeton University Press: 601–638.

Timasheff, Nicholas S. (1965). The Attempt to Abolish the Family in Russia. *Comparative Family Systems*. M. F. Nimkoff, ed. Boston, Houghton Mifflin: 55–63.

Tope, Trimbak Krishna and Ursekar, Harihar Sitaram (1950). *Why Hindu Code? A Historical, Analytical and Critical Exposition of the Hindu Code Bill*. Lonavla, Dist. Poona, Dharma Nirnaya Mandal.

Toungara, Jeanne Maddox (1994). "Inventing the African Family: Gender and Family Law Reform in Côte d'Ivoire." *Journal of Social History* 28(1): 37–61.

Traer, James F. (1980). *Marriage and the Family in Eighteenth-Century France.* Ithaca, NY, Cornell University Press.

Treitel, Andrew (1995). "Conflicting Traditions: Muslim 'Shari'a' Courts and Marriage Age Regulation in Israel." *Columbia Human Rights Law Review* 26(2): 403–438.

Triger, Tzvi (2005). Remembrance of Laws Past: Israel's Adoption of Religious Marriage and Divorce Law as a Means for Reviving the Jewish People's Lost Manliness. *Trials of Love.* H. Naveh and O. Ben-Naftali, eds. Tel Aviv, Ramot Pub.: 173–225 [in Hebrew].

Tsadik, Daniel (2003). "The Legal Status of Religious Minorities: Imami Shi'i Law and Iran's Constitutional Revolution." *Islamic Law and Society* 10(3): 376–408.

Tsimhoni, Daphne (1993). *Christian Communities in Jerusalem and the West Bank since 1948: An Historical, Social, and Political Study.* Westport, CT, Praeger.

Tsuk, Dalia (2001). "The New Deal Origins of American Legal Pluralism." *Florida State University Law Review* 29: 189–268.

Tucker, Robert C. (1978). *The Marx-Engels Reader.* New York, WW Norton & Co.

Tully, James (1995). *Strange Multiplicity: Constitutionalism in an Age of Diversity.* Cambridge; New York, Cambridge University Press.

Turner, Bryan (1990). "Outline of a Theory of Citizenship." *Sociology and Social Research* 24(2): 189–217.

Twining, William (2001). *Globalisation and Legal Theory.* Evanston, Northwestern University Press.

(2009). *Human Rights, Southern Voices: Francis Deng, Abdullahi an-Naim, Yash Ghai and Upendra Baxi.* Cambridge, UK; New York, Cambridge University Press.

Tyagi, Ruchi (2001). *Secularism in Multi-Religious Indian Society.* New Delhi, Deep & Deep.

US Department of State (2003). "Israel and the Occupied Territories." *2003 Human Rights Reports.* Accessed in Dec., 2006, from www.state.gov/g/drl/rls/hrrpt/2003/27929.htm.

(2010) Report on International Religious Freedom.

Uma, Saumya (2004). "Interpreting Muslim Law." *Combat Law* 3(4): 29–33.

Upadhyaya, Prakash Chandra (1992). "The Politics of Indian Secularism." *Modern Asian Studies* 26(4): 815–853.

Van der Vyver, J. D. and Witte, John (1996). *Religious Human Rights in Global Perspective: Religious Perspectives.* Cambridge, MA, M. Nijhoff Publishers.

Vanderlinden, Jacques (1989). "Return to Legal Pluralism: Twenty Years Later." *Journal of Legal Pluralism* 28: 149–157.

Vatikiotis, P. J. (1969). *The Modern History of Egypt.* New York, Praeger.

(1978). *Nasser and his Generation.* New York, St. Martin's Press.

Vatuk, Sylvia (2001). Where Will She Go? What Will She Do? Paternalism toward Women in the Administration of Muslim Personal Law in Contemporary India. *Religion and Personal Law in Secular India: A Call to Judgment*. G. J. Larson, ed. Bloomington, Indiana University Press: 226–248.

(2005). Moving the Courts: Muslim Women and Personal Law. *The Diversity of Muslim Women's Lives in India*. Z. Hasan and R. Menon, eds. New Brunswick, NJ, Rutgers University Press: 18–56.

(2008). "Islamic Feminism in India: Indian Muslim Women Activists and the Reform of Muslim Personal Law." *Modern Asian Studies* 42(2–3): 489–518.

Venkata Subbarao, G. C. and Subba Rao, T. V. (2002). *Family Law in India: Hindu Law and Mahommedan Law*. Hyderabad, Andra Pradesh, S. Gogia and Co.

Verhelst, Thierry (1968). *Safeguarding African Customary Law: Judicial and Legislative Processes for its Adaptation and Integration*. Los Angeles, African Studies Center, UCLA.

Verma, Ratna, ed. (1997). *Family Courts in India: An Appraisal of Strength and Limitation*. New Delhi, Inter-India Publications.

Villalón, Leonardo Alfonso (1995). *Islamic Society and State Power in Senegal: Disciples and Citizens in Fatick*. Cambridge University Press.

Viorst, Milton (1998). *In the Shadow of the Prophet: The Struggle for the Soul of Islam*. New York, Anchor Books.

Vitalis, Robert (1995). *When Capitalists Collide: Business Conflict and the End of Empire in Egypt*. Berkeley, University of California Press.

Vitta, Edoardo (1947). *The Conflict of Laws in Matters of Personal Status in Palestine*. Tel-Aviv, S. Bursi.

Wadud, Amina (1995). "Towards a Qur'anic Hermeneutics of Social Justice: Race, Class and Gender." *Journal of Law and Religion* 12(1): 37–50.

Wardi, Chaim (1950). *Christians in Israel: A Survey*. Jerusalem, Ministry of Religious Affairs, Govt. of Israel.

Washington Post and Times Herald (1955, Dec. 19). "Egypt's Catholics Protest," p. 4.

Waterbury, John (1983). *The Egypt of Nasser and Sadat: The Political Economy of Two Regimes*. Princeton University Press.

Watson, Alan (1981). *The Making of the Civil Law*. Cambridge, MA, Harvard University Press.

(1984). "An Approach to Customary Law." *University of Illinois Law Review* 3: 561–576.

Webb, Edward (2007). *Civilizing Religion: Jacobin Projects of Secularization in Turkey, France, Tunisia, and Syria*. Ph.D. thesis, University of Pennsylvania, Philadelphia.

Weber, Max (1954). *Max Weber on Law in Economy and Society*. Cambridge University Press.

(1978). *Economy and Society: An Outline of Interpretive Sociology*. Berkeley, University of California Press.

Weiss, Susan (2002, Aug. 12). "Loud Talk, Small Stick," *The Jerusalem Report*, p. 54.

(2009). "Divorce: The Halakhic Perspective." *Jewish Women: A Comprehensive Historical Encyclopedia*. Accessed in April, 2010, from http://jwa.org/encyclopedia/article/divorce-halakhic-perspective.

Welchman, Lynn (1990). Family Law under Occupation: Islamic Law and the Shari'a Courts in the West Bank. *Islamic Family Law*. C. Mallat and J. F. Connors, eds. London, Graham & Trotman: 93–115.

(2000). *Beyond the Code: Muslim Family Law and the Shari'a Judiciary in the Palestinian West Bank*. Boston, Kluwer Law International.

(2003). "In the Interim: Civil Society, the Shari'a Judiciary and Palestinian Personal Status Law in the Transitional Period." *Islamic Law and Society* 10 (1): 35–69.

(2004). Legal Context: Shari'a Courts and Muslim Family Law in the Transitional Period. *Women's Rights and Islamic Family Law: Perspectives on Reform*. L. Welchman, ed. London, Zed Books: 99–111.

Westermarck, Edward Alexander (1922). *The History of Human Marriage*. New York, The Allerton Book Co.

Westreich, Avishalom (2010). "Annulment of Marriage (Hafka'at Kiddushin): Re-examination of an Old Debate 2008" [cited April 2010]. Available from www.mucjs.org/Annulment.pdf.

Wheelock, Keith (1960). *Nasser's New Egypt: A Critical Analysis*. New York, Praeger.

Wiber, Melanie (1993). *Politics, Property and Law in the Philippine Uplands*. Waterloo, ON, Wilfred Laurier University Press.

Wieacker, Franz (1995). *A History of Private Law in Europe with Particular Reference to Germany*. Oxford, Clarendon Press.

Williams, Rina Verma (2006). *Postcolonial Politics and Personal Laws: Colonial Legal Legacies and the Indian State*. New Delhi; Oxford, Oxford University Press.

Winter, Michael (1995). Islam and the State: Pragmatism and Growing Commitment. *Egypt from Monarchy to Republic: A Reassessment of Revolution and Change*. S. Shamir, ed. Boulder, CO, Westview Press: 44–58.

Witte, John and Green, M. Christian (2012). *Religion and Human Rights: An Introduction*. Oxford University Press.

Women Living under Muslim Laws (2006). *Knowing Our Rights: Women, Family, Laws, and Customs in the Muslim World*. Nottingham, UK, The Russell Press.

Woodman, Gordon (1999). The Idea of Legal Pluralism. *Legal Pluralism in the Arab World*. B. Dupret, M. Berger and L. Al-Zwaini, eds. The Hague, Kluwer Law International: 3–19.

(2004). *The One True Law, or One among Others? The Self Image of English Common Law.* Paper presented at the Commission on Folk Law and Legal Pluralism 14th International Congress, Fredericton, NB.

Woods, Patricia (2001). *Courting the Court: Social Visions, State Authority, and the Religious Law Debates in Israel.* Ph.D. thesis, University of Washington, Seattle.

(2004). Gender and the Reproduction and Maintenance of Group Boundaries: Why the "Secular" State Matters to Religious Authorities in Israel. *Boundaries and Belonging: States and Societies in the Struggle to Shape Identities and Local Practices.* J. S. Migdal, ed. Cambridge University Press: 226–249.

(2008). *Judicial Power and National Politics: Courts and Gender in the Religious-Secular Conflict in Israel.* Albany, NY, SUNY Press.

Working Group on the Status of Palestinian Women in Israel (1997). "NGO Report: The Status of Palestinian Women Citizens of Israel." Accessed in Oct., 2010, from www.adalah.org/eng/intladvocacy/pal_women1.pdf.

Wright, Martin (1952). *British Colonial Constitutions, 1947.* Oxford, Clarendon Press.

WUNRN (Jan. 2007). "Shariat Courts Protected under Muslim Personal Law." Accessed from www.wunrn.com/news/2007/01_07/01_22_07/012707_india2.htm.

Yadin, Uri (1966). The Law of Succession and other Steps towards a Civil Code. *Studies in Israel Legislative Problems.* G. Tedeschi and U. Yadin, eds. Jerusalem, Magnes Press, Hebrew University: 104–133.

Yanai, Nathan (1996). "The Citizen as Pioneer: Ben-Gurion's Concept of Citizenship." *Israel Studies* 1(1): 127–143.

Yazbak, Heba (2007). "Statistical Data: The Proportion of Young Arab Women Married under 19 between Years 2000 and 2007." Accessed in Jan., 2011, from www.pstatus.org/?todo=projects&pid=00000023&pcatid=21&sid=4 [in Arabic].

Yiftachel, Oren (1997). "Israeli Society and Jewish–Palestinian Reconciliation: Ethnocracy and its Territorial Contradictions." *Middle East Journal* 51(4): 505–519.

(1999). "Ethnocracy: The Politics of Judaizing Israel/Palestine." *Constellations* 6(3): 364–390.

Yılmaz, Ihsan (2005). *Muslim Laws, Politics and Society in Modern Nation States: Dynamic Legal Pluralisms in England, Turkey and Pakistan.* Aldershot, Ashgate.

Yoaz, Yuval (2006, April 7). "State vs. Religion: Dramatic Ruling Curbs Rabbinic Court Powers." *Ha'aretz.* Accessed in Oct., 2012, from www.haaretz.com/print-edition/news/state-vs-religion-dramatic-ruling-curbs-rabbinic-court-powers-1.184773.

Young, Crawford (1994). *The African Colonial State in Comparative Perspective.* New Haven, CT, Yale University Press.

Young, Iris Marion (1990). *Justice and the Politics of Difference.* Princeton University Press.

(2000). *Inclusion and Democracy.* Oxford University Press.

Yuval-Davis, Nira, Anthias, Floya, *et al.* (1989). *Woman-Nation-State.* New York, St. Martin's Press.

Zahalka, Iyad (2009). *The Shari'a Courts between Adjudication and Identity.* Tel Aviv, Israel Bar Publishing House [in Hebrew].

(2010a). "The Challenge of Administering Justice to an Islamic Minority Living in a Non-Moslem State: The Shari'a Courts in Haifa, Israel." [Unpublished paper, on file with author.]

(2010b). *The Guide of Islamic Judiciary – Personal Status.* Tel Aviv, Israel Bar Publishing House [in Arabic].

Zarchin, Tomer (2010). "Controversial Civil Union Bill up for Discussion." Accessed in Jan., 2011, from www.haaretz.com/print-edition/news/controversial-civil-union-bill-up-for-discussion-1.264360.

Zavos, John (2002). *The Emergence of Hindu Nationalism in India.* New Delhi, Oxford University Press.

Zeghal, Malika (1999). "Religion and Politics in Egypt: The Ulema of Al-Azhar, Radical Islam, and the State (1952–1994)." *International Journal of Middle East Studies* 31(3): 371–399.

Ziadeh, Farhat Jacob (1968). *Lawyers, the Rule of Law and Liberalism in Modern Egypt.* Hoover Institution on War, Revolution, and Peace, Stanford University.

Zimmerman, Carle C. (1940). "Types of Families – Communist, Fascist, Democratic." *Marriage and Family Living* 2(1): 12–15.

Zucker, Norman L. (1973). *The Coming Crisis in Israel: Private Faith and Public Policy.* Cambridge, MA, MIT Press.

Zulficar, Mona (1999). "The Islamic Marriage Contract in Egypt." [Unpublished paper, on file with author.]

(2004). "Egypt: New Signs of Progress for Women in Egypt." Accessed in April, 2007, from www.wluml.org/english/newsfulltxt.shtml?cmd%5B157%5D=x-157-85801.

Zweigert, Konrad and Kötz, Hein (1998). *Introduction to Comparative Law.* Oxford, Clarendon Press.

INDEX

accountability, 218–219
Ackerly, Brooke, 69
Afshari, Reza, 68
Agudat Yisrael, 94–95, 98, 99
agunah, 11, 71, 102, 104, 105–106, 205
Alemy-Kabha, Nasreen, 89, 114
All India Muslim Personal Law Board
    (AIMPLB), 73, 183, 191, 195–200
All India Muslim Women Personal Law Board
    (AIMWPLB), 73, 198–199
Ambedkar, Babasaheb, 160, 172, 174, 176, 177
Amber, Shaista, 198–199
An-Naim, Abdullahi Ahmed, 43, 46, 68, 69, 72
Armenian communities, 77, 90, 119, 135
Asa-El, Amotz, 101–102
Atashi, Zeidan, 92
Atatürk (Mustafa Kemal), 34, 56, 135
Austin, Granville, 173
Australia, 23
Austria, 21
authoritarianism. *See* technocratic-
    authoritarian regimes
authority. *See* state control
Ayodhya, 183, 186, 187, 188, 189, 199
Ayubi, Nazih, 128
Ayyar, Alladi Krishnaswami, 172

Babri Masjid (Ayodhya), 183, 186, 187, 188,
    189, 199
Bahadur, Mahboob Ali Baig Sahib, 173
Bahadur, Pocker Sahib, 173
Baha'i, 10, 58, 78, 164
Baharatiya Janata Party (BJP), 185–187
Bangladesh, 189, 200, 202, 219, 220
Bangladesh Rural Advancement Committee
    (BRAC), 219, 220
Barelvi Muslims, 199
Barzilai, Gad, 51, 179
Belgium, 21
Bellefonds, Linant de, 127
Ben-Dahan, Rabbi Eliyahu, 105, 110
Ben-Gurion, David, 96, 100, 101
Benda-Beckmann, Keebet von, 65
Benhabib, Seyla, 49, 179
Benin, 219

Bennani, Farida, 116
Berger, Maurits, 123, 124, 139, 144, 145
Bharatiya Muslim Mahila Andolan (BMMA),
    72
Bibawy, Father Ishaia, 147
Botman, Selma, 135
Bourguiba, Habib, 37
Boyden, Michael, 108
Brison, Ronny, 104–105, 110
Buddhism, 163–168, 176

Canada, 23
capitalism, 26
CEDAW
    Article 2, 225
    Article 5, 225
    Article 7, 222
    Article 9, 223
    Article 16, 222–223
    Article 29, 223
    Egypt and, 212
    India and, 218, 225–226
    Israel and, 218, 222–223
    reservations, 218, 222–226
    signatories, 64
chador, 60
Chaldeans, 77, 119, 135
Chanock, Martin, 68
children's rights, 57
China, 27
Cohen, Rabbi Shear Yishuv, 110
Cohn, Bernard, 163
Cohn, Haim, 101
colonialism
    Egypt. *See* Egypt
    India. *See* India
    Israel. *See* Israel
    legacy, 13, 25–26
    personal status systems and, 3–4
    post-colonial nation-building, 19–42
    religious strategies, 78
Copts. *See* Egypt
Crecelius, Daniel Neil, 131, 135
cultural relativism, 67, 221
Cyril VI, Pope, 135

Books in the series

Diseases of the Will
Mariana Valverde

The Politics of Truth and Reconciliation in South Africa: Legitimizing the Post-Apartheid State
Richard A. Wilson

Modernism and the Grounds of Law
Peter Fitzpatrick

Unemployment and Government: Genealogies of the Social
William Walters

Autonomy and Ethnicity: Negotiating Competing Claims in Multi-Ethnic States
Yash Ghai

Constituting Democracy: Law, Globalism and South Africa's Political Reconstruction
Heinz Klug

The Ritual of Rights in Japan: Law, Society, and Health Policy
Eric A. Feldman

The Invention of the Passport: Surveillance, Citizenship and the State
John Torpey

Governing Morals: A Social History of Moral Regulation
Alan Hunt

The Colonies of Law: Colonialism, Zionism and Law in Early Mandate Palestine
Ronen Shamir

Law and Nature
David Delaney

Social Citizenship and Workfare in the United States and Western Europe: The Paradox of Inclusion
Joel F. Handler

Law, Anthropology and the Constitution of the Social: Making Persons and Things
Edited by Alain Pottage and Martha Mundy

Judicial Review and Bureaucratic Impact: International and Interdisciplinary Perspectives
Edited by Marc Hertogh and Simon Halliday

Immigrants at the Margins: Law, Race, and Exclusion in Southern Europe
Kitty Calavita

Mitigation and Aggravation at Sentencing
Edited by Julian Roberts

Institutional Inequality and the Mobilization of the Family and Medical Leave Act: Rights on Leave
Catherine R. Albiston

Authoritarian Rule of Law: Legislation, Discourse and Legitimacy in Singapore
Jothie Rajah

Law and Development and the Global Discourses of Legal Transfers
Edited by John Gillespie and Pip Nicholson

Law against the State: Ethnographic Forays into Law's Transformations
Edited by Julia Eckert, Brian Donahoe, Christian Strümpell, and Zerrin Özlem Biner

Transnational Legal Process and State Change
Edited by Gregory C. Shaffer

Legal Mobilization under Authoritarianism: The Case of Post-Colonial Hong Kong
Edited by Waikeung Tam

Complementarity in the Line of Fire: The Catalysing Effect of the International Criminal Court in Uganda and Sudan
Sarah M. H. Nouwen

Political and Legal Transformations of an Indonesian Polity: The Nagari from Colonisation to Decentralisation
Franz von Benda-Beckmann and Keebet von Benda-Beckmann

CPSIA information can be obtained
at www.ICGtesting.com
Printed in the USA
LVOW04s1757021215

465071LV00013B/219/P